P9-CJC-081

DATE DUE

DE 18 '98			
MY 1 5 '02			
JE 8 '04			
OC 27 '05			
MO 3 '08			

DEMCO 38-296

Page 21

Rescorla-Wagner
model Math Thing

CONTEMPORARY LEARNING THEORIES:
Pavlovian Conditioning and the Status of Traditional Learning Theory

Page 34 contingency

CONTEMPORARY LEARNING THEORIES:
Pavlovian Conditioning and the Status of Traditional Learning Theory

Edited by
STEPHEN B. KLEIN
Fort Hays State University
ROBERT R. MOWRER
Angelo State University

LEA LAWRENCE ERLBAUM ASSOCIATES, PUBLISHERS
1989 Hillsdale, New Jersey   Hove and London

Riverside Community College
Library
4800 Magnolia Avenue
Riverside, CA 92506

BF 319 .C577 1989

Contemporary learning
theories

Copyright © 1989 by Lawrence Erlbaum Associates, Inc.
All rights reserved. No part of this book may be reproduced in any form, by photostat, microform, retrieval system, or any other means without the prior written permission of the publisher.

Lawrence Erlbaum Associates, Inc., Publishers
365 Broadway
Hillsdale, New Jersey 07642

Library of Congress Cataloging in Publication

Contemporary learning theories—pavlovian conditioning and the status of traditional learning theory.

Includes bibliographies and indexes.
1. Classical conditioning. 2. Learning in animals.
3. Psychology, Comparative. I. Klein, Stephen B. II. Mowrer, Robert R.
BF319.C577   1989   156′.31526   88-33419
ISBN 0-89859-915-6

Printed in the United States of America
10 9 8 7 6 5 4 3 2

Dedicated to
Dora, David, and Jason
and
Gail, Chelsea, and Shawna

Contents

CONTEMPORARY LEARNING THEORIES:
Instrumental Conditioning Theory and the Impact of Biological Constraints on Learning

Contents

Preface

Theoretical interpretations of the learning process have concerned experimental psychologists for well over 100 years and have been a dominant force in psychology in general. Many of the initial theories, such as those of Hull and Tolman, attempted to capture the entire essence of learned behavior—the age of global theories of learning. In the past 10 to 15 years, theoretical concepts of the way in which human and non-human organisms learn or acquire information have undergone a dramatic metamorphosis. This change has involved moving from the broad, all-encompassing theories of Hull, Tolman, Guthrie and Thorndike to more specific, focused theories.

Most learning texts available to upper level students reviewing various theories of learning cover the traditional theories in detail, while only casually addressing more contemporary theories. Detailed treatment of these modern theories is available but can be found only by searching through a variety of sources (i.e., book chapters, review articles or a series of research articles). Feeling that there is a definite need to put all of these ideas into a single easily accessible medium, we contacted many noted modern learning theorists who graciously agreed to provide a discussion of their most recent research and theorizing. The result is a two-volume text dealing with the most up-to-date conceptualizations of the learning process. This first volume describes the ideas of sixteen psychologists on Pavlovian conditioning and modifications of traditional learning theory. The companion second volume presents the views of seventeen psychologists on instrumental conditioning and biological constraints on learning.

The material in this two volume text is appropriate for several different audiences. It could be used in an upper division learning theories course, a graduate learning theories class, or as reference text for researchers. We hope that the ideas of these noted psychologists will be as enlightening and stimulating to you as it has been to us.

Stephen B. Klein
Robert R. Mowrer

Contributors

ANDY G. BAKER, McGill University, Montreal
SUSAN E. BRANDON, Yale University
WILLIAM BROOKS, Rutgers University
ANTHONY DICKINSON, University of Cambridge
PAULA DURLACH, McMaster University
GEOFFREY HALL, University of York
ROBERT HONEY, University of York
STEPHEN B. KLEIN, Fort Hays State University
DONALD J. LEVIS, SUNY—Binghamton
LOUIS D. MATZEL, SUNY—Binghamton
PIERRE MERCIER, Laval University
RALPH R. MILLER, SUNY—Binghamton
ROBERT R. MOWRER, Angelo State University
ARTHUR TOMIE, Rutgers University
ALLAN R. WAGNER, Yale University
BARBARA ZITO, Rutgers University

THEORIES OF PAVLOVIAN
CONDITIONING

1 Traditional Learning Theory and the Transition to Contemporary Learning Theory

Robert R. Mowrer
Angelo State University
Stephen B. Klein
Fort Hays State University

I. BEHAVIORISM AND AN INTEREST IN LEARNING

This volume discusses the learning process and theories developed to explain this process. Learning is defined as a relatively permanent change in the probability of exhibiting a specific behavior. This change in behavioral potential occurs as the result of experience, either successful or unsuccessful.

Dating back to the beginning of this century psychologists have been keenly interested in learning—an important player in the area of psychology called behaviorism. Many different views of learning have been proposed by the behaviorists; this chapter briefly examines traditional learning theory. From the 1930s to the late 1960s, behavior theorists developed global theories of learning; that is, theories that attempted to explain all aspects of the learning process. Although this approach provided much information about learning, more contemporary theorists investigate and describe specific aspects of the learning process. We first discuss the global theories of the early behaviorists. After this description of traditional learning theory, we examine the reasons why contemporary learning theorists have abandoned global inclusive theories of learning in favor of more specific learning principles. This 2-volume set presents the ideas and research of 29 noted contemporary learning theorists. Volume one deals with contemporary thinking in Pavlovian conditioning and the current status of traditional learning theory. The second volume examines contemporary approaches to instrumental conditioning and the influence of biological processes on learning.

II. THE ERA OF GLOBAL THEORIES OF LEARNING

Behaviorism is a school of psychology that emphasizes the role of experience

3

in governing human behavior. According to behaviorists, we possess instinctual motives, but the important determinants of our behavior are learned. Acquired drives typically motivate us; our actions in response to these motives are also learned through our interaction with the environment. For example, a behaviorist assumes that your motivation to attend school is a learned one, and that your behaviors while you are attending school are also learned. One main goal of the behaviorist is the delineation of the laws governing learning—a concern that has dominated academic psychology for generations. For much of this century, behaviorists have proposed global explanations of learning; that is, a single view that could explain the learning of all behaviors. Let's next briefly examine four major global learning theories.

Clark Hull taught at Yale University from the early 1930s till his death in 1952. Even after his death, his view dominated behavior theory through the influence of his close colleague Kenneth Spence and their students until the late 1960s. More recently, the perspectives of two other traditional learning theories, Edward Tolman and Edwin Guthrie, have been appreciated. We examine the theories of learning of Hull-Spence, Guthrie, and Tolman next. Although their ideas do not have the same impact as they did in the 50s and 60s, they still tell us something important about the learning process.

Hull-Spence Learning Theory

The Concept of Drive.   In 1918, Robert Woodworth introduced the concept of *drive* to psychology, defining the term as an intense internal force that motivates behavior. The Hull-Spence learning theory was based on the assumption that an intense internal arousal, drive or D, automatically motivates behavior. Hull (1943) proposed that drive could be either unconditioned or acquired. Deprivation, for example, is one unconditioned source of drive. According to Hull, in order for an animal or person to survive, their internal biological systems must operate effectively. A deficit in these internal systems threatens survival, and represents one antecedent condition which motivates an adjustment to restore the biological systems to normal.

Intense environmental events are another unconditioned source of drive. Hull asserted that intense environmental events, such as electric shock or loud noise, motivate behavior by activating the internal drive state. The electric shock or the loud noise may be aversive, but they do not necessarily threaten the animal's survival. Thus, drive can be induced by circumstances that are intense although not life threatening.

Hull suggested that through classical conditioning, environmental events can acquire the ability to produce internal drive. According to this view, the association of environmental cues with the antecedent conditions which produce an unconditioned drive state causes the development of a conditioned drive state. Once this conditioned drive state has developed, these cues can induce internal arousal and thus can motivate behavior on subsequent occasions, even in the absence of the unconditioned drive-inducing stimuli.

The Development of Habit Strength.   What determines which behavior is elicited when an animal is aroused? In Hull's view, drive motivates behavior, but each specific instrumental action depends on the environment—or, environmental events direct behavior. But which behavior does a specific stimulus elicit? Hull thought that when an animal or human is motivated, the environmental cue automatically elicits a response; the response with the strongest innate habit strength ($_sU_R$) to that stimulus will occur. If that response reduces the drive state, the bond between the stimulus and response is strengthened; thus, in Hull's view, habit stength ($_sH_R$) is increased as the result of drive reduction. Further, Hull proposed that as behavior produces drive reduction, the habit strength increases.

Can an animal's behavior change after it has become habitual? According to Hull, unsuccessful behavior causes drive to persist, and all activity is temporarily suppressed—a process he referred to as *reactive inhibition*. If the drive state persists, the unsuccessful habitual behavior will occur again when the reactive inhibition declines. However, the continued failure of the habit to reduce drive leads to a permanent or *conditioned inhibition*. Conditioned inhibition is specific to a particular response and acts to reduce the excitatory strength of the dominant habit. The continued failure of a behavior to reduce drive causes the second strongest response in the *habit hierarchy* to become the dominant habit. If this second behavior is successful (produces drive reduction), the response's habit strength increases and the response will again be elicited when the animal is motivated. The conditioned inhibition process will be repeated if the second habit in the hierarchy is also ineffective; thus, the animal will continue down the habit hierarchy until a successful response is discovered.

The Influence of Incentive Motivation.   In 1943, Hull suggested that the value of reward influenced the strength of the S–R bond; a more valuable reward produced greater drive reduction and, therefore, a stronger habit. Once the habit was established, the likelihood of behavior depended on the animal's drive level, but not value of reward. However, various studies (e.g., Crespi, 1942) showed that the value of the reinforcer has an important influence on motivation level. For example, Crespi (1942) found that shifts in reward magnitude (increases or decreases) produced a rapid change in rats' runway performance for food. If reward magnitude influenced only learning level, as Hull has suggested, the animal's change in runway speed should have been gradual. The rapid shift in the rats' behavior indicates that reward magnitude influenced their motivation; the use of higher reward magnitude increased the rats' motivation level and a decreased reward magnitude lowered motivation.

The results of these experiments convinced Hull in 1952 that reward magnitude or K, affects the intensity of instrumental behavior. Kenneth Spence (1956) detailed how incentive value influences an animal's motivation level. Spence suggested that when a reward is obtained, the reward elicits a goal response (Rg). For example, food elicits saliva. This internal response produces an internal stimulus state (S_g) which motivates consummatory behavior; thus, the animal eats the food.

Spence thought that during the first few experiences, the environmental cues (for example, the goal box) present during reward became associated with reward and subsequently produced a conditioned or anticipatory goal response (r_g). This conditioned goal response then causes internal stimulus changes (s_g) which motivate instrumental appetitive behavior. After the establishment of the r_g to the goal box, the sight of the goal box will elicit the r_g-s_g mechanism, which then motivates the animal to approach the goal box. Thus, the animal is motivated to obtain reward even though it may not be able to see the reward when it starts to respond. According to Spence, the strength of the animal's motivation to obtain reward intensifies as the strength of the r_g-s_g increases on every reinforced trial.

The level of responding is influenced by the magnitude of the reward used during conditioning. Because a large reward creates a more intense R_g than does a smaller reward, Spence assumed that the environmental cues associated with the large reward produce a stronger r_g than if paired with a small reward. This idea conforms to basic classical conditioning principles: The strength of a CR is dependent upon US intensity; the stronger the US, the greater the CR. Spence's incentive motivation concept is supported by observations (e.g., Crespi, 1942) that performance level is higher with greater reward.

Spence's anticipatory goal mechanism indicates that Pavlovian conditioning is responsible for the influence of reward value on the intensity of instrumental appetitive behavior. Other psychologists (see Amsel, 1958; D'Amato, 1970) have adopted this conditioning approach to explain an animal's motivation to avoid frustrating or painful circumstances.

Guthrie's Contiguity Theory

The Role of Reinforcement.   Edwin Guthrie (1935, 1959) proposed that contiguity was sufficient to establish an S–R association. According to Guthrie, if a response occurs when a particular stimulus is present, the stimulus and response will automatically become associated without the necessity of reward. Guthrie assumed that many responses can become conditioned to a stimulus, and the response exhibited just prior to reward will be associated with the stimulus and will be exhibited when the stimulus is experienced again. Why does the reward act to increase responding? In Guthrie's view, once the appropriate response is exhibited, the reward acts to change the stimulus context (internal and/or external) which was present prior to reward. Any new actions will be conditioned to this new stimulus circumstance, therefore allowing the appropriate response to be produced by the stimulus context when it is experienced again. Thus, reward functions to prevent further associations from being conditioned, rather than to strengthen an S–R association.

What if reward is delayed? According to Guthrie, reward must be presented immediately after the appropriate response if that response is to occur on the next stimulus exposure. With delayed reward, actions occurring after the appropriate response, but before reward, will be exhibited later when the stimulus context is again encountered. Therefore, immediate reward prevents the acquisition of competing S–R associations.

The Influence of Punishment.   How did Guthrie explain the effect of punishment on behavior? When effective, punishment decreases the likelihood that the punished behavior will be repeated. However, in Guthrie's view, punishment, like reward, changes the stimulus context, but its behavioral effect is a decrease rather than an increase in the preceding behavior. To explain this opposite effect, Guthrie assumed that punishment functions like a stimulus rather than a reward; that is, punishment is an unconditioned stimulus capable of eliciting a number of responses, such as crying, pouting, or fleeing. If the response elicited by punishment terminates the adversity, it will become conditioned to the stimulus context in which punishment occurred. When this stimulus circumstance is encountered again, the conditioned response will be elicited. If this anticipatory response is effective, punishment will not occur. However, if the response which terminates punishment does not prevent punishment, the animal or person will not be able to avoid but only escape punishment.

An All-or-none Theory of Learning.   According to Guthrie, learning occurs in a single trial; that is, the strength of an S–R association reaches its maximum value following the first pairing of the stimulus and a response. You might wonder why Guthrie believes that learning could occur on a single trial when it is obvious that the efficiency and strength of behavior (or both) improve with successful experience. Guthrie did not deny that behavior improves with successful experience; however, he rejected the Hullian view that the strength of the S–R bond slowly increases with successful experience. According to Guthrie, there are three reasons for the gradual improvement in performance. First, although many potential stimuli are present during the initial conditioning, only a portion of these stimuli will be active (or attended to). The exact stimuli present when an animal or person responds varies from trial-to-trial. For a stimulus attended to during a particular trial to produce a specific response, this stimulus must have been attended to during a previous response. Changes in attention can lead to changes in behavior despite prior conditioning. Thus, behavior may change from trial-to-trial, but this change may reflect an attentional process rather than a learning process. Second, many different stimuli can become conditioned to produce a particular response. As more stimuli become able to elicit a response, the strength of the response will increase. However, this increased intensity is not caused by an increased strength of a S–R association, but rather by the increased number of stimuli able to produce the response. Third, a complex behavior consists of many separate responses. In order for the behavior to be efficient, each response element must be conditioned to the stimulus. As each element is conditioned to the stimulus, the efficiency of behavior will improve. According to Guthrie, the more varied the stimuli, the responses, or both, which must be associated to produce effective performance, the more that practice will be necessary for behavior to be efficient.

Tolman's Expectancy Theory

The Concept of an Expectancy.   Edward Tolman's (1932, 1959) view of learning contrasts with the mechanistic views described earlier. Tolman did not envision behavior as reflecting an automatic response to an environmental event but rather believed that human behavior has both direction and purpose. According to Tolman, behavior is goal-oriented because people are motivated either to approach a particular reward or to avoid a specific aversive event. In addition, people are capable of understanding the structure of the environment. There are (1) paths leading to goals, and (2) tools which can be employed to obtain these goals. Through experience, people gain an expectation of how to use these paths and tools in order to reach goals. Although Tolman used the terms *purpose* and *expectation* to describe the process which motivates human behavior, he did not mean that individuals are aware of either the purpose or the direction of behavior. He theorized that people act *as if* particular action was expected to lead to a specific goal.

According to Tolman, behavior is not only goal-oriented, but specific outcomes are expected to follow specific behaviors. For example, you expect that going to a favorite restaurant will result in a great meal. If you do not obtain this goal, you will continue to search for the reward and will not be satisfied with a lesser valued goal object. Thus, if the favorite restaurant is closed, you will not accept any restaurant, but instead choose a suitable alternative. Also, certain events in the environment convey information about where goals are located. Tolman thought that people are able to reach goals only after learning the environmental signs leading to reward or punishment. Thus, you know where your favorite restaurant is located and use this information to guide you to that restaurant.

Tolman suggested that people do not have to be reinforced in order to learn. However, expectations will not be translated into behavior unless the individual is motivated. Tolman proposed that motivation has two functions: (1) It produces a state of internal tension which creates a demand for the goal object, and (2) it determines the environmental features to which the individual will attend. For example, if you are not hungry, you are less likely to learn where food is located than if you are starving. However, tension does not possess the mechanistic quality which it did in Hull's theory. According to Tolman, expectations control the directions of drives. Therefore, when motivated, people do not respond in a fixed, automatic or stereotyped way to reduce drive, but rather behavior will remain flexible enough to enable a goal to be reached.

The Search for Reward and Cognitive Maps.   Tolman (1948) asserted that animals and people expect reinforcement to occur in a certain place and then they follow the paths leading to that place. According to Tolman, as animals and people explore their environment, a mental representation, called a *cognitive map*, of their environment develops; this cognitive map guides their exploration through the environment to reward. In contrast, Hull proposed that environmental cues elicit specific motor responses which have led to reinforcement in the past. Which view is valid? Under normal conditions, we cannot differentiate whether our expectations or habits will lead us to reward.

The Influence of Reward Magnitude.   According to Tolman, the value of the goal influences the intensity of motivation; people are more motivated to obtain a large reward than a small one. Tolman referred to the motivational qualities of a reward as *incentive motivation*. In addition, Tolman (1959) suggested that environmental events can acquire motivational properties through association with either a primary drive or a reinforcer. Suppose that a hungry child sees a cheeseburger (primary drive). According to Tolman, the ability of hunger to motivate behavior transfers to the cheeseburger. Tolman called this transference process *cathexis*, a concept he borrowed from psychoanalytic theory. As a result of cathexis, the cheeseburger is now a preferred goal object, and this child, even when not hungry, will be motivated to obtain a cheeseburger in the future. The preference for the cheeseburger is a positive cathexis. In contrast, our avoiding a certain food could reflect a negative cathexis. In Tolman's opinion, our association of that food with an unpleasant experience leads us to think of this food as an aversive object. Recall our discussion of conditioned drives; Tolman's cathexis concept is very similar to Hull's view of acquired drive. Tolman's equivalence belief principle is also like Hull's acquired incentive concept. Animals or people react to a secondary reinforcer (or subgoal) as they do to an original goal object. For instance, the motivation to obtain money reflects the belief in the equivalence of money to a desired goal object such as food.

People are not only motivated to obtain reward, but also to expect a specific reinforcer. An individual will not accept a lesser valued reward when expecting to receive a desired one, and will continue to act until the desired reward is obtained. Many animals studies demonstrating the incentive motivational process have been reported since Tinkelpaugh's (1928) study. Tinkelpaugh taught primates to obtain a banana by choosing the container that had a banana under it. The subsequent placement of a piece of lettuce, rather than a banana, under the correct container produced a typical response: The primates refused to eat the lettuce, a less preferred food than bananas, and continued to search the room for the expected banana and shrieked at the experimenters to indicate their displeasure.

Skinner's Behaviorism

The Irrelevance of Theory and the Importance of a Behavior Analysis.   The work of B.F. Skinner, a noted American psychologist, spans more than half a century and has contributed greatly to our understanding of the learning process. Yet, Skinner's behaviorism, often referred to as *behaviorist methodology*, is quite different from theories advocated by the other behaviorists we have discussed in this chapter. In his 1938 text, *The Behavior of Organisms*, Skinner asserted that the goal of behaviorism should be to identify and isolate the environmental factors that govern behavior. Further, Skinner stated that a particular behavior will be understood only if it can be predicted and controlled. He also suggests that the ability to predict and control a behavior is dependent upon understanding the circumstance governing the occurrence of the behavior. Skinner's first step toward this goal was to examine the variables responsible for a rat's behavior—pressing a lever for food—in an operant chamber. His analysis of the rat's behavior explained the environmental factors influencing the rat's responding. Skinner then expanded his analysis of behavior to include other animals, humans, situations and behaviors, which differed greatly from operant chambers and bar pressing. For example, in his 1957 text, *Verbal Behavior*, Skinner argued that people do not have an instinctive capacity for ''expressing our ideas.'' Instead, he believed that verbal behavior, like any other instrumental behavior, is controlled by differential reinforcement and punishment administered by significant others, such as parents and friends.

How does Skinner's view differ from those of the behaviorists that were described earlier? Skinner (1938) asserted that the use of theory and ''theoretical constructs'' does not contribute to our understanding of behavior. In fact, he argued that theory can actually hamper the accumulation of knowledge. In Skinner's view, the search for evidence to validate a particular theory of behavior interferes with the functional analysis of the variable controlling the behavior, and, thereby, precludes the discovery of the environmental variables which control responding. Consider the following example to illustrate Skinner's approach. As we have discovered, many psychologists have speculated that stimulus–response associations are strengthened as the result of reinforcement, and years of research have been devoted to validating this view. According to Skinner, understanding the ''theoretical construct'' underlying the strengthening effect of reward on stimulus–response associations is useful only in that it indicates that reinforcement is one environmental variable which can control how frequently a specific behavior occurs in a particular context.

The Concept of a Contingency between Behavior and Reinforcement. In 1938, Skinner identified two types of learning, *respondent* and *operant* conditioning. Respondent conditioning refers to the learning situation investigated by Pavlov: The conditioned and unconditioned stimuli are paired, and the conditioned stimulus subsequently elicits the conditioned response. In this type of learning, the animal or human passively responds to an environmental stimulus. Respondent behaviors are primarily internal responses in the form of emotional and glandular reactions to stimuli. However, Skinner was most interested in operant conditioning. He asserted that in operant conditioning, an animal or human actively interacts with its environment to obtain reward. Operant behavior is not elicited by a stimulus: Rather, in anticipation of the consequences of the behavior, an animal or person voluntarily performs a specific behavior if that behavior has previously produced reinforcement. Skinner called this relationship between behavior and reinforcement a *contingency*. The environment determines contingencies, and the animal or human must perform the appropriate behavior in order to obtain a reinforcer.

It should be noted that a contingency is not necessarily a perfect relationship between behavior and reinforcement. An individual may have to exhibit several or many responses in order to gain reinforcement. In order to respond effectively, the animal or person must be sensitive to the degree of relationship between behavior and reinforcement. Skinner's (1938) concept of *schedule of reinforcement* was based on the observation that contingencies differed and that animals sensitive to the exact contingency behave differently when confronted with different contingencies (see Ferster & Skinner [1957] for a complete review of this literature). Animals and people can also recognize that there is no relationship between behavior and reinforcement. This situation can lead to feelings of helplessness and depression. A more detailed discussion of contingency learning is presented by Maier (1989).

III. THE TRANSITION TO CONTEMPORARY LEARNING THEORY

Dissatisfaction with Global Theories of Learning

Can a Single Theory Explain the Learning Process? The preceding sections have revealed a diversity of views about the fundamental nature of the learning process. Hull, and Skinner, emphasized reinforcement mechanisms for the acquisition of behavior, Tolman suggested that cognitions were learned during an animal's exploration of its environment, and Guthrie proposed that contiguity was sufficient for learning to occur. Since the early 1960s global theories of learning have become less popular and research has tended to focus on more specific aspects of the learning process. There are probably several reasons for this change in the focus of learning research, including skepticism that the fundamental nature of learning could ever be answered completely (Bolles, 1979).

Most of the global theories of the 1930s through the 1950s dealt with aspects of instrumental conditioning rather than classical conditioning. This emphasis reflected the belief that classical conditioning was a fairly simple, reflexive type of learning and the mechanisms governing the acquisition of conditioned responses were believed to be fairly well understood. In addition, Hull, Tolman, and others demonstrated that most responses were not classically conditionable. Thus, it was concluded that classical conditioning was applicable only to certain behaviors (reflexes) (Mowrer, 1947; Skinner, 1938). It was even posited that there was no such thing as a separate phenomenon of classical conditioning. Hull (1943) argued that in a typical classical conditioning study of salivation, it could not be determined whether the dog salivated to the bell because the bell was associated with food or because the food pellet reinforced salivation. If the latter is correct, the situation is analogous to instrumental conditioning.

Current thinking, however, assumes that there are two distinct paradigms (classical and instrumental conditioning), each with different efficiencies in modifying various behaviors. This recognition of a dual response system may lead to difficulties in developing one single, unitary theory to explain the entire range of learned behavior. Further, it has been argued that these two paradigms interact in many learning situations leading to theories encompassing both Pavlovian and instrumental responding (Hull, 1943; Mowrer, 1960). Thus, there are at least three potential forms of learning: classical, instrumental, and a combination of the two.

A Greater Interest in Specific Learning Processes

A Renewed Investigation of Classical Conditioning.   As previously stated, classical conditioning had been thought of as a relatively simple, reflexive type of learning and that the mechanisms were fairly well understood. However, research beginning in the 1960s indicated that classical conditioning was far from simple and the mechanisms involved elusive. Further, until recently, classical conditioning was considered less important than instrumental conditioning as it had only limited application (Skinner, 1938). One of the most significant changes in the study of conditioning since 1960 was the realization that classical conditioning may have a much wider range of effect on behavior than was initially realized (Mackintosh, 1983).

The critical experiment that led to this change in thinking about Pavlovian conditioning was conducted by Brown and Jenkins (1968) using a procedure that became known as autoshaping. They discovered that rather than going through the elaborate process of shaping a pigeon to peck a key, it was possible to train the pigeon to peck the key by simply illuminating the response key followed by the presentation of food. Food reward was presented regardless of the bird's behavior. Within about 50 training trials, the birds would reliably approach and peck the key. Although this finding is difficult to explain in terms of operant conditioning, it is easily interpreted in terms of classical conditioning. In this situation, the lighted key serves as a CS, the food as the US, and pecking as the CR. While this is not the only interpretation, it is a plausible one (see Mackintosh, 1983, for more detail). In addition, Hearst and Jenkins (1974) have provided evidence that a wide variety of behaviors both in the lab as well as in the animal's natural environment may be interpreted in terms of classical conditioning. Chapter 7 by Tomie, Brooks, and Zito will have a good deal more to say about the autoshaping phenomenon.

A second reason for the renewed interest in classical conditioning involves the experimental precision inherent in the classical conditioning paradigm. For an experimenter interested in specifying precise relationships which occur in learning, this paradigm has a significant advantage (Wagner, 1969). A final reason for the renewed interest in classical conditioning is a rebirth of interest in inhibitory conditioning. A significant portion of Pavlov's seminal work, *Conditioned Reflexes* (1927) is devoted to the discussion of inhibition (what he called internal inhibition). Most of the work undertaken by Hull, and Skinner, involved strengthening of new responses. In contrast, Hull proposed that inhibition was merely though of as a reduction of excitatory strength. However, inhibitory conditioning appears to involve more than just response reduction and a clearer understanding of this process is necessary for a comprehensive concept of learning. A greater discussion of inhibitory conditioning can be found in chapters 2 and 3 of this volume.

The Emergence of Psychobiological Accounts of Learning

Probably the single most influential factor causing the transition from global, all encompassing theories to the more specific, contemporary theories has been the impact of research on biological constraints on learning. One of the basic assumptions of traditional learning theory has been the generality of the phenomena across all stimuli and responses. According to Skinner (1938): "the general topography of operant behavior is not important, because most if not all specific operants are conditioned. I suggest that the dynamic properties of operant behavior may be studied with a single reflex" (pp. 45–46). Likewise, according to Pavlov (1928): "any natural phenomenon chosen at will may be converted into a conditioned stimulus...any visual stimulus, any desired sound, any odor and the stimulation of any part of the skin" (p. 86).

There are a large number of research findings which are at odds with the above assumptions. Since we cannot cover all of these in detail, we will briefly discuss several of the more important ones. Certainly one of the most significant examples of research that called the generality of laws of learning into question was conducted by John Garcia (see Garcia & Koelling, 1966). In this study Garcia utilized a number of CSs (light, noise, and flavor) and two USs (shock or illness) and combined them in a 2 x 2 design. Specifically, the light + noise was paired with shock or illness, and the flavor was paired with shock or illness. The results were not in accord with those predicted by the general laws of conditioning view. Garcia and Koelling found that there was little or no association established between the light+tone and illness. Conversely, a strong association developed between flavor and illness. Likewise, there was little or no association between flavor and shock, while a strong association was found for light+tone and shock.

According to Pavlov (1928), there should have been no difference in the associability of these stimuli. Not only did Garcia and Koelling provide a rejection of the general laws by demonstrating that not all stimuli and responses are equally associable, they also showed another assumption of traditional learning theory to be incorrect. A basic premise of traditional learning theory was that for an association to be established between a CS and a US there must be fairly close temporal contiguity between the two. This time period, between the offset of the CS and the onset of the US, was believed to be in the range of seconds. Any longer than this and no conditioning will occur. Garcia, Clark, and Hankins (1973) showed that an association between a flavor CS and the illness US could be established even when 24 hr separated the CS and US presentations. Although these data stirred up considerable debate, it appears clear that flavor aversion learning is itself a different form of learning not accounted for by general laws.

These findings led Seligman (1970) to propose the concept of "preparedness." Seligman suggests that the biological equipment of a given species determines what an animal will or will not learn. This biological predisposition may render an animal prepared, unprepared, or contraprepared to learn a specific association. Specifically, preparedness refers to the situation in which the animal's biological character facilitates learning; unprepared is when the biological character neither facilitates nor retards learning and contraprepared is when this character prevents learning. Other examples of where an animal's biological character affects learning are detailed by LoLordo and Droungas (1989).

The Acceptance of a Cognitive View

Edward Tolman (1932, 1959) rejected the mechanistic viewpoint of Thorndike, Hull, and Guthrie. Instead, he argued that behavior has both direction and purpose in that we understand the structure of the environment. Tolman used the terms purpose and expectation to describe motivational processes. He claimed we act as if we expect a particular action to lead to a specific goal. Tolman's view was not particularly popular during the 1950s and it was not until the late 1960s that the cognitive viewpoint began to gain wider appeal.

One of the leading contemporary cognitive theorists is Robert Bolles (1972, 1979). He has suggested that as a result of our interaction with the environment, we form two types of expectancies which lead us to reinforcement or avoid punishment. Anytime a biologically important event occurs, such as the presentation of food or water, it occurs in the presence of environmental stimuli which may or may not become associated with obtaining food or water. Bolles labels the biologically important event S* and the environmental stimuli S. For an S–S* expectancy to develop (environmental stimuli causing the animal to expect food or water), S must reliably predict the occurrence of S*. While contiguity is necessary, it is not sufficient for an expectancy to develop. Events must occur consistently together before the S–S* expectancy will be established. Further, when more than one environmental stimulus is present, the most reliable S will become associated with S*.

The second type of expectancy has been called an R–S* expectancy. This expectancy refers to the understanding of the responses necessary to obtain reward or avoid punishment (S*). According to Bolles, our S–S* expectancies predict the potential occurrence of a biologically significant event and R–S* expectancies lead us to a particular goal. (See Chapter 9 by Dickinson for a recent elaboration of expectancy theory.)

Another example of the acceptance of a more cognitive view comes from recent work by Allan Wagner (1976, 1978, 1981). The original Rescorla-Wagner model (1972) argued that subjective representations of event contingencies are not what guides behavior. While still maintaining an S–R viewpoint, Wagner has modified the model to include such notions as surprise, rehearsal, expectancies, and memory. We now have a concept of the animal as an active information processor, quite different from earlier S–R notions that the organism is passive. A more detailed description of Wagner's learning theory is presented in Chapter 6.

The above are only two examples of a trend toward a more cognitive approach to learning. We will see throughout this text a continued appeal to cognitive mechanisms in detailing the learning process.

A Glimpse of Things to Come!

The following chapters represent a discussion of the current research and theorizing by a number of the most prominent researchers today. Chapter 2, provided by Paula Durlach reviews the original Rescorla-Wagner model (1972) followed by a comparison of this associative theory with a comparator theory of Pavlovian conditioning. The third chapter, authored by Ralph Miller and Louis Matzel, describes evidence supportive of a comparator theory. In Chapter 4, by Andy Baker and Pierre Mercier, attentional processes involved in Pavlovian conditioning are discussed in relation to retrospective processing and cognitive representations. Geoff Hall and Robert Honey continue with the focus on attention from a perceptual and associative point-of-view in Chapter 5. Allan Wagner and Susan Brandon present a revision of SOP theory of Pavlovian conditioning in Chapter 6. Chapter 7, provided by Arthur Tomie, William Brooks, and Barbara Zito discusses the phenomenon of autoshaping or sign tracking.

While preceding chapters deal primarily with classical conditioning, the second major section concerns itself with revisions of traditional learning theory. Chapter 8 by Donald Levis discusses two-factor theory and its relation to psychopathology. The final chapter (9) by Anthony Dickinson describes the current status of expectancy theory and the role predictiveness plays in the learning process.

Volume 2 of this set deals with instrumental conditioning and begins with a chapter by the editors contrasting traditional and contemporary issues. Chapter 2 by James Allison deals with the nature of reinforcement by looking at such concepts as learning vs. performance, response deprivation and related corollary issues. Chapter 3 by Russell Church discusses timing behavior in nonhuman animals. In Chapter 4, Steve Maier reviews the history and current status of learned helplessness theory. Still within the framework of instrumental conditioning, Chapter 5 by Franco Vaccarino, Stephen Glickman, and Bernard Schiff looks at the biological basis of reinforcement, discussing such topics as the function of reinforcement, evolutionary and ecological perspectives, and species characteristics, ending with a discussion of neurophysiological mechanisms of reinforcement.

The second general section of volume two focuses on biological constraints in learning. The initial Chapter (7) by Vincent LoLordo and Anastasia Droungas reviews the general process view concerning the area of biological constraints. This is followed by chapter 8 authored by John Garcia, Ken Rusiniak and Linda Brett which covers the evolutionary approach to biological constraints in learning. In Chapter 8, Anthony Riley and Cora Wetherington look at polydipsia and how this relates to an animal model of drug abuse. Finally, we end the discussion of biological constraints with Chapter 9 by William Timberlake providing us with a behavior system approach to learning including a discussion of the evolutionary aspect of behavior systems.

REFERENCES

Amsel, A. (1958). The role of frustrative nonreward in noncontinuous reward situations. *Psychological Bulletin, 55*, 102–119.

Bolles, R. C. (1972). Reinforcement, expectancy and learning. *Psychology Review, 79*, 394–409.

Bolles, R. C. (1979). *Learning theory* (2d ed.). New York: Holt, Rinehart & Winston.

Brown, P. L., & Jenkins, H. M. (1968). Authoshaping of the pigeon's key peck. *Journal of the Experimental Analysis of Behavior, 11*, 1–8.

Crespi, L. P. (1942). Quantitative variation of incentive and performance in the white rat. *American Journal of Psychology, 55*, 467–517.

D'Amato, M. R. (1970). *Experimental psychology: Methodology, psychophysics, and learning.* New York: McGraw-Hill.

Ferster, C. B., & Skinner, B. F. (1957). *Schedules of reinforcement.* New York: Appleton-Century-Crofts.

Garcia, J., Clark, J. C., & Hankins, W. G. (1973). Natural responses to scheduled rewards. In P. P. G. Bateson & P. H. Klopfer (Eds.), *Perspectives in ethology.* New York: Plenum.

Garcia, J., & Koelling, R. A. (1966). Relation of cue to consequence in avoidance learning. *Psychonomic Science, 4*, 123–124.

Guthrie, E. R. (1935). *The psychology of learning*. New York: Harper.

Guthrie, E. R. (1959). Association by contiguity. In S. Koch (Ed.), *Psychology: A study of a science, Vol. 2.* New York: McGraw-Hill.

Hearst, E., & Jenkins, H. M. (1974). *Sign tracking: The stimulus-reinforcer relation and direct action.* Austin, TX: Monograph of the Psychonomic Society.

Hull, C. L. (1943). *Principles of behavior.* New York: Appleton.

Hull, C. L. (1952). *A behavior system.* New Haven: Yale University Press.

LoLordo, V. M., & Droungas, A. (1989). Selective associations and adaptive specializations: Food aversion and phobias. In S. B. Klein & R. R. Mowrer (Eds.). *Contemporary learning theories: Instrumental conditioning theory and the impact of biological constraints on learning.* Hillsdale, NJ: Lawrence Erlbaum Associates.

Mackintosh, N. J. (1983). *Conditioning and associative learning.* Oxford: Oxford University Press.

Maier, S. F. (1989). Learned helplessness: Event covariation and cognitive changes. In S. B. Klein & R. R. Mowrer (Eds.). *Contemporary learning theories: Instrumental conditioning theory and the impact of biological constraints on learning.* Hillsdale, N J : Lawrence Erlbaum Associates.

Mowrer, O. H. (1947). On the dual nature of learning—A reinterpretation of "conditioning" and "problem solving." *Harvard Educational Review, 17,* 102–148.

Mowrer, O. H. (1960). *Learning theory and behavior.* New York: Wiley.

Pavlov, I. (1927). *Conditioned reflexes.* Oxford: Oxford University Press.

Pavlov, I. (1928). *Lectures on conditioned reflexes: The higher nervous activity of animals* (Vol. 1). H. Grantt (Trans.). London: Lawrence and Wishart.

Rescorla, R. A., & Wagner, A. R. (1972). A theory of Pavlovian conditioning: Variations in the effectiveness of reinforcement and non-reinforcement. In A. H. Black & W. F. Prokasy (Eds.), *Classical conditioning II.* New York: Appleton-Century-Crofts.

Seligman, M. E. P. (1970). On the generality of laws of learning. *Psychological Review, 44,* 406-418.

Skinner, B. F. (1938). *The behavior of organisms. An experimental analysis.* New York: Appleton-Century-Crofts.

Skinner, B. F. (1957). *Verbal behavior.* New York: Appleton.

Spence, K. W., (1956). *Behavior theory and conditioning.* New Haven, CT: Yale University Press.

Tinklepaugh, O. L. (1928). An experimental study of representative factors in monkeys. *Journal of Comparative Psychology, 8,* 197-236.

Tolman, E. C. (1932). *Purposive behavior in animals and men.* New York: Century.

Tolman, E. C. (1948). Cognitive maps in rats and men. *Psychological Review, 55,* 189-208.

Tolman, E. C. (1959). Principles of purposive behavior. In S. Koch (Ed.), *Psychology: A study of a science* (Vol. 2). New York: McGraw-Hill.

Wagner, A. R. (1969). Stimulus selection and a "modified continuity theory." In G. H. Bower & J. T. Spence (Eds.), *The psychology of learning and motivation* (Vol. 3). New York: Academic Press.

Wagner, A. R. (1976). Priming in STM: An information processing mechanism for self-generated or retrieval-generated depression in performance. In T. J. Tighe & R. N. Leaton (Eds.), *Habituation: Perspectives from child development, animal behavior and neuropsychology.* Hillsdale, NJ: Lawrence Erlbaum Associates.

Wagner, A. R. (1978). Expectancies and the priming of STM. In S. H. Hulse, H. Fowler, & W. K. Honig (Eds.), *Cognitive processes in animal behavior.* Hillsdale, NJ: Lawrence Erlbaum Associates.

Wagner, A. R. (1981). SOP: A model of automatic memory processing. In R. R. Miller & N. E. Spear (Eds.), *Information processing in animals: Memory mechanisms.* Hillsdale, NJ: Lawrence Erlbaum Associates.

Woodworth, R. S. (1918). *Dynamic psychology,* New York: Columbia University Press.

Learning and Performance in Pavlovian conditioning: Are failures of contiguity failures of learning or performance?

2

Paula J. Durlach
McMaster University

The primary motivation behind a great deal of research and theorizing in Pavlovian conditioning has been to provide an account of certain "failures of contiguity." That is, to explain why the same degree of CS–US contiguity does not necessarily produce the same degree of performance to the CS (e.g., Gibbon & Balsam, 1981; Kamin, 1969; Mackintosh, 1975; Pearce & Hall, 1980; Rescorla, 1968; Rescorla & Wagner, 1972; Wagner, 1969, 1981). For example, although repeated pairings of a CS, X, and a US typically result in the development of conditioned responding to X, if X is accompanied by another salient cue (A) on the occasion of those pairings, the degree of conditioned responding elicited by X alone will not be as great (A is said to overshadow X; Kamin, 1969; Pavlov, 1927). Moreover, A's own relation with the US affects its ability to interfere with conditioning to X. Separate reinforced presentations of A will enhance A's ability to interfere with conditioning to X (blocking), whereas separate nonreinforced presentations will reduce it (Wagner, 1969). Even in the absence of an explicit interfering cue, the same number of CS–US pairings will not necessarily support the same level of conditioned responding. Factors such as the time between CS–US pairings and the rate at which the US occurs in the absence of the CS also seem to have an effect (e.g., Terrace, Gibbon, Farrell, & Baldock, 1975; Rescorla, 1968, 1969).

Assuming that conditioned responding is a reflection of underlying learning, one interpretation of results such as these is that mere CS–US pairing is not sufficient for associative learning. Instead, the learning depends on the relative predictiveness or relative validity of the CS (Mackintosh, 1965; Rescorla, 1968; Sutherland, 1964; Wagner, 1969). A CS will gain value only to the extent that it provides information (about the occurrence of the US) that was not available from some other source. Several contemporary theories of associative learning were born out of this interpretation (e.g., Mackintosh, 1975; Pearce & Hall, 1980; Rescorla & Wagner, 1972; Sutherland & Mackintosh, 1971; Wagner, 1981). Those theories attempt to detail how the individual events that occur in a conditioning situation are combined or intergrated by the subject so as to produce emergent sensitivity to relative validity. Although there has been disagreement as to whether the "failures of contiguity" that are indicative of this sensitivity are best accounted for by variations in CS processing (e.g., Mackintosh, 1975; Pearce & Hall, 1980) or by variations in US processing (e.g. Rescorla & Wagner, 1972; Wagner, 1981), until recently, there was general concensus that the failures to be explained were failures of learning.

An alternative possibility, however, is that at least some failures of contiguity represent not failures of learning, but failures of performance (where "learning" refers to the strength of the CS–US association and "performance" refers to the behavioral expression of that association). That is, CS–US contiguity might be sufficient for learning a CS–US association; it might be the expression of that learning that is sensitive to relative informativeness. For example, Balaz, Gerstin, Cacheiro, and Miller (1982) have suggested that blocking is explicable not in terms of a failure to associate the blocked stimulus and the US, but rather as a failure to retrieve that association at the time of test. As a second example, Estes (1969), Gibbon (1981), and Jenkins, Barnes, and Barrera (1981) have all suggested that the failure to observe the acquisition of conditioned responding (despite CS–US pairings) when the US occurs at a high rate in the absence of the CS, reflects not a failure of the CS to become associated with the US, but rather a failure of the CS to elicit conditioned responding when presented in a context that itself is well associated with the US. Recently, these ideas have been expressed in the form of various formulations that I shall refer to collectively as comparator theories (e.g., Estes, 1969; Gibbon & Balsam 1981; Jenkins et al., 1981; Miller & Schachtman, 1985a, 1985b; see Chapter 3, this volume for a discussion of comparator theory).

The purpose of this chapter is to examine whether certain failures of contiguity are best understood as failures of learning or as failures of performance. The comparator theory interpretation of various conditioning phenomena is contrasted with one particular learning theory interpretation, that provided by the Rescorla-Wagner model (Rescorla, 1972; Rescorla & Wagner, 1972; Wagner & Rescorla, 1972). The decision to restrict the discussion of a learning interpretation to this particular theory was based largely on the ease of exposition that such restriction permits. The Rescorla-Wagner model has been one of the most influential contempory theories of associative learning, and so should be quite familiar to many readers; moreover, it allows relatively unambiguous predictions about how learning should proceed in a wide range of conditioning situations. This discussion does not propose to establish whether the Rescorla-Wagner model, per se, represents the best selective learning interpretation of conditioning, but rather whether an explanation of failures of contiguity in terms of selective learning is more or less appropriate than an explanation in terms of selective performance.

I. THE RESCORLA-WAGNER MODEL

The basic intuition the Rescorla-Wagner model attempts to express is that expected reinforcers are less effective than surprising reinforcers. The very same US can be differentially effective in producing conditioning, depending upon the extent to which its occurrence is well predicted by available antecedent stimuli. Hull (1943) had suggested (although in different language) that to the extent a CS was well associated with a US, each subsequent CS–US pairing would produce a smaller increment in conditioned value (producing a negatively accelerated learning curve). The important modification of this idea, suggested by Wagner (1969) and implemented in the Rescorla-Wagner model, was that changes in the conditioned value of a CS, X, resulting from an X–US pairing, were not only due to the extent of prior learning about X, but were also due the extent of prior learning about the entire stimulus complex in which X was embedded. Whether the US is expected on the basis of what has been learned about X, or on the basis of what has been learned about some other stimulus occurring concurrently with X, the consequences for further learning about X are the same.

More formally, the model proposes that change in the associative value of X may represented as

$$\Delta V_x = \alpha_x \, \beta \, [\lambda - \bar{V})$$

where $\bar{V}$ represents the total associative strength of all stimuli present. This is calculated by a simple sum of the strengths of the components, so that the total strength of an AX compound would be $V_A + V_x$. λ represents the asymptotic level of associative strength that the US will support, with $\lambda = 0$ representing nonreinforcement. From the formula it can be seen that it is not the absolute strength of the US (λ) that determines changes in V_x, but rather the discrepancy between the obtained and anticipated US ($\lambda - \bar{V}$) that determines such changes.

Alpha (α) and Beta (β) are parameters that influence the rate of change, and are allowed to take on values between 0 and 1. Alpha represents the salience of an individual CS component (in the above equation, the salience of X). Thus, different stimuli may acquire associative strength at different rates despite equal reinforcement if they differ in alpha. Beta represents the salience of the US, thus allowing for the possibility that the rate of learning will be influenced by the nature of the US.

Notice that V can take on negative as well as positive values. Positive values correspond to conditioned excitation whereas negative values correspond to conditioned inhibition. Notice also that V is in principle unbounded; however, in practice, repeated application of the discrepancy ($\lambda - \bar{V}$) will tend to force $\bar{V}$ towards λ.

For the Rescorla-Wagner model, all the interesting aspects of conditioning take place at the level of learning. Learning is assumed to map into performance by a rule that maintains ordinality, so that larger V values should correspond to more vigorous or more probable conditioned responding. The specific mapping rule, however, might depend on the experimental situation, and in fact might be different for different stimuli within the same situation. For all intents and purposes, however, performance is considered a rather direct window on associative value.

II. COMPARATOR THEORIES

The basic intuition that comparator theories (e.g., Balsam, 1984; Estes, 1969; Gibbon & Balsam, 1981; Jenkins et al., 1981; Miller & Schachtman, 1985a, 1985b) attempt to express is that subjects learn about every CS–US relation they experience. Conditioned performance, however, is not a direct window on this learning. CS–US contiguity will produce learning regardless of whether other available cues also predict the occurrence of the US; but unless the CS is presented under conditions favorable for the behavioral expression of that learning, the knowledge of the CS–US relation will remain behaviorally silent. Conditioned performance is not determined by the associative value of the CS per se, but rather by the value of the CS *relative* to the value of its context. Performance to the CS is generated by a mechanism that *compares* the strengths of the CS and its context (hence the name comparator theories). Only if the occurrence of the CS produces a significant change in the level of expectation (for the US) from that which was produced from the context alone will it influence behavior. To the extent the value of the CS exceeds the value of its context, the more likely the CS will be to elicit a conditioned response. To the extent the value of the context exceeds the value of the CS, the more likely the CS will be to inhibit a conditioned response (Balsam 1984; Miller & Schachtman, 1985b).

The various specific theories that I have included in this category of comparator models actually differ somewhat in what is meant by "its context." In the accounts proposed by Gibbon and Balsam (1981) and Jenkins et al., (1981), the "context" is literally the experimental context (the static cues of the experimental chamber). In contrast, Miller and Schachtman (1985a, 1985b) and Estes (1969) suggest that the context used for comparison could be the experimental context; but it could also be another punctate stimulus. This would depend on whether the CS of interest was presented in isolation or in compound with other punctate stimuli during training. Thus, one position endows the experimental context per se with special status, whereas the other does not.

Miller and Schachtman's position differs from the other comparator formulations in another respect as well. According to Gibbon and Balsam and Jenkins et al. performance to a CS is determined by a comparison between the value of the CS and the value of the context in which the CS is presented (the test context). In contrast, Miller and Schachtman have suggested that the comparison is made specifically with the context in which the CS gained its value (the training context). These two possibilities merge into one when the training context and the test context are one and the same, as in experiments in which all procedures are implemented in a single context. The two positions make divergent predictions, however, when conditioned responding is examined in a context different from that in which the CS–US relationship is presented. Consider a subject that receives a light-food relationship in context A, but subsequently encounters the light in context B. At issue is whether the subject's conditioned responding to the light in B will be influenced by the current value of B (the test context) or the current value of A (the training context).

Gibbon and Balsam suggest that to influence performance the light must produce some change in the level of expectation produced by B. In contrast, Miller and Schachtman view the subject as retrospectively reevaluating the significance of the light, according to the current value of A. For example, if the value of A were reduced between light-food pairings (in A) and encountering the light in B, the effect of that reduction should be to enhance the subject's "confidence" that it was the light (and not A) that reliably produces food.

Although subsequent discussion considers both these possibilities, a detailed description of only Gibbon and Balsam's (1981) comparator theory is presented, it being the only version of comparator theory that has been formulated at least as precisely as the Rescorla-Wagner model.

Gibbon and Balsam's comparator theory grew out of the observation that, in autoshaping at least, the interreinforcement interval has a substantial influence on the rate of acquisition of conditioned responding. Calling the average duration between successive reinforcer presentations Cycle time (C), and the average duration the CS is present during each interreinforcement interval Trial time (T), Gibbon and Balsam review a range of findings that imply that speed of acquisition can be predicted quite well by the ratio, C/T. They note that no matter how arrived at, equal values of C/T seem to produce equal rates of acquisition. In essence their model suggests that this is because animals compare the average delay to reinforcement in the presence of the signal (T) with the average delay in the context overall (C). Responding to the CS occurs only if the CS indicates a reduction in the wait till the next reinforcer (i.e., when C/T is large).

The animal must learn these average delays till reinforcement. Associative value (or expectancy) is acquired according to a negatively accelerating function, which reaches an asymptote inversely related to C (for the context) or T (for the CS). More formally, for any stimulus, X, the change in the value of X due to an X–US pairing can be represented by

$$\Delta V_x = \alpha_x \, (\lambda/D - V_x)$$

where λ represents the amount of expectancy the US is able to support, and D represents the *cumulative* time X has been present since the last US presentation. As can be seen from the formula, changes in the value of X depend only on X's own relationship with the US; as long as X is sometimes contiguous with the US, the associative value of X will approach a value inversely proportional to the average cumulative time X is present in each cycle (or the average cycle time itself if X is the context). One further assumption made is that learning about the context reaches asymptote very much sooner than learning about the CS; that is, the salience of the context, α_c, is assumed to be much larger than the salience of punctate CSs. Conditioned performance is assumed to depend on the ratio of CS value to context value; because at asymptote, the value of the CS is λ/T and the value of the context is λ/C, that ratio reduces to C/T.

III. TRIAL SPACING

One of the phenomena that Gibbon and Balsam were concerned to account for was the effect of trial spacing on speed of acquisition. Acquisition of conditioned responding is typically faster the more spaced are CS–US pairings (e.g., Terrace et al., 1975). The trial spacing effect can be thought of as a failure of contiguity in that the same number of CS–US pairings produces a different amount of conditioned responding depending only on how far apart those pairings are scheduled to occur. The question is: Is this due to a failure on the part of subjects to learn the same thing about the CS in the two situations, or is it merely due to a failure of performance?

According to the Rescorla-Wagner model, the difference in acquisition rates on massed versus spaced schedules reflects a difference in the speed with which the CS–US association is learned. Early CS–US pairings are assumed to endow both the CS and the context with conditioned value, but intertrial periods are assumed to afford loss of contextual value. The longer the intertrial interval (ITI), the greater the opportunity for context extinction. The consequence is that contextual value should be higher the more massed the schedule of CS–US presentations. Recall that according to the Rescorla-Wagner model, increments in associative strength to a CS depend on the strength of the entire stimulus complex within which the CS is presented. To the extent that concurrent cues are well associated with the US, they will interfere with learning about the CS. The model assumes that any stimulus, the context included, can have such an interfering role. The implication is that if context value is greater under massed than spaced conditions, there should be more interference with CS–US learning under massed than spaced conditions.

Gibbon (1981) argues that the effect of trial spacing is better (and more naturally) accounted for by his model. The longer the ITI, the greater C and thus the greater the C/T ratio. The greater the C/T ratio, the more rapidly should conditioned performance emerge. Besides predicting this qualitative relation between trial spacing and acquisition speed, Gibbon and Balsam's model is remarkably accurate in predicting precisely how variations in T, C, and the probability of the US given the CS affect when conditioned responding will emerge in autoshaping (cf. Gibbon & Balsam, 1981); this is a feat that is difficult for the Rescorla-Wagner model (cf. Gibbon, 1981).

Let us be perfectly clear about how the Gibbon-Balsam model portrays the situation, however. According to Gibbon and Balsam (and Jenkins et al.), when T is held constant but C is increased, this does not change the associative value of the CS (determined by T alone). Only the value of the context is affected. Faster acquisition is observed the more spaced the training conditions not because the associative value of the CS is greater, but because the value of the CS *relative* to the value of the context is greater.

In summary, the trial spacing effect is viewed as a performance effect by the comparator theories but as an associative effect by the Rescorla-Wagner theory. The mere observation of an effect of trial spacing, of course does not speak to which position is correct. What is required is an evaluation of performance to differently trained CSs under equivalent contextual conditions. If the trial spacing effect is due only to context-mediated performance factors, CSs trained under different ITI conditions should elicit the same degree of performance when presented in contexts equated in value. In contrast, if the trial spacing effect is due to differences in CS–US learning, then a CS trained under spaced conditions should elicit greater performance than a CS trained under massed conditions, not only during training, but also when tested in contexts equated in value.

Rescorla and Durlach (1987) evaluated these predictions by training pigeons with two keylight CSs. Both CSs were consistently followed immediately by access to food; however, CS-short was presented with a 10-sec ITI whereas CS-long was presented with a 2-min ITI. To accomplish this the birds were given training with each CS in separate sessions and in discriminably different contexts (distinguished by liners in the chambers). The left panel of Fig. 2.1 shows that, as expected, birds acquired keypecking faster to CS-long than to CS-short, although by the end of training the two CSs elicited equivalent rates of keypecking. The question of interest, however, was not how birds would respond to the CSs in their training contexts, but rather how they would respond to them in a common, third context. During the test in the third context, CS-short and CS-long were presented intermixed, with each CS equally often preceded by a 10-sec or 2-min ITI. No food was presented during the first session of testing; however, every trial was reinforced during the second session. The right panel of Fig. 2.1 shows the performance of birds during each of these sessions. The results support the assertion that trial spacing affects learning about the CS; when the CSs were presented in the same context, birds responded more to CS-long than CS-short. Testing the CSs in the same transfer context revealed a difference in CS value that was not apparent from an examination of the final levels of performance in the training contexts.

It should be noted that although these test results are in accord with the predictions of the Rescorla-Wagner model, they could also be accommodated by Miller and Schachtman's version of comparator theory. For their version, performance to the CS is inversely related to the value of the *training* context, not the test context. Therefore, despite equivalent learning about CS-long and CS-short, their version would still predict different levels of performance when these CSs are tested in the same transfer context, assuming that CS-short's training context was of higher value than CS-long's. A recent experiment by Wagner and Larew (1985) is not subject to such an interpretation, however. Using the conditioned emotional response (CER) procedure with rats, Wagner and Larew established two different signals for shock within the *same* context. CS-short was regularly preceded by an ITI of 60 sec, whereas CS-long was regularly preceded by an ITI of 600 sec. Performance to the CSs was examined during separate test sessions interposed between every 4 sessions of training. During these tests, no shock was presented and both CSs were presented at common long ITIs (12 to 18 min). By the third test session, rats evidenced substantially more fear to CS-long than to CS-short.

At first blush, these results may seem difficult not only for comparator theories, but also for the Rescorla-Wagner model. If differential context value is supposed to be the basis of the trial spacing effect (whether associative or not), how could Wagner and Larew have obtained such an effect when the two CSs were trained in the same context? The Rescorla-Wagner model can easily accommodate these results with the assumption that, during training, there were

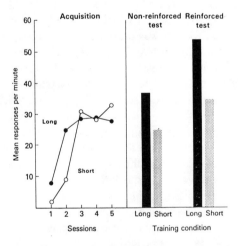

FIG. 2.1.   Effect of ITI on autoshaped keypecking. The left panel shows response rates during acquisition with two different keylights presented either with a 10-s (short) or 2-min (long) ITI, and in different contexts. The right panel shows response rates to these CSs tested under nonreinforcement and reinforcement with a mixed ITI in a third context. From Rescorla & Durlach (1987). Reprinted by permission.

consistent local variations in the value of the context, resulting from differential opportunities for context extinction before CS-short and CS-long trials. After all, it is the assumption that longer ITIs provide greater opportunity for context extinction that leads the Rescorla-Wagner model to predict a trial spacing effect in the first place.

Such an appeal to local variation in the value of the context cannot save the Miller and Schachtman version of comparator theory, however. Recall that Wagner and Larew tested in the training context at a common ITI. Therefore at the time of *testing* there should not have been any consistent difference in the value of the context for CS-short and CS-long. Differential performance during the test, then, must reflect differential learning. (Ignoring the possibility that there may have been more generalization decrement for CS-short tested at a long ITI, than for CS-long.)

One final set of experiments on trial spacing is of interest in the context of the present discussion. Kaplan (1984) gave pigeons an autoshaping procedure in which a 12-sec keylight CS was regularly followed by a 12-sec trace interval, and then access to food. Different groups of pigeons were distinguished by the ITI with which their trials were presented (15, 30, 60, 120, or 240 sec). Kaplan measured the birds' tendency to approach or withdraw from the keylight CS, both during training and in a final test session that was identical to training except that no food was presented. Approach to the keylight is generally interpreted as evidence of conditioned excitation, whereas withdrawal is interpreted as evidence of conditioned inhibition (Kaplan & Hearst, 1985; Wasserman, Franklin, & Hearst, 1974). Not surprisingly, the groups tended to show greater approach, the longer the ITI. The group trained with the 15-sec ITI, however, actually showed significant withdrawal from the keylight. The implication of this result is that not only did the CS in the 15-sec condition fail to become a conditioned excitor, instead it became a conditioned inhibitor.

These results have been interpreted as posing problems for the Rescorla-Wagner model. As already outlined, the model does anticipate less conditioned excitation the shorter the ITI; however, on a simple analysis, it would not predict an actual switch to conditioned inhibition. Recall that conditioned inhibitory value accrues when there is a negative discrepancy between the value of the CS complex and the reinforcer that actually occurs. If we conceptualize the trace procedure as consisting of context and CS compound trials that are reinforced (CX+) and context alone trials that are nonreinforced (C−), it is easy to see that C will better overshadow X the shorter the ITI (the fewer C− occasions). However, it is not apparent how the CX complex could ever come to "overpredict" the US such that X could gain inhibitory value. Alternatively, we could conceive of trace conditioning as an explicitly unpaired procedure. In this case, we might conceptualize the experiment as consisting of CX− trials, C+ trials (when the trace is reinforced) and C− trials. In this case, we can see that X might become more inhibitory the shorter the ITI (the fewer C− occasions); however, it is not apparent how with long ITIs X could ever become excitatory.

While posing apparent problems for the Rescorla-Wagner model, Kaplan's (1984) results fit quite well with the modified comparator theory suggested by Balsam (1984). Balsam modified the comparator ratio so as to allow the model to deal with procedures in which a trace separates CS offset from US onset. In the revised model, learning about the CS approaches an asymptote that is a weighted average of expectancy appropriate if there were no trace (i.e., as if the CS continued during the trace), and expectancy in the context. The weights for these values are the actual CS and trace durations, respectively. The new comparator ratio becomes $C/T - [(G/T) \times (C/T - 1)]$, where C represents Cycle time, T represents the duration of CS onset to US onset, and G represents the duration of the trace. Notice that when G is 0 this reverts back to the C/T ratio. Besides assuming that large comparator ratios increase the probability that the CS will act as a conditioned excitor, Balsam also added the assumption that small ratios increase the probability that the CS will act as a conditioned inhibitor. This (along with similar assertions made by Miller and Schachtman) is a rather radical formulation, for it suggests that conditioned excitation and conditioned inhibition are not two different kinds of learning (cf. Konorski, 1948; Rescorla 1979), or opposite ends of a single continuum (Wagner & Rescorla, 1972). Rather, the same CS can act as a conditioned excitor or as a conditioned inhibitor depending only on the excitatory value of the context.

One prediction that can be made from this formulation is that manipulation of the value of the context following training with Kaplan's trace procedure should have consequences for subsequent performance to the CS. For example, recall that the trace procedure administered with a long ITI resulted in a CS that elicited approach; however, inflating the value of the context following such training should make the CS subsequently elicit withdrawal. Analogously, although when administered with a 15-sec ITI the trace procedure produced a CS that elicited withdrawal, this same CS should elicit approach subsequent to a reduction in the value of the context.

Kaplan (1985) evaluated this latter prediction. Three groups of pigeons were given training in which a 12-sec CS was followed by a 12-sec trace interval, and then access to food. The ITI, on average, was 15 sec. As in his previous experiment, Kaplan found that with this procedure, birds withdrew from the CS. Subsequent to this training, Kaplan executed procedures intended to deflate the value of the context. Two groups of birds were given daily sessions in the experimental context. For one group, no events were scheduled to occur. For the other group, food presentations occurred on the average once every 267 sec. Recall that in Kaplan's original experiment, the trace procedure produced conditioned approach when given at ITIs of 120 or 240 sec; therefore a cycle time of 267 sec should be favorable for producing conditioned approach. The third group of birds was simply left in their homecages during this period. According to the comparator theory, when subsequently tested with the CS, the two groups of birds that received the context manipulation should show approach, whereas the homecage group should continue to show withdrawal. In fact, although both context manipulation groups tended to show less withdrawal than the homecage group, they certainly did not approach the CS. That exhibition of withdrawal was weakened by extinguishing the context is consistent with the suggestion that conditioned inhibition will only be operative in an excitatory context (Kaplan & Hearst, 1985; Lysle & Fowler, 1985; Rescorla, 1979; Wagner, 1981). This finding, however, hardly provides evidence that the same CS can be both an excitor and an inhibitor, depending on the context. Thus the strong claim that birds learn the same thing under different spacing conditions in Kaplan's original experiment seems to be incorrect.

Perhaps it is now appropriate to reconsider the Rescorla-Wagner interpretation of Kaplan's (1984) results. We saw that on any simple analysis, the Rescorla-Wagner model cannot explain how the same contiguity relation between CS and US could produce excitation at one ITI but inhibition at another ITI. All that is required, however, is a rather more sophisticated analysis of the situation. For example, instead of containing only two stimuli, the CS (X) and the context (C), suppose the situation is conceived of as containing three stimuli: X, C, and T, the trace of X. The procedure can then be conceived of as consisting of CX − trials, CT + trials, and C − trials. T, the trace of X should in some sense be similar to X and so we should expect substantial stimulus generalization between the two; however, since T is merely the *memory* of X, it might be expected to be low in salience (low alpha). Let us consider what might happen with a short ITI (few C − episodes). If the salience of T is lower than the salience of C, C should overshadow T, and should itself be fairly valuable. Therefore, when the CX compound is nonreinforced, inhibition should accrue to X. In contrast, when the ITI is long, the context will be less valuable (because there is more opportunity for context extinction). This means not only that the context will be less effective at overshadowing T so that T should become quite excitatory, but also that CX − occasions will be rather ineffective at producing inhibition to X. In fact, with substantial generalization between X and T, X should act as an excitor.

This explanation is, admittedly, post hoc. It shoud be noted that it is not the only available explanation (e.g., Wagner & Larew, 1985). In any event, the results reviewed earlier, suggest that the trial spacing effect is not merely a performance effect, as suggested by comparator theories, but reflects differences in associative learning. The same contiguity relationship results in different degrees of learning, depending upon the rate at which that relationship is experienced.

IV. US-PREEXPOSURE AND US-POSTEXPOSURE

It is a common finding that exposure to the US on its own, prior to experience with CS-US pairings, interferes with acquisition of conditioned responding to the CS (e.g., Baker, Mercier, Gabel, & Baker, 1981; Balsam & Schwartz, 1981;

Randich & LoLordo, 1979; Tomie, 1976). Like the effect of trial spacing, this US-preexposure effect can be thought of as a failure of contiguity; the same number of CS-US pairings results in different degrees of conditioning, depending on whether the US was preexposed or not. Although nonassociative factors might contribute to the US-preexposure effect in some instances (cf. Randich & LoLordo, 1979), there is substantial evidence that in general, the effect has an associative basis. In particular, it has been suggested that US-preexposure supports context-US learning, which interferes with subsequent excitatory conditioning in the preexposure context.

One explanation of the US-preexposure effect is the context-blocking hypothesis (e.g., Tomie, 1981). This account suggests that during US-preexposure, the context gains associative value and, therefore, because it is a valuable cue present at the time of CS-US pairings, is able to block learning about the CS. There is, in fact, good evidence that the effect does depend on the conditioned value of the context in which the CS-US pairings occur. For example, interposing context extinction between US-preexposure and CS-US pairings tends to reduce or eliminate the retarding effect of the preexposures (Baker et al., 1981; Batson & Best, 1979; Tomie, 1981). Likewise, changing contexts between US preexposure and CS-US pairings seems to undermine the effect (Baker et al., 1981; Batson & Best, 1979; Randich & Ross, 1985; Tomie, 1981). But evidence concerning the importance of the conditioned value of the context at the time of CS-US pairings does not provide unique support for the context-blocking interpretation. Comparator theories also explain the US-preexposure effect in terms of context conditioning.

According to the comparator theories, CS-US learning will proceed in the same manner whether the US is preexposed or not; however, US-preexposure is expected to produce context conditioning. This means that, at least early in acquisition, the value of the CS relative to the value of the context should be less following preexposure than following no preexposure. This in turn means that performance to the CS should be reduced (Balsam, 1982).

Once again then, we have a difference in conditioned responding that is viewed as a difference in CS-US learning by the Rescorla-Wagner model but as only a difference in performance by comparator models. The majority of experiments examining the US-preexposure effect evaluate responding to the CS in the context in which acquisition occurred. Therefore, although there are many results that support the assertion that the effect depends on context conditioning, most of these experiments are uninformative about whether the effect of context value is on CS-US learning or performance to the CS. For example, extinguishing the context between US exposure and CS-US training might reduce the retardation effect because it reduces the ability of the context to block CS-US learning. On the other hand, it might reduce the effect because, by reducing context value, it enhances the CS's relative value.

There are several ways to tease these two possibilities apart. One way is to unconfound the potential effects of context value at the time of training from their effects at the time of testing. In other words, performance to the CS must be assessed in contexts of equivalent value for all training conditions. Fortunately, there are a few recent experiments that meet this requirement.

Randich and Ross (1985) and Ayres, Bombace, Shurtleff, and Vigorito (1985) used a conditioned suppression procedure in which rats were preexposed to shock USs and then given pairings of an auditory CS and shock either in the same context as preexposure, or in a different context. Then the rats were tested for fear to the CS either in the pairing context or the alternate context. The results indicated that the location of testing had little effect. Rats showed less fear to the CS when preexposure and pairing occurred in the same context compared with when preexposure and pairing occurred in different contexts; and it didn't matter much where the rats were tested. Grau & Rescorla (1984) found analogous results with pigeons, using an autoshaping procedure. These results suggest that the US-preexposure effect is not explainable only in terms of differences in the value of the test context.

An alternative way to test the context-blocking hypothesis versus the comparator account is to manipulate the value of the context *subsequent* to CS-US pairings rather than prior to CS-US pairings. According to the context-blocking account, it is the value of the context at the time of CS-US pairings that influences the learning of the CS-US relation. Therefore only preacquisition exposure to the US in the training context, and not postacquisition exposure, should interfere with conditioned responding. In contrast, according to comparator theories, whether the context gains its value prior to or subsequent to CS-US pairings should be of little consequence. Both should interfere with conditioned responding to the CS.

Experiments that have examined the effect of postacquisition exposure to the US are generally unfavorable to the comparator position. In autoshaping, postacquisition food presentations have either had no detectable effect (e.g., Jenkins & Lambos, 1983; Kaplan & Hearst, 1985), or have actually facilitated responding to the CS (e.g., Durlach, 1983). For example, in an unpublished experiment carried out in collaboration with James Grau, I gave pigeons different rates of food presentations subsequent to discriminative autoshaping. During autoshaping, a green keylight CS was paired with food on 50% of its occurrences, and a white keylight CS was never paired with food. Birds were then assigned to one of four groups, distinguished by the number of food presentations given during each of 12 postacquisition sessions; groups received either 0, 1, 5, or 15 food presentations during each 30-min session. Finally, we re-presented birds with the green and white CSs during a nonreinforced test session. Responding during that test is illustrated in Fig. 2.2. We found a clear and reliable *direct* relation between the rate of postacquisition reinforcement and performance to green (S+). Other results suggest that such facilitatory effects are specific to the context of postacquisition exposure; that is, when birds were given postacquisition food presentations in one context but not in another, they subsequently responded more in the food than the no food context (e.g., Durlach, 1983; Grau & Rescorla, 1984).

These results are clearly in conflict with the predictions of comparator theories; those theories suggest we should have found an inverse relation between context value and performance.

The results shown in Fig. 2.2 seem difficult for Miller and Schachtman's comparator theory, as well as for the accounts proposed by Gibbon and Balsam (1981) and Jenkins et al. (1981). This is because autoshaping, postacquisition food presentations, and testing were all carried out in the same context (i.e., the training and testing context were one and the same). Miller and Schachtman have argued, however, that the value of the *test* context could actually summate with the value of the CS, making performance more likely, the higher the value of the context (rather than less likely). When the training context and the test context are one and the same, both summation and comparator factors might operate making it difficult to predict whether performance should be inversely or directly related to the value of the context. This will depend, presumably, on the relative strengths of these proposed performance factors. Because of these two factors, the only way to unambiguously test Miller and Schachtman's theory is to train with the CS in one context, manipulate the value of that context, and then test, not in the training context, but in a second context equated across groups for the potential summation factor.

Miller and Schachtman (1985b) carried out such a test, using a lick suppression preparation but failed to find evidence for their theory. Rats were initially given noise-shock pairings such that noise was paired with shock on some percentage of its presentations. Rats were subsequently assigned to two groups. One group was given unsignaled shocks in the conditioning context, the other was not. Finally all rats were tested for lick suppression to the noise in a second context (where they had had previous experience drinking). No effect of the postac-

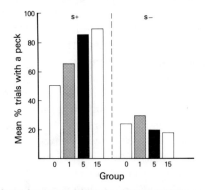

FIG. 2.2.   Effect of postacquisition food presentations on autoshaped key-pecking. The left and right panels show mean percent trials with a response to S+ and S−, respectively, during a nonreinforced test. 0, 1, 5, and 15 indicate the number of food presentations given during each of 12 30-min postacquisition sessions, which intervened between discrimination training and testing.

quisition shocks was found in that rats exhibited equivalent levels of suppression to the noise.

In similar experiments, Marlin (1982) found results antithetical to Miller and Schachtman's predictions. Also using lick suppression, Marlin gave her rats lick training in one context, and then tone-shock pairings in a separate context. She subsequently gave rats unsignaled shock presentations, either in the tone conditioning context, or in yet a third context. Finally, rats were tested for fear to the tone in the original lick training context. Rats that received the unsignaled shocks in the same context as conditioning exhibited *more* fear to the tone than rats that received the unsignaled shocks in a different context from conditioning. In a companion experiment, Marlin used the same procedures except that now instead of unsignaled postconditioning exposures to shock, she gave context extinction, either in the conditioning context or a third context. As before, she examined fear to the tone in the licking context. Rats that had been given extinction of the fear conditioning context were *less* fearful of the tone than rats given extinction of the alternate context. Marlin interpreted her results as evidence for within-compound CS-context associations. According to this interpretation, changes in the value of the context should, by association, produce corresponding changes in the value of the CS. This is just the opposite of the effects required to support the Miller and Schachtman formulation. Indeed, perhaps at this point it is worth considering just how Miller and Schachtman's comparator mechanism could operate. If performance to the CS is meant to be inversely related specifically to the value of its own training context, then there must be some sort of association between the CS and its training context in order for the comparator mechanism to "know" which CS to compare with which context. But from what we know of such associations (e.g., Rescorla, 1980; Rescorla & Durlach, 1981), changes in the value of one associate directly (and not inversely) affect the value of the other.

The experiments on the effect of postacquisition exposure to the US, which were reviewed earlier, yielded results that were unsupportive of either version of comparator theory. Exposure to the US (in the training context or the test context) following CS-US pairings does not have the same detrimental effect on conditioned performance as exposure to the US (in the training context) prior to CS-US pairings. Instead of trying to reproduce the US-preexposure effect by giving the US after acquisition, as opposed to before, Matzel, Brown, and Miller (1987) attempted to reduce the US-preexposure effect by giving context extinction subsequent to US-preexposure and CS-US pairings. Using a lick suppression procedure with rats, they gave shock preexposure in two distinctive contexts (A and C). Rats were then given fear conditioning in which a noise CS was paired with shock in context A. Rats were then given simple exposure either to context A (Group DA), context C (Group DC), or else remained in their homecages (Group ND). Finally all rats were tested for fear to the noise in yet a third context, B (where A and B, not A and C, were counterbalanced). Rats given extinction in context A prior to testing (Group DA) exhibited more fear to the noise during the test in context B than rats given either extinction in context C or no context extinction. In other words, extinction of fear in the pairing context (A), but not the other preexposure context (C), seemed to reduce the effect of shock preexposure on fear to the noise. These results are compatible with the view that the US-preexposure effect is due, at least in part, to a modulation of the exhibition of fear by the value of the training context at the time of testing. Matzel et al.'s (1987) conclusion as to the mechanism of their effect would be even more secure if they had shown that the enhancement of fear by postacquisition context extinction was specific to *non*reinforced context exposure; it is possible that postacquisition context conditioning would have had a similar, or even greater enhancing effect on manifest fear to the noise.

The data summarized in this section seem more favorable to the context blocking account of the US-preexposure effect than to the comparator account. Although factors besides context blocking might contribute to the US-preexposure effect (cf. Baker, Singh, & Bindra, 1985; Randich & LoLordo, 1979), the only evidence in support of the claim that a comparator-like process is one of them is the study by Matzel et al. (1987).

V. CONTINGENCY

The last section examined the effect of exposure to the US in the conditioning context before or after CS-US pairings. The present section is concerned with how intermixing US presentations with CS-US pairings affects learning and performance to the CS. A schedule of CS-US pairings that would otherwise produce robust conditioned responding can be made completely ineffective by the addition of a sufficient number of unsignaled US presentations in the ITI (Gamzu & Williams, 1973; Rescorla, 1968; Jenkins et al., 1981). An example of this effect is illustrated in Fig. 2.3 (taken from Durlach, 1983). One group of pigeons was given autoshaping with a keylight CS that was followed by food 25% of the time. This resulted in a substantial amount of conditioned responding, as illustrated by the curve for Group 25. A second group of pigeons was also given this same schedule of CS-food pairings; however, in addition, they were given several unsignaled food presentations in the ITI. Extra food presentations were given sufficiently often so as to make food occurrence equally likely in the presence and the absence of the CS. Pigeons in this group (Group Unsignaled) failed to show any evidence of acquisition to the CS. Despite the fact that the two groups of birds experienced the same number of reinforced and nonreinforced CS presentations, they showed very different levels of conditioned performance. Results such as this have led to the suggestion that it is the correlation or contingency between a CS and US, and not merely their cooccurrence, that determines whether conditioning will take place (e.g., Dickinson, 1980; Rescorla, 1968).

In general, when the US is more likely to occur in the presence of the CS than its absence (a positive contingency), the CS becomes a conditioned excitor (Rescorla, 1968). When the US is more likely to occur in the absence of the CS than its presence (a negative contingency), the CS becomes a conditioned inhibitor (Baker, 1977; Rescorla, 1969; Witcher & Ayres, 1980). When the US is equally likely to occur whether the CS is present or not (a 0 correlation or random relation) the CS appears to gain little value either way (Durlach, 1983; Rescorla, 1968).

According to the Rescorla-Wagner model, USs that occur in the absence of the CS have an impact on learning about the CS because they influence the conditioned value of the context. Recall once again that changes in the associative value of a CS depend not only on its own relation with the US, but also on the relation that concurrently present stimuli have with the US. Because the context is always concurrent with stimuli that occur within it, the context's relation with the US in the absence of the CS will affect what can be learned when the CS is present. When the US occurs in conjunction with the CS, but never in its absence (as for Group 25 in Fig. 2.3), the context should be rather poorly associated with the US because it is nonreinforced in isolation during the ITI. If this arrangement is modified by the addition of ITI USs, however, the context would be expected to maintain a value directly related to the frequency of the extra USs. To the extent that contextual value is maintained, CS-US learning will be disrupted. Should the frequency of ITI USs be sufficient to maintain such a high

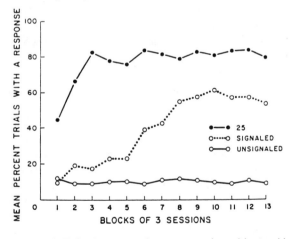

FIG. 2.3. Effect of ITI food presentations on autoshaped keypecking. For all groups, the CS was paired with food 25% of the time. For Groups Signaled and Unsignaled, food was also presented in the ITI. For Group Signaled, those extra food occurences were signaled by a tone, whereas for Group Unsignaled, they were unsignaled. From Durlach (1983). Copyright 1983 by the American Psychological Association. Reprinted by permission.

contextual value that the context actually loses value in the presence of the CS, the CS will not only fail to become excitatory, it will actually become inhibitory. In summary, the Rescorla-Wagner model suggests that the same schedule of CS-US pairings can produce different learning (about the CS) depending on the rate of US occurrence in the absence of the CS. This sensitivity to contingency is caused by the competition between CS and context for associative strength (Rescorla, 1972; Rescorla & Wagner, 1972).

Comparator theories suggest that it is performance, not learning, that is sensitive to contingency. According to this view, contiguity is sufficient for learning; as long as the schedule of CS-US pairings is the same, learning about the CS is the same. However, like the Rescorla-Wagner model, comparator theories suppose that degrading CS-US contingency by the addition of ITI USs results in a context of higher value. In the language of the Gibbon-Balsam model, T is held constant, but C is reduced, so the C/T ratio is reduced. In other words, although CS-US learning is unaffected, the value of the CS relative to the value of the context is less, and so performance is less. At very low relative values, the CS is expected to act as a conditioned inhibitor (Balsam, 1984; Miller & Schachtman, 1985b). This last assumption suggests that associative learning can be described soley in terms of excitatory associations, and that conditioned inhibition is merely a performance effect.

As with previous "failures of contiguity" that have been discussed, both the Rescorla-Wagner model and the comparator models assume that the effect of contingency is mediated by context conditioning. What if there were some way to undermine this context-US learning? According to the Rescorla-Wagner model one way to do this should be to signal the ITI USs with some other stimulus. This is because contemporaneous stimuli are supposed to compete with one another for associative strength. Signaling the ITI USs should provide a strong competitor for the context, and so should reduce the amount of context-US learning produced by the ITI USs. If the context-US learning is reduced, the context's ability to compete with the original (target) CS should also be reduced.

In contrast to the Rescorla-Wagner model, the comparator models do not expect signaling ITI USs to alleviate the response decrement they produce. According to this view, concurrent stimuli are learned about independently. Therefore, US presentations in a context should have the same effect on context conditioning whether the USs are signaled or not. Because context value should be the same with and without signals, performance to the target CS should be the same with and without signals.

The curve labeled Group Signaled in Fig. 2.3 shows the outcome of such a signaling manipulation. Birds in Group Signaled were treated just like birds in Group Unsignaled except that all their ITI food presentations were signaled by a 10-sec tone (Birds in all three groups had had prior experience with tone-food pairings). Although the effect emerged only gradually, the signaling procedure was effective in reducing the response decrement produced by the ITI USs. Similar effects of signaling ITI shocks in the conditioned suppression preparation with rats have been shown by Rescorla (1972, 1984b). Not only does signaling reduce the detrimental effect of ITI USs on excitatory conditioning, it also reduces their beneficial effect on inhibitory conditioning when the target CS and US are explicitly unpaired (Baker, 1977; Fowler, Kleiman, & Lysle, 1985). Signaling also seems an effective way of reducing the US-preexposure effect; when the preexposure USs are signaled, subsequent acquisition of conditioned responding is improved, compared with the unsignaled condition (Baker et al., 1981; Grau & Rescorla, 1984; Randich, 1981).

In an attempt to provide converging evidence that signaling the US does indeed reduce context conditioning, several experimenters have tried to assess context value by examining the subject's response to the context on its own. Despite certain failures to find an effect of signaling on the subject's response to the context (e.g., Balsam, 1984, Rescorla, Durlach, & Grau, 1985), there is evidence that signaling does reduce context value. For example, Baker et al. (1981) found rats' lever press responding for food to be less disrupted by signaled than unsignaled shocks. And given the choice, rats show less avoidance of a context in which shocks had previously been signaled as opposed to randomly related to a signal (Fanselow, 1980; Odling-Smee, 1975, 1978).

It is possible that failures to find such effects are due more to the lack of sensitivity of the measure of context value than to the absence of the effect itself (cf. Ayres et al., 1985; Rescorla et al., 1985). Moreover, the possibility of context-CS, as well as context-US associations, may obscure the usefulness of such measures. For example, general activity is often used to index context-food associations in autoshaping; but besides being influenced by rate of food presentations, context elicited conditioned activity can also be influenced by the current value of keylights that have been presented in the context (Rescorla, 1984a). The implication is that signaling food might reduce first-order context-food learning, but also produce second-order, context-CS learning; thus, an effect of signaling on activity might be difficult to detect.

The observation of a signaling effect supports the claim that a CS does compete with the context for associative strength. The possibility remains, however, that the differences illustrated in Fig. 2.3 are only differences in performance, not learning. Although the comparator position was incorrect in claiming that signaling would not have an effect on responding, it could still be correct in claiming that the observed differences are all in performance. For example, suppose CS/context competition were asymmetric so that a CS could interfere with context-US learning, but a context could not interfere with CS-US learning, just performance to the CS. Then signaling the ITI USs would have an effect on performance to the target CS, but not its association with the US. By now, the reader should be familiar with one method of testing this possibility. Responding to the CS must be assessed, not in the original training context, for which the different groups might have different opinions, but rather in a new test context that has been deliberately equated in value for all groups. If the birds learned the same thing about the target CS in the Signaled and Unsignaled conditions, the groups should respond equally to the CS in such a transfer context.

In order to examine this question, I tested pigeons in transfer contexts following training with the signaled or unsignaled ITI US procedures (Durlach, 1983). The transfer contexts (distinguished by liners) were treated identically for the two groups so that differences in performance could not be attributed to differences in what the birds had learned about the contexts, but would have to be due to differences in what the birds had learned about the CS. Testing actually involved the use of two transfer contexts, one where birds were accustomed to a high rate of food (40 presentations per 20-min session) and one where they were accustomed to never obtaining food. This permitted an opportunity to evaluate the effect of context value per se on performance. Activity in each context was measured during context discrimination training to verify that birds learned which context was which.

The results of training and testing are shown in Fig. 2.4. The left panel shows that, as before, birds in Group Signaled acquired conditioned keypecking whereas birds in Group Unsignaled did not. The right panel shows performance in the transfer contexts; during that test, the CS was presented in simple extinction. The two left bars show responding for the two groups in the high valued context; the two right bars show responding in the low valued context. Regardless of which context birds were tested in, those from Group Signaled responded more than those from Group Unsignaled. In fact, as during training, birds in Group Unsignaled responded hardly at all. This pattern implies that signaling the ITI foods indeed did affect CS-US learning and not merely performance to the CS.

Examining the effect of context value per se on performance, for the birds that were responding (Group Signaled), performance was greater in the high valued context than in the low valued context. This result fits with the results I presented earlier (Fig. 2.2); in autoshaping, responding seems to be directly related to the value of the test context. This is just the opposite of the kind of performance effect anticipated by the Gibbon and Balsam (1981) and Jenkins et al. (1981) formulations.

Although the above results are incompatible with a theory that views performance to the CS as an inverse function of the value of the test context, they do not rule out Miller and Schachtman's suggestion that performance is inversely related to the value of the training context. An unpublished experiment by Fairless (reported by LoLordo, Fairless, & Stanhope, 1985) speaks to this issue. Two groups of pigeons were given experience with a keylight and food presented in a random relation (R-Ext and R-HC). A third group experienced the same food presentations, but no CS presentations (US-Ext). Subsequently, Groups R-Ext and US-Ext were given several sessions of context extinction (in the training context), whereas Group R-HC stayed in the homecages. Finally, all birds were given a savings test in which the CS was positively related to food. If birds learned

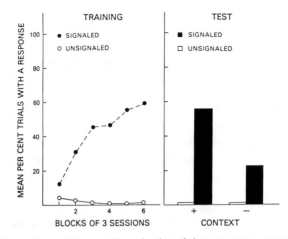

FIG. 2.4 Effect of the conditioned value of the context on autoshaped keypecking after training with signaled or unsignaled ITI food presentations. The left panel shows mean percent trials with a response during training with signaled or unsignaled ITI food presentations. The right panel shows mean percent trials with a response during testing, when the CS was presented in extinction and in a transfer context of high value (+) or low value (−). From Durlach (1983). Copyright 1983 by the American Psychological Association. Reprinted by permission.

to associate the CS and US as a result of chance pairings in the random schedule, birds in Group R-Ext should show faster acquisition than birds in Group US-Ext, for whom the CS was novel. In fact, both Groups R-Ext and US-Ext met an acquisition criterion of 3 consecutive trials with a peck sooner than Group R-HC, showing that the extinction manipulation was effective; however, birds in Groups R-Ext and US-Ext acquired at the same rate. Thus extinguishing the training context did not unmask CS-US learning. An analogous result was found by Keller, Ayres, and Mahoney (1977) in the conditioned suppression preparation with rats; after 2 sessions of exposure to a random CS/shock relation, rats were, if anything less suppressed to the CS if they had 34 subsequent sessions of context extinction than if they had waited 34 days in the homecages before testing.

These data on the effect of signaling ITI USs and of testing the CS in an extinguished context suggest that the Rescorla-Wagner model does a fairly good job at accounting for the mechanisms underlying sensitivity to contingency. Degrading a positive contingency by adding ITI USs disrupts learning. This disruption occurs because the extra USs produce so much context conditioning that the context blocks learning about the CS. If we can reduce the amount of context conditioning, say by signaling the extra USs, then the decrement in learning about the CS will be reduced as well. Reducing the value of the context after exposure to an uncorrelated schedule does not have the same effect.

The experiments discussed above illustrated that the addition of ITI USs can undermine an effective excitatory conditioning procedure. An even denser scheduling of ITI USs should actually result in inhibitory conditioning to the CS. For example, Miller and Schactman (1985a, 1985b) present evidence that in a lick suppression procedure with rats, a CS paired with shock 33% of the time acts as a conditioned excitor if no ITI shocks are scheduled during training, but acts as a conditioned inhibitor (i.e., passes summation and retardation tests) if ITI shocks are scheduled with a probability of .67 during training. The question is, do the rats learn the same thing about the CS in these two situations or not? If they do, we should be able to manipulate the value of the context subsequent to the different training procedures so as to get the CS trained with the positive contingency to act as an inhibitor or to get the CS trained with the negative contingency to act as an excitor.

Evidence relevant to the first possibility was presented in the preceding discussion on the effects of exposure to the US alone following CS-US pairings. Recall that there was little evidence to suggest that postacquisition exposure to the US undermined excitatory performance, let alone that it changed excitation into inhibition.

LoLordo, et al. (1985) addressed the second possibility using the autoshaping procedure with pigeons. Two groups of birds were trained with the same number of CS presentations and the same rate of food presentations in the absence of the CS (1.19/min). The difference between the groups was that for one (Group Unpaired), the CS was never paired with food whereas for the other (Group Paired), the CS was paired with food (at an average rate of .57/min of CS). Both procedures produced withdrawal to the CS. The test involved presenting the CS in a second context where the birds had been accustomed to receiving a low rate of food (.16/minute). If the test context serves as the comparison for the CS in determining performance, the comparator position might expect the birds in the paired group to approach and peck the pretrained CS upon its initial presentation in the low valued context; but LoLordo et al. found that this did not induce the birds in Group Paired to approach or peck the pretrained CS.

This finding in itself is not strong evidence against the comparator position because we cannot be certain that LoLordo et al.'s pairing parameters (about 20% reinforcement of a 20-sec CS), in the absence of ITI food presentations, would support acquisition. LoLordo et al. went on, however, to do a savings test in which the pretrained CS and a novel CS were now paired with food. This resulted in a cross-over interaction, in that birds in Group Paired met an acquisition criterion sooner for the pretrained CS than the novel CS, whereas birds in Group Unpaired met criterion sooner for the novel CS than the pretrained CS. These results nevertheless provide only weak support for the view that birds in Group Paired came to associate the pretrained CS with food during training, because none of the pairwise comparisons were reliable (e.g., Group Paired did not reach criterion for the pretrained CS significantly faster than Group Unpaired).

LoLordo et al.'s experiment is similar in strategy to the experiment by Kaplan (1985), which was described in the section on trial spacing. Recall that Kaplan

(1985) also failed to induce approach to an inhibitory CS (i.e., one that elicited withdrawal) merely by extinguishing the training context. This failure carries somewhat more weight because Kaplan has shown that the same CS-US relation that produced withdrawal when presented at a short ITI, produced approach when presented at a long ITI (Kaplan, 1984).

Miller and Schachtman found some support for their theory in the results of an experiment that involved giving rats context extinction subsequent to training with a negative contingency between noise and shock. During initial training, the probability of shock given noise was .33, whereas the probability of shock in the absence of the noise was .67 (In a separate experiment, Miller and Schachtman showed that this was an effective arrangement for producing conditioned inhibition to the noise). In a different context, rats were given clicker-shock pairings such that every clicker presentation was paired with shock and shock never occurred in the absence of the clicker. Subsequent to these experiences, half of the rats were given extinction of the context in which the noise had previously been trained. Finally, all rats were tested in yet a third context for lick suppression to the clicker-noise compound. Rats that had received extinction of the noise's training context had longer latencies to complete the criterion number of licks than rats that had not. Miller and Schachtman interpreted this to mean that extinction of the noise's training context made the noise a less effective conditioned inhibitor. But Miller and Schachtman neither tested the noise alone, nor compared responding to the clicker-noise compound with responding to the clicker alone. Therefore, these results do not really speak to whether extinction of the noise's training context actually turned the noise into a fear-eliciting stimulus. In summary, there is no good evidence that inhibition produced from a negative contingency or a short ITI is really excitation masked by a valuable context.

VI. TRANSITIONS IN CONTINGENCY

According to the Rescorla-Wagner model, transition from a positive to a zero or negative contingency should produce loss of associative strength to the CS. Consider the case where a positive relation is switched to a random relation merely by the addition of ITI USs. As a result of involvement in the initial positive contingency, the CS (X) should have relatively high, and the context (C) relatively low, associative value. The total associative strength present when the CS is present $(V_x + V_c)$ should be close to λ. When ITI USs are added, V_c should increase and $(V_x + V_c)$ will come to exceed λ. Because $\lambda - (V_x + V_c)$ will be negative, V_x and V_c should decline. The ITI USs will tend to maintain a high V_c, however; therefore a redistribution of associative values should occur such that V_x should become relatively low and V_c relatively high. Essentially, transition from a positive to a 0 contingency should produce unlearning of the CS-US relation in spite of continued contiguity.

There is some evidence that a redistribution of associative strength does take place as a result of transition from a positive to a 0 contingency. First, after such a switch, the CS typically ceases to elicit conditioned responding. For example, Keller et al. (1977) found that an uncorrelated schedule of tones and shocks that contained a local positive correlation at the beginning of the schedule resulted in conditioned fear to the tone (by rats) if only brief exposure to the schedule was given; however, extended exposure to the schedule resulted in a loss of fear to the tone (see also Rescorla, 1972). Second, experiments examining the interaction of punctate CSs (rather than CS and context) provide evidence that "overexpectation" of the US does lead to a reduction in conditioned value despite continued contiguity with reinforcement (Kamin & Gaioni, 1974; Kremer, 1978; Rescorla, 1970). For example, Rescorla (1970) separately paired a tone and a light with shock. After rats acquired substantial fear to both CSs, the CSs were presented in simultaneous compound and reinforced. This led to a reduction in the fear elicited by each component, compared to control conditions that administered no compound training. According to the Rescorla-Wagner model, this decrement in the value of the elements occurred because the total strength of the compound exceeded the level supportable by the US. Discrete trial situations also provide evidence that, without changing the schedule of reinforcements and nonreinforcements of the target CS itself, changing the relation that other CSs have with the US can lead to a loss in the value of the target (e.g., Wagner, Logan, Haberlandt, & Price 1968).

Particularly troublesome for the Rescorla-Wagner model, however, is the finding that, in autoshaping with pigeons, transition from a positive to a 0 or negative contingency does not necessarily lead to a loss of associative strength. Although conditioned keypecking may cease during the nonpositive contingency, it subsequently recovers if the CS is presented in simple extinction. (e.g., Durlach, 1986; Epstein & Skinner, 1980; Lindblom & Jenkins, 1981). For example, I gave pigeons training in which a keylight CS was reinforced 50% of the time; this led to a high rate of conditioned responding. Subsequently, the keylight was presented in an explicitly unpaired relation with food for 15 sessions. The effects of the explicitly unpaired procedure are shown in the left panel of Fig. 2.5 (Durlach, 1986). As anticipated by the model, this treatment eliminated conditioned responding. Unanticipated by the model, however, was the reaction of the birds when all food presentations were omitted. The right panel of Fig. 2.5 shows that when all food presentations were omitted, keypecking recovered. Similar recovery effects have been found during simple extinction subsequent to a transition from a positive to a 0 contingency (Epstein & Skinner, 1980; Lindblom & Jenkins, 1981). In some cases this recovery seems to be complete, i.e., the birds respond as much in extinction as birds that experienced the initial positive contingency but no intervening phase with the 0 contingency (e.g., Lindblom & Jenkins, 1981).

On the face of it, this recovery phenomenon seems to fit well with the comparator formulation. After a switch to a 0 contingency, context value should in-

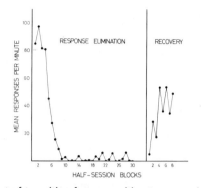

FIG. 2.5   Effect of transition from a positive to a negative contingency on autoshaped keypecking. The left panel shows mean rate of responding during the negative contingency (in which the CS and US were explicitly unpaired). The right panel shows mean rate of responding when the CS was subsequently presented in simple extinction. From Durlach (1986). Copyright 1986 by the American Psychological Association. Reprinted by permission.

crease. The value of the CS relative to the value of the context should decrease, and so, a corresponding decline in performance should occur. A subsequent switch to simple extinction should produce a reduction in the value of the context. If context value declines more rapidly than CS value, there should be at least a temporary increase in the value of the CS relative to the value of the context, and therefore a temporary recovery of responding.

If the comparator interpretation is correct, recovery ought to be maximized by extinction of the context between the response elimination treatment and the final recovery phase (in which the CS is presented in simple extinction). In agreement with this prediction, Kaplan and Hearst (1985) found that recovery of approach, following response elimination via an explicitly unpaired procedure, could be facilitated by extinction of the training context prior to testing (in the training context). I have found analogous results, illustrated in Fig. 2.6. In this experiment, birds were first given 24 sessions in which a white keylight was paired with food according to a 25% reinforcement schedule. The contingency was then lowered to 0 by adding ITI food presentations. As shown in the left curve in the left panel of Fig. 2.6, this reduced responding, but not completely. To eliminate keypecking more completely, all pairings of the keylight and food were dropped, so that during the last 6 sessions of response elimination the keylight and food were explicitly unpaired (right curve in left panel of Fig. 2.6).

Concurrent with training with the white keylight in an unlined context, birds were given experience with 2 other contexts where they would ultimately be tested. As in the signaling experiment described earlier, these contexts were distinguished by liners and birds were accustomed to receiving a high rate of food in one (30 per 20-min session) and no food in the other. Sessions in the lined con-

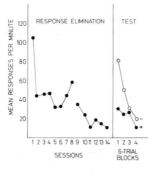

FIG. 2.6   Effect of context value on autoshaped keypecking after a transition from a positive to an nonpositive contingency. During response elimination (left panel), the CS was first uncorrelated (sessions 1–8) and then negatively correlated (sessions 9–14) with food. During the test (right panel) the CS was presented in extinction in a transfer context of high value (+) or low value (−).

texts occurred in the afternoons, whereas sessions in the unlined context occurred in the mornings. Figure 2.7 shows the activity measured during the first 5 min of each session in the lined contexts (before any food was scheduled to occur). As can be seen in the figure, birds were more active in the food (+) than the no-food (−) context.

During the test, half of the birds received nonreinforced keylight presentations in the high valued context (+) and the rest received them in the low valued context (−). As can be seen in the right panel of Fig. 2.6, there was some recovery of keypecking in both contexts, compared with the end of response elimina-

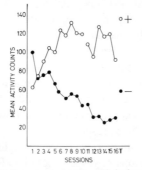

FIG. 2.7   Mean activity counts measured during the first 5 min of each session during context discrimination training and testing (T). In one context (+) pigeons received 30 food presentations during the last 15 min of each 20-min session. In the other context (−), birds never received food. Contexts were distinguished by liners. Over the first 20 days of context discrimination training birds received one session (+ or −) per day; over the last 6 days, birds received one session in each context (+ and −) per day.

tion. More importantly, however, there was a large effect of context value. Birds tested in the low valued context responded more than those tested in the high valued context.

These results are in agreement with those of Kaplan and Hearst (1985) and further show that manipulation of the training context, per se, is not necessary to obtain this comparator-like effect. These results, however, are not in agreement with the effects of context value on performance in autoshaping that were presented earlier (e.g., Figs. 2.2 & 2.4). Those results indicated a direct relation between test context value and performance to a simple excitor. I will have more to say about this discrepancy later on; for the moment, however, notice that the observation of a direct relation for a simple excitor, but an inverse relation for an ''eliminated'' excitor probably means that these performance effects are not explicable merely in terms of competing responses elicited by the test context. Context-elicited competing responses would be expected to have the same effect on performance regardless of the history of the tested CS.

Although the above results are in keeping with the predictions of the comparator view, there are several aspects of the recovery phenomenon that cannot be accounted for by that position. First, if response elimination due to the transition from a positive to a nonpositive contingency is supposed to be due soley to the resulting increase in contextual value, then response loss should not be specific to the CS involved in the nonpositive contingency. In fact, mere postacquisition exposure to a high rate of food in the context should also produce equivalent response elimination. As discussed in an earlier section, postacquisition context conditioning has, if anything, a facilitatory effect on performance in autoshaping. In addition, I have found that after concurrently training two excitors, subsequent exposure to an explicitly unpaired procedure involving only one of them had no detrimental effect on performance to the other (Durlach, 1986).

A second problem is that the comparator view predicts recovery not only when a positive contingency is followed by a 0 contingency and then simple extinction, but also when a 0 contingency applied from the outset is followed by simple extinction. Lindblom and Jenkins (1981) showed that no such recovery occurs; and as discussed at length in the preceding section, taking a CS that has been involved only in a 0 or negative contingency with food and presenting it in a low valued context (whether the training context or a transfer context) does not induce performance to the CS (Durlach, 1983; Kaplan & Hearst, 1985; LoLordo et al., 1985). In order to observe recovery, the CS must itself at one time have elicited excitatory responding.

Finally, although the comparator position expects recovery following response elimination procedures that retain CS-US pairings, it is not clear that it would also expect recovery subsequent to response elimination via an explicitly unpaired procedure (as illustrated in Fig. 2.5). In an explicitly unpaired procedure, the CS and US are never paired, so the CS might be expected to lose associative value. Although Balsam's (1984) version of comparator theory can deal with this situation by treating it like a trace conditioning procedure, it encounters the same problems as discussed above; i.e., it cannot account for why an explicitly un-paired procedure applied in the absence of prior excitatory training does not result in recovery (Durlach, 1986).

The recovery phenomenon is problematic for both the Rescorla-Wagner model and for comparator models. The crucial question seems to be, does the bird learn anything about the CS during the response elimination treatment, and if so, what? One way to approach this question is to examine whether a CS that has under-gone a response elimination treatment has properties that are different from one that has not. We have already seen one such difference; performance to an "elimi-nated" CS is inversely related to the value of the test context, whereas perfor-mance to a simple excitor is directly related to the value of the test context. The problem comes in characterizing what sort of learning might account for this difference.

The Rescorla-Wagner model expects that decrements in associative value should occur subsequent to a transition from a positive to a nonpositive contingency. This is because there should be a negative discrepancy between the reinforcer presented and the reinforcer expected. The solution to explaining the recovery phenomenon might come in recognizing that such decremental learning might occur, but not detract from excitation in the way envisaged by the model. The Rescorla-Wagner model does not recognize decremental learning and inhibition as being a process independent of incremental learning and excitation. Both con-tribute to the same hypothetical construct, V. A stimulus is either excitatory ($V > 0$) or inhibitory ($V < 0$); and the animal has no representation of whether the current V for that stimulus was obtained through an increment or a decrement (i.e., there is independence of path). This is a unique stance in the realm of learning theory, however. The more commonly adopted position is that a CS can have both excitatory and inhibitory associations, which interact to produce performance. (Hull, 1943; Konorski, 1967; Pavlov, 1927; Pearce & Hall, 1980; Wagner, 1981). The independence of incremental and decremental learning is achieved by allow-ing them to accumulate separately (i.e., V_E for increments and V_I for decre-ments). According to this view inhibition can be acquired without the loss of excitation.

These dual-process theories, nevertheless, also have trouble accounting for the recovery effect. This is because they view conditioned behavior as reflecting the net associative value ($V_E - V_I$), perhaps modulated by performance factors like motivation or contextual value, P. In other words, the likelihood of excitato-ry performance might be expressed as

$$\text{Probability of a CR} = P \times (V_E - V_I) \text{ for } V_E > V_I$$

Whenever V_I is greater than or equal to V_E, the stimulus will never elicit a con-ditioned response. In contrast, the recovery phenomenon suggests that an expres-sion such as

$$\text{Probability of CR} = (P_E \times V_E) - (P_I * V_I)$$

might be more appropriate. That is, the influence of inhibition on behavior might be modulated by performance factors *before* inhibition detracts from excitation. In this case V_I might be greater than or equal to V_E, but if P_I sufficiently attenuates the impact of V_I, the stimulus can still elicit a CR.

The recovery phenomenon suggests that, for pigeons anyway, inhibition can be acquired without the loss of excitation. If we examine how inhibition "behaves" in the pigeon autoshaping situation, it appears plausible that the recovery effect can be explained in terms of a separate inhibitory process, whose influence on performance is governed by the associative value of the context. Hearst and his colleagues have provided evidence that the influence of inhibition on performance in this paradigm seems to depend on either the recent occurrence of food or a strong expectation for food. Using withdrawal as a measure of conditioned inhibition, Bottjer (1982) found that the withdrawal that develops to a CS trained in a negative CS-US contingency goes away when the CS is presented in simple extinction. It can also be made inoperative by presenting the CS in an extinguished context (Kaplan & Hearst, 1985). In either case, however, it can be reinstated merely by reintroducing food or even an excitatory CS (Kaplan & Hearst, 1985). It is possible then, that the recovery effect can be accounted for by this same inhibitory mechanism. During the course of the response elimination treatment, the repeated occurrence of food keeps the inhibition operative; during simple extinction, in the absence of background excitation, the inhibition becomes inactive (i.e., no longer influences behavior).

The dual-process view presented above might explain the recovery phenomenon, but it encounters difficulty in also accounting for simple extinction. The traditional view of extinction is that response loss is due to the superimposition of inhibition on excitation (e.g., Hull, 1943; Pavlov, 1927; Wagner & Larew, 1985); but according to the proposed explanation, inhibition (in pigeons at least) should only influence behavior in an excitatory context. Because during simple extinction context value should decline, the proposed view cannot account for response loss during simple extinction without postulating yet some other inhibitory mechanism.

An entirely different explanation of the finding that (in autoshaping) performance to a simple excitor is directly related to the value of the test context, whereas performance to an "eliminated" excitor is inversely related to the value of the test context is that during the elimination procedure, birds learn to use either the presence or absence of food, or the value of the context itself, as a conditional cue. In the absense of food (or in a low-valued context), the CS is treated as an excitor, but in the presence of food (or in a high-valued context), it is not. Although attempts to assess this possibility have not yielded supportive results (e.g., Durlach, 1986, Experiments 3 & 4; Lindblom & Jenkins, 1981, Experiment 5), its intuitive appeal makes it difficult to dismiss. In any event, the recovery phenomenon remains problematic for both selective learning and selective performance accounts of conditioning.

VII. OVERSHADOWING AND BLOCKING

The preceding discussion has concentrated on failures of contiguity that have been blamed, one way or another, on differences in learning about the experimental context. This final section is concerned with failures of contiguity that have been blamed on the presence of another, punctate CS, namely, overshadowing and blocking. Overshadowing refers to the finding that when a CS (X) is used to signal a US, less conditioned responding develops to X if, at the time of X-US pairings, X is accompanied by some other stimulus (AX+) than if X occurs in isolation (X+). Blocking refers to the finding that when the compound AX is used to signal a US, less conditioned responding develops to X if A had been previously established as a good signal for the US than if A is novel. In all three cases (X+, AX+, AX+ preceded by A+) the relationship between X and the US is the same; however, performance to X, as seen if X is subsequently tested in isolation, is different. Although there has been much debate about whether these phenomena are best accounted for by a theory that postulates competition for associative strength (e.g., the Rescorla-Wagner model) or that postulates changes in attention (e.g., Mackintosh, 1975; Pearce & Hall, 1980), until recently, there has been little question that overshadowing and blocking represented differences in X-US learning.

The possibility that blocking and overshadowing represent performance effects rather than associative effects is suggested by a version of comparator theory that views performance as inversely related to the value of the *training* context. If contiguity is sufficient for learning, then X+ and AX+ procedures should endow X with the same associative value; however, if A is regarded as the training context for X in the AX+ procedure, but the background stimuli are regarded as the training context for X in the X+ procedure, then X+ and AX+ procedures will result in the training contexts (of X) having different values. Because the background stimuli are nonreinforced in the absence of X but A is not, the comparator context should be more valuable following AX+ than X+. This means that conditioned performance to X should be less following AX+ than X+ (i.e., overshadowing). Blocking follows from the assumption that pretraining A will make A even more valuable; the more valuable is A, the less able should be X to elicit performance. In general, if X is trained in compound with A, the comparator model predicts that performance to X should be inversely related to the value of A.

A few recent experiments have demonstrated that extinction of A following AX+ training does enhance conditioned performance to X (Kaufman & Bolles, 1982; Matzel, Schachtman, & Miller, 1985; Matzel, Shuster, & Miller, 1987).

For example, Matzel et al. (1985) gave rats pairings of a tone-light (TL) compound with shock, as well as pairings of a clicker (C) and shock. Subsequently, rats were given extinction of T (Group ET), extinction of C (Group EC), or extinction of the chamber only (Group 0). When tested for suppression of licking in the presence of L, rats in Group ET had longer latencies to complete a criterion number of licks than rats in Group 0, and latencies for Groups 0 and EC were not reliably different. If group ET were more suppressed than Group EC, it would suggest that this effect was specific to extinction of L's training partner; however, this difference was only marginally significant, making conclusions about specificity only tenuous.

Although these "unovershadowing" results fit with the comparator predictions that postacquisition extinction of one element of a training compound should enhance performance to the other, they are in direct conflict with a number of other experimental results that show just the reverse. Typically, postacquisition extinction of one element of a training compound has a corresponding decremental effect on performance to the other (e.g., Durlach & Rescorla, 1980; Holland & Ross, 1981; Marlin, 1982; Rescorla & Cunningham, 1978; Rescorla & Durlach, 1981; Schweitzer & Green, 1982; Speers, Gillan, & Rescorla, 1980). For example, Schweitzer and Green (1982) gave rats pairings of a tone-light compound and shock, followed by several sessions of context only ($-$), shock only ($+$), the tone only (T$-$), or the tone paired with shock (T$+$). When subsequently given extinction with the light alone, rats that had been given T$-$ met an extinction criterion *sooner* than controls ($+$ and $-$), whereas rats that had been given T$+$ met the criterion later than controls. In other words, treatment of T had a corresponding effect on L, not an opposite effect on L. These results, and others like them, seem best interpreted in terms of within-compound associations (cf. Rescorla and Durlach, 1981). According to this interpretation, associations between elements of a compound allow changes in the the value of one to have a similar impact on the value of the other.

The conflict in the data presented above (e.g., Matzel et al., 1985 vs. Schweitzer & Green, 1982) might be explained in terms of the presence or absence of within-compound associations; perhaps when within-compound associations are present they overwhelm the comparator effect. One method to evaluate this possibility might be to use procedures known to be unfavorable to the formation of within-compound associations; however, these procedures might also obscure the comparator mechanism. As previously mentioned, this version of comparator theory requires some kind of link or association between the target stimulus and its training context in order for the comparator mechanism to operate. Any procedure intended to destroy or prevent within-compound associations (e.g., separate element presentations) might also upset the potential comparator relation between the elements as well.

Alternatively, it is possible that the unovershadowing effect is actually a "closet" reminder effect mediated by within-compound associations (Miller,

Kasprow, & Schachtman, 1986). Miller and his colleagues (Balaz et al., 1982; Kasprow, Cocheiro, Balaz, & Miller, 1982; Schachtman, Gee, Kasprow, & Miller, 1983) have found that in their lick suppression preparation, a *few* nonreinforced exposures to the target CS following a blocking or overshadowing procedure actually enhanced the fear produced by that same CS during a subsequent test. They suggest this occurs because the nonreinforced CS presentations facilitate retrieval of the training events. If nonreinforced presentations of the target CS seem to enhance subsequent performance to that CS, it seems plausible that nonreinforced presentations of an associate of that CS might have a similiar effect.

The second prediction of Miller and Schachtman's comparator model is that enhancing the value of A subsequent to AX+ training should decrement performance to X (compared to no treatment of A). Kamin (1969), in fact, provided some evidence for this backward blocking effect. He found that 8 LN+ trials resulted in less fear to L if 16 N+ trials were interposed between compound conditioning and L testing, than if L were tested immediately after compound conditioning; however, Kamin attributed these results to forgetting (referring to undescribed control groups establishing this). In general, attempts to obtain backward blocking in animal conditioning have been unsuccessful (e.g., Matzel et al., 1987, personal communications from A.G. Baker, and from G.C. Preston). Note however, that backward blocking should only occur, according to the comparator model, if A+ subsequent to AX+ did enhance the value of A. In other words, if AX+ training produced an A of asymptotic value, further A+ training would be expected to have no effect. Some failures of backward blocking have not merely been null results, however; the Schweitzer and Green (1982) study referred to earlier found the reverse. Recall that they found that pairings of T and shock subsequent to TL-shock pairings enhanced fear to L, relative to control groups. Many of the relevant experiments available compare post-AX+ A+ training with post-AX+ A− training; as mentioned before, the typical finding is that if postacquisition manipulation of A has any effect on performance to X, it is that X changes in the same manner as A; X elicits more performance after A+ than after A− (Rescorla & Durlach, 1981).

One demonstration of backward blocking comes from a human learning experiment (Shanks, 1985). In this experiment, subjects fired shells at tanks (on a video screen) while the tanks drove through an invisible minefield. When the subjects fired, tanks might explode because they were hit by a shell (and the shell was effective) or because they hit a mine, but the subjects couldn't tell which (the AX+ phase where A is the minefield and X is the shells). At the end of the experiment, subjects were asked to judge the effectiveness of the shells (test of X). In the backward blocking condition, subjects were allowed to observe the destructiveness of the minefield alone (A+) before making their judgment about the shells; in the control condition, subjects were not given this observation period. The results were that subjects in the backward blocking condition judged the shells as less effective than subjects in the control condition. Many aspects of this experiment make it of questionable relevance to animal learning, however. The instructions emphasized the either/or aspect of the destruction of the tank (either minefield or shell) and so may have set subjects to make reciprocal judgments of the effectiveness of the two. Moreover, the instructions explicitly pointed out that the observation period (of the minefield alone) would be helpful in making a judgment about the shells. Finally use of a meaningful or structured situation like this probably predisposed subjects against forming the type of within-compound associations (between A and X) discussed above.

In conclusion, the evidence that overshadowing and blocking are merely performance effects due to a comparator mechanism seems rather weak. Some of the unovershadowing results are favorable, but there are also many results that are unfavorable. The conditions under which unovershadowing does and does not occur require further attention.

VIII. CONCLUDING COMMENTS

The pairing of a CS and a US provides an opportunity for associative learning. The question pursued by this chapter has been whether that opportunity is always taken advantage of. The same contingency relation seems to result in different degrees of conditioned responding to the CS, depending on the relations that other stimuli have with the US. The present discussion has been concerned with whether, for certain cases, these differences in behavior reflect differences in the way the same learning is mapped into performance, or rather differences in the learning itself. In particular, comparator accounts were contrasted with the associative account offered by the Rescorla-Wagner model. Within this theoretical context, the associative position seemed to provide a better characterization of the phenomena that were examined.

That context value at the time of CS-US pairings affects the rate of acquisition of conditioned responding is fairly well established. The more valuable the context, the slower the emergence of conditioned responding. The question examined repeatedly in this chapter has been whether contextual value affects the learning of a CS-US association, or rather whether contextual value merely affects the performance based on equivalent underlying learning. Examination of conditioned performance after different training procedures, but under conditions in which the potential influence of contextual value is equated, is one strategy for assessing these two possibilities. This removes any potential differential effect of context value on performance that might have been inherent in the different training procedures. If differential performance is still observed under equivalent test conditions, it suggests that the difference reflects a difference in underlying learning. For example, Rescorla and Durlach (1987) found that an effect of trial spacing on performance was evident not only during training, but also when the CSs were presented under mixed ITI conditions in a common transfer context. Because the potential influence of context value at the time of testing was the same for both CSs, their results suggest that the effect of trial spacing on performance cannot be accounted for only by difference in the value of the test context. Other experiments that have utilized this strategy have also found that differences in performance resulting from different training conditions tend to be maintained under equivalent testing conditions (e.g., Ayres et al., 1985; Durlach, 1983; Grau & Rescorla, 1984).

A second strategy is to examine conditioned performance after identical training procedures, but under conditions in which the potential influence of context value on performance has been deliberately manipulated subsequent to training. This allows the opportunity to assess whether context value does indeed affect performance in the manner predicted. For example, after training with a target-CS intermixed with signaled ITI USs, Durlach (1983) examined performance to the target-CS either in a context of high value or a context of low value. Contrary to the predictions of comparator theory, performance during that test was greater in the higher valued context. Utilization of this strategy has tended to yield results unfavorable to the comparator positions (e.g., Jenkins & Lambos, 1983; Kaplan, 1985; Miller & Schachtman, 1985a, 1985b; Rescorla et al., 1985; Schweitzer & Green, 1982), although there are some notable exceptions (e.g., Matzel et al., 1985, 1987).

One issue that has cropped up several times in the course of this chapter concerns whether a CS of a given history (e.g., one trained in a negative contingency) might act as an inhibitor under some test conditions but as an excitor under others. The evidence reviewed suggested that although a reduction in the value of the training or testing context might lead to a diminution in exhibition of inhibitory tendencies, it did not unmask the presence of excitatory tendencies (e.g., Kaplan, 1985; Kaplan & Hearst, 1985; LoLordo et al., 1985; Miller & Schachtman, 1985a, 1985b). But there is other evidence relevant to this question which has not heretofore been mentioned. Mackintosh and Cotton (1985) used a variant of the standard feature negative discrimination procedure (A+, AX−) for producing conditioned inhibition. Instead of signaling the complete omission of the US, however, the feature (X) predicted a decrease in the quality of the US. Rats received discrete trial operant training in which a tone alone signaled the availability of 20% sucrose solution, whereas a tone-light compound signaled the availability of only an 8% sucrose solution. The light acted as a conditioned inhibitor in a summation test with a clicker that had also signaled the 20% sucrose solution (i.e., the light reduced responding to the clicker); however, in a separate experiment they found that the light acted as a conditioned excitor (i.e., it enhanced responding to the clicker) if the clicker had been trained as a signal for only 2% sucrose solution.

Nelson (1987) found a similar effect when she manipulated probability (instead of quality) of reward. Lever pressing was rewarded on every trial signaled by a tone alone, but only on 50% of the trials signaled by a tone-light compound. When the light was subsequently presented in a summation test with a clicker, the light suppressed responding if the clicker had been trained as a signal for a 90% reinforcement schedule, but accelerated responding if the clicker had been trained as a signal for only a 15% reinforcement schedule.

That the feature (light) gained inhibitory properties when it signaled a reduction in the quality or probability of reward is consistent with the idea that inhibition results from a negative discrepancy between the predicted and obtained reward, as indicated by the Rescorla-Wagner model. However, the fact that the feature exerted a different effect on performance depending upon the reinforcement history of the stimulus with which it was compounded poses problems for that model. According to the Rescorla-Wagner model, a stimulus can only be excitatory ($V > 0$) or inhibitory ($V < 0$), but not both.

In contrast, the comparator model proposed by Balsam (1984) predicts that the same stimulus might act as an excitor when tested in a context of substantially lower value than its own, but as an inhibitor when tested in a context of substantially higher value than its own. According to this view, stimuli are only more or less excitatory, but the behavioral effect of a stimulus is determined by its relative rather than its absolute value. If punctate stimuli are allowed to act as contexts, then this comparator view is quite content with the finding that the feature in the above experiments acts as an inhibitor when tested with a clicker that signaled a higher probability of reinforcement but as an excitor when tested with a clicker that signaled a lower probability of reinforcement.

A problem with the comparator account becomes apparent, however, when the results obtained from Mackintosh and Cotton's and Nelson's control groups are considered. Besides the feature-negative discrimination, their experiments included control groups in which the light alone signaled the lower valued reward (e. g., Tone-100%, Light-50%). According to comparator theory, there is no reason why the light trained in this simple discrimination procedure should, during the summation test, produce behavior any different from a light trained in the feature negative discrimination (e.g., Tone-100%, Tone-Light-50%). This is because it is only the light's own relation with the US that should influence learning about the light, and this is the same for the two procedures. In contrast with this expectation, when the test clicker was trained with a higher value (or probability) reinforcer than the light, the light trained in the feature negative discrimination invariably acted as an inhibitor (i.e., suppressed responding to the clicker), whereas the light trained in the simple discrimination invariably acted as an excitor (i.e., accelerated responding to the clicker). Thus the comparator model cannot account for the fact that the light acquires dual behavioral tendencies only when it is trained in the feature negative procedure.

The theoretical problems raised by these "incomplete reduction in reward" experiments are analogous to those raised by the recovery phenomenon discussed earlier. Both phenomena seem to demand a dual-process view of learning in which the same stimulus can be endowed with both excitatory and inhibitory associations. However, they also point to inadequacies in currently available dual-process formulations (e.g., Pearce & Hall, 1980; Wagner, 1981), for according to these theories, performance should always reflect the stronger of the two associations. In contrast, what is required is a dual-process theory in which the influence of inhibition on performance can be modulated independently of the influence of excitation.

Finally, it should be mentioned that although the foregoing discussion has tended to dispute specific versions of comparator theory, there is no dispute about the spirit behind that theory. The comparator view serves to emphasize the distinction between what the subject knows and how the subject behaves, and urges consideration of the possibility that our subjects know more than their behavior might suggest. The comparator theorists are in some sense in a position analogous to that of early cognitive learning theorists who attempted to demonstrate, contrary to the dogma of the time, that learning about the relation between two neutral stimuli could occur (Brogden, 1939). That a rat could learn that a light cooccurred with a tone was not obvious merely from changes in the rat's response to the light; some special manipulation forcing the behavioral expression of this learning needed to be found (e.g., pairing the tone with shock). Likewise, contrary to current dogma that animals only learn about valid or predictive relations between CSs and USs (Pearce & Hall, 1980; Rescorla & Wagner, 1972; Wagner, 1981), comparator theories suggest that animals learn about all the stimulus relations they experience, whether predictive or not. That a rat might learn that a CS cooccurs with a US despite the fact that the CS and US are uncorrelated is not obvious merely from changes in the rat's response to the CS. But some special manipulation might be found for revealing that the rat does have this knowledge. The particular manipulations reviewed in this paper were not terribly successful in uncovering latent learning; but early attempts to obtain evidence for sensory preconditioning were not overly impressive either (Rescorla, 1980). As Dickinson (1980) points out, "although we can conclude with confidence that a behavioral change shows that learning has occurred, . . . we cannot assume that nothing is learned in the absence of a behavioural change" (p. 15). Thus, we can never be entirely confident that the failure of contiguity to produce behavioral change implies a failure of learning.

ACKNOWLEDGMENT

This chapter is dedicated to my foster family: all the members of the University of Cambridge Department of Experimental Psychology animal learning laboratory from 1983–1987.

REFERENCES

Ayres, J. J. B., Bombace, J. C., Shurtleff, D., & Vigorito, M. (1985). Conditioned suppression tests of the context-blocking hypothesis: Testing in the absence of the preconditioned context. *Journal of Experimental Psychology: Animal Behavior Processes, 11,* 1-14.

Baker, A. G. (1977). Conditioned inhibition arising from a between-session negative correlation. *Journal of Experimental Psychology: Animal Behavior Processes, 3,* 144-158.

Baker, A. G., Mercier, P., Gable, J., & Baker, P. A. (1981). Contextual conditioning and the US preexposure effect in conditioned fear. *Journal of Experimental Psychology: Animal Behavior Processes, 7,* 109-128.

Baker, A. G., Singh, M., & Bindra, D. (1985). Some effects of contextual conditioning and US predictability on Pavlovian conditioning. In P. D. Balsam & A. Tomie (Eds.), *Context and learning* (pp. 73-104). Hillsdale, NJ: Lawrence Erlbaum Associates.

Balaz, M. A., Gerstin, P., Cacheiro, H., & Miller, R. R. (1982). Blocking as a retrieval failure: Reactivation of associations to a blocked stimulus. *Quarterly Journal of Experimental Psychology, 34B,* 99-113.

Balsam, P. D. (1982). Bringing the background to the foreground: The role of contextual cues in autoshaping. In M. Commons, R. Herrnstein, & A. Wagner (Eds.), *Quantitative analyses of behavior, Vol. 3: Acquisition* (pp. 141-171). Cambridge, MA: Ballinger.

Balsam, P. D. (1984). Relative time intrace conditioning. In J. Gibbon & L. Allan (Eds.), *Timing and time perception* (pp. 211-227). New York: New York Academy of Science.

Balsam, P. D., & Schwartz, A. L. (1981). Rapid contextual conditioning in autoshaping. *Journal of Experimental Psychology: Animal Behavior Processes, 7,* 382-393.

Batson, J. D., & Best, P. J. (1979). Drug-preexposure effects in flavor-aversion learning: Associative influence by conditioned environmental stimuli. *Journal of Experimental Psychology: Animal Behavior Processes, 5,* 273-283.

Bottjer, S. W. (1982). Conditioned approach and withdrawal behavior in pigeons: Effects of a novel extraneous stimulus during acquisition and extinction. *Learning and Motivation, 13,* 44-67.

Bouton, M. E., & Bolles (1985). Contexts, event-memories, and extinction. In P. D. Balsam & A. Tomie (Eds.), *Context and learning* (pp. 133-166). Hillsdale, NJ: Lawrence Erlbaum Associates.

Bouton, M. E., & King, D. A. (1986). Effect of context on performance to conditioned stimuli with mixed histories of reinforcement and nonreinforcement. *Journal of Experimental Psychology: Animal Behavior Processes, 12,* 4-15.

Brogden, W. J. (1939). Sensory pre-conditioning. *Journal of Experimental Psychology, 25,* 323-332.

Dickinson, A. (1980). *Contemporary animal learning theory.* Cambridge, England: Cambridge University Press.

Durlach, P. J. (1982, April). Direct measurement of context conditioning in the pigeons. *Proceedings of the 53rd Annual Meeting of the Eastern Psychological Association,* Baltimore, MD.

Durlach, P. J. (1983). Effect of signaling intertrial unconditioned stimuli in autoshaping. *Journal of Experimental Psychology: Animal Behavior Processes, 9,* 374-389.

Durlach, P. J. (1986). Explicitly unpaired procedure as a response elimination technique in autoshaping. *Journal of Experimental Psychology: Animal Behavior Processes, 12,* 172-185.

Durlach, P. J., & Rescorla, R. A. (1980). Potentiation rather than overshadowing in flavor-aversion learning: An analysis in terms of within-compound associations. *Journal of Experimental Psychology: Animal Behavior Processes, 6,* 175-187.

Epstein, R., & Skinner, B. F. (1980). Resurgence of responding after cessation of response-independent reinforcement. *Proceedings of the National Academy of Science, 77,* 6251-6253.

Estes, W. K. (1969). New perspectives on some old issues in association theory. In N. J. Mackintosh & W. K. Honig (Eds.), *Fundamental issues in associative learning* (pp. 162–189). Halifax: Dalhousie University Press.

Fanselow, M. S. (1980). Signaled shock-free periods and preference for signaled shock. *Journal of Experimental Psychology: Animal Behavior Processes, 6,* 65–80.

Fowler, H., Kleiman, M. C., & Lysle, D. T. (1985). Factors affecting acquisition and extinction of conditioned inhibition suggest a "slave" process. In R. R. Miller & N. E. Spear (Eds.), *Information processing in animals: Conditioned inhibition* (pp. 113–150). Hillsdale, NJ: Lawrence Erlbaum Associates.

Gamzu, E., & Williams, D. (1973). Associative factors underlying the pigeon's key pecking in autoshaping. *Journal of Experimental Analysis of Behavior, 19,* 225–232.

Gibbon, J. (1981). The contingency problem in autoshaping. In C. M. Locurto, H. S. Terrace, & J. Gibbon (Eds.), *Autoshaping and conditioning theory* (pp. 285–308). New York: Academic Press.

Gibbon, J., & Balsam, P. D. (1981). Spreading association in time. In C. M. Locurto, H. S. Terrace, & J. Gibbon (Eds.), *Autoshaping and conditioning theory* (pp. 219–253). New York: Academic Press.

Grau, J. W., & Rescorla, R. A. (1984). Role of context in autoshaping. *Journal of Experimental Psychology: Animal Behavior Processes, 10,* 324–332.

Holland, P. C., & Ross, R. T. (1981). Within-compound associations in serial compound conditioning. *Journal of Experimental Psychology: Animal Behavior Processes, 7,* 228–241.

Hull, C. L. (1943). *A behavior system.* New York: Appleton-Century-Crofts.

Jenkins, H. M., Barnes, R. A., & Barrera, F. J. (1981). Why autoshaping depends on trial spacing. In C. M. Locurto, H. S. Terrace, & J. Gibbon (Eds.), *Autoshaping and conditioning theory* (pp. 255–284). New York: Academic Press.

Jenkins, H. M., & Lambos, W. A. (1983). Test of two explanations of response elimination by non-contingency reinforcement. *Animal Learning and Behavior, 11,* 302–308.

Kamin, L. J. (1969). Selective association and conditioning. In N. J. Mackintosh & W. K. Honig (Eds.), *Fundamental issues in associative learning* (pp. 42–64). Halifax: Dalhousie University Press.

Kamin, L. J., & Gaioni, S. J. (1974). Compound conditioned emotional response conditioning with differentially salient elements in rats. *Journal of Comparative and Physiological Psychology, 87,* 591–597.

Kaplan, P. S. (1984). Temporal parameters in trace autoshaping: From excitation to inhibition. *Journal of Experimental Psychology: Animal Behavior Processes, 10,* 113–126.

Kaplan, P. S. (1985). Explaining the effects of relative time in trace conditioning: A preliminary test of a comparator hypothesis. *Animal Learning and Behavior, 13,* 233–238.

Kaplan, P. S., & Hearst, E. (1985). Contextual control and excitatory versus inhibitory learning: Studies of extinction, reinstatement, and interference. In P. D. Balsam & A. Tomie (Eds.), *Context and learning* (pp. 195–224). Hillsdale, NJ: Lawrence Erlbaum Associates.

Kasprow, W. J., Cocheiro, H., Balaz, M. A., & Miller, R. R. (1982). Reminder-induced recovery of associations to an overshadowed stimulus. *Learning and Motivation, 13,* 155–166.

Kaufman, M. A., & Bolles, R. C. (1982). A nonassociative aspect of overshadowing. *Bulletin of the Psychonomic Society, 18,* 318–320.

Keller, R. J., Ayres, J. J. B., & Mahoney, W. J. (1977). Brief vs. extended exposure to truly random control procedures. *Journal of Experimental Psychology: Animal Behavior Processes, 3,* 53–65.

Konorski, J. (1948). *Conditioned reflexes and neuron organization.* Cambridge, England: Cambridge University Press.

Konorski, J. (1967). *Integrative activity of the brain.* Chicago: Chicago University Press.

Kremer, E. F. (1978). The Rescorla-Wagner model: Losses in associative strength in compound conditioned stimuli. *Journal of Experimental Psychology: Animal Behavior Processes, 4,* 22–36.

Lindblom, L. L., & Jenkins, H. M. (1981). Responses elicited by noncontingency or negatively contingent reinforcement recover in extinction. *Journal of Experimental Psychology: Animal Behavior Processes, 7,* 175–190.

LoLordo, V. M., Fairless, J. A., & Stanhope, K. J. (1985). The effect of context upon responses to conditioned inhibitors. In F. R. Brush & J. B. Overmier (Eds.), *Affect, conditioning, and cognition* (pp. 131–144). Hillsdale, NJ: Lawrence Erlbaum Associates.

Lysle, D. T., & Fowler, H. (1985). Inhibition as a "slave" process: Deactivation of conditioned inhibition through extinction of conditioned excitation. *Journal of Experimental Psychology: Animal Behavior Processes, 11,* 71–94.

Mackintosh, N. J. (1965). Selective attention in animal discrimination learning. *Psychological Bulletin, 64,* 124–150.

Mackintosh, N.J. (1975). A theory of attention: Variation in the associability of stimuli with reinforcement. *Psychological Review, 82,* 276–298.

Mackintosh, N. J., & Cotton, M. M. (1985). Conditioned inhibition from reinforcement reduction. In R. R. Miller & N. E. Spear (Eds.), *Information processing in animals: Conditioned inhibition* (pp. 89–111). Hillsdale, NJ: Lawrence Erlbaum Associates.

Marlin, N. A. (1982). Within-compound associations between the context and the conditioned stimulus. *Learning and Motivation, 13,* 526–541.

Matzel, L. D., Brown, A. M., & Miller, R. R. (1987). Associative effects of US preexposure: Modulation of conditioned responding by an excitatory training context. *Journal of Experimental Psychology: Animal Behavior Processes, 13,* 65–72.

Matzel, L. D., Schachtman, T. R., & Miller, R. R. (1985). Recovery of an overshadowed association achieved by extinction of the overshadowing stimulus. *Learning and Motivation, 16,* 398–412.

Matzel, L. D., Shuster, K., & Miller, R. R. (1987). Covariation in conditioned response strength between stimuli trained in compound. *Animal Learning and Behavior, 15,* 439–447.

Miller, R. R., Kasprow, W. J., & Schachtman, T. R. (1986). Retrieval variability: Sources and consequences. *American Journal of Psychology, 99,* 145–218.

Miller, R. R., & Schachtman, T. R. (1985a). The several roles of context at the time of retrieval. In P. D. Balsam & A. Tomie (Eds.), *Context and learning* (pp. 167–194). Hillsdale, NJ: Lawrence Erlbaum Associates.

Miller, R. R., & Schachtman, T. R. (1985b). Conditioning context as an associative baseline: implications for response generation and the nature of conditioned inhibition. In R. R. Miller & N. E. Spear (Eds.), *Information processing in animals: Conditioned Inhibition* (pp. 51–88). Hillsdale, NJ: Lawrence Erlbaum Associates.

Nelson, K. J. (1987). Conditioned inhibition from incomplete reduction in the probability of reinforcement. *Quarterly Journal of Experimental Psychology, 39B,* 365–391.

Odling-Smee, F. J. (1975). The role of background stimuli during Pavlovian conditioning. *Quarterly Journal of Experimental Psychology, 27,* 201–209.

Odling-Smee, F. J. (1978). The overshadowing of background stimuli by an informative CS in aversive Pavlovian conditioning with rats. *Animal Learning and Behavior, 6,* 43–51.

Pavlov, I. P. (1927). *Conditioned reflexes.* London: Oxford University Press.

Pearce, J. M., & Hall, G. (1980). A model of Pavlovian learning: Variations in the effectiveness of conditioned but not unconditioned stimuli. *Psychological Review, 87,* 532–552.

Randich, A. (1981). The US preexposure phenomenon in the conditioned suppression paradigm: A role for conditioned situational stimuli. *Learning and Motivation, 12,* 321–341.

Randich, A., & Haggard, D. (1983). Exposure to the unconditioned stimulus alone: Effects upon retention and acquisition of conditioned suppression. *Journal of Experimental Psychology: Animal Behavior Processes, 9,* 147–159.

Randich, A., & LoLordo, V. M. (1979). Associative and nonassociative theories of the US pre-exposure phenomenon: Implications for Pavlovian conditioning. *Psychological Bulletin, 86,* 523–548.

Randich, A., & Rescorla, R. A. (1981). The effect of separate presentations of the US on conditioned suppression. *Animal Learning and Behavior, 9,* 56–64.

Randich, A., & Ross, R. T. (1985). Contextual stimuli mediate the effects of pre- and postexposure to the unconditioned stimulus in conditioned suppression. In P. D. Balsam & A. Tomie (Eds.), *Context and learning* (pp. 105–132). Hillsdale, NJ: Lawrence Erlbaum Associates.

Rescorla, R. A. (1968). Probability of shock in the presence and absence of the CS in fear conditioning. *Journal of Comparative and Physiological Psychology, 66*, 1–5.

Rescorla, R. A. (1969). Conditioned inhibition of fear. In N. J. Mackintosh & W. K. Honig (Eds.), *Fundamental issues in associative learning* (pp. 65–89). Halifax: Dalhousie University Press.

Rescorla, R. A. (1970). Reduction in the effectiveness of reinforcement after prior excitatory conditioning. *Learning and Motivation, 1*, 372–381.

Rescorla, R. A. (1972). Informational variables in Pavlovian conditioning. In G. H. Bower (Ed.), *The psychology of learning and motivation, Vol. 6* (pp. 1–46). New York: Academic Press.

Rescorla, R. A. (1973). Effect of US habituation following conditioning. *Journal of Comparative and Physiological Psychology, 82*, 137–143.

Rescorla, R. A. (1974). Effect of inflation of the unconditioned stimulus value following conditioning. *Journal of Comparative and Physiological Psychology, 86*, 101–106.

Rescorla, R. A. (1979). Conditioned inhibition and extinction. In A. Dickinson & R. A. Boakes (Eds.), *Mechanisms of learning and motivation* (pp. 83–110). Hillsdale, NJ: Lawrence Erlbaum Associates.

Rescorla, R. A. (1980). *Pavlovian second-order conditioning*. Hillsdale, NJ: Lawrence Erlbaum Associates.

Rescorla, R. A. (1984a). Associations between Pavlovian CSs and context. *Journal of Experimental Psychology: Animal Behavior Processes, 10*, 195–204.

Rescorla, R. A. (1984b). Signaling intertrial shocks attenuates their negative effect on conditioned suppression. *Bulletin of the Psychonomic Society, 22*, 225–228.

Rescorla, R. A., & Cunningham, C. L. (1978). Within-compound flavor associations. *Journal of Experimental Psychology: Animal Behavior Processes, 4*, 267–275.

Rescorla, R. A., & Durlach, P. J. (1981). Within-event learning in Pavlovian conditioning. In N. E. Spear & R. R. Miller (Eds.), *Information processing in animals: Memory mechanisms* (pp. 81–112). Hillsdale, NJ: Lawrence Erlbaum Associates.

Rescorla, R. A., & Durlach, P. J. (1987). The role of context in intertrial interval effects in autoshaping. *Quarterly Journal of Experimental Psychology, 39B*, 35–40.

Rescorla, R. A., Durlach, P. J., & Grau, J. W. (1985). Contextual learning in Pavlovian conditioning. In P. D. Balsam & A. Tomie (Eds.), *Context and learning* (pp. 23–56). Hillsdale, NJ: Lawrence Erlbaum Associates.

Rescorla, R. A., & Wagner, A. R. (1972). A theory of Pavlovian conditioning: Variations in the effectiveness of reinforcement and nonreinforcement. In A. H. Black & W. F. Prokasy (Eds.), *Classical conditioning II: Current theory and research* (pp. 64–99). New York: Appleton-Century-Crofts.

Schachtman, T. R., Gee, J., Kasprow, W. J., & Miller, R. R. (1983). Reminder-induced recovery from blocking as a function of the number of compound trials. *Learning and motivation, 14*, 154–164.

Schweitzer, L., & Green, L. (1982). Reevaluation of things past: A test of the "retrospective hypothesis" using a CER procedure with rats. *Pavlovian Journal of Biological Science, 17*, 62–68.

Shanks, D. R. (1985). Forward and backward blocking in human contingency judgement. *Quarterly Journal of Experimental Psychology, 37B*, 1–21.

Sherman, J. E. (1978). US inflation with trace and simultaneous fear conditioning. *Animal Learning and Behavior, 6*, 463–468.

Speers, M. J., Gillan, D. J., & Rescorla, R. A. (1980). Within-compound associations in a variety of compound conditioning procedures. *Learning and Motivation, 11*, 135–149.

Sutherland, N. S. (1964). Visual discrimination in animals. *British Medical Bulletin, 29*, 54–59.

Sutherland, N. S., & Mackintosh, N. J. (1971). *Mechanisms of animal discrimination learning*. New York: Academic Press.

Terrace, H. S., Gibbon, J., Farrell, L., & Baldock, M. D. (1975). Temporal factors influencing the acquisition and maintenance of an autoshaped keypeck. *Animal Learning and Behavior, 3*, 53–62.

Tomie, A. (1976). Interference with autoshaping by prior context conditioning. *Journal of Experimental Psychology: Animal Behavior Processes, 2*, 323–334.

Tomie, A. (1981). Effect of unpredictable food on the subsequent acquisition of autoshaping: Analysis of the context-blocking hypothesis. In C. M. Locurto, H. S. Terrace, & J. Gibbon (Eds.), *Autoshaping and conditioning theory* (pp. 181–215). New York: Academic Press.

Wagner, A. R. (1969). Stimulus selection and a "modified continuity theory" (pp. 1–41). In G. H. Bower & J. T. Spence (Eds.), *The psychology of learning and motivation, Vol. 3*. New York: Academic Press.

Wagner, A. R. (1981). SOP: A model of automatic memory processing in animal behavior. In N. E. Spear & R. R. Miller (Eds.), *Information processing in animals: Memory mechanisms* (pp. 5–48). Hillsdale, NJ: Lawrence Erlbaum Associates.

Wagner, A. R., & Larew, M. B. (1985). Opponent processes and Pavlovian inhibition. In R. R. Miller & N. E. Spear (Eds.), *Information processing in animals: Conditioned inhibition* (pp. 223–266). Hillsdale, NJ: Lawrence Erlbaum Associates.

Wagner, A. R., Logan, F. A., Haberlandt, K., & Price, T. (1968). Stimulus selection in animal discrimination learning. *Journal of Experimental Psychology, 76*, 171–180.

Wagner, A. R., & Rescorla, R. A. (1972). Inhibition in Pavlovian conditioning: Application of a theory. In R. A. Boakes & M. S. Halliday (Eds.), *Inhibition and learning* (pp. 301–336). London: Academic Press.

Wasserman, E. A., Franklin, S. R., & Hearst, E. (1974). Pavlovian appetitive contingencies and approach vs. withdrawal to conditioned stimuli in pigeons. *Journal of Comparative and Physiological Psychology, 86*, 616–627.

Witcher, E. S., & Ayres, J. J. B. (1980). Systematic manipulation of CS-US pairings in negative CS-US correlation procedures in rats. *Animal Learning and Behavior, 8*, 67–74.

3 Contingency and Relative Associative Strength

Ralph R. Miller
Louis D. Matzel
State University of New York at Binghamton

The intellectual roots of traditional learning theories can be found in the principles of associationism advanced by the British empiricist philosophers of the 17th, 18th, and 19th centuries (e.g., John Locke, David Hume, & John Stuart Mill). They viewed the problem of how experience causes specific changes in subsequent behavior as essentially answerable in terms of mental links, called associations, between internal representations of contiguous events, that is, events that occur in temporal and spatial proximity to one another. Although Pavlov (1927) was primarily interested in the physiological underpinnings of learning, at the psychological level of analysis he too subscribed to contiguity as the central tenet of associationism despite his concern with the relative weakness of simultaneous conditioning compared to forward conditioning. Today, most theories of learning are couched in the language of associationism with the various theories being differentiated by their choices of qualifiers and additions to contiguity, e.g., whether reinforcement (Hull, 1943) or surprise (Rescorla & Wagner, 1972) are necessary in addition to contiguity and whether reactivation of the mental representation of a past event can act as a surrogate for the event itself (Gordon, 1983; Riccio & Ebner, 1981).

One consequence of this associationist tradition has been a continuing emphasis on the mechanisms underlying the acquisition of information and relative neglect of the many other steps that must occur between the pairing of two events and any subsequent change in behavior, e.g., storage in passive memory, retrieval from passive memory, and response generation. So strong is this bias that students of the consequences of prior experience are said to study *learning* as opposed to *the acquisition and processing of information by living organisms*, which in fact is really the issue at hand. (Please forgive our awkward alternative to *learn-*

ing, but the lack of a simple name for it indicates just how prevalent the focus on acquisition is.)

In recent years, investigators of human cognitive processes have begun to show considerable interest in the extra-acquisition aspects of information processing (e.g., Anderson, 1983). Although researchers who have focused on the fundamentals of information processing in animals have been more hesitant to leave the appealing simplicity of traditional associationism, new data are rendering purely associative models of information processing less and less viable. Miller, Kasprow, and Schachtman (1986), for example, have summarized evidence for the importance of retrieval mechanisms in the processing of acquired information by animals.

This chapter is primarily concerned with the generation of conditioned responses, a topic that all complete theories concerning the processing of acquired information must address. However, owing in large part to the biases of associationism, response rules traditionally have received little attention in contemporary learning theories. Rescorla and Wagner (1972), for instance, state only that responding is monotonically related to associative strength, that is, response strength and associative strength vary in the same direction. However, linearity of associative strength and response strength, that is, direct proportionality, is often implicit in their interpretations of data. Whether linear or merely monotonic, such simple response rules are not sufficient to explain behavioral differences between experimental groups. As we will soon see, somewhat more complex rules for responding can have considerable explanatory value, thereby lightening the explanatory burden on the other steps in the information processing sequence, particularly the greatly overburdened acquisition process.

I. CONTINGENCY THEORY OF LEARNING

Contiguity theory is centrally concerned with the number of pairings of the conditioned stimulus (CS) with the unconditioned stimulus (US). In its simplest form, it does not attach any importance to presentations of the CS or US alone. As early as Pavlov (1927), it was recognized that presentations of the CS alone intermixed with the CS–US pairings of training (i.e., partial reinforcement) were detrimental to conditioned responding, presumably because extinction of the CS occurred on those trials lacking the US. The pervasiveness of the phenomenon of extinction resulted in the concept of contiguity being modified to emphasize the percentage of *recent* CS presentations that were reinforced, as opposed to merely the total number of reinforced pairings. However, just as presentations of the CS alone during training attenuate conditioned responding, so too do presentations of the US alone (Dweck & Wagner, 1970; Rescorla, 1968). To address these inadequacies of contiguity theory, Rescorla (1968, 1969b) formulated what has come to be called *contingency theory*. Rescorla's contingency theory takes into account not only the presence and absence of the US on trials in which the

CS is present, but also the presence and absence of the US on trials in which the CS is omitted.

Stated more formally, Rescorla proposed that organisms are sensitive to the probability of the US occurring in the presence of the CS, that is, $P(US|CS)$, and to the probability of the US occurring in the absence of the CS, that is, $P(US|no\text{-}CS)$, and that associative strength, which Rescorla assumed mapped directly into response strength, reflects the difference between these two probabilities. The transformation from perceived probabilities to associative strength and hence response strength is illustrated in Fig. 3.1. If we assume a fixed duration CS, the percentage of recent CSs that have been reinforced (divided by 100 to obtain probabilities) is plotted on the ordinate (vertical axis). Then the session time during which the CS is absent is partitioned into temporal intervals equal to the CS duration and the percentage of these recent no-CS intervals that have been reinforced (again divided by 100) is plotted on the abscissa (horizontal axis). Thus, any stable set of CS presentations and US presentations can be plotted on the *contingency space* depicted in Fig. 3.1, which takes into account all reinforced and nonreinforced CS occurrences and all reinforced and nonreinforced intervals in which the CS was absent. Within Rescorla's framework, the occurrence of the US in the absence of the CS effectively serves to condition the apparatus cues (also known as background, contextual, or situational stimuli).

When $P(US|CS) = P(US|no\text{-}CS)$, the events map onto the diagonal line of the contingency space. This line is referred to as the *line of indifference* because the CS is uninformative concerning the likelihood of the US occurring under these circumstances. All points on the line of indifference represent a zero correlation

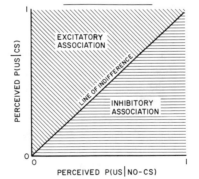

FIG. 3.1.   Contingency theory states that any consistent set of events can be plotted as a point in the contingency space depicted here. Points above the line of indifference are presumed to result in excitatory associations and points below the line of indifference are presumed to result in inhibitory associations. The strength of the resultant excitatory and inhibitory associations are assumed to be proportional to the perpendicular displacement of the representative point from the line of indifference. After Rescorla (1968).

between the CS and US, that is, presentations of the CS and US that occur randomly with respect to one another. Rescorla (1967) has suggested that truly random presentations of the CS and US constitute the ideal control treatment in studies of classical conditioning because it provides control subjects with exposures to the CS and US that are equal in number to the experimental subjects that experience positive (or negative) correlations of the CS and US. However, randomness is meaningful only with a large number of trials. With small numbers of trials, initial pairings or initial nonpairings could result in the CS acting like a conditioned excitor or conditioned inhibitor, respectively (Benedict & Ayres, 1972; Kremer, 1971), just as two or three flips of a coin could result in all heads or all tails as opposed to an equal distribution of each. Furthermore, the likelihood of transient excitation or inhibition would be augmented by differential *associabilities* (i.e., inherent predisposition to accrue associative strength) of the CS and contextual cues allowing the perception of one probability to be completed in fewer trials than the other. Despite these difficulties with the truly random control, it still constitutes one of the better controls for Pavlovian conditioning.

Rescorla's contingency theory postulates that the associative strength of a CS is determined by a comparison between $P(US|CS)$ and $P(US|no\text{-}CS)$. When $P(US|CS)$ is larger than $P(US|no\text{-}CS)$, the CS will be a conditioned excitor (i.e., it will elicit excitatory responding) and when $P(US|CS)$ is smaller than $P(US|no\text{-}CS)$, the CS will be a conditioned inhibitor (i.e., it will pass summation and retardation tests for inhibition). The greater the inequality between $P(US|CS)$ and $P(US|no\text{-}CS)$, the greater will be the observed excitation or inhibition. In terms of Fig. 3.1, conditioned excitation will occur when the training situation maps into the triangular space above the line of indifference, with the degree of excitation being directly proportional to the distance between the point representative of the training situation and the line of indifference. Similarly, contingency theory states that conditioned inhibition will occur when the training situation maps into the triangular space below the line of indifference with the degree of inhibition being directly proportional to the distance between the point representative of the training situation and the line of indifference. Stated in informational terms, the associative strength of a CS reflects the degree to which the CS announces an increase or decrease in the likelihood of the US relative to the likelihood of the US in the absence of the CS. Of course this analysis assumes that accurate perception of $P(US|CS)$ and $P(US|no\text{-}CS)$ has occurred. To the extent that extraneous factors (e.g., differential associabilities) produce an error in the subject's perception of $P(US|CS)$ or $P(US|no\text{-}CS)$, the perceived values of these probabilities rather than their true values will determine the associative strength of the CS.

For purposes of later comparisons between models, it should be emphasized that in Rescorla's contingency theory the associative strength of a CS is determined by a comparison of $P(US|CS)$ and $P(US|training\ context)$ *that occurs at the time of training*. Later in this chapter, we shall examine this assumption. For the moment, it suffices to say that contingency theory in many instances makes accurate predictions across a number of species concerning conditioned responding when CSs and either appetitive or aversive USs have been intermingled, provided there is a moderately large number of trials. The full implications and breadth of contingency theory are best represented by Gibbon, Berryman, and Thompson (1974), who among other things present an extension of contingency theory to concurrent free-operant responding, that results in Herrnstein's (1970) Matching Law. Thus, contingency theory must be viewed as an elegant and largely successful effort to correct contiguity theory's failure in handling unsignaled USs.

Despite contingency theory's relative success in predicting the consequences of exposure to various correlations of a CS and US, it suffers from a number of deficiencies. First, it does not address interactions between stimuli that are compounded during acquisition. Thus, Rescorla's contingency theory does not predict phenomena such as overshadowing and blocking. This omission prompted Rescorla's collaborative efforts with Wagner to develop the Rescorla-Wagner (1972) model; however, Rescorla did not abandon contingency theory in that many of his views on contingency and the nature of conditioned responding were built into the Rescorla-Wagner model (see Chapter 2 by Durlach for a review of this model). Furthermore, as will be seen, the other models discussed in this chapter can all trace their ancestry to contingency theory (and consequently, to contiguity theory).

A second failing of contingency theory is that it predicts that delivery of a given US will either increment the perception of $P(US|CS)$ or $P(US|no\text{-}CS)$, but not both. If $no\text{-}CS$ is equated with the background cues, this is equivalent to saying that the CS will totally overshadow the background cues on those reinforced trials on which the CS is present. Unfortunately, the data concerning this issue are indecisive. Sometimes overshadowing is seen (e.g., Durlach, 1983, Grau & Rescorla, 1984), and sometimes it is not (Gibbon & Balsam, 1981; Jenkins, Barnes, & Barrera, 1981). Future research can be expected to delineate the conditions under which CSs will overshadow background cues. The erroneous prediction of consistent overshadowing of the context by CSs was one of the bases for the subsequent development of the timing theories of learning and performance that we discuss later.

A third failing of contingency theory is its inability to cope with various manipulations of temporal duration (see Gibbon et al., 1974). This is evident in the rather arbitrary assumption that, during conditioning sessions, intervals lacking the CS are decomposed by the subject into epochs of duration equal to the CS duration. Although it may seem farfetched to assume that an animal would process information in this manner, in practice this assumption has been rather successful. The reason for this success is that the successful transformation of differences between $P(US|CS)$ and $P(US|no\text{-}CS)$ into behavior requires multiplication by a constant. This transformation corrects for the error in presuming that the CS duration is the basic unit of time for psychological process (i.e., the psychological moment), provided that the psychophysical function for time perception is linear. Nevertheless, an accurate description of the data is not necessarily indicative of an accurate description of the underlying mechanism. More serious is the inability of contingency theory to deal with variable CS durations and with no-CS intervals that are not integer multiples of the CS duration. This failing was a primary impetus for development of the timing theories of learning and performance that we describe later in this chapter.

A fourth failing of contingency theory is that it, like the Rescorla-Wagner (1972) model, assumes that conditioned excitation and conditioned inhibition are mutually exclusive, that is, a training situation maps into a single point in contingency space (see Fig. 3.1) that can result in conditioned excitation *or* conditioned inhibition, but not both. However, Matzel, Gladstein, and Miller (in press) trained rats with a white noise CS and footshock US on a negative contingency schedule with partial reinforcement of the noise, specifically, $P(US|CS) = .33$, $P(US|no-CS) = .68$. Consistent with Rescorla's predictions, the white noise passed both summation and retardation tests for conditioned inhibition. However, the partially reinforced conditioned inhibitor also passed a standard test for conditioned excitation (also see Mackintosh & Cotton, 1985; Tait & Saladin, 1986). Simultaneous excitation and inhibition is a problem for any theory that views excitation and inhibition as opposite ends of a single dimension of associative strength (e.g., Rescorla & Wagner) or as independent dimensions that fully summate prior to response generation to yield either an effective excitor *or* an effective inhibitor (e.g., Hull, 1943; Pavlov, 1927). However, the observation that a CS can function simultaneously as an inhibitor and as an excitor is not a problem for models that regard excitatory and inhibitory tests as measuring partially independent aspects of the CS (e.g., Miller & Schachtman's 1985 comparator hypothesis of response generation).

A fifth failing of contingency theory is that it assumes that $P(US|CS)$ and $P(US|no-CS)$ are compared at the time of training to yield an S-R association. Consequently, changes in $P(US|no-CS)$ following completion of CS training should not alter conditioned responding to the CS. However, Kaplan and Hearst (1985), Miller and Schachtman (1985), and Kasprow, Schachtman, and Miller (1987) have found that extinction of the CS conditioning context following completion of inhibitory training will decrease conditioned inhibition as measured on both summation and retardation tests given outside of the training context. This observation is a primary basis for the comparator hypothesis of response generation, which is described later in this chapter.

A sixth failing of contingency theory is built into its own fabric rather than arising from data. In stating that $P(US|CS)$ and $P(US|no-CS)$ are perceived and compared at the time of CS training to yield the associative strength of the CS, contingency theory fails to consider that these two probabilities cannot be instantaneously sensed, but are abstractions resulting from the processing of the *memories* of several events distributed over time. Hence, there must necessarily be some sort of memory of the individual training events (i.e., CS–US associative memories, CS-alone memories, US-alone memories, and memories of the conditioning context in the absence of both the CS and US). This is equivalent to saying that rather than perceived values of $P(US|CS)$ and $P(US|no–CS)$ being the fundamental bases of memories, memories are the bases for these probabilities (although derived, higher order memories and consequent response tendencies might well be dependent on these probabilities). As associations must precede perception of the probabilities that are assumed to be involved in determining conditioned responding, the question arises under what conditions does the subject conclude CS training is over and "calculate" the probabilities which determine responding in the presence of the CS. Contingency theory as described by Rescorla does not address this issue. However, as a subject never knows whether there will be another training trial, it seems reasonable to assume that these "calculations" are performed anew for each CS presentation to determine if a response should be made and the underlying memories of prior events are largely retained for subsequent updating if and when additional training occurs. The timing theories and the comparator hypothesis to be discussed both make this assumption and the experiments cited in the preceding paragraph give substance to the suggestion of repeated recalculation of associative strength.

This extended discussion of the faults of contingency theory is meant to put contingency theory into its historical perspective. It was quite successful in its primary purpose of giving weight to the occurrence of unpaired CS and US presentations as well as intervals lacking either stimulus. Moreover, the newer models soon to be described (as well as the Rescorla-Wagner, 1972, model) were all developed as a result of the insights provided by contingency theory as well as its failings.

II. TIMING THEORIES OF LEARNING AND PERFORMANCE

Simple contiguity theory has had to be qualified in order to account for phenomena such as the effects of unpaired CSs and USs, variable intertrial intervals, simultaneous and backward pairings, and higher order conditioning. Nevertheless, the need for temporal and spatial proximity to form associations is so compelling that no serious model of learning fails to incorporate the principles of contiguity in some form. (Herrnstein's, 1970, Matching Law might appear to be an exception, but it is primarily a theory of motivation rather than learning.) For timing and spacing to influence information processing, they must be perceived. Space perception has been an important research topic since the inception of experimental psychology. Time perception, although not totally neglected in the past (e.g., Harzem, 1969), has not received equivalent attention, particularly with respect to its impact upon learning. Recently, however, Gibbon and Church and their colleagues, among others, have attempted with considerable success to correct this deficit (see Church, 1989, for background on psychological mechanisms of timing).

Underlying this increased interest in the perception of time as it relates to learning is the Scalar Expectancy Theory (SET) of Gibbon (1977). In essence, SET posits that the variance in temporal estimation is directly related to the duration of the interval being estimated (specifically, the variance is assumed to be proportional to the square of the mean interval being estimated). This assumption generates Weber's Law and successfully describes considerable animal timing data. Gibbon and Balsam (1981) apply SET to Pavlovian conditioning and particularly autoshaping. Basically, they define *cycle time* (C) as the time from the offset of one presentation of the reinforcer to the onset of the next presentation of the reinforcer and *trial time* (T) as the total time the CS is present between reinforcements of the CS. Rate of acquisition of conditioned responding is equated with the *expectancy ratio* (r), which is defined as $r = C/T$. A value for r is "computed" for each new presentation of the US. Hence, learning is an automatic consequence of the subject's perception of T and C, which depends on r, and $r = C/T$ is also the response rule for SET.

Both C and T represent averages of waiting time for the US based on many trials rather then merely the immediately preceding trial. This is a matter of some consequence in that Jenkins et al. (1981) have shown that a cluster of reinforced trials with a short intertrial interval is as effective as spaced trials provided prior experience has established a long average US cycle time. Moreover, this same experiment demonstrates that the effectiveness of a CS–US pairing is not an inverse function of the subject's *momentary* expectation of the US based on when within the average US cycle the pairing occurs. A cluster of CS–US pairings early in the average US cycle, when the US should be unexpected, has the same effect as when the pairings occur later in the US cycle, when the US should be expected.

Notably, SET rejects the traditional notion that in continuously reinforced forward conditioning the interval between US offset and CS onset is extratrial time, that is, an intertrial interval. Rather, C for the next trial begins with US offset. Learning as a result of reinforcement is "spread" independently to all stimuli presented since the last reinforcement with the associative increment being inversely proportional to T, the total time that the particular CS was present since the last reinforcement, that is, $r = C/T$. Thus, the model also successfully predicts Gibbon and Balsam's demonstration that one 10-sec CS presented immediately prior to a US will subsequently evoke a CR comparable to that seen after the two 5-sec CSs are presented with only the latter one being terminated with the US (see Fig. 3.2). This prediction, the generality of which has been reasonably well confirmed in a number of autoshaping studies, is counterintuitive in that SET suggests that the temporal location of the unpaired CS with respect to the impending CS–US pairing is irrelevant so long as it occurs since the immediately preceding US. However, SET does not totally abandon contiguity in that the waiting time in the presence of the CS (T) is based on total exposure to the CS *until a US occurs in the presence of the CS*. Unsignaled USs will contribute to (i.e., reduce) cycle time (C), but will not terminate the integration of CS durations used to determine T. Although both SET and contingency theory state that responding to the CS will be inversely related to the frequency of unsignaled USs, SET's emphasis on the total duration of exposure to the CS between reinforcements of the CS is in sharp contrast to contingency theory's emphasis on numbers of reinforced and nonreinforced presentations of the CS.

The equation $r = C/T$ provides a surprisingly good fit to numerous acquisition curves, largely but not exclusively from the pigeon autoshaping literature. Without any further assumptions, Gibbon and Balsam (1981) predict both the faster rate of acquisition and, if masking by ceiling effects is avoided, greater asymptotic level of associative responding seen with spaced (distributed) training trials relative to massed trials (e.g., Gibbon, Baldock, Locurto, Gold, & Terrace, 1977). Rather than relying on traditional mechanisms such as differential rehearsal time and interference, SET succeeds merely by equating C with the intertrial interval plus the stimulus duration (T). That is, with a CS of fixed duration, the C/T ratio increases as the session length increases (provided that the number of CS–US pairings remain constant). In practice, this prediction says that responding will be better after distributed trials than after massed trials, an effect readily obtained with both animals and humans (Spence & Norris, 1950). However, the confirmation of this particular prediction is not compelling evidence for SET because most other models of conditioning and performance are as successful in predicting this phenomenon.

Another example of the success of SET is seen in Jenkins and Shattuck's (1981) reexamination of some of Rescorla's early data in support of contingency theory. Rescorla (1968) showed that excitatory responding to the CS was attenuated when unsignaled US were inserted between the CS–US pairings. He interpreted this as a consequence of augmenting P(US|no–CS). However, Rescorla's origi-

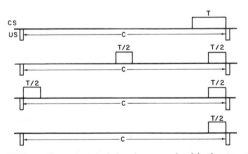

FIG. 3.2.   SET predicts that training in accord with the top three time lines will result in conditioning at the same rate and slower than training in accord with the bottom time line. Available evidence appears consistent with these expectations. After Gibbon and Balsam (1981).

nal data were confounded by a change in the overall density of the US. Using conditioned suppression of barpressing for food by rats as did Rescorla (1968), Jenkins and Shattuck (1981) successfully replicated Rescorla's results, but also included subjects for which the added USs were signaled with the target stimulus. Surprisingly, the attenuation in responding was found to occur even when the added USs were signaled by the target CS. Thus, more CS–US pairings in the same length session proved detrimental to conditioned responding. In the framework of SET, the added USs decreased the cycle time (i.e., time between USs) without increasing the already asymptotic ability of the CS to predict the US. In other words, the expectation of the US in the presence of the context was increased while the expectation of the US in the presence of the CS remained constant, thereby reducing the C/T ratio and attenuating the response to the CS. Indicative of the generality of these observations, Jenkins et al. (1981) report comparable effects using pigeons on an autoshaping task. These experiments also demonstrate a lack of overshadowing of the context by a punctate CS, which is consistent with SET's assumption of independent associative acquisition for all cues present at US onset. (The validity of this assumption is considered later.)

SET correctly predicts that partial reinforcement will result in slower acquisition than continuous reinforcement under some schedules, but not others. Specifically, if the partial reinforcement schedule is generated by taking the reinforcement schedule of the consistently reinforced control subjects and omitting some of the USs, acquisition is uneffected relative to the control animals because both T and C are increased (Gibbon, Farrell, Locurto, Duncan, & Terrace, 1980). However, if the partial reinforcement schedule is produced by adding nonreinforced CSs to the CS–US pairings scheduled for the consistently reinforced control subjects, acquisition will be retarded because T is being increased without any change in C (Wasserman, Diech, Hunter, & Nagamatsu, 1977).

As previously mentioned, conditioned responding according to SET depends on the expectation of the US in the presence of the CS relative to the expectation of the US in the presence of the background cues. Presumably, the subject maintains over the course of training and through any retention intervals separate expectations of the US (i.e., associations) for the CS and the context. This contrasts with contingency theory, which assumes that at the time of training the subject compares the perceived values of P(US|CS) and P(US|no–CS) to obtain a likelihood of emitting a CR in the presence of the CS. In other words, in SET separate CS–US and context–US associations are maintained with a comparison of these associations occurring with each presentation of the CS, whereas in contingency theory the comparison takes place at the time of CS training and results in a single CS–CR association that is retained over any retention interval. Experiments bearing on these opposing views are examined later in this chapter.

Having briefly described some of SET's successes, we now turn to its failings. First, SET predicts that responding to a CS will be inversely proportional to the associative strength of the context. Consequently, USs delivered before or after CS training should be as detrimental to responding to the CS as unsignaled USs delivered during CS training (provided recency effects do not attenuate the effects of USs presented prior to CS training). Consistent with this prediction, unsignaled USs delivered prior to CS training are well known to interfere with conditioned responding (e.g., Randich & LoLordo, 1979). Rather, it is USs after CS training that fail to have their predicted detrimental effect upon responding to the CS. Responding to the CS appears to be impervious to such treatment (e.g., Kaplan & Hearst, 1985; Miller & Schachtman, 1985).

Extinction poses another problem for SET. According to SET, T and C are recalculated upon each US presentation. Hence, any procedure that lacks a US presentation should have no effect on responding to the CS. This poses no problem for partial reinforcement schedules, but fails to predict extinction of conditioned responding as a consequence of CS-alone presentations. Partly to rectify this omission, Jenkins et al. (1981) have proposed the *Relative Waiting Time* (RWT) hypothesis. The RWT hypothesis is quite similar to SET except that it focuses on time since the last US rather than time until the next US. Thus, RWT, unlike SET, is able to explain extinction. However, RWT lacks the quantitative specificity of SET and shares with SET all of SET's other failings.

The timing models of learning and performance (SET and RWT) are both unable to predict the retarded acquisition of conditioned responding that is observed following pretraining exposure to the CS alone (latent inhibition; see Lubow & Moore, 1959). Although CS preexposure might be expected to add to T in the case of SET, C/T and hence the rate of learning are indeterminant prior to the first US. One way that the timing models could accommodate the CS preexposure effect is to make the added assumption that pre-US exposure to the context does not contribute to C, but that pre-US exposure to the CS does contribute to T. Although this assumption may sound arbitrary, it is consistent with data reported by Jenkins et al. (1981). Nevertheless, the timing models in their original forms are not able to explain the effects of CS preexposure.

A central assumption of both timing models is that they, contrary to the Rescorla-Wagner (1972) model, predict no competition between a CS and a context for associations based on a particular CS–US pairing in that context. Thus, C is based strictly on US density regardless of whether or not the US presentations are signaled. Punctate stimuli are assumed not to overshadow or block the context in its coming to predict the US. Both Gibbon and Balsam (1981) and Jenkins et al. (1981) give numerous examples of this with pigeons in autoshaping situations. On the other hand, considerable data demonstrating blocking of the context by punctate cues have also been presented (e.g., Durlach, 1983; Grau & Rescorla, 1984). Clearly, overshadowing and blocking of background cues are not consistent phenomena, and we have not yet identified the circumstances under which they occur. However, SET and RWT are as erroneous in saying that overshadowing and blocking of context will never occur as the Rescorla-Wagner model is in saying that they will always occur.

A further failure of the timing models is that they do not predict responding when the CS is terminated prior to the onset of the US, that is, trace conditioning. Both models state that the clock that measures T is reset to zero only when a US occurs in the presence of a CS. Hence, the timing models treat trace conditioning procedures as identical to explicitly unpaired presentations of the CS and US. (Although SET is unable to predict trace conditioning, Balsam, 1984, has developed a variation of SET in which expectancy of a US is transmitted to a CS across an interstimulus interval in inverse proportion to the duration of the interval.)

Another shortcoming of both SET and RWT is the logic underlying the presumed timing mechanism that determines C and T. Both models suggest that a stimulus is timed with respect to the occurrence of a US and that a later comparison of this duration to that for the context determines the rate of conditioning. However, Roberts (1983) has presented data which suggests that animals do not arbitrarily time all stimuli. Rather, they appear to time only biologically relevant stimuli. According to Roberts, a stimulus that has no predictive value concerning the occurrence of a US is not timed. This observation has led Roberts to conclude that the underlying logic of SET and RWT is flawed. That is, it appears that the establishment of a conditioned association must precede, as opposed to result from, the animal's timing of the stimulus.

Despite the several failures of SET and RWT, these models are unique in their ability to *explain* CS duration effects rather then merely compensate for them by using a smaller associative growth constant for longer CSs, a strategy that has predictive but not explanatory value. Moreover, the timing models provide a novel and stimulating perspective concerning the role of time in learning and performance.

III. THE COMPARATOR HYPOTHESIS
OF PERFORMANCE

The comparator hypothesis (Miller & Schachtman, 1985) began as an attempt to extend contingency theory and, driven by data, ended by adopting one of the central tenets of SET. In contingency theory, the comparison of P(US|CS) with P(US|no–CS) is assumed to occur at the time of training. Moreover, although contingency theory does not directly address the consequences of training in one context and testing in another, the assumption that the comparison takes place during training (i.e., before testing) requires that P(US|no–CS) refer to the training context as opposed to any dissimilar test context.

Miller and Schachtman (1985) and Kasprow et al. (1987) both performed experiments to determine whether the CS was compared to the training context or to the test context. Training of the CS always occurred in what they called Context A, whereas testing occurred either in Context A or Context B. Using a lick suppression procedure with water-deprived rats, a 30-sec CS was reinforced with footshock on 50% of its occurrences in Context A, that is (PUS|CS) = .50. During CS training in Context A, subjects spent an equal amount of time in Context B. Time in Contexts A and B was conceptually divided into 30-sec intervals to match the CS duration. For some subjects, 53% of the no−CS intervals during CS training sessions in Context A included an unsignaled footshock. This presumably resulted in conditioning of Context A but not Context B, that is, P(US|training context) = .53, P(US|Context B) = 0. For other subjects, the same density of unsignaled footshock was administered, but in Context B rather than in Context A, that is, P(US|training context) = 0, P(US|Context B) = .53. Additional subjects received no unsignaled shocks, that is, P(US|training context) = P(US|Context B) = 0. Procedures were used that minimized direct responding to the context summating with responding to the CS. The general design of these studies is illustrated in Table 3.1.

Conditioned fear of the CS as indicated by interruption of ongoing drinking when the CS was presented (i.e., conditioned suppression) is represented in Fig. 3.3. To summarize, regardless of where testing occurred, unsignaled shocks in the training context attenuated manifest fear of the CS relative to that seen with either no unsignaled shocks or unsignaled shocks administered in Context B. Thus, these studies indicate that, to determine responding to a CS, the associative strength of the CS is compared to the associative strength of the CS training context rather than that of the test context, a conclusion which is entirely consistent with the assumptions of contingency theory as well as the Rescorla-Wagner model (1972).

TABLE 3.1
Group Treatments[a] During Six Daily Conditioning Subsessions

Group	Subsessions					
	1	2	3	4	5	6
USA-A	B(−)	B(−)	A(24+)	A(3N+,3N−)	A(24+)	B(−)
NUSA-A	B(−)	B(−)	A(−)	A(3N+,3N−)	A(−)	B(−)
USB-B	B(−)	A(−)	B(24+)	A(3N+,3N−)	B(24+)	A(−)
NUSB-B	B(−)	A(−)	B(−)	A(3N+,3N−)	B(−)	A(−)
USA-B	B(−)	B(−)	A(24+)	A(3N+,3N−)	A(24+)	B(−)
NUSA-B	B(−)	B(−)	A(−)	A(3N+,3N−)	A(−)	B(−)
USB-A	B(−)	A(−)	B(24+)	A(3N+,3N−)	B(24+)	A(−)
NUSB-A	B(−)	A(−)	B(−)	A(3N+,3N−)	B(−)	A(−)

(after Kasprow, Schachtman, & Miller, 1987)
[a]A and B = distinctly different contexts, (−) = No treatment, (24+) = 24 unsignaled shocks, (3N+, 3N−) = 3 out of 6 white noise presentations terminated with shock.
[b]USA = 48 unsignaled shocks in Context A per day.
USB = 48 unsignaled shocks in Context B per day.
NUSA = No unsignaled shocks in Context A = Control groups for USA
NUSB = No unsignaled shocks in Context B = Control groups for USB
Last letter of group designation = test location.

In contrast, the timing models are silent concerning whether cycle time reflects expectation of the US in the training context or the test context. However, the timing models posit that the response to a given CS is "computed" anew for each presentation of the CS based on a comparison of the current values of C and T, that is, C/T. Hence, it is possible that the context-US association that underlies C could reflect either the associative strength of the training context or the test context. A number of researchers have incorrectly assumed that Gibbon and Balsam (1981) meant C to refer the current (i.e., test) context, as opposed to the context in which the CS was trained.

Although the studies just described found that the predictive value of the CS is compared to that of the training context as opposed to the test context, they did not determine when the comparison took place. If the comparison stimulus had been the test context, the comparison would necessarily have to occur at the time of testing because the context for a specific CS test is not known to the subject until the time of testing. But with the training context serving as the comparator stimulus for the CS, in principle the comparison could occur at either the time of training, as assumed by contingency theory, or at the time of testing, as assumed by the timing models.

In a second set of experiments, Miller and Schachtman (1985) and Kasprow et al. (1987) investigated whether the presumed comparison between P(US|CS) and P(US|no-CS) took place at the time of training or at the time of testing. Their tactic consisted of deflating (i.e., extinguishing) the CS training context *following* negative contingency conditioned inhibition training (+/X−) of the CS. Of

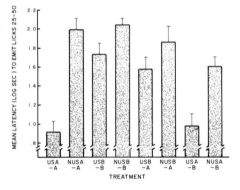

FIG. 3.3.   Conditioned lick suppression to the white noise CS as a function of the presence or absence of unsignaled shock (US vs. NUS), which context the animal was in when unsignaled shock (or its absence) was administered (Context A or Context B), and where testing occurred (-A or -B). The CS was intermittently reinforced with shock in Context A. Fear was reduced by unsignaled shocks given in the CS training context (A) regardless of where testing occurred. After Kasprow, Schachtman, and Miller (1987).

interest was the effect of this manipulation upon the manifest conditioned inhibitory value of the CS as seen in retardation and summation tests. Using conditioned lick suppression in water-deprived rats as before, all subjects first experienced the CS reinforced one-third of the time and the absence of the CS (i.e., the training context alone) reinforced two-thirds of the time, such that $P(US|CS) = .33$ and $P(US|no-CS) = .67$. Preliminary tests determined that a CS so trained was slow in becoming a conditioned excitor when later consistently paired with the US (i.e., retardation), and attenuated responding when paired with a known excitor for the same US (i.e., negative summation). Hence, this training appeared to make the CS a conditioned inhibitor. However, the same tests following deflation of the CS training context found that the deflation manipulation reduced the retardation and the negative summation effects, despite testing having occurred in a neutral context to avoid summation effects with the CS training context differentially affecting the various groups. Of particular note is that attenuation of negative summation occurred even when the CS training context was deflated after the end of CS training and the loss of retardation occurred even when the training context was deflated after both the CS inhibitory training and the CS–US pairings of the retardation test. This reduction in conditioned inhibition is inconsistent with the Rescorla-Wagner (1972) model in that Rescorla and Wagner, although allowing the CS training context to influence conditioning of the CS through such mechanisms as blocking of the CS by the context, posit that once training of a CS has determined its associative strength, conditioned responding to the CS is independent of the associative strength of the training context.

Collectively, these two sets of observations give rise to the comparator hypothesis, which states that *responding to a CS will be directly related to the associative value of the CS at the time of testing and inversely related to the associative value of the CS training context at the time of testing.* The description of conditioned responding offered by the comparator hypothesis is sometimes difficult to understand because it assumes that the comparison is to the training context even when testing (and hence the comparison) occurs in a different context. Presumably, the CS presentation at the time of testing reactivates both the CS–US association and the CS–comparator stimuli association, the latter of which in turn reactivates the comparator stimuli–US association. In stating that CS–US associations will be manifest in behavior as an excitatory response only when the corresponding comparator stimuli–US associations are relatively weak, the comparator hypothesis is suggesting that many associations are latent. In this regard, the comparator hypothesis is consistent with a growing body of literature that emphasizes the existence of a large reservoir of latent learning that can be revealed with the appropriate experimental manipulations (e.g., see Miller et al., 1986).

Unlike the Rescorla-Wagner (1972) model which equates conditioned inhibition with negative associations, in the framework of the comparator hypothesis, all associations are positive. Behavior indicative of conditioned inhibition is assumed to reflect the CSs having an excitory association to the US that is weaker than the training context's excitatory association to the US, that is, the CS predicts a decrease in the likelihood of the US occurring relative to the training context in the absence of the CS. Correspondingly, behavior indicative of conditioned excitation reflects a CS that predicts an increase in the likelihood of the US relative to its comparator stimuli. Owing to the comparison taking place at the time of testing, the comparator hypothesis is to be viewed as a response rule. To provide a complete theory of conditioned behavior, the comparator hypothesis must be wedded to a theory of acquisition, the details of which might incorporate many of the principles of the Rescorla-Wagner model for instance. However, with a response rule such as the comparator hypothesis, which (as we shall see) can explain a number of behavioral phenomena, there will be less of an explanatory burden on any accompanying theory of acquisition.

The comparator hypothesis has a great deal in common with SET, but the two models are not identical. The features that distinguish the comparator hypothesis from SET include:

1. SET is silent concerning what happens when training and testing occur in dissimilar contexts, whereas the comparator hypothesis explicitly states that the CS is always compared to stimuli that were in evidence at the time of prior CS presentations (i.e., cues present at training).

2. SET, with its focus on US cycle time, assumes that the associative value of the CS is compared exclusively to that of the context for the session, whereas the comparator hypothesis posits that all stimuli in which the CS has been embedded will contribute to the comparator term. Thus, the comparator hypothesis permits punctate cues to be part of the comparator term.

3. The comparator hypothesis, unlike SET, provides a framework for explaining conditioned inhibition.

4. SET says that C and T and consequently the derived response potentials are revalued only upon presentation of a US; hence, SET predicts that extinction of the context following CS training is not possible and therefore the extinction operation would have no effect on responding to the CS. In contrast, the comparator hypothesis predicts that extinction of the CS and the context can occur and that in the latter instance it will attenuate behavior indicative of inhibition and enhance behavior indicative of excitation. While SET predicts the existence of latent associations to a CS given more excitatory training context, it does not anticipate the enhanced response to the CS that is often observed following deflation of the training context.

5. SET, with its assumption that US associations to a CS and to the CS's training context are formed independently of each other during each CS–US pairing and each context–US pairing, denies that the CS or the context can block one another, whereas the comparator hypothesis, in acknowledgment of the incon-

sistent evidence concerning this issue (e.g., Durlach, 1983; Gibbon & Balsam, 1981, Grau & Rescorla, 1984; Jenkins et al., 1981), is intentionally silent on this issue. Specifically, the comparator hypothesis is a response rule and makes no claims concerning acquisition.

6. SET is specific about the mathematical form of the comparison (i.e., $r = C/T$) whereas the comparator hypothesis is intentionally vague, thereby lending itself only to predictions of rank order between groups rather than predictions of specific performance levels.

By generally accepted definition, a conditioned inhibitor is a stimulus that "passes" a negative summation test *and* a retardation test (Hearst, 1972; Rescorla, 1969a). Specifically, on a summation test, a conditioned inhibitor decreases responding to a known conditioned excitor when compounded with it, and on a retardation test, a conditioned inhibitor is slower to become a conditioned excitor as result of CS–US pairings than if the stimulus were associatively neutral. Traditional views of conditioned inhibition have assumed the existence of inhibitory associations that take the form of negative CS–US associations, CS–no US associations, or elevated the threshold for reactivating a representation of the US (Konorski, 1948, 1967; Pavlov, 1927; Rescorla & Wagner, 1972). Each of these conceptualizations is able to explain how a putative conditioned inhibitor comes to "pass" inhibitory summation and retardation tests. The comparator hypothesis, in taking the position that behavior indicative of conditioned inhibition arises from a positive CS–US association that is weak relative to the corresponding comparator stimuli–US association, implies that inhibitory *associations* do not exist. In rejecting traditional views of conditioned inhibition that have proven successful in describing summation and retardation test performance, the comparator hypothesis has an obligation to offer alternative explanations of summation and retardation test performance by a putative conditioned inhibitor.

Schachtman, Brown, Gordon, Catterson, and Miller (1987) have analyzed retardation test performance following inhibitory training and concluded that the comparator process complemented by such well-established phenomena as the CS preexposure effect, blocking by the training context, and US habituation can collectively explain retardation. Prior studies have commonly controlled for some but not all of these possible sources of retardation at the same time. The contribution of the putative comparator process to retardation performance arises when, as a result of inhibitory training, the comparator stimulus for the CS (the training context in the case of $+/X-$ inhibitory training) is highly excitatory at the beginning of the CS–US pairings that constitute the retardation test. Consequently, these subjects do not begin to respond to the CS in an excitatory fashion until the associative value of the CS has approached or exceeded that of the comparator stimuli. In contrast, naive control subjects start the CS–US pairings of the retardation test with the comparator stimuli neutral. Consistent with the comparator process contributing to the retardation performance that is seen following inhibitory training, Schachtman et al. found that extinction of the comparator stimuli *following* the CS–US pairings of the retardation test eliminated the retardation effect as thoroughly as extinction of the comparator stimuli *prior to* the retardation test pairings. Moreover, they found that following negative contingency inhibitory training ($+/X-$), retardation was a consequence of giving the CS–US retardation test pairings in the excitatory context and was not CS specific. That is, retardation was also seen with a novel CS, provided that the CS–US pairings used to assess retardation occurred in the training context used for $+/X-$ inhibitory training. These observations, as well as similar ones by Kaplan and Hearst (1985), are problematic for the Rescorla-Wagner (1972) model and contingency theory. In contrast, the timing models simply do not address conditioned inhibition.

Although Schachtman et al. (1987) have succeeded at explaining retardation following inhibitory training without recourse to inhibitory associations, there is not yet as well documented an alternative explanation of negative summation. Kasprow et al. (1987) have proposed several mechanisms within the framework of the comparator hypothesis to explain summation test performance following inhibitory training, but supportive evidence does not exist at this time.

There are several phenomena that the comparator hypothesis has been uniquely successful in explaining. For example, the US–preexposure effect refers to the deficit in conditioned responding following CS–US pairings that is seen as a consequence of presenting the US alone prior to the pairings (Randich & LoLordo, 1979). The common explanation of this response deficit is that it is due to an acquisition failure arising at the time of CS training from blocking of the CS–US association by the already excitatory context. The primary evidence supporting the blocking interpretation is that the observed retardation can be attenuated by either extinguishing the context before the retardation test pairings or by changing contexts between the US alone presentations and the retardation test pairings. The comparator hypothesis is readily able to explain both of these observations in terms of performance failure that arises from the excitatory value of the CS training context at the time of testing. Differentiating the two explanations, Matzel, Brown, and Miller (1987) have found that extinction of the training context *after* the CS–US test pairings eliminates much of the performance deficit. This observation is predicted by the comparator hypothesis, which says that responding to a CS will be inversely related to the associative value of the training context at the time of testing. But it is inconsistent with the blocking interpretation of the US preexposure effect because blocking presumably occurs at the time of the CS–US pairings.

Another observation that lends itself to explanation by the comparator hypothesis is the ''extinction'' of conditioned inhibition. Although the Rescorla-Wagner (1972) model predicts that presentation of a conditioned inhibitor alone following inhibitory training should reduce the inhibitory value of the CS (i.e., make the negative associative value of the CS less negative), Zimmer-Hart and Rescorla (1974) found no such attenuation in manifest inhibition. The comparator hypothesis assumes that a "conditioned inhibitor" is an excitatory stimulus more weakly associated to the US than is the training context and that the magnitude of behavior indicative of inhibition is directly proportional to the difference in the US associative strength between the CS and the training context. Consequently, operational extinction of the inhibitor should *increase* manifest inhibition provided that the putative inhibitor's excitatory strength is greater than zero at the beginning of "extinction" and that care is taken not to simultaneously extinguish the training context. Such increases in inhibition have been reported (e.g., DeVito & Fowler, 1986; Miller & Schachtman, 1985). Presumably, Zimmer-Hart and Rescorla failed to see an increase in inhibition because to produce conditioned inhibition they used an explicitly unpaired procedure that resulted in the CS having zero associative strength. Thus, their lack of an increase in inhibition can be viewed as a floor effect.

Just as the comparator hypothesis predicts that associative deflation (extinction) of the CS training context following CS conditioning will attenuate manifest inhibition, so too does it predict that deflation of the training context will increase excitatory responding to the CS. Although unpublished data from our laboratory suggests that this predicted increase in excitation is not as ubiquitous across parameters as the effect of context deflation on inhibition, there are several published examples of such an effect. One instance is provided by Balsam (1985) who found that autoshaping with pigeons failed to produce responding when the trials were massed, but subsequent extinction of the training context resulted in conditioned keypecking. Similarly, the previously cited study of the US preexposure effect by Matzel et al. (1987), which used an aversive US, as well as a comparable one by Timberlake (1986), which used an appetitive US, demonstrated recovery from the US–preexposure deficit as a result of postconditioning extinction of the CS training context. Paralleling these examples in an instrumental framework, Dickinson and Charnock (1985) found that an operant response by rats for a liquid reinforcer in a context in which free liquid is occasionally administered is enhanced if the free liquid is eliminated (i.e., the context extinguished) after the completion of instrumental training.

Another instance of enhanced responding to a CS as consequence of extinction of its comparator stimulus is provided by Kaufman and Bolles (1981) and Matzel, Schachtman, and Miller (1985) who found, using conditioned suppression in rats, that following reinforced trials with a compound stimulus which produced overshadowing, extinction of the overshadowing stimulus restored responding to the overshadowed stimulus. Appropriate control groups demonstrated that this effect was specific to extinction of the overshadowing stimulus as opposed to extinction of any other excitatory stimulus. Presumably, during the compound stimulus presentations, the overshadowing stimulus became one component of the comparator stimulus for the overshadowed stimulus. Consequently, extinction of the overshadowing stimulus effectively deflated the comparator stimulus for the overshadowed stimulus.

The findings of Kaufman and Bolles (1981) and Matzel et al. (1985) not only demonstrate increased excitatory responding following deflation of the comparator, they also illuminate the nature of comparator stimuli. Apparently, not only can the diffuse, protracted background cues of the CS training context contribute to the effective comparator stimulus, punctate stimuli presented proximal to the target CS also can play a comparator role. Consistent with this conclusion, Lysle and Fowler (1985) have found that, following Pavlovian conditioned inhibition training (A+/AX−), extinction of the A stimulus reduces the inhibitory behavior elicited by X.

Having described several successes of the comparator hypothesis, we turn now to its failings. As already mentioned, the comparator hypothesis predicts that extinction of a conditioned excitor's comparator stimuli should increase the CS's manifest excitatory value and does so at least in some cases of overshadowing (Kaufman & Bolles, 1981; Matzel et al., 1985) and US preexposure (Matzel et al. 1987). However, based on unpublished data this effect is not consistently seen following excitatory conditioning of a CS embedded in unsignaled presentation of the US. These observations have not been sufficiently extensive to permit identification of the factors that determine when extinction of the comparator stimuli will enhance excitation and when it will not. But that there are any circumstances under which excitation is not augmented is an embarrassment to the comparator hypothesis.

A second and more consistent failure of the comparator hypothesis in its basic formulation is seen in the apparent failure of inflation of the comparator stimuli following CS training to either decrease manifest conditioned excitation or increase manifest conditioned inhibition (Jenkins & Lambos, 1983; Miller & Schachtman, 1985). This lack of effect of inflation of the comparator stimuli following CS training is in marked contrast to the fulfillment of the comparator hypothesis' predictions concerning inflation of the comparator stimuli before or during CS training, that is, US preexposure effect and contingency effects, respectively. Of course, these successful predictions concerning inflation of comparator stimuli before and during CS training are also predicted by other models including contingency theory and the timing models. In response to the asymmetry between the effects of post-CS training inflation and deflation, Miller and Schachtman (1985) have suggested that subjects retain memories of both the past and present associative status of comparator stimuli and that the comparator stimulus' current value is used to determine responding following post-CS comparator deflation, but its value during CS training is used following post-CS comparator inflation. This suggestion, which can be regarded as a variant of the basic comparator hypothesis, is clearly post hoc and consequently not particularly satisfying. However, in partial support of this view, Miller and Matzel (1987) review a large body of data indicating that subjects retain the complete associative history of a stimulus as opposed to just its current associative status (as is assumed by all contemporary models of conditioning including that of Rescorla-Wagner, 1972). This conclusion notwithstanding, acceptance of the notion that associative history is remembered does not explain why an old comparator associative value is used following post-CS training inflation and the new value is used after post-CS training deflation.

The failings of the comparator hypothesis may appear fewer than those of contingency theory and the timing models. However, the comparator hypothesis is the newest of the models and consequently the least tested. Moreover, it is a conservative model that addresses only the generation of unconditioned responses, thereby leaving it largely immune from attack based on acquisition phenomena.

IV. CONCLUSIONS

All of the models that we have reviewed in this chapter emphasize the history of the CS *relative* to that of the context. The failings of each of these models make evident that none of them embody completely valid principles. Yet, each model has addressed with considerable success some existing deficits of the other models (including that of Rescorla & Wagner, 1972) and has inspired research that has resulted in important empirical observations. In providing less than a fully accurate description of acquired behavior but having considerable heuristic value, these models have much in common with the Rescorla-Wagner (1972) model.

Given the failings of these models, there are three strategies available to researchers. First, we can ignore the failings and continue to use the models as heuristic devices in gathering new data that might some day inspire a new, more successful model. Second, we can focus on the failings of one of the models and test various modifications of the model that are proposed to address the apparent failing. Such modifications usually take the form of qualifiers or additional postulates. These can be thought of as placing *bandaids* on a model. To the extent that a few bandaids correct all existing deficits, the effort can be constructive. But when the number of bandaids becomes large, the model loses the attractiveness provided by simplicity. A good model is one that is easier to remember than the data that it explains. Third, the models can be abandoned. This strategy is constructive only when another model is available as an alternative. In a theoretical vacuum, there is no basis for doing one experiment instead of another. Given the infinite number of possible experiments, theories provide essential direction.

Some models are as briefly lived as a flash in a pan, whereas others have a longevity measured in years. (Newton's mechanics are still used to obtain accurate predictions concerning certain, relatively broad classes of events.) Although we believe that each of the three models described in this chapter still have considerable heuristic value for contemporary researchers, new models ultimately replace old ones. When this does occur, it does not mean that the old theories were unsuccessful. Success of a model is measured in terms of longevity and heuristic contribution. Fashion dictates "down with the old, up with the new." This tends to obscure our intellectual debts. The rarely cited British empiricists gave us both associationism, which is alive and well although not without contemporary competition, and still existing overemphasis of acquisition processes. Clark Hull (1943), who is today regarded as passé, provided us with the first formal model in learning theory as well as a number of variables that are still important today. Science is an ongoing process and our models are merely steps along the way.

ACKNOWLEDGMENTS

This chapter was prepared with the support of NSF Grant BNS 86-00755. Thanks are due Steve Hallam, Karl Shuster, and Joshua Sloat for their comments on an early draft of the manuscript.

REFERENCES

Anderson, J. R. (1983). *The architecture of cognition*. Cambridge, MA: Harvard University Press.

Balsam, P. D. (1984). Relative time in trace conditioning. *Annals of the New York Academy of Sciences, 423*, 211–227.

Balsam, P. D. (1985). The functions of context in learning and performance. In P. D. Balsam & A. Tomie (Eds.), *Context and learning* (pp. 1–21). Hillsdale, NJ: Lawrence Erlbaum Associates.

Benedict, J. D., & Ayres, J. J. B. (1972). Factors affecting conditioning in the truly random control procedure in the rat. *Journal of Comparative and Physiological Psychology, 78*, 323–330.

Church, R. M. (1989). Theories of timing behavior. In S. B. Klein & R. R. Mowrer (Eds.), *Contemporary learning theories: Instrumental conditioning theory and the impact of biological constraints on learning*. Hillsdale, NJ: Lawrence Erlbaum Associates.

DeVito, P. L., & Fowler, H. (1986). Effect of contingency violations on the extinction of a conditioned fear inhibitor and a conditioned fear excitor. *Journal of Experimental Psychology: Animal Behavior Processes, 12*, 99–115.

Dickinson, A., & Charnock, D. J. (1985). Contingency effects with maintained instrumental reinforcement. *Quarterly Journal of Experimental Psychology, 37B*, 397–416.

Durlach, P. J. (1983). The effect of signaling intertrial USs in autoshaping. *Journal of Experimental Psychology: Animal Behavior Processes, 9*, 374–389.

Dweck, C. S., & Wagner, A. R. (1970). Situational cues and correlation between CS and US as determinants of the conditional emotional response. *Psychonomic Science, 18*, 145–147.

Gibbon, J. (1977). Scalar expectancy theory and Weber's law in animal timing. *Psychological Review, 84*, 279–325.

Gibbon, J., Baldock, M. D., Locurto, C. M., Gold, L., & Terrace, H. S. (1977). Trial and intertrial durations in autoshaping. *Journal of Experimental Psychology: Animal Behavior Processes, 3*, 264–284.

Gibbon, J., & Balsam, P. (1981). Spreading association in time. In C. M. Locurto, H. S. Terrace, & J. Gibbon (Eds.), *Autoshaping and conditioning theory* (pp. 219–253). New York: Academic Press.

Gibbon, J., Berryman, R., & Thompson, R. L. (1974). Contingency spaces and measures in classical and instrumental conditioning. *Journal of the Experimental Analysis of Behavior, 21*, 585–605.

Gibbon, J., Farrell, L., Locurto, C. M., Duncan, H. J., & Terrace, H. S. (1980). Partial reinforcement in autoshaping with pigeons. *Animal Learning and Behavior*, *8*, 45–59.

Gordon, W. C. (1983). The malleability of memory in animals. In R. L. Mellgren (Ed.), *Animal cognition and behavior* (pp. 399–426). New York: North Holland.

Grau, J. W., & Rescorla, R. A. (1984). Role of context in autoshaping. *Journal of Experimental Psychology: Animals Behavior Processes*, *10*, 324–332.

Harzem, P. (1969). Temporal discrimination, In R. M. Gilbert & N. S. Sutherland (Eds.), *Animal discrimination learning*. New York: Academic Press.

Hearst, E. (1972). Some persistent problems in the analysis of conditioned inhibition. In R. A. Boakes & M. S. Halliday (Eds.), *Inhibition and learning* (pp. 5–39). London: Academic Press.

Herrnstein, R. J. (1970). On the law of effect. *Journal of the Experimental Analysis of Behavior*, *13*, 243–266.

Hull, C. L. (1943). *Principles of behavior*. New York: Appleton-Century-Crofts.

Jenkins, H. M., Barnes, R. A., & Barrera, F. J. (1981). Why autoshaping depends on trial spacing. In C. M. Locurto, H. S. Terrace, & J. Gibbon (Eds.), *Autoshaping and conditioning theory* (pp. 255–284). New York: Academic Press.

Jenkins, H. M., & Lambos, W. A. (1983). Tests of two explanations of response elimination by noncontingent reinforcement. *Animal Learning and Behavior*, *11*, 302–308.

Jenkins, H. M., & Shattuck, D. (1981). Contingency in fear conditioning: A reexamination. *Bulletin of the Psychonomic Society*, *17*, 159–162.

Kaplan, P. S., & Hearst, E. (1985). Excitation, inhibition, and context: Studies of extinction and reinstatement. In P. D. Balsam & A. Tomie (Eds.), *Context and learning* (pp. 195–224). Hillsdale, NJ: Lawrence Erlbaum Associates.

Kasprow, W. J., Schachtman, T. R., & Miller, R. R. (1987). The comparator hypothesis of conditioned response generation: Manifest conditioned excitation and inhibition as a function of relative excitatory associative strengths of CS and conditioning context at the time of testing. *Journal of Experiment Psychology: Animal Behavior Processes*, *13*, 395–406.

Kaufman, M. A., & Bolles, R. C. (1981). A nonassociative aspect of overshadowing. *Bulletin of the Psychonomic Society*, *18*, 318–320.

Konorski, J. (1948). *Conditioned reflexes and neural organization*. Cambridge, England: Cambridge University Press.

Konorski, J. (1967). *Integrative activity of the brain: An interdisciplinary approach*. Chicago: University of Chicago Press.

Kremer, E. F. (1971). Truly random and traditional control procedures in CER conditioning in the rat. *Journal of Comparative and Physiological Psychology*, *76*, 441–448.

Lubow, R. E., & Moore, A. U. (1959). Latent inhibition: The effect of nonreinforced exposure to the conditioned stimulus. *Journal of Comparative and Physiological Psychology*, *52*, 415–419.

Lysle, D. T., & Fowler, H. (1985). Inhibition as a "slave" process: Deactivation of conditioned inhibition through extinction of conditioned excitation. *Journal of Experimental Psychology: Animal Behavior Processes*, *11*, 71–94.

Mackintosh, N. J., & Cotton, M. M. (1985). Conditioned inhibition from reinforcement reduction. In R. R. Miller & N. E. Spear (Eds.), *Information processing in animals: Conditioned inhibition* (pp. 89–111). Hillsdale, NJ: Lawrence Erlbaum Associates.

Matzel, L. D., Brown, A. M., & Miller, R. R. (1987). Associative effects of US preexposure: Modulation of conditioned responding by an excitatory training context. *Journal of Experimental Psychology: Animal Behavior Processes*, *13*, 65–72.

Matzel, L. D., Gladstein, L., & Miller, R. R. (in press). Conditioned excitation and conditioned inhibition are not mutually exclusive. *Learning and Motivation*.

Matzel, L. D., Schachtman, T. R., & Miller, R. R. (1985). Recovery of an overshadowed association achieved by extinction of the overshadowed stimulus. *Learning and Motivation*, *16*, 398–412.

Miller, R. R., Kasprow, W. J., & Schachtman, T. R. (1986). Retrieval variability: Sources and consequences. *American Journal of Psychology*, *99*, 145–218.

Miller, R. R., & Matzel, L. D. (1987). Memory for associative history of a CS. *Learning and Motivation*, *18*, 118–130.

Miller, R. R., & Schachtman, T. R. (1985). Conditioning context as an associative baseline: Implications for response generation and the nature of conditioned inhibition, In R. R. Miller & N. E. Spear (Eds.), *Information processing in animals: Conditioned inhibition* (pp. 51–88). Hillsdale, NJ: Lawrence Erlbaum Associates.

Pavlov, I. P. (1927). *Conditioned reflexes*. London: Oxford University Press.

Randich, A., & LoLordo, V. M. (1979). Preconditioning exposure to the unconditioned stimulus affects the acquisition of a conditioned emotional response. *Learning and Motivation*, *10*, 245–277.

Rescorla, R. A. (1967). Pavlovian conditioning and its proper control groups. *Psychological Review*, *74*, 71–80.

Rescorla, R. A. (1968). Probability of shock in the presence and absence of CS in fear conditioning. *Journal of Comparative and Physiological Psychology*, *66*, 1–5.

Rescorla, R. A. (1969a). Pavlovian conditioned inhibition. *Psychological Bulletin*, *72*, 77–94.

Rescorla, R. A. (1969b). Conditioned inhibition of fear resulting from negative CS–US contingencies. *Journal of Comparative and Physiological Psychology*, *67*, 504–509.

Rescorla, R. A., & Wagner, A. R. (1972). A theory of Pavlovian conditioning: Variations in the effectiveness of reinforcement. In A. H. Black & W. F. Prokasky (Eds.), *Classical conditioning II: Current research and theory* (pp. 64–99). New York: Appleton-Century-Crofts.

Riccio, D. C., & Ebner, D. L. (1981). Postacquisition modification of memory, In N. E. Spear & R. R. Miller (Eds.), *Information processing in animals: Memory mechanisms* (pp. 291–317). Hillsdale, NJ: Lawrence Erlbaum Associates.

Roberts, S. (1983). Properties and function of an internal clock. In R. L. Mellgren (Ed.), *Animal cognition and behavior* (pp. 345–397). New York: North-Holland.

Schachtman, T. R., Brown, A. M., Gordon, E., Catterson, D., & Miller, R. R. (1987). Mechanisms underlying retarded emergence of conditioned responding following inhibitory training: Evidence for the comparator hypothesis. *Journal of Experimental Psychology: Animal Behavior Processes*, *13*, 310–322.

Spence, K. W., & Norris, E. B. (1950). Eyelid conditioning as a function of the inter-trial interval. *Journal of Experimental Psychology*, *40*, 716–720.

Tait, R. W., & Saliadin, M. E. (1986). Concurrent development of excitatory and inhibitory associations during backwards conditioning. *Animal Learning & Behavior*, *14*, 133–137.

Timberlake, W. (1986). Unpredicted food produces a mode of behavior that affects rats' subsequent reactions to a conditioned stimulus: a behavior-system approach to context blocking. *Animal Learning and Behavior*, *14*, 276–286.

Wasserman, E. A., Deich, J. D., Hunter, N. B., & Nagamatsu, L. S. (1977). Analyzing the random control procedure: Effects of paired and unpaired CSs and USs on autoshaping the chick's keypeck with heat reinforcement. *Learning and Motivation*, *8*, 467–487.

Zimmer-Hart, C. L., & Rescorla, R. A. (1974). Extinction of a Pavlovian conditioned inhibitor. *Journal of Comparative and Physiological Psychology*, *86*, 837–845.

4

Attention, Retrospective Processing and Cognitive Representations

A. G. Baker
McGill University

Pierre Mercier
Laval University

I. HISTORICAL CONTEXT

It is easy to forget that the traditional associationist theories of learning, like those of Thorndike, Hull, and Guthrie were theories of knowledge as well as of behavior. These theories attempted to specify the mechanism by which stimuli came to influence responses. The stimuli and responses studied were chosen for their simplicity[1] partly because that is a good place to start but mostly because it was believed that an understanding of more complex behaviors could later be achieved by building from the simpler level. These theorists never denied that language is a complex behavior or that insight and creativity required an elaborate knowledge structure. What they did deny was that these phenomena were to be primitives in a theoretical system. To use modern terminology they would argue that these phenomena were perhaps emergent properties of simpler processes.

This attempt to explain very complex phenomena with very simple elements was the main beauty of the theories. They were originally very elegant and parsimonious. But, as we soon argue, this simplicity was also their downfall. It is often said that S–R psychologists did not believe in memory. This is not logically possible because a theory of learning must also be a theory of memory as illustrated in the three necessary stages of learning shown in Fig. 4.1. The animal is first trained (the input stage), something about the training is stored (memory), and then learning is assessed in the test (output) phase of the experiment.

Nevertheless, this criticism does get at an essential feature of the models. A simple S–R approach such as that of Guthrie (1959) claims that learning, in the

---

[1]The organisms chosen for study, mostly nonhumans, is also an issue but we defer discussion of this point until we come to evolutionary considerations at the end of the chapter.

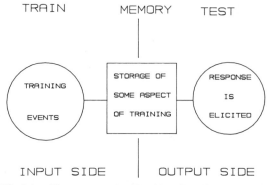

FIG. 4.1.   Three stages involved in a learning experiment.

form of an S–R bond, occurs whenever a stimulus and a response occur contiguously. Later, learning is shown and the presence of a memory is confirmed when the stimulus elicits the response. Some of the details of an experiment described in simple S–R terms are shown in Fig. 4.2. The response is determined by the presence of the S–R bond and that bond is formed at the time of the original stimulus-response pairing. Subsequently when a stimulus evokes that response its form has already been determined. In this system, the response evocation phase and the memory process are essentially passive in that they directly react to the stimulation. *Memory* consists of these bonds and there is no subsequent processing of information to speak of. Put somewhat differently the *decision* about performance occurs on input to memory and memory passively accumulates the inputs.

This analysis of S–R learning is an oversimplification because any theory must allow for learning that occurs at separate times to interact. The organism must *decide* which of several learned responses to perform. With these early associative theories the decisions were, however, very mechanistic or automated. In the

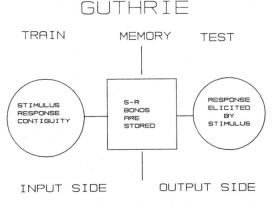

FIG. 4.2.   Guthrie's model for direct stimulus-response learning.

case of Guthrie the response that was associated with the most stimulus elements of the situation would occur (again this is a cross between an oversimplification and paraphrasing). With other theories there might be a simple comparison of habit strengths or associative levels. The crucial point is that even though a choice is made in these experiments, the interesting part of the process goes on during input.

An S–R reinforcement theory such as Hull's (1943) has the same features as Guthrie's theory but there is an extra *decision* stage at the time of input to memory. As Fig. 4.3 illustrates, an S–R association will be formed only if a reinforcement stamps it in. This general approach to learning and memory may be contrasted to that of more *cognitive* psychologists such as Tolman (1959), which is illustrated in Fig. 4.4.

According to Tolman learning does occur on the input side of memory, as it must, but this learning is fairly automatic. The animal forms a *cognitive map* (S–S associations) of the environment and perhaps a number of stimulus-response-outcome expectancies (S_1-R_1-S_2 associations) during training. The interesting part of his model comes about when it is time to respond. The animal then retrieves the cognitive map from memory, processes this information, and makes a response decision. In Tolman's psychology, the response to be made is determined very late—on the performance end of memory—in contrast to the S–R associationists who would claim that the form and type of response that could be evoked is determined by the formation of associative bonds during training.

Thus, these models generally agreed on the association as the basic unit of learning. However, some theorists felt the need to include extra processes to increase the flexibility of their systems. In Tolman's model for instance, the system allows for more varied *decisions* by accumulating a lot of information first and processing whatever elements are needed at a later time.

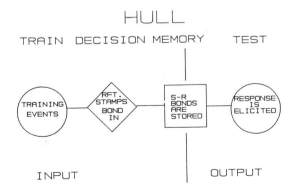

FIG. 4.3.   Hull's stimulus-response model where reinforcement is required to obtain learning.

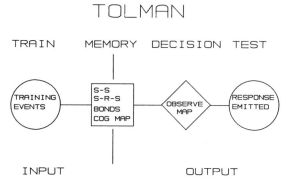

FIG. 4.4.   Tolman's retrospective memory model.

II. SELECTIVE ASSOCIATIONS: THE NEED FOR MORE FLEXIBILITY

Although Tolman and his associates presented compelling evidence for his model, the simple S–R models survived fairly intact until a number of experiments during the 1960s suggested that the associative process was indeed very flexible. Several phenomena were reported in which it looked like the animals might be retrospectively evaluating what they had learned and selectively using the information.

Kamin's (1969) blocking experiment is perhaps the prototypical demonstration of what has been termed selective associations. The experiment used the conditioned emotional response paradigm (CER) in which a conditioned stimulus (CS) is paired with shock. Any fear or anxiety that is imparted to the CS by these pairings is measured by its ability to suppress a food motivated behavior such as lever pressing. In Kamin's experiment two groups of animals were exposed to eight trials in which a stimulus compound (NL) composed of a diffuse overhead light (L) and a white noise (N) was paired with a shock. The main difference between the groups was that the *blocked* group was first exposed to 16 noise-shock trials before the reinforced compound trials, whereas the control group only received the compound trials.

The crucial feature of this experiment was that the animals in both groups received the same number of light-shock pairings. A simple associative model would predict that both groups should show similar learning about the light. The results, however, did not confirm this prediction. When tested with light alone, the animals in the control group exhibited considerable suppression reflecting what they had learned about the light. The blocked group which had received previous noise-shock pairings showed little suppression. Previous experience with noise-shock pairings had *blocked* learning about the light in this group.

In another experiment Wagner, Logan, Haberlandt, and Price (1968) exposed rats in two groups to two compound stimuli (T_1L and T_2L) each consisting of a common light (L) and one of two tones (T_1 and T_2) which differed in pitch.

In each of the groups, the animals were reinforced on 50% of these compound trials. The critical difference was that one group, the uncorrelated group, was reinforced on half of the T_1L trials and half of the T_2L trials whereas the correlated group was always reinforced on T_1L trials but was never reinforced on T_2L trials. Following extensive training on these discriminations, the amount of responding controlled by the stimuli was assessed by presenting each of them alone. The interesting results were those for the light which had been reinforced 50% of the time in each group. In the uncorrelated group in which all stimuli were reinforced 50% of the time, the light was shown to control considerable responding; however, in the correlated group, in which T_1 was a perfect predictor of the reinforcer, the light controlled relatively little responding even when ·presented alone.

The similar feature of the two preceding experiments is that a stimulus was reinforced an equivalent number of times in two groups yet the animals conditioned very differently to it. In each experiment, the presence of a stimulus that predicted more of the shocks seemed to prevent conditioning to a second stimulus. On the face of it, it looked like the animals were assessing the relative predictiveness of two stimuli and then deciding to respond to the best predictor at the expense of the other stimulus.

To integrate these data, Rescorla and Wagner (1972) proposed a model that had many of the features of Hull's (1943). It is a reinforcement model in which associative strength accrues to conditioned stimuli in trial-by-trial increments as a linearly decreasing function of the current value of the CS. More formally, $\Delta Va = \alpha\beta(\lambda - Va)$, where ΔVa is the change in associative strength to CSa, Va is the current strength of the CS, λ is the limit to V, and α and β are learning rate parameters specific to the CS and the US respectively.

To account for selective associations, it is further assumed that a given reinforcer can only support a limited amount of associative strength and that the various stimuli in a compound compete for this associative strength. In other words, a limitation is imposed on input processing, resulting in what has been termed reciprocal overshadowing. The associative strength accruing to one CS is a proportion of what remains to be learned. Formally, $\Delta Va = \alpha\beta(\lambda - \Sigma V)$ where ΣV represents the total associative strength of all stimuli present on a given trial. Any conditioning to a stimulus other than CSa will inflate the value of ΣV thereby leaving less room for conditioning to CSa. Thus, blocking occurred in the situations described above because the preconditioned noise or tone had already acquired all of the available associative strength; so little was left to be attached to the light (refer to Chapter 2 of this volume for a detailed description of the Rescorla-Wagner theory).

It is important to point out that although the Rescorla-Wagner model was much more flexible than previous conceptualizations, it was still a reinforcement model because associations were seen to be stamped in by reinforcement. The critical aspect of learning occurred on the training trials, and responding during the test was simply determined by the accumulated associative strength up to that point.

Important *decisions* in learning were again assumed to occur during training. Our account oversimplifies the theory but the important point is that it too was an input based model.

Another kind of account of the selective association results that is more germane to the present discussion is based on variations in attention. In addition to the basic expression of incremental associative strength, many selective attention theories propose that the associability of the CS (i.e., the learning rate parameter α) can change with experience. Note that the Rescorla-Wagner model did allow for changes in α resulting from experience but it did not provide an explicit mechanism for the change (Wagner & Rescorla, 1972, p. 326).

The specific mechanism for changing α differs from one attentional theory to another but the emphasis placed on these changes in associability is a major feature differentiating attentional and nonattentional models of associative learning. Many attentional theories formulated prior to 1975 (e.g., Lovejoy, 1968; Mackintosh, 1965; Sutherland, 1964; Sutherland & Mackintosh, 1971; Trabasso & Bower, 1968; Zeaman & House, 1963) share the assumption that, during the course of conditioning, attention paid to relevant stimuli increases while attention to irrelevant stimuli decreases. A subject learning about a given stimulus will increasingly attend to it if the stimulus consistently predicts its consequences, i.e., the presence or the absence of the US. However, the decrease in attention to irrelevant stimuli does not occur independently of the increase to other stimuli; rather stimuli are presumed to compete for attention. Consequently, any increase in attention to one or a group of stimuli will cause a decrease in attention to the others. This has been termed the inverse hypothesis of attention (Thomas, 1970), and it provides the mechanism for controlling the value of parameter α.

On the surface at least, the inverse hypothesis deals with some important selective attention problems such as blocking. According to an attentional analysis, the effect of the early training is to increase attention paid to the pretrained CS to the detriment of the other element of the compound. Notice we are already beginning to reach the limits of credibility for it is difficult to imagine that even rats lack the resources to attend to two simultaneous CSs whose duration is often as long as 3 min.

The idea of a limited capacity input system as an argument for the inverse hypothesis is not very tenable in view of the relative simplicity of the tasks where selective conditioning occurs. Yet its successful predictions and parsimony keep it a central part of many theories. This is partly what led Mackintosh (1975) to propose a modified mechanism for controlling the variation in attention. He suggested that attention to a CS might increase if that CS was a more accurate predictor of its consequences than all other stimuli on the same trial, and that attention would decrease when the CS predicted its consequence less accurately. The formal rule is: $\Delta Va = \alpha(\lambda - Va)$; α is positive if $|\lambda - Va| > |\lambda - V\Sigma|$ and α is negative if $|\lambda - Va| < = |\lambda - V\Sigma|$, where $V\Sigma$ represents the associative value of all other stimuli on the trial. This rule based formulation specifies a symmetrical mechanism for augmenting and diminishing attention. It accounts for block-ing effects while avoiding the implausibility of limited input processing capability.

Hall and Honey describe the fate of the Mackintosh model and some of its descendants more fully in Chapter 5 of this volume. Most relevant to our discussion is the observation that this model is also an input side model. Variations in performance are due to variations in learning brought about by variations in attention on the learning trials. Again performance on the test is determined fairly automatically by the amount of associative strength that has been accrued to the controling stimulus during input. The output is generated accordingly. As we will see in the section on latent inhibition, the Pearce and Hall model (1980) which is closely related to Mackintosh's also emphasizes the notion of limited input processing.

III. LEARNED IRRELEVANCE AND THE NEED FOR RETROSPECTIVE PROCESSING

In 1973, Mackintosh reported a series of experiments that formed the foundation for much of our work and that in our minds cried out for the development of a model of learning that included retrospective processing. Mackintosh's experiments arose from some seminal correlation learning experiments reported by Rescorla (1966, 1967).

In these experiments, Rescorla demonstrated that the amount of conditioning ac-cruing to a stimulus was not only a function of the number of temporally contiguous pairings of the CS and US but was also a function of the correlation or contingency between the events. That is, conditioning seemed to occur only if the CS gave information concerning the occurrence of the US. If the CS predicted a relatively high level of US occurrences then excitatory conditioning occurred. If the CS predicted the absence of the US then inhibitory conditioning occurred. Finally if the CS and US were uncorrelated no conditioning occurred regardless of the number of contiguous CS–US pairing (but see Quinsey, 1971; and Benedict & Ayres, 1972).

Because Rescorla's experiments demonstrate that animals are sensitive to the contingency between events and not just temporal contiguity, they suggest that the animals might be indulging in retrospective processing. If the animals are some-how calculating the correlation between the events then they must, at the point of the calculation, be considering the contents of memory. In order to calculate a correlation or a contingency it is necessary to have some representation of the number of times the two events occurred together and apart and the number of times or amount of time that neither occurred. Such correlations would need to be calculated at the time of the test. Much like Tolman's (1959) model, this is an output oriented formulation in which the animal is seen to *passively* gather data and then make an active decision at the time of performance. Behavior is not constrained by limitations on learning during training but by decisions made at the time of performance.

This is by no means the only account of Rescorla's data. A far more popular one claims that the learning in his experiments is a special case of selective associations. More specifically, the lack of associations to the CS in the uncorrelated CS/US case would be an example of overshadowing involving the experimental context, i.e. the conglomerate of nonspecific cues formed by the experimental chamber and test situation as a whole. Such an analysis requires only the additional assumption that the context has many of the properties of a conventional stimulus. The context can condition, extinguish, and compete with other stimuli for associations like conventional stimuli. Thus, in the case of uncorrelated CS/US presentations, the context is seen to be paired with all of the USs and ultimately comes to control all of the associative strength at the expense of the discrete CS. Again it can be seen that this is an input based explanation. The context is seen to become conditioned and then blocks learning about the CS. A crucial feature about these input oriented explanations is that they imply that, because there is no performance to the CS following uncorrelated CS/US presentations, then there is no learning and thus this stimulus must have the same *cognitive* status as a novel stimulus. This is called the independence of path assumption (cf. Rescorla & Wagner, 1972).

The alternative retrospective processing account would argue that although the animal may not behave in the presence of an uncorrelated CS, it still has a reservoir of *knowledge* about its experience with the CS. Mackintosh (1973) carried out a proactive interference experiment and we ourselves have carried out many more, which we feel strongly support the notion of an output based retrospective processing mechanism.

A typical example of these experiments was reported by Baker and Mackintosh (1977), using a conditioned licking paradigm. In this paradigm, rats are trained by exposing them to pairings of a CS with presentations of water through a drinking tube that is always present in the apparatus. Conditioned responding is assessed by measuring the amount of licking to the tube that occurs during the CS, in anticipation of the water. This experiment consisted of a preexposure phase followed by a training phase in which a tone CS was paired with water. The control group received no exposure to the tone and water before training. The tone alone and water alone groups were exposed to the tone and water respectively prior to training. Finally, the critical group was exposed to uncorrelated presentations of the tone and water. Following this treatment, the animals in all groups received 10 pairings of the tone and water per day for 8 days.

The results of the experiment were straightforward. The animals' performance on the final conditioning day is shown in Fig. 4.5. It is quite clear that the uncorrelated group showed considerably less responding to the tone than the other groups. Mackintosh called this retarded conditioning "Learned Irrelevance." He claimed that during exposure to the uncorrelated tone and water presentations

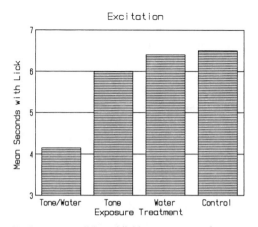

FIG. 4.5. Excitatory conditioned licking to a tone after preexposure to Tone alone, Water alone, Tone/Water uncorrelated or no preexposure (Control). From Baker & Mackintosh (1977).

the animals learned that the tone was irrelevant as a predictor of the US. This knowledge suppressed attention to the CS and thus the animals learned little about it during later training.

Again it can be seen that Mackintosh's account is input based. He is claiming that something about the preexposure retards acquisition of conditioning to the tone. Contrary to this, we would argue that the critical feature of the learned irrelevance explanation is that it must reflect a retrospective conditioning process. If the animal is *deciding* that the tone is irrelevant then it must in some sense be calculating a correlation between the tone and water. In order to do this, and to keep updating things during exposure and training, the animal must be keeping track of at least some data about its experiences with the tone and water and then performing some mental computations on this knowledge at the time of performance. In our terminology, the animal has formed a temporal cognitive map of its experiences and is retrospectively processing this information.

Our explanation of this experiment is not the only or even the most parsimonious description of the results. It could be argued that during exposure to the tone and water the animals simply learned to be inactive during the tone. If this inactivity transferred to the tone-water training phase then we would expect retarded performance in the uncorrelated group. A second experiment that extended the generality of our results and provided evidence against this learned inactivity hypothesis involved interference with the acquisition of conditioned inhibition. In the conditioned inhibition procedure, the to-be-inhibitory stimulus is paired in compound with an excitatory stimulus and the compound is not reinforced. As the stimulus becomes inhibitory, responding to the compound decreases (the animal is *less* active). Thus any inactivity that is conditioned to the stimulus should enhance rather than interfere with the stimulus's ability to decrease responding.

The critical feature of the two experiments taken together is that in the first experiment interference with excitatory conditioning came about because the animals licked *less* than controls and in the present experiment any interference with inhibition should come about because the animals lick *more* than controls. Such results should eliminate most alternative explanations of the data that rely on a simple transference of response tendencies.

The design of the experiment was very similar to the previous one. In order to provide an excitatory stimulus to be used in compound with the preexposed tone, the animals were first exposed to pairings of a light with water. Following this, the animals were divided into four groups and given the same four exposure treatments as the animals in the previous experiment (i.e., no exposure control, tone alone, water alone, and tone/water uncorrelated). In the final test phase of the experiment, the animals were required to learn a discrimination between the light which was again paired with water and a compound of the light and the tone which was never paired with water.

Our expectation was that if the animals in the uncorrelated group learned that the tone and water were uncorrelated then they should have difficulty learning that the tone predicted the absence of water. As Fig. 4.6 indicates, this expectation was confirmed.

This figure shows the level of responding to the tone-light compound on the last day of the test. It can be clearly seen that the animals that had been exposed to uncorrelated tone/water presentations responded much more to the compound than the controls. It must be remembered that this higher level of *activity* comes about because the animals have failed to learn that the tone signals that they will not be reinforced. It should also be mentioned that there were no reliable differences in the animals' response levels to the light on the light-water trials so these

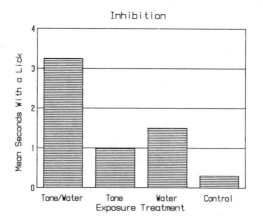

FIG. 4.6.   Licking to a tone-light compound during inhibitory conditioning, after preexposure to Tone alone, Water alone, Tone/Water uncorrelated, or no preexposure (Control). From Baker & Mackintosh (1977).

differences genuinely reflect differential tendencies for the tone to inhibit behavior elicited by the light.

This experiment rules out alternative explanations of learned irrelevance that would emphasize the role of nonassociative factors such as activity deficits in the interference. We claim that the critical feature of the interference in these experiments is that the animals learn specifically that the CS and US are uncorrelated and this knowledge interferes with future performance. Thus, the important thing about preexposure is not simple the exposure to the CS and US but the specific experience with the lack of correlation or contingency.

An alternative explanation of our results would point out that exposure to the CS alone causes interference with conditioning and so does exposure to the US alone. These proactive interference effects are called latent inhibition and the US preexposure effect. There are theoretical accounts of each of these phenomena that do not call upon retrospective processing. It is thus possible that the interference that we call learned irrelevance is not a unitary effect of the lack of correlation between the CS and the US but is the sum of latent inhibition and US preexposure. But let us have a closer look at what we know about these two phenomena to better judge the kind of explanation just offered.

IV. US EXPOSURE

Presentation of the US alone exerts a strong influence on the outcome of conditioning. For instance, it has been frequently observed, in a variety of conditioning paradigms (e.g., human and rabbit eyelid conditioning, conditioned emotional response, conditioned taste aversion, and autoshaping), that repeated presentations of unsignaled USs prior to conditioning can retard future conditioning based on that US (see Randich & LoLordo, 1979, for a review; Baker, Mercier, Gabel, & Baker, 1981). US alone stimulation intermixed with paired CS–US trials during acquisition can also reduce the amount of conditioning (e.g., Gamzu & Williams, 1973; Jenkins, Barnes, & Barrera, 1981; Rescorla, 1968). As well, under certain conditions, postconditioning exposure to the US alone will reduce the magnitude of the conditioned response (Randich & Rescorla, 1981; Rescorla, 1974).

The common feature of these manipulations is that they all reflect a degradation in the contingency between the CS and the US and show that subjects are sensitive to this degradation. We would like to claim that the degraded contingency is what the subject learns and that this information controls the speed of acquisition and the asymptotic level of performance. In other words, the subject fully learns the relationship between the CS and the US and behaves accordingly. In contrast to this, modern selective attention theories propose that any US alone trial changes the extent to which a CS is an accurate or inaccurate predictor of its consequences and that this change limits the amount of associative strength that could be gained on the next trial.

Attentional and nonattentional associative theories of learning attempt to account for the interference caused by US alone trials by appealing to background or contextual stimuli and ascribing them a blocking role. In the case of exposure to the US prior to conditioning, the contextual stimuli would be reinforced, building up associative strength and/or increasing attention to them. When conditioning is later carried out in the same environment, the contextual stimuli are said to receive more attention than is usually the case thus reducing the possibility of conditioning to the discrete CS. The same analysis can be used in the case of extra US trials interspersed with paired CS–US trials where the competition for attention would be spread and maintained throughout conditioning instead of being sequential and transient as in preexposure. Nonattentional theories would make essentially the same analysis based on stimulus competition but without recourse to the concept of attention. Thus if one is prepared to consider that contextual stimuli might behave the same as discrete CSs, the inverse hypothesis or reciprocal overshadowing would apparently allow associative theories to deal with exposure to extra USs.

But are these theories successful? If conditioning the context is blocking learning about the CS, then any reduction in associative strength of the context should bring a corresponding reduction in interference. Tomie (1976a, 1976b) and Baker and Mackintosh (1979) have provided indirect evidence consistent with this by showing that either signaling the US during preexposure (with a CS other than the test stimulus) or carrying out exposure in a context different from the test context, both treatments which should reduce context conditioning, would reduce the interference effects. However, more direct measurement of conditioning to the context provides a different picture.

In a series of experiments using signaling and context-change procedures to reduce the US preexposure effect in a conditioned emotional response task, Baker et al. (Baker, Mercier, Gabel, & Baker, 1981; Baker & Mercier, 1982a, 1982b) have assessed fear of the context directly by measuring how much suppression of operant responding it caused. They have shown that contrary to the context blocking hypothesis, specific reductions of interference did not always correspond to equivalent reductions in fear of the context.

Figure 4.7a shows the success of four associative manipulations in reducing contextual conditioning. In these experiments fear is measured by its ability to suppress ongoing responding for food so low scores represent more fear or more conditioning than higher scores. It can be seen from the figure that exposure to shocks (Group SH) produced substantial contextual fear compared to the controls (CONT). It is also apparent that signaling the shocks with a discrete CS (CS–SH, the CS was a 60 sec light), exposing the animals in another context (O.B., the animals were exposed in other boxes), removing some of the contextual stimuli following exposure (CS/SH, a light stimulus was removed), or extinguishing the context following exposure (EXT, the animals were exposed to the context for several sessions between exposure and conditioning) all reduced contextual fear but in differing amounts.

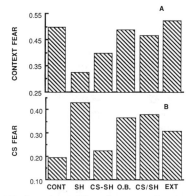

FIG. 4.7. Panel B shows conditioned suppression to a clicker without prior treatment (Cont) or after exposure to unsignaled shocks (Sh), shocks signaled with a discrete CS (CS→Sh), shocks signaled with a session-long CS (CS/Sh), unsignaled shocks delivered in a context different from test (Other Box), or unsignaled shocks followed by exposure to the context alone (Extinction). Panel A shows fear of contextual stimuli prior to the conditioning phase shown in Panel A. From Baker & Mercier (1982a).

Because each of these treatments reduced contextual fear then each should reduce the ability of shock preexposure to reduce or interfere with conditioning to a discrete CS, in this case a clicker, paired with shocks. The theory also predicts that the treatments that most markedly reduce contextual fear should most markedly reduce interference with conditioning. Observation of Fig. 4.7a would indicate that signaling the shocks with a discrete CS (CS–SH) should be least effective in reducing interference because it is the least effective treatment in reducing context fear. The results of conditioning to the clicker following the exposure treatments are shown in Fig. 4.7b and they are inconsistent with this prediction. It is clear that rather than being the least effective procedure at reducing the interference with conditioning caused by exposure to the US signaling the US was the most, and arguably the only, effective procedure. Contrary to the predications of the context blocking hypothesis the level of interference with conditioning following exposure to the US does not appear to be a simple function of the level of conditioning to contextual cues.

A parallel set of observations has been reported by Durlach (1982) who found that signaling intertrial USs reduced interference with autoshaping while a more direct index of contextual conditioning, namely general activity, seemed relatively unaffected by the signaling procedure. Similar evidence is available in conditioned licking (Baker, Bindra, & Singh, 1985). These data directly challenge the context blocking hypothesis as the mechanism for competition among cues.

Another challenge may come from the reduction in conditioned responding that is sometimes observed after postconditioning exposure to the US alone. In conditioned suppression, this postconditioning effect is related to the number and intensity of the extra USs, and inversely related to the delay between the last exposure to the US alone and the test of the target CS (Randich & Haggard, 1983). To our knowledge, the effect has not yet been submitted to context shifts, but it is difficult to imagine how postconditioning exposure to the US could retroactively interfere with input processing of the CS–US relationship.

We propose an alternative theoretical approach to the US exposure effect (see Baker & Mackintosh, 1979; Baker & Mercier, 1982a), inspired in part by Mackintosh's (1975) rule based model in that the emphasis is on making decisions about relevant and irrelevant stimuli. This approach postulates an intrinsic tendency for the subjects to search for contingencies in the environment, i.e., to examine salient stimuli in relation to one another and determine what correlations exist between them. In US preexposure, the subjects learn that US alone trials are unrelated to any other specific cue in the immediate environment. The knowledge about these US alone trials is simply *memorized* and it later interferes with learning a paired CS–US relationship based on the same US because the overall contingency between the CS and US pair is reduced by the memory of prior US alone trials. The interference is not caused by reduced processing but by conflicting information. Signaling the US during exposure thus reduces the interference because it reduces the overall unpredictability of the US. There must be an upper limit to input capacity but we prefer to relegate it to situations where a larger number of salient and relevant cues would result in a more obvious overload on processing.

Interspersing unsignaled USs with CS–US pairings during conditioning also degrades the overall correlation between stimuli and thus degrades performance as well. Additionally, the notion of retrospective processing where current information is compared with past data would also regard postconditioning exposure to the US as a case of degraded contingency as long as the episodes of exposure and test are sufficiently similar to conditioning to maintain continuity of experience. Postexposure to a stronger US might not result in reduced responding because the US is perceived as an independent experience. A longer time interval between postexposure and final test (Randich & Ross, 1985) might also separate the experiences and limit retrospective processing.

Note how this position suggests two processes for determining the response. The organism calculates the contingency between events within some time frame and an analysis of the results of these calculations determines the ultimate response. But, separately, the animal decides how big this frame is or what data to include in the analysis. Thus in some instances the animal might include all of the experimenter's events in the analysis but at other times only some of them. Anything that might mark or emphasize the posttraining, pretraining or any added events might make the animal ignore them in its analysis of the contingency. (This is much like the traditional concept of stimulus generalization decrement.) Research should be directed at determining when animals are likely to include all the events and when they assign them to different frames for analysis.

What then is the role of contextual stimuli? According to our position, the subjects can and often do learn a relationship between the background and the US particularly when no other more salient cue signals those USs and there is ample evidence that such learning takes place (Balsam, 1985). That relationship is only significant or predictive in the larger context of the subjects' global experience. Within an experimental session, USs are associated with more discrete cues, and the subjects have no difficulty representing both relationships.

The idea that performance is controlled by comparative evaluation of more than one information source is not unique to our approach. For instance, scalar expectancy theory (Gibbon & Balsam, 1981), predicts that, in US preexposure, conditioning to the background and conditioning to the target CS develop independently and that responding to the CS will emerge only when CS associative strength reaches a sufficient threshold above background level. That threshold is of course lower when no US alone trials occur. Durlach (1982) has specifically tested this position and found that in autoshaping, pigeons responded less in a context where no food had occurred than in an equivalent context previously associated with food. She interpreted this finding as incompatible with a strict performance model such as Gibbon-Balsam's but consistent with a model where US alone trials modify learning (such as Rescorla-Wagner, 1972), not just performance.

Our correlational approach claims that the representation of the overall CS–US contingency is modified after retrospective evaluation and performance or output is controlled accordingly. Contextual conditioning may develop separately but may also modulate the output depending on what information the context carries. Thus the correlational view points toward empirical tests of the role of the context in framing the continuity of experience rather than toward considering it just as any other CS.

But let us now examine another kind of isolated cue presentation that hampers conditioning: latent inhibition.

Latent Inhibition

Latent inhibition is the retardation in conditioning observed after preexposure to the CS alone. Like the US exposure phenomenon, it has been observed in a variety of conditioning situations (Lubow, 1973).

Early attentional theories were poorly equipped to account for latent inhibition. They might have claimed that the CS would become an irrelevant stimulus as a result of predicting neither the presence nor the absence of the US during preexposure. Consequently, less and less attention would be paid to the CS and conditioning would proceed slowly when the CS would finally begin to be consistently followed by the US. However, as we have already pointed out, the early formulations only stated that attention was paid to relevant stimuli at the expense of the irrelevant ones. No mechanism was offered to allow for an independent decrease in attention. Mackintosh's (1975) formulation is better equipped in this regard. The model states that attention to a given CS will decrease unless that CS is a more accurate predictor of the US than any other stimulus in the conditioning situation.

Attentional approaches predict that if attention to the CS could be maintained during preexposure, then latent inhibition should be reduced or even eliminated. A number of experiments have attempted to corroborate this prediction by accompanying the CS with another stimulus during exposure. At best these procedures have had mixed success at reducing latent inhibition. Mercier and Baker (1985) have criticized the successful reports (Doré, 1980; Lubow, Schnur, & Rifkin, 1976; Lubow, Wagner, & Weiner, 1982; Szakmary, 1977) on methodological and logical grounds, and they have reported a series of experiments where latent inhibition was not reduced.

The rationale for experiments in which an exposed CS is signaled or is a signal for another CS is similar to that for signaling the US in US preexposure experiments. Forming an association between the two stimuli either keeps up attention to them or it blocks or overshadows context–CS associations which might retard conditioning. There is little problem in interpreting cases where adding a stimulus during exposure reduces latent inhibition. If, however, adding a CS during exposure does not reduce latent inhibition we do not know whether latent inhibition is insensitive to the signaling manipulation in general or whether the animals just did not learn the CS–CS association or were insensitive to one of the stimuli. We have completed a series of experiments in which signaling did not reduce latent inhibition and in which we were able to use sensory preconditioning to unequivocally demonstrate that the animals had both noticed the stimuli and formed an association between them during preexposure.

Sensory preconditioning was originally reported by Brogden (1939) and it involves pairing two neutral stimuli (CS_1–CS_2). Following this pairing, one of the stimuli is paired with a traditional reinforcer such as a shock (CS_2–Sh). In a final test phase the animal is presented with the other stimulus (CS_1). On this test it is typically found that part of the conditioned response to CS_2 has transferred to CS_1. With appropriate controls this test demonstrates that the animals have noticed and associated the two neutral stimuli during the CS_1–CS_2 pairings. The first two stages of a sensory preconditioning experiment are very similar to a latent inhibition experiment and are logically identical to the treatment used in attempts to demonstrate that signaling reduces latent inhibition. Animals are exposed to two neutral stimuli one signaling the other and then one of them is reinforced. These animals are compared to a group in which the stimuli are independently presented. We took advantage of this similarity to demonstrate that the animals had indeed noticed and associated the stimuli in an experiment in which signaling did not reduce latent inhibition.

Figure 4.8 shows the results of one of these experiments in which we attempted to reduce latent inhibition to a clicker by signaling it with a light. Four groups

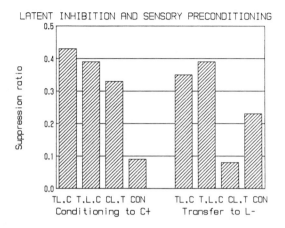

FIG. 4.8.   Left: Conditioned suppression to a clicker after exposure to clicker, light and tone presented independently (C,L,T), clicker-light compound and independent tone (CL,T), tone-light compound and independent clicker (TL,C) or minimal expsoure (CON). Right: Sensory preconditioning to the light after the treatments above. From Mercier & Baker (1985).

were exposed to either separate presentation of tones, lights, and clickers (Group T,L,C), tone-light compounds and separate clickers, (TL,C), clicker-light compounds and separate tones (CL,T, this is the critical group in which the light might reduce latent inhibition to the clicker), or were minimally exposed to all three stimuli. Figure 4.8 shows that compared to the controls all three groups exposed to the clicker showed similar amounts of latent inhibition. In the final phase of the experiments when all groups were tested with the light Group CL,T showed strong suppression to the light indicating sensory preconditioning and showing that although the light and clicker must have been attended to and associated during exposure this was not sufficient to reduce latent inhibition.

This is not to say that the interference caused by CS preexposure can never be reduced, it seems that it can sometimes be reduced through manipulations of the context (Baker & Mercier, 1982c) and generalization decrement (Mackintosh, 1973). As it stands though, the signaling procedure is not nearly as effective in reducing latent inhibition as it is in reducing the US preexposure effect.

Even if for some yet unknown reason, the signaling procedure could be made effective under a specific set of circumstances, the attentional interpretation of latent inhibition considered so far is faced with a major difficulty when the results of Hall and Pearce (1979) are considered. They have shown that conditioning can be retarded even when the CS is reinforced with a low intensity US during preexposure. This observation is partly responsible for their proposed reduced associability model.

Pearce and Hall's model (1980) is largely inspired from Mackintosh's (1975) attention theory. They propose that the associability of a stimulus *decreases* if it consistently predicts a consequence. Stimulus associability is said to depend upon the absolute difference between the maximum associative strength available (λ) and the current associative strength of all cues present ($\alpha_n = |\lambda_{n-1} - \Sigma V_{n-1}|$) while the change in associative strength (for cue A) itself depends on its associability and on the maximum associative strength available ($\Delta V_A = K^*\alpha_A^*\lambda$, where K is a constant determined by the strength of A). As more and more reinforced trials are experienced, the quantity $|\lambda_{n-1} - \Sigma V_{n-1}|$ becomes smaller, reducing α and limiting any further increments in associative strength. The effect of including a low intensity reinforcer during preexposure would be to reduce the associability of the CS (α) while overt responding remains at a low or even subthreshold level.

While the model would logically handle nonreinforced preexposure in the same manner, its basic equation leads it to predict a preexposure effect in less trials than is empirically warranted: the basic equation reduces associability to zero in one nonreinforced trial. To solve this problem, Pearce and Hall have proposed an averaging mechanism whereby the amount of reduction in α is a function of accumulated data over a number of trials. Pearce, Kaye, and Hall (1982) have extended this principle to account for partial reinforcement effects. It should be noted that allowing the animal to compute a weighted average over trials is not a *simple and uncontentious* addition to Pearce and Hall's model. Calculating an average requires that the animal store data concerning recent events and then make calculations on these data. This is just another form of retrospective processing, and requiring it to account for such a fundamental empirical finding as latent inhibition certainly reduces the parsimony of the Pearce-Hall model.

This process of averaging over trials is very similar to the retrospective processing which we propose. However, we do not believe that it results in reduced associability or diminished learning. As we have mentioned before, we suggest that subjects scan their memory for information about past events, compare that information with the stimulation on the current trial, and regulate output accordingly. In the case of latent inhibition, retrospective processing informs the subject that the current CS signaled no significant event in the recent past. As with US preexposure, the experience of CS alone trials is nevertheless memorized. When these trials are later included in evaluating the overall CS–US contingency, the net effect is to reduce the perceived correlation. The development of the full conditioned response is thus retarded as a result of this discrepancy in the information. Mercier (1985) has proposed a similar analysis of the interference caused by low intensity reinforced preexposure, where the conflicting information would arise from knowledge of the different US intensities. Exposed animals would be faced with the ambiguous information that the CS had predicted both a strong and a weak CS. The resulting response would reflect this conflict and would thus be weaker than that produced by animals whose only experience was with a constant intensity US paired with the CS.

Thus the distinctive features of the retrospective mechanism as exposed so far are that: (1) learning itself is not diminished following exposure to the CS or the US, only performance is modified according to available evidence regarding the stimuli involved; (2) instead of postulating a limited capacity processor, we suggest that the system encodes many aspects of the stimulation (e.g., rate, intensity, contingency) and that all these aspects contribute to the determination of the output. A change in any of these is a potential source of interference. One advantage of this approach is that it has the potential of explaining US and CS interference effects with a common mechanism. The Pearce and Hall formulation would apparently require a separate although similar mechanism to account for US exposure.

This call for integration brings us back full circle to learned irrelevance. We ended our section on learned irrelevance by mentioning how it could at least logically be argued to result from the sum of the US and CS exposure effects. Let us first consider an empirical test of that hypothesis. Knowing as we do that the interference caused by exposure to the US alone can be largely eliminated by signaling the US during exposure, it should in principle be possible to eliminate the independent contribution of US exposure to learned irrelevance. Baker and Mackintosh (1979) did just that. Using a CER preparation, they exposed one group of animals to uncorrelated clickers and shocks (Cl/Sh). A second group was exposed to the same schedule of uncorrelated clickers and shocks but the shocks were all signaled with a light (Cl/L→Sh). A reference group was exposed to clickers alone (Cl). As depicted in Fig. 4.9, the signaling of the shocks in the Cl/L→Sh group produced just as much interference as plain exposure to uncorrelated clickers and shocks. This suggests that the interference results from learning the uncorrelated relationship between the clicker CS and the shock US, and not from the sum of two separate exposure effects.

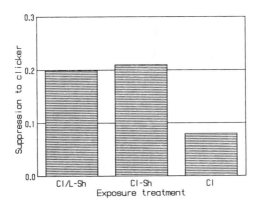

FIG. 4.9. Conditioned suppression to a clicker after exposure to clicker alone (Cl), uncorrelated clickers and unsignaled shocks (Cl-Sh) or uncorrelated clickers and signaled shocks (Cl/L-Sh). From Baker & Mackintosh.

Aside from this empirical test however, attempting to explain learned ir-relevance as the sum of latent inhibition and US exposure would not further our understanding by much since, as we hope to have shown above, the latter two phenomena are also best explained in terms of retrospective processing.

V. SOME OTHER EVIDENCE FOR RETROSPECTIVE PROCESSING

We have argued from our own research on proactive interference effects that there is a strong case for retrospective processing in classical conditioning. There have been several, to our minds quite compelling demonstrations of retrospec-tive processing carried out in other labs. The first of these demonstrations was a control condition in Kamin's (1969) series of experiments on blocking. It will be recalled that in the blocking experiment, prior reinforced experience with one member (N) of a compound stimulus (NL) blocked future suppression to the sec-ond. The traditional associative explanations of this phenomenon claimed that something about the initial training of the noise blocked or prevented processing of the light. This argument is an input based account because although previous experience with the noise is involved it acts upon the formation of the associative bond during training. Put more simply, blocking is seen as a learning deficit and not as a performance effect.

If this account is true a necessary feature of the blocking experiment must be that the organism has had its experience with the noise prior to the point where it modulates *learning* about the light. None of the traditional blocking control groups are relevant to this point. Kamin (1969) did, however, report an appropriate test of the possibility that blocking might be at least partially an output based or retrospective processing phenomenon. In one experiment, he reported the results of a group of animals that had received what we call the backward blocking proce-dure. These animals were first exposed to reinforced presentations of the noise-light compound followed by reinforced trials to the noise alone. Subsequent to this the animals were tested for suppression to the noise.

The crucial feature of this experiment is that the animals in the backward block-ing group had identical experience with the noise and light compound up until the last light presentation. These two groups must have learned the same amount about the light up to that point. Following compound training, the light was never presented again for either group until the test. If, as the input based models would have it, associations are formed and modulated on conditioning trials the two groups should show equivalent suppression to the light. The results did not con-firm this prediction. The animals in the backward blocking group showed sub-stantially less suppression to the light than the NL control group. Although the effect was not as strong as in a forward blocking experiment, subsequently rein-forced noise trials did *block* suppression to the light.

There are alternative explanations for the backward blocking effect. Kamin (1969) himself argued that the reductions in suppression could result from retroactive interference from the shock presented between compound training and test or from the passage of time. He also claimed that he had run controls for these effects and they they had shown that backward *blocking* was an artifact. To our knowledge he has never reported the results of these control procedures or for that matter specified what they actually were.

If there is something in the *backward blocking* result it provides compelling evidence for retrospective processing. During compound training the animal becomes afraid of the light. Subsequently the animal discovers that the noise is a better predictor of shocks and *decides* that the light is not an adequate cause. Because of the importance of the backward blocking result, we have tried to replicate it in our lab, with mixed results. This is not surprising because backward blocking tends to be opposed to the rather strong tendency towards primacy in conditioning.

There seems to be some sort of behavioral *inertia*; that is, once an organism strongly makes up its *mind* about something, it is rather difficult to change it. For instance Baker and Baker (1985) have argued that although it is possible to change an excitor into an inhibitor and vice versa this is generally quite difficult. This is another argument against the independence of path that is found in many input based theories. Regardless of the level of behavior controlled by a stimulus at the present time, the history of that stimulus and other stimuli is crucial in determining future changes in learning and performance. Thus we find the sometimes surprisingly large and long-lasting interference with conditioning in procedures like learned helplessness, learned irrelevance, and latent inhibition.

These points aside, it is not surprising to find only limited success in asking an animal to change its "mind" about a stimulus that it has decided is fear producing. There are, however, several other more robust demonstrations that suggest that blocking's cousin overshadowing may be influenced by retrospective mechanisms. In an overshadowing experiment, a compound stimulus is paired with shock and it is found that one, or sometimes both stimuli, reduces conditioning to the other. This result is taken by input based models as suggesting that conditioning is retarded because the stimuli must share some limited resource like attention or associative strength and thus learning on the input trials is reduced. The alternative is that the animal *learns* about both stimuli but later decides that one was the more likely *cause* of the US.

Clearly, both theories make equivalent predictions about the result of the test in overshadowing but the latter leaves open the possibility that the animal might "change its mind" about the elements of the compound. Kaufman and Bolles (1981) carried out an experiment that tested this. They gave animals a number of reinforced pairings of a compound which had been chosen so that one element overshadowed the other. Following these compound trials the stronger "overshadowing" stimulus was extinguished. When the weaker, previously "overshadowed," stimulus was later tested, it was found to control more conditioning than the same stimulus in a group which had not had the stronger stimulus extinguished. This result clearly implies that the nonreinforced experience with the stronger stimulus caused the animal to retrospectively *decide* that the weaker but now more highly correlated stimulus was the *true cause* of the US. Or, as Bouton and Bolles (1985) might argue, the true cause of the shock in the reinforced compound is ambiguous but the extinction of the stronger stimulus might *disambiguate* the *cause* and induce responding to the weaker stimulus.

This one experiment does not stand in isolation. The basic result has been replicated in Ralph Miller's lab (Miller & Schachtman, 1985a, 1985b; refer to Chapter 3, this volume) as one of a series of experiments designed to demonstrate that phenomena like blocking and overshadowing are performance effects. He argues that in both blocking and overshadowing the animals do store a representation of the blocked or overshadowed stimulus as being paired with the US only this representation or memory is not subsequently manifested in behavior. Extinguishing the overshadowing stimulus or various *reminder* treatments such as separate presentations of the CS or US cause this memory to be manifested. Although truly retrospective, Miller's theoretical explanations of these results differ from ours in that they essentially call upon comparisons of habit strength as the mechanism of retrospection and thus would have trouble accounting for findings such as learned irrelevance, latent inhibition or the classical maze learning results of Tolman and his associates.

Thus, in addition to our work on learned irrelevance, the US preexposure effect, and latent inhibition, these experiments provide evidence for the presence of a fairly general decision making mechanism on the output side of memory.

VI.   THE VALUE OF A RETROSPECTIVE PROCESSING ACCOUNT: HUMAN JUDGMENT PROCESSES

We have been careful to call our musings about output based processes an approach or an orientation rather than a theory because it certainly is not a theory. Theories are testable but the notion of animals retrospectively *thinking* about their representations of the world almost certainly is not. An animal in a backward blocking experiment might cogitate on its overall experience with the stimuli and accordingly change its mind about the blocked stimulus but, on the other hand, it might not. Either of these outcomes is consistent with a naive retrospective processor. If the animal takes all of its experience into account then that is fine but if it does not that is no problem either. Extinguishing the overshadowing stimulus could cause the rat to *think* that the overshadowed stimulus is the best *cause* of the US and this might be reflected by an increase in responding or it might think that the extinction trials herald a new "US-free" era and therefore it would be even less afraid of the overshadowed stimulus than before. Even "counterintuitive'' predictions or, for that matter, any evidence supporting input based models are no problem because most believers in naive retrospection would feel no uneasiness with the proposition that retrospection is a recently *evolved* ability that is in some sense laminated onto the traditional, even S–R learning processes. Retrospection is a tautological system and we are left with a homunculus inside the rat's head making decisions for the real rat. We are as much in the dark concerning the decision processes of this little internal rat as we are for the real rat.

This is why the experiments of *cognitive* animal learners like ourselves and Tolman are almost always negative in nature. The experiments attack various tenets of input based theories, and usually find them wanting but they rarely investigate any predictions that are driven by their own position. Perhaps that is why the associationists hold the theories in such contempt.

As theory, retrospective processing has little value; but as an orientation or approach it is of considerable use. Certainly without it phenomena such as latent learning, learned helplessness, and learned irrelevance would not have been studied very extensively. But beyond the empirical relevance of these approaches is the observation made by many philosophers of science that the questions asked by scientists often reflect their own and their scientific culture's theoretical position. This can influence the structure of the data base in psychology and it can even lead the field astray. As an example of the weakness and strength of the input based models, we would like to consider several experiments in human judgment processes carried out by Anthony Dickinson and David Shanks (Dickinson, Shanks, & Evenden, 1984; Shanks, 1985; see Chapter 9, this volume) and our as yet unpublished and even uncompleted response to them.

A common finding in the study of human judgment processes is that humans often do not act like natural statisticians. They make systematic errors (e.g., Nisbett & Ross, 1980; Tversky & Kahneman, 1978). These results are quite puzzling to many scientists and as yet no strong theoretical position has arisen to account for these biases. In a typical judgment experiment, human observers are exposed to a contingency or correlation between two events and are then asked to estimate the correlation or causal relation between them. Generally speaking, people are quite good at estimating strong positive or negative contingencies, but their performance breaks down when the correlation between the events is not perfect. This reduction in performance is most marked with cases of zero contingencies with fairly dense frequencies of presentations of events.

Dickinson, Shanks, and Evenden (1984) observed the methodological similarity of asking humans to judge contingencies between events, and experiments in classical conditioning in which animals are asked to form associations between events. In both types of experiment, the organism is asked to extract the correlation between events and respond accordingly. There is at least a superficial resemblance between rats' and humans' reactions to these problems. It will be recalled that Rescorla carried out a series of experiments in which he varied the correlation between the CS and the US and that he found very little evidence of responding in animals which had been exposed to a lack of correlation between these events. This does not, however, tell the whole story because other researchers (e.g., Benedict & Ayres, 1972; Quinsey, 1971) found that in some instances, particularly when faced with very dense schedules of preexposure, the animals would show excitatory conditioning when exposed to uncorrelated events. Further, in most cases, this excitatory conditioning is transient and goes away with extended training.

Dickinson, Shanks, and Evenden devised a human contingency judgment task in which subjects were asked to judge the effectiveness of shells that they shot at a tank in a video game. The subjects were told that the shells were not perfectly effective and that they might only cause the tank to explode some of the time. In addition, the tank was said to be traversing a mine field and it might hit a mine and explode at any time regardless of whether or not a shell had hit it. The observer could not tell from any explosion whether it was due to an effective shell or to a mine. This situation thus had the elements for presenting correlations between the shells and the explosions. Explosions could occur either in the presence or the absence of a hit. If many more explosions occurred following hits than misses then the shells were effective. If the tank blew up with the same frequency in the presence and the absence of hits then there was a zero contingency and the shells were said to be ineffective.

The possibility of a negative correlation between the shells and the explosions was provided by stating that if the tank was hit by an ineffective shell it might alert the driver of the tank to danger and he might be more likely to avoid a mine and thus the shells might reduce the probability of an explosion.

The best metric for describing such a binary contingency is the difference between the conditional probability of an explosion given a hit and that given a miss. Figure 4.10 shows a contingency table describing the task as well as how this

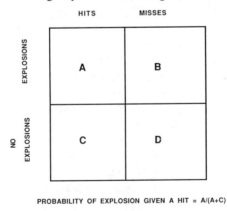

FIG. 4.10.   Contingency table for tank experiments.

measure (ΔP) is calculated. In Shanks and Dickinson's experiments a typical positive contingency between the shells and explosions would involve the tank blowing up 75% of the time given a hit (conditional probability = .75) and 25% of the time given a miss (conditional probability = .25). This would represent a contingency (ΔP) of .50. A typical dense noncontingent procedure would require equal conditional probabilities of .75 and a less dense procedure would require probabilities of .25 (ΔPs = 0). Finally a negative contingency with a ΔP of −.50 might have the conditional probability an explosion of given a hit of .25 and given a miss of .75.

When subjects are exposed to these contingencies and are asked to judge the effectiveness of the shells on a scale ranging from −100 to +100 they typically perform rather well. Figure 4.11 shows a replication of this result that was carried out in our laboratory. The subjects did well on both the positive and negative contingencies. However, their performance on the dense 75:75 and less dense 25:25 zero contingencies shows a systematic bias. The subjects evaluated the shells as being effective in the more dense contingency and as being negatively effective in the less dense contingency. There is even some evidence that the excitatory tendency found in the over evaluation of the high density zero contingency goes away with trials. In addition to this, Dickinson et al. (1984) carried out an experiment that was somewhat analogous to blocking and found what appeared to be blocking by the experimental context.

The data from Fig. 4.11 are quite compelling: human decision making shows a learning curve much like that found in conditioning studies, there is a similar density dependent bias in estimates, and it appears possible to show a blocking effect. With this in mind, Shanks and Dickinson have suggested that these judgments are best characterized by an input based description such as the Rescorla-Wagner or Pearce-Hall models. They even showed that a reasonable simulation of human performance on their task could be derived from either model.

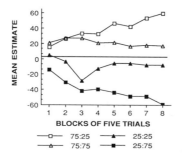

FIG. 4.11. Estimates of contingency between tank explosions and hits when the actual contingency is positive (probability of explosion given a hit = .75 and probability of explosion given a miss = .25), negative (.25:.75), null with a high density of events (.75:.75), or null with a low density (.25:.25). From Baker & Berbrier (unpublished).

This input based description differs very much from the more traditional conceptualization of the human as a statistician, although at times a not very good one. The former view claims that learning will only occur on input trials and the latter might argue that the subject will form a representation of the world and make a judgment from that representation. For the output based model the only function of the trials is to get the data into memory.

A fundamental difference between the approaches is that because the cognitive view states that the organism makes a representation of the world then the instructions must accurately describe the world and the contingency. Input models, on the other hand would argue that the only important thing on any one trial is the contiguity between the stimuli, responses, and reinforcements; thus the *description* of the task is not important, only the trialwise occurrence of events is. The importance of this distinction is better understood by analyzing some logical errors in Shanks and Dickinson's task.

We will first consider the positive (75:25) contingency. Shanks and Dickinson correctly claim that the true difference in the conditional probability of an explosion given a hit and a given a miss was .5. The subjects, however, were not asked to judge this probability. Rather they were asked to judge the *effectiveness* of the shells which, it turns out, is not .5 but is .67. This arises because there are two possible causes of each explosion—a mine or a shell. We know the effectiveness of the mines is .25 because that is the probability of an explosion on trials in which the tank has not been hit by a shell and because the second cause (the shell) is absent any explosion must be caused by a mine. But the proportion of explosions given a hit includes explosions caused by both the shells and the mines. On a given trial when the tank has been hit by a shell it might explode because the shell was effective or if the shell was ineffective the tank might blow up because it hits a mine. This description, however, is not complete because it ignores a third possibility and that is that on some trials on which the tank would have hit a mine and exploded it would also have been hit by an effective shell. These trials on which there is the joint occurrence of positive instances of both events are ignored by Shanks and Dickinson. The problem is more clearly described another way. On trials in which the tank has been hit by a shell it will blow up 25% of the time anyway because it would hit a mine. It is on the other 75% of the trials that the tank would not have hit a mine that we can see the actual effectiveness of the shells. Because the addition of shells to the mines (by hitting the tank) increases the percentage of explosions from 25% to 75% then we know that the true effectiveness of the shells must be .67 (the shells cause the tank to explode on two thirds of the 75% of trials on which the tank would not have hit a mine and thus increasing the overall probability of an explosion to 75%).

A second problem with the description of the tank task involves the possibility of the shells having a dual effect. If the tank is hit by a less than perfect shell it might explode on some trials but on those that the shell is ineffective it might warn the tank and actually reduce the likelihood that the tank would hit a mine. Given this possibility what is meant by the true effectiveness becomes ambiguous. In the 25:25 contingency the shells could have no effect and thus the tank would blow up 25% of the time because of the mines or the shells could cause some explosions but on trials in which they did not explode they could warn the driver and thus reduce the likelihood that the tank would hit a mine. In both cases the net effectiveness might be 0 but the constituent positive effectiveness (will the shell explode?) and negative effectiveness (will the shell make the driver more wary?) of the shell can vary.

When we mentioned these difficulties to David Shanks (personal communication) he responded by pointing out that these logical problems are only a difficulty if the subjects form cognitive representations of the world to make the judgments. If the only role of a trial is to cause the habit strength of some response or association to change then there is no problem—a reinforcement is a reinforcement. Retrospective processing does not have this luxury. A complex and ambiguous description of the task may interfere with the formation of a representation and thus influence judgments.

To evaluate this possibility Baker and Berbrier (1987) devised a task that was not so ambiguous and which represented a pure binary contingency as represented in Fig. 4.10. The only cause of the explosions was the mines. They were a special kind of mine that needed to *see* the tanks to explode them. In this task the subject was asked to try to influence the mines' effectiveness by camouflaging (painting) the tanks. If the camouflage was effective the tank would be safer in the minefield. If, however, the paint made the tank easier rather than harder to see the tank would be less safe in the minefield and thus would be explode more often.

The subjects, McGill undergraduates, were exposed to the four contingencies described earlier. The results were very similar to those shown in Fig. 4.11 with one important exception. There was no longer any statistical evidence in support of the learning curve that is the necessary consequence of the subjects gradually acquiring associative strength.

We would argue from this data that the learning curve is a consequence of the ambiguous description of the world used by Shanks and Dickinson. In our experiment, subjects behaved as if they developed representations of their experience with the experimental events and used rule-based strategies (retrospective processing) to make their estimates. In some sense the subjects may have made an internal contingency table like that shown in Fig. 4.10 and used it to make their estimate.

This is one case where the retrospective processing approach is more parsimonious than the input models. This is so because there is a rich tradition of research in human contingency judgments which has used designs in which the subjects do not gather data as they do in Shanks and Dickinson's and our experiments but are presented with already tabulated contingency tables (e.g., Nisbett & Ross,

1984; Tversky & Kahneman). In these experiments just as in ours, it was found that people are often fairly accurate judges but they also make errors. Because the data in these experiments are not presented to the subjects in a sequential fashion the results are not amenable to analysis by input based models. There are no trials for habit strength to build up on. Dickinson et al. (1984) acknowledged this and argued that some other cognitive mechanism must be involved in these judgments.

This is no problem for the retrospective processor because all the contingency table approach does is provide the subject with a ready made contingency table or temporal cognitive map that may be used to make decisions. We are presently carrying out experiments in which we compare subjects who receive data in a sequential manner with others receiving the same data presented already tabulated.

Important questions that must be answered include: Is the representation formed in sequential tasks as accurate as in tasks using tabulated data? Do subjects selectively ignore some aspects of the data if they must gather it themselves in a sequential task? Do they use the same rules with both sorts of data? These questions outline a psychophysics of retrospective representations. They are without doubt radically different questions than would be asked by a scientist testing input oriented models.

VII. SOME CONCLUSIONS AND THOUGHTS ON MAKING COMPARISONS ACROSS SPECIES

We began this rather lengthy discussion with the argument that animals must have a very much richer representation of the world than attentional or other input based models would allow. Rats *must* retrospectively process at least some of the data from their experience. Even more fundamentally, their classical conditioning systems must have retrospective abilities. We then hopped to humans making judgments about rather fuzzy data concerning tanks and shells. It is obvious that we feel these data belong together but what is the justification?

At first one might think that we are arguing that the two processes share the same mechanism much like a naive radical behaviorist might once have argued that much of human behavior shared the same mechanisms as operant conditioning. This type of thinking is fundamentally invalid because it uses an invalid evolutionary analysis. The implication of that analysis is that rats are in some sense primitive men and thus it must be possible to find the primitive precursors to our thought processes in these little ''humans.'' This reasoning is weak because humans are not descendants of rats. Our common ancestors are extinct and rats are in no sense ''primitive''; they are modern animals which have evolved and are adapted to their particular ecological niche just as we are to ours. If we think of rats as our ancestors we are barking up the wrong evolutionary tree. Any cognitive system in rats let alone whatever does Pavlovian conditioning is not an ancestor of our cognitive processes but something that has evolved and is adaptive for the rat.

There is an easy and elegant way out of this impasse and that is to consider the *function* of the systems. If the ability to make contingency judgments is of some use to us then there must be selective pressures for us to develop the ability to extract causal or correlational information from the environment and make adaptive (Note: this does not always mean correct!) judgments or atttributions of cause.

But the Pavlovian conditioning system also must extract causal information in an imperfect world. The rat needs to *know* when to be anxious, when to have an aversion, and even when to salivate. If it is adaptive there must be a selective pressure to make these attributions. And this at the very least is where the parallel lies.

If different systems have evolved to solve similar information processing problems the solutions may be analogues, in the evolutionary sense. Thus evolution may have used very similar solutions to these similar problems. In general, both systems are pretty accurate in their attributions but they both make mistakes. Some of these mistakes are very similar. For example, both systems "think" high density but zero contingencies to be positive.

At the very least the rich recent history in animal learning research in selective attributions (i.e., blocking, etc.) should provide a valuable reservoir of ideas, techniques, and theories for those wishing to study human judgment. And it is possible that there is much more in the analogy than just that.

REFERENCES

Baker, A. G., & Baker, P. A. (1985). Does inhibition differ from excitation: Proactive interference, contextual conditioning, and extinction. In R. R. Miller & N. S. Spear (Eds.), *Information processing in animals: Conditioned inhibition* (pp. 151–184). Hillsdale, NJ: Lawrence Erlbaum Associates.

Baker, A. G., & Berbrier, M. (1987). *Judgments of a 2X2 contingency table: Rules, associations and the learning curve.* Unpublished manuscript, McGill University, Montréal, Canada.

Baker, A. G., Bindra, D., & Singh, M. (1985). Some effects of contextual conditioning and US predictability on Pavlovian conditioning. In P. D. Balsam & A. Tomie (Eds.), *Context and learning* (pp. 73–104). Hillsdale, NJ: Lawrence Erlbaum Associates.

Baker, A. G., & Mackintosh, N. J. (1977). Excitatory and inhibitory conditioning following uncorrelated presentations of CS and UCS. *Animal Learning and Behavior, 5,* 315–319.

Baker, A. G., & Mackintosh, N. J. (1979). Preexposure to the CS alone, US alone, or CS and US uncorrelated: Latent inhibition, blocking by context or learned irrelevance. *Learning and Motivation, 10,* 278–294.

Baker, A. G., & Mercier, P. (1982a) Prior experience with the conditioning events: Evidence for a rich cognitive representation. In M. L. Commons, R. J. Herrnstein, & A. R. Wagner (Eds.), *Quantitative analyses of behavior III: Acquisition* (pp. 117–144). Cambridge, MA: Ballinger.

Baker, A. G., & Mercier, P. (1982b). Manipulations of the apparatus and response context may reduce the US preexposure interference effect. *Quarterly Journal of Experimental Psychology, 34B,* 221–234.

Baker, A. G., & Mercier, P. (1982c). Extinction of the context and latent inhibition. *Learning and motivation, 13*, 391–416.

Baker, A. G., Mercier, P., Gabel, J., & Baker, P. A. (1981). Contextual conditioning and the US preexposure effect in conditioned fear. *Journal of Experimental Psychology: Animal Behavior Processes, 7*, 109–128.

Balsam, P. D. (1985). The functions of context in learning and performance. In P. D. Balsam & A. Tomie (Eds.), *Context and learning* (pp. 1–22). Hillsdale, NJ: Lawrence Erlbaum Associates.

Benedict, J. O., & Ayres, J. J. B. (1972). Factors affecting conditioning in the truly random control procedure in the rat. *Journal of Comparative and Physiological Psychology, 78*, 323–330.

Bouton, M. E., & Bolles, R. C. (1985). Contexts, event-memories, and extinction. In P. D. Balsam & A. Tomie (Eds.), *Context and learning* (pp. 133–166). Hillsdale, NJ: Lawrence Erlbaum Associates.

Brogden, W. J. (1939). Sensory pre-conditioning. *Journal of Experimental Psychology, 25*, 223–232.

Dickinson, A., Shanks, D. R., & Evenden, J. L. (1984). Judgement of act-outcome contingency: The role of selective attribution. *Quarterly Journal of Experimental Psychology, 36A*, 29–50.

Doré, F. Y. (1980). *Inhibition latente: Apprentissage du caractère non-prédictif d'un événement* [Latent inhibition: Learning about events that predict nothing]. Paper presented at 48th annual conference of the French-Canadian Association for the Advancement of science, Québec, Canada.

Durlach, P. J. (1982). Pavlovian learning and performance when CS and US are uncorrelated. In M. L. Commons, R. J. Herrnstein, & A. R. Wagner (Eds.), *Quantitative analyses of behavior III: Acquisition* (pp. 179–194). Cambridge, MA: Ballinger.

Gamzu, E. R., & Williams, D. R. (1973). Associative factors underlying the pigeon's key pecking in autoshaping procedures. *Journal of Experimental Analysis of Behavior, 19*, 225–232.

Gibbon, J., & Balsam, P. (1981). Spreading association in time. In L. C. Locurto, H. S. Terrace, & J. Gibbon (Eds.), *Autoshaping and conditioning theory*. New York: Academic Press.

Guthrie, E. R. (1959). Association by contiguity. In S. Koch (Ed.), *Psychology: A study of a science* (vol 2). New York: McGraw-Hill.

Hall, G., & Pearce, J. M. (1979). Latent inhibition of CS during CS-US pairings. *Journal of Experimental Psychology: Animal Behavior Processes, 5*, 31–42.

Hull, C. L. (1943). *Principles of behavior*. New York: Appleton.

Jenkins, H. M., Barnes, R. A., & Barrera, F. J. (1981). Why autoshaping depends on trial spacing. In L. C. Locurto, H. S. Terrace, & J. Gibbon (Eds.), *Autoshaping and conditioning theory*. New York: Academic Press.

Kamin, L. J. (1969). Predictability, surprise, attention, and conditioning. In B. A. Campbell & R. M. Church (Eds.), *Punishment and aversive behavior*. New York: Appleton-Century-Crofts.

Kaufman, M. A., & Bolles, R. C. (1981). A nonassociative aspect of overshadowing. *Bulletin of the Psychonomic Society, 18*, 318–320.

Lovejoy, E. (1968). *Attention in discrimination learning*. San Francisco: Holden-Day.

Lubow, R. E. (1973). Latent inhibition. *Psychological Bulletin, 79*, 398–407.

Lubow, R. E., Schnur, P., & Rifkin, B. (1976). Latent inhibition and conditioned attention theory. *Journal of Experimental Psychology: Animal Behavior Processes, 2*, 163–174.

Lubow, R. E., Wagner, M., & Weiner, I. (1982). The effects of compound stimulus preexposure of two elements differing in salience on the acquisition of conditioned suppression. *Animal Learning and Behavior, 10*, 483–489.

Mackintosh, N. J. (1965). Selective attention in animal discrimination learning. *Psychological Bulletin, 64*, 124–150.

Mackintosh, N. J. (1973). Stimulus selection: Learning to ignore stimuli that predict no change in reinforcement. In R. A. Hinde & J. S. Hinde (Eds.), *Constraints on learning* (pp. 75–100). London: Academic Press.

Mackintosh, N. J. (1975). A theory of attention: Variations in the associability of stimuli with reinforcement. *Psychological Review, 82*, 276–298.

Mercier, P. (1983). *Latent inhibition and habituation during sensory preconditioning*. Unpublished doctoral dissertation, McGill University.

Mercier, P., & Baker, A. G. (1985). Latent inhibition, habituation, and sensory preconditioning: A test of priming in short-term memory. *Journal of Experimental Psychology: Animal Behavior Processes, 11*, 485–501.

Miller, R. R., & Schachtman, T. R. (1985a). The several roles of context at the time of retrieval. In P. D. Balsam & A. Tomie (Eds.), *Context and learning* (pp. 167–194). Hillsdale, NJ: Lawrence Erlbaum Associates.

Miller, R. R., & Schachtman, T. R. (1985b). Conditioning context as an associative baseline: Implications for response generation and the nature of conditioned inhibition. In R. R. Miller & N. E. Spear (Eds.), *Information processing in animals: Conditioned inhibition* (pp. 51–88). Hillsdale, NJ: Lawrence Erlbaum Associates.

Nisbett, R. E., & Ross, L. (1984). *Human interference: Strategies and shortcomings of social judgment*. Englewood Cliffs, NJ: Prentice-Hall.

Pearce, J. M., & Hall, G. (1980). A model for Pavlovian learning: Variations of conditioned but not unconditioned stimuli. *Psychological Review, 87*, 532–552.

Pearce, J. M., Kaye, H., & Hall, G. (1982). Predictive accuracy and stimulus associability: Development of a model for Pavlovian learning. In M. L. Commons, R. J. Herrnstein, & A. R. Wagner (Eds.), *Quantitative analyses of behavior III: Acquisition* (pp. 241–256). Cambridge, MA: Ballinger.

Quinsey, V. L. (1971). Conditioned suppression with no CS-US contingency in the rat. *Canadian Journal of Psychology, 25*, 69–82.

Randich, A., & Haggard, D., (1983). Exposure to the unconditioned stimulus alone: Effects upon acquisition and retention of conditioned suppression. *Journal of Experimental Psychology: Animal Behavior Processes, 9*, 147–159.

Randich, A., & LoLordo, V. M. (1979). Associative and non-associative theories of the UCS preexposure phenomenon: Implications for Pavlovian conditioning. *Psychological Bulletin, 86*, 523–548.

Randich A., & Rescorla, R. A. (1981). The effects of separate presentations of the US on conditioned suppression of instrumental responding. *Animal Learning and Behavior, 9*, 56–64.

Randich, A., & Ross, R. T. (1985). Contextual stimuli mediate the effects of pre- and postexposure to the unconditioned stimulus on conditioned suppression. In P. D. Balsam & A. Tomie (Eds.), *Context and learning* (pp. 105–132). Hillsdale, NJ: Lawrence Erlbaum Associates.

Rescorla, R. A. (1966). Predictability and number of pairings in Pavlovian fear conditioning. *Psychonomic Science, 4*, 383–384.

Rescorla, R. A. (1967). Pavlovian conditioning and its proper control procedures. *Psychological Review, 74*, 71–80.

Rescorla, R. A. (1968). Probability of shock in the presence and absence of the CS in fear conditioning. *Journal of Comparative and Physiological Psychology, 66*, 1–5.

Rescorla, R. A. (1974). Effect of inflation of the unconditioned stimulus value following conditioning. *Journal of Comparative and Physiological Psychology, 86*, 101–106.

Rescorla, R. A., & Wagner, A. R. (1972). A theory of Pavlovian conditioning: Variations in the effectiveness of reinforcement and non-reinforcement. In A. H. Black & W. F. Prokasy (Eds.), *Classical conditioning II: Current research and theory*. New York: Appleton-century-Crofts.

Shanks, D. R. (1985). Continuous monitoring of human contingency judgment across trials. *Memory and cognition, 13*, 158–167.

Sutherland, N. S. (1964). The learning of discrimination by animals. *Endeavours, 23*, 69–78.

Sutherland, N. S., & Mackintosh, N. J. (1971). *Mechanisms of animal discrimination learning*. New York: Academic Press.

Szakmary, G. A. (1977). A note regarding conditioned attention theory. *Bulletin of the Psychonomic Society, 9*, 142–144.

Thomas, D. R. (1970). Stimulus selection, attention, and related matters. In J. H. Reynierse (Eds.), *Current issues in animal learning*. Lincoln: University of Nebraska Press.

Tolman, E. C. (1959). Principles of purposive behavior. In S. Koch (Ed.), *Psychology: A study of a science* (vol 2). New York: McGraw-Hill.

Tomie, A. (1976a). Interference with autoshaping by prior context conditioning. *Journal of Experimental Psychology: Animal Behavior Processes, 2,* 323–334.

Tomie, A. (1976b). Retardation of autoshaping: Control of contextual stimuli. *Science, 192,* 1244–1246.

Trabasso, T. R., & Bower, G. H. (1968). *Attention in learning: Theory and research.* New York: Wiley.

Tversky, A., & Kahneman, D. (1978). Causal thinking in judgment under uncertainty. In B. Butts & J. Hintikka (Eds.), *Logic, methodology and philosophy of science.* Dordrecht, Holland: D. Reidel.

Wagner, A. R., Logan, F. A., Haberlandt, K., & Price, T. (1968). Stimulus selection in animal discrimination learning. *Journal of experimental psychology, 76,* 171–180.

Wagner, A. R., & Rescorla, R. A. (1972). Inhibition in Pavlovian conditioning: Applications of a theory. In R. A. Boakes & M. S. Halliday (Eds.), *Inhibition and learning.* London: Academic Press.

Zeaman, D., & House, B. J. (1963). The role of attention in retardate discrimination learning. In N. R. Ellis (Ed.), *Handbook of mental deficiency: Psychological theory and research* (pp. 159–223). New York: McGraw-Hill.

5 Perceptual and Associative Learning

Geoffrey Hall
Robert Honey
University of York

I. INTRODUCTION

The associative account of learning has at its heart just a single concept—the notion that the central representations of events can become linked so that activation of one can excite its associate. Of course any adequate theory of learning needs to consider other things—the exact conditions in which the events need to be presented for an association to be formed; how excitation of a representation produces changes in behavior; and so on. But these other issues, although they have been the subject of much debate among theorists, remain secondary matters. Only inhibitory learning, with its implication that associations might inhibit rather than excite representations, and, more recently "occasion-setting" (Holland, 1982; Rescorla, 1985) with its implication that associations might act on other associations rather than on event-representations, have challenged the simplicity of the basic conception.

This attempt to deal with a major part of an animal's cognitive functioning armed with just a single explanatory tool may seem naive, and some have called for a radically different approach to the study of learning that dispenses with the notion of association (e.g., Bouton & Bolles, 1985). On the other hand, it is difficult not to be impressed by the rigor of some associative theories and the wide range of phenomena that they have managed to encompass (see e.g., Rescorla & Wagner, 1972). Equally impressive has been the ability of these theories to deal with phenomena that seem, at first sight, to lie beyond their scope, an ability that prompted us to ask (Hall, 1983) whether there were *any* forms of learning that were not reducible to association formation. The purpose of this chapter is to attempt to answer this question by examining what seem to us to

117

constitute some of the more obvious and analytically tractable examples of (possibly) nonassociative learning. Our intention is to explore the limits of associative theory and to specify what new mechanisms must be added to it in order to achieve comprehensiveness. We must acknowledge the possibility that these new mechanisms might turn out to be powerful enough to supplant associationism altogether. We can be equally sure, however, that associative theory will not submit without a fight when confronted with a learning phenomenon that purports to be outside its scope.

The phenomena that seem to us most relevant in this context lie at the interface between perception and learning. The experimenter perceives a certain set of events in the experimental situation (stimuli: a light, a tone, an electric shock; responses: a peck, a lever press) and assumes that associations can be formed between their central representations. But the system of representation used by another animal (or another individual) may be quite different from that of the experimenter; and if it is, our associative theorizing will be rendered impotent. Consideration of this issue has been revived in recent years by the work of Rescorla (e.g., 1980, 1986) but the problem has always been with us. As soon as an adequately formulated associative theory of discrimination learning appeared (Spence, 1936) it was attacked on just these grounds by "noncontinuity" theorists (see, e.g., Lashley & Wade, 1946, who criticized continuity theory for assuming that "there is little or no organization of the various aspects of a stimulus during initial conditioning," p. 72). Since then there has been a steady supply of critics (e.g., Dodwell, 1961; Lawrence, 1963; Mackintosh, 1965; Sutherland, 1959) ready to insist that it is not possible to devise a theory of learning without an accompanying theory of stimulus "coding" or analysis. A theory of learning that cannot specify the precise nature of the events that the animal has learned about will not be able to predict the circumstances in which the newly acquired behavior will reappear (e.g., Taylor, 1964).

One partial solution to this problem is to accept that the effective stimulus must be defined experimentally. When an animal has come to emit a conditioned response when confronted with one event we can test it with a range of others and note which do and which do not evoke the response. The effective stimulus can then be identified as some feature held in common by events of the first sort. Why this particular feature should be "dominant" (Lashley's, 1942, terminology) is an important issue but associative theorists (if they are narrow minded enough) could hand this problem over to the student of perception and carry on with their theorizing. Such a strategy is only acceptable, however, if the coding of the stimulus display is determined solely by the animal's "internal organizing tendencies" (Lashley, 1942). But many theorists (including Lashley himself, e.g., Lashley & Wade, 1946) have supposed that the nature of perceptual organization can change as a result of experience. If they are right it implies the existence of a process that no theory of learning can afford to ignore. Accordingly, we concentrate in this chapter on the effects of experience on perceptual organization. Later sections discuss possible mechanisms; we begin, however, by surveying some of the empirical phenomena that our theories need to explain.

II. MODIFICATION OF PERCEPTUAL ORGANIZATION

Much of the empirical work on perceptual learning comes from procedures sufficiently remote from those used in studies of animal learning (see, e.g., Gibson, 1969) to have had little impact on associative theory. The largest body of directly relevant work arose out of the continuity/noncontinuity controversy and consists of studies of the transfer effects produced by discrimination training. These experiments concentrate on one aspect of the noncontinuity position—the possibility that the attention paid to certain aspects of a complex event might be modified by training. The possibility that experience might be necessary for the various aspects of a complex event to be perceived at all (for "perceptual differentiation" to occur) has been acknowledged by workers in this tradition (e.g., Sutherland & Mackintosh, 1971, pp. 52–55) but has not been subject to much empirical investigation. We review studies of the effects of discrimination training only briefly, partly because they have been reviewed extensively elsewhere (Sutherland & Mackintosh, 1971) but also because rather better evidence comes from somewhat simpler experiments that look at the effects of mere exposure to a stimulus on subsequent learning. Examples of these experiments are outlined in the second part of this section of the chapter.

Effects of Discrimination Training

According to attentional theories, discrimination learning serves not only to change the associations that underlie performance but also to modify attention, so that the cues (Lawrence, 1949), or the dimension on which they differ (Sutherland & Mackintosh, 1971), become dominant. This change in attention should reveal itself in the rapid learning of some new task in which the same cues are relevant. The problem with this experimental design is to ensure that the positive transfer observed is indeed the result of attentional changes. Several strategies have been tried, none with complete success.

In Lawrence's (1949) original study of the acquired distinctiveness of cues the same stimuli were used in initial training and in the transfer test but new response requirements were imposed. His assumption that this procedure ensured that the positive transfer he observed was based on familiarity with the stimulus has been undermined by the later demonstration (Siegel, 1967) that specific patterns of response acquired in training will transfer to and influence learning in the test stage. In an attempt to avoid such effects, Hall and Pearce (1978) investigated the effects of prior Pavlovian training on stimuli subsequently used as cues in an instrumental successive discrimination. They found no sign of acquired distinctiveness. Rather, subjects given initial Pavlovian discrimination training learned the test problem less well than subjects that had experienced uncorrelated presentations of the cues and the Pavlovian reinforcer in the first stage.

An alternative experimental strategy leaves the response requirement the same in the two stages of training but changes the stimuli in such a way as to eliminate the role of direct associative transfer. Thus in an intradimensional shift, a pigeon might initially learn a discrimination between red and green and then be transferred to a blue-yellow discrimination. Generalization of associative strength from the original training cues might endow both blue and yellow with some strength but, with appropriately chosen hues, the two cues will not differ in this regard. Positive transfer from the first to the second discrimination can thus be ascribed to an enhanced tendency to attend to color. Unfortunately the experimental evidence for such transfer is mixed. In an experiment using an elaboration of the design just described, Mackintosh and Little (1969) found learning of an intradimensional shift to be rapid but subsequent studies using closely similar designs (Couvillon, Tennant, & Bitterman, 1976; Hall & Channell, 1985a) have failed to replicate the finding. The reason for the discrepancy is obscure but it is enough to undermine our faith in the effect that has been cited as "perhaps the best evidence that transfer between discrimination problems may be partly based on increases in attention" (Mackintosh, 1974, p. 597).

A third strategy pits associatively based transfer against the supposed effects of attentional transfer. When a rat is required to learn the reversal of its original discrimination task, transfer based on associations will retard new learning. The observation that overtraining on the original task can facilitate reversal learning (e.g., Mackintosh, 1969) has been taken as showing that attention to the relevant stimulus dimension is so strongly established by overtraining that it outweighs any other effects. Unfortunately for this interpretation it has since become clear that the effects of overtraining can be quite general and are not restricted to transfer tasks involving the same relevant dimension as the original task (Hall, 1974). That is, overtraining can indeed supply a source of positive transfer that can outweigh the retardation produced by a reversal but we have no reason to suppose that the positive effect derives from an increase in attention to the relevant cues.

There are a few other phenomena thought to support the case (see Sutherland & Mackintosh, 1971, chapter 6) but enough has been said already to make one cautious about accepting the reality of acquired distinctiveness effects. Indeed some of the evidence seems to suggest that training might actually cause cues to lose distinctiveness. Better evidence on these possibilities comes from studies of the effects of nonreinforced preexposure.

Exposure Learning

Mere exposure to a stimulus can modify the behavior it evokes and the ease with which it is subsequently learned about (Hall, 1980). Evidently some sort of learning goes on during exposure and since no explicit contingency is arranged between the target stimulus and other events the scope for explaining these effects in associative terms is restricted (although not, as we shall see, entirely eliminated).

Discrimination learning after stimulus exposure.   Although there is little evidence for the acquired distinctiveness of cues from studies using explicit discrimination training, positive transfer effects have been generated by a procedure in which the subjects simply received exposure to the relevant cues. In its original form (Gibson & Walk, 1956) this procedure was one in which immature rats were given prolonged exposure to a pair of objects (such as a cut-out triangle and circle) in their home cages before being required to learn a simultaneous discrimination with these objects as the cues. Later research has shown, however, that home-cage exposure is just as effective when the subjects are adults as when they are immature (Hall, 1979), and that exposure need not be as prolonged as in the original study. Channell and Hall (1981) found positive transfer in rats given exposure for just 1 hour a day for 40 days (Gibson & Walk, 1956, gave exposure for 24 hours a day over 90 days).

The study by Channell and Hall, (1981, Experiment 3) further showed that the nature of the transfer produced by this exposure learning procedure depends on the context in which exposure occurs. One group of subjects received daily exposure to the stimuli (plaques bearing horizontal and vertical stripes) and was also given 1 hour's exposure each day to the jumping stand in which discrimination training was subsequently to be given. A second group received exposure to the stimuli but these were presented in the jumping stand itself. A control group received exposure to the apparatus only. Figure 5.1 shows the performance of these groups when required to learn a simultaneous horizontal-vertical discrimination in the jumping stand. Exposure to the stimuli in the home cage facilitated learning whereas animals that received exposure in the apparatus were retarded with respect to the control group.

Habituation and latent inhibition.   Examples of positive transfer after exposure to the stimuli are relatively infrequent, but negative transfer, apparently equivalent to that shown by the subjects of Fig. 5.1 that received exposure in the apparatus, has been demonstrated many times in a range of conditioning procedures. In the simplest demonstration, animals are given initial habituation training (repeated nonreinforced presentations of a stimulus) and it is found that subsequent classical conditioning with that stimulus used as the CS (conditioned stimulus) tends to be retarded. The phenomenon has been called "latent inhibition" (Lubow, 1973).

The results of a slightly more complex demonstration of these effects (more complex in that the experiment was designed to allow us to assess the role of contextual variables) are shown in Fig. 5.2 and 5.3. In this experiment (Hall & Channell, 1985b, Experiment 2) rats in group E received presentations of a 10-s

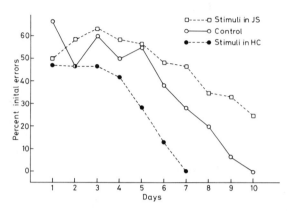

FIG. 5.1. Acquisition of a simultaneous horizontal-vertical discrimination in a jumping stand (group mean daily error scores). One group had received preexposure to the stimuli in the apparatus (JS); one group had received preexposure in their home cages (HC); the control group received no preexposure to the stimuli. See Channell & Hall (1981).

light, 8 times per session for 18 sessions. (Rats in group C received exposure to the training context but not to the light.) The rats' initial response was to turn toward the light and rear in front of it, behavior that we scored as an OR (orienting response). But with repeated presentation the likelihood of an OR gradually declined (Fig. 5.2; E gp). Such long-term habituation of unconditioned responding is an ubiquitous phenomenon and itself implies the existence of a learning process that may be nonassociative in nature (e.g., Sokolov, 1963).

The effect of habituation training on subsequent associative learning is shown in Fig. 5.3. The results of a second stage of training given to the rats whose habituation performance are depicted in Fig. 5.2. In this second stage, presentations of the light continued as before but were followed by food delivery. The increasing ratio score indicates conditioning—an increasing tendency to approach the site of food delivery in the presence of the light which is now acting as a CS. The rats received two conditioning sessions per day, one in the context (A) used for habituation and one in a different context (B) with which they were familiar but in which the light had not previously been presented. (The two contexts differed in level of background noise and in the type of odorant added to them.) Conditioning in the different context proceeded normally: the performance of group E in context B matches that of subjects in group C for whom the light was novel. But conditioning in the original context proceeded only slowly—an instance of latent inhibition.

The context-specificity of latent inhibition has only recently been established (Channell & Hall, 1983; Lovibond, Preston, & Mackintosh, 1984) but the basic effect is as ubiquitous and robust as habituation itself. And although a change of context between preexposure and conditioning can abolish the latent inhibi-

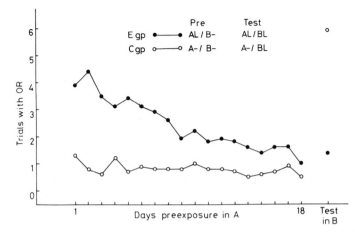

FIG. 5.2. Group mean trials per session on which an orienting response (OR) occurred during preexposure in context A and test in context B. All subjects received two sessions per day. The E group experienced the light (L) in A but not in B during preexposure (Pre); the C group received the light in neither context. On the test session the light was presented in B for all subjects. After Hall & Channell (1985b).

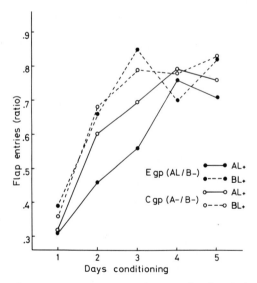

FIG. 5.3. Group mean responses to the magazine flap during the light expressed as a ratio of response rate in the absence of the light. For all subjects the light was reinforced (L+) in both context A and context B. For the prior treatment given to the E and C groups see Figure 2. After Hall & Channell (1985b).

tion effect there is, as yet, no evidence from experiments using orthodox classical conditioning procedures (cf. Lubow, Rifkin, & Alek, 1976) that preexposure combined with a change of context can actually facilitate subsequent conditioning; that is, there is no parallel to the positive transfer seen after home-cage preexposure.

Conclusion.   These experiments show that animals learn something as a consequence of mere exposure to stimuli that can modify their performance (usually for the worse but in some circumstances for the better) when subsequently trained by orthodox associative learning procedures. Our task now is to supply an account for these phenomena that is also capable of encompassing the basic facts of associative learning itself. Such an account needs to explain why some preexposure procedures help later learning when others hinder; also how the effects of a given procedure can be modified by changing contextual and other variables. Since, however, accounts of latent inhibition and habituation have, for the most part, developed independently of any consideration of the facilitatory effects of exposure learning, we may begin by considering the two sets of phenomena separately.

III.   MECHANISMS FOR REDUCING ASSOCIABILITY

Latent inhibition has generally been interpreted as showing that habituation training causes a stimulus to lose associability. And since the dominant theories of habituation (Groves & Thompson, 1970; Sokolov, 1963) rely on nonassociative mechanisms, to accept them would seem to imply a nonassociative basis for the loss of associability. The theory for Pavlovian conditioning proposed by Pearce and Hall (1980) included an attempt to specify the mechanism whereby such a loss might occur.

A Partly Nonassociative Theory

The theory put forward by Pearce and Hall (1980) has as a central concept the notion of associative strength and proposes that this strength will increase when an effective CS and an effective US occur together. But this theory (in common with a number of other attentional theories, e.g., Frey & Sears, 1978; Mackintosh, 1975) allows that the effectiveness of a CS can change with experience. The learning process involved in this change, although dependent on associative mechanisms, is not in itself associative in nature but consists of a change in the value of learning rate parameter (designated α) associated with the CS.

The impetus for the model came from the evidence (some of it cited above) showing that CS effectiveness can indeed change and from the observation that there was very little evidence of any change other than a decline. Accordingly, we proposed that the α-value of a novel stimulus tends to be high (its exact value being determined by stimulus intensity or salience) but that it will decline as the stimulus becomes familiar. We allowed however that lost associability might be restored to some extent when a familiar stimulus is presented along with some new event (such as when the US is introduced in the test phase of a latent inhibition experiment).

More formally, associability was held to be determined as follows:

$$\alpha^n = |\lambda^{n-1} - V^{n-1}|$$

where α^n represents the associability of a given CS after trial n, λ^{n-1} the magnitude of the US (if any) presented on the preceding trial, and V^{n-1} the associative strengths of stimuli associated with the US representation. In habituation training the values of λ and V will be zero and α will fall to zero. When a reinforcer is introduced, as on the first trial of a latent inhibition experiment, a discrepancy between the values of λ and V will occur and α will increase for the next trial. It should be noted that loss of associability is not restricted to the habituation procedure. In any case in which the outcome of a CS (λ) matches what is expected (V), α will fall to zero. Thus in the simplest conditioning procedure where the CS is consistently paired with a given US, associability will decline as V grows. Far from acquiring distinctiveness, the cue will lose it. An experiment by Hall and Pearce (1979) has been taken to demonstrate just this point (see also: Ayres, Moore, & Vigorito, 1984; Kasprow, Schachtman, & Miller, 1985; Schachtman, Channell, & Hall, 1987). In this study animals were given extensive preexposure to a CS presented in conjunction with a weak electric shock as the US. Some associative strength was acquired but nonetheless conditioning was retarded when, in a second stage of training, an increase in reinforcer magnitude allowed further learning to be observed.

In an elaboration of the basic theory, Pearce, Kaye, and Hall (1982) acknowledged that associability is not (as Equation 1 implies) determined solely by events on the preceding trial. Associability does not fall to zero after just one habituation trial and is unlikely to be fully restored by a single reinforced trial in the conditioning phase of a latent inhibition experiment. Rather, α needs to be determined by some sort of average of the values for a number of preceding trials. We therefore modified Equation 1 as follows:

$$\alpha^n = \Gamma|\lambda^{n-1} - V^{n-1}| + (1 - \gamma)\alpha^{n-1}$$

The value of the parameter $\gamma\Delta$ (which lies between 0 and 1) will determine the extent to which the outcome is weighted in favor of events occurring on the immediately preceding trial.

The essential notion that this formalization tries to capture is that the associability of a stimulus will be determined by how well the consequences of that stimulus are predicted. An animal needs to attend to and learn about a stimulus only when its consequences are not fully expected. The implication of this view is that associability will *not* be lost when a stimulus is followed by inconsistent consequences. We have examined this implication in a range of experimental preparations.

Stimulus Associability and Predictive Accuracy

Inconsistent reinforcement and transfer.   Pearce, Kaye, and Hall (1982) reported an experiment using the conditioned suppression procedure that examined the effects of extensive preexposure to a tone on subsequent conditioning with the tone as the CS. For one group of rats during preexposure, the tone was consistently followed by a low intensity shock; for a second group this shock was presented on only half of the trials. Two control groups received identical experience of shock but for these animals the CS was a light rather than a tone. (See Fig. 5.4). In a second stage of training, all subjects received two trials per day with the tone predicting a shock of higher intensity. Group mean suppression ratios are presented in Fig. 5.4 which shows that continuous reinforcement in stage 1 engendered more suppression than did partial reinforcement. This difference remained, for the groups pretrained with the tone, on the initial trials of stage 2. But as conditioning progressed, the rate of acquisition of suppression proved to be greater in the group (Tone PRf) trained with partial reinforcement. This difference was not a consequence of the difference between the two tone groups in their experience of the shock during stage 1—the two light-preexposed groups learned readily and at the same rate.

The slow learning of group Tone CRf constitutes a confirmation of the results of Hall and Pearce (1979) that we have interpreted as showing latent inhibition

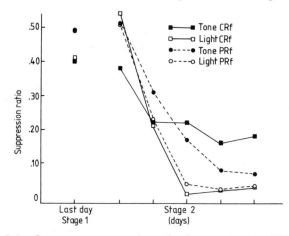

FIG. 5.4.   Group mean suppression ratios for rats given partial (PRf) or continuous (CRf) reinforcement with a weak shock in Stage 1. In Stage 2 all subjects received conditioning with the tone and a stronger shock. From Pearce, Kaye & Hall (1982).

in a CS. The results for group Tone PRf show that this latent inhibition effect will be attenuated when the reinforcement presented during preexposure is inconsistent. Pearce et al. (1982) present a computer simulation of these procedures using the formal model of which Equation 2, above, is a part. They found (for a range of parameters) that partial reinforcement, although it may generate less net associative strength than continuous reinforcement, leaves the value of α high. The positive transfer produced by this latter factor is enough to ensure rapid acquisition in a second stage of conditioning.

The orienting response.   The value of the parameter α determines the readiness with which a CS will enter into associations and to that extent may be regarded as representing an aspect of attention. It is possible (although not necessary), therefore, that other aspects of attention might be determined by α. In particular we have examined the possibility that the behavioral OR shown by rats (and described above) might serve as a direct index of the value of α. Certainly the OR shows some of the right properties—it has a high likelihood of occurrence when the stimulus is first presented and tends to decline with repeated nonreinforced presentations (Fig. 5.2). The extent to which the likelihood of an OR depends on how well the eliciting stimulus predicts its consequences has been studied by Kaye and Pearce (1984, Experiment 2; see also Pearce et al., 1982).

In this experiment, three groups of rats were initially trained to drink milk delivered by a dipper. They next received training in which a 10-s light was presented 6 times per session. The first of these constituted a preexposure session in which the unconditioned effects of the light were monitored. For the remaining 14 sessions one group of subjects (group C) received reinforcement (milk) after every trial with the light, one group (P) received a 50% reinforcement schedule, the third group (N) received no reinforcers. Each rat's behavior was monitored twice during each trial and the percentage of observations yielding an OR was noted. The results are presented in Fig. 5.5.

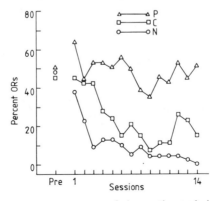

FIG. 5.5. Group mean percentages of observation periods on which an OR to a light was observed for groups receiving partial (P), continuous (C) or no (N) reinforcement. After Pearce, Kaye & Hall (1982).

When it was first presented the light evoked an OR on about half of the observations. With further nonreinforced presentations, the OR habituated (confirming the result shown in Fig. 5.2). Although it occurred more slowly, habituation was also seen in group C, as a result consistent with the view that α will decline when a CS predicts a consistent consequence and that the OR reflects the value of α. More significant for this interpretation is the behavior shown by the subjects receiving partial reinforcement. In these animals the OR continued to occur at a high level throughout training, a result that we interpret as showing that a stimulus that fails to predict its consequences accurately will continue to receive attention.

These results sit comfortably with the suggestion that α is determined by the principles embodied in Equation 2 and that α determines the likelihood of an OR. There is, however, a body of evidence (largely from studies of the effects of changes in context) that constitutes a challenge to this conclusion and we consider these issues next.

The Role of Context

The extent to which the effects of habituation training are specific to the context in which the training was given is important for at least two reasons. First, in those studies that have demonstrated positive transfer, preexposure has usually been given in a context different from that used for conditioning. Is it possible, then, that a change of context might somehow enhance the associability of a preexposed stimulus? Second, although we have interpreted the phenomena described above in terms of a nonassociative learning process, associative accounts still remain possible. In particular, the theory proposed by Wagner (1976; extensively developed in Wagner, 1981) provides a powerful account both of latent inhibition and of habituation in terms of the formation of an association between the preexposed stimulus and the context.

According to Wagner, in bare outline, an event that is novel will receive processing and thus evoke both an unconditioned response (UR) and be available to enter into associations. A familiar stimulus will be one that has formed associations with other stimuli. Presentation of these other stimuli will activate a representation of the target event making that event itself less likely to receive processing. Thus in the habituation procedure an association will be formed between the experimental context and the target stimulus. The presentation of the contextual stimuli will then stop the target event from evoking its UR and from entering readily into new associations. No special process of perceptual learning is invoked.

Dissociating habituation and latent inhibition.   Hall and Channell (1985b) showed how repeated exposure to a light caused habituation of the OR (Fig. 5.2) and retarded subsequent conditioning in the same context (Fig. 5.3). The fact that conditioning proceeded normally when conducted in a context different from that used for preexposure accords with Wagner's interpretation and further implies that the habituated OR should also have been restored by this contextual change. Our experiment was designed to allow us to test this implication. The isolated point for group E on the right of Fig. 5.2 shows the ORs recorded on a single test session on which the familiar light was presented in a new context. There is no sign of dishabituation. It should be added that the OR will be restored when the test context is quite novel (Hall & Channell, 1985b, Experiment 1)—the results of Fig. 5.2 come from an experiment in which the subjects had been made familiar with the test context in the absence of the light before the test session. But this latter procedure is not one that allows the formation of an association between the test context and the light and so dishabituation is predicted by Wagner (1976, 1981) in this case too.

This dissociation of habituation and latent inhibition is open to the relatively trivial interpretation that speed of conditioning is merely a more sensitive measure of the status of the light than is the likelihood of occurrence of an OR. Accordingly, Hall and Schachtman (1987) have conducted a study using procedures that we suspected might be effective in restoring the habituated OR (the supposedly less sensitive measure) while leaving latent inhibition intact. There were three basic conditions of preexposure. Subjects in one condition (L/HC) received 16 days of habituation training to the light followed by a 16-day retention interval spent in the home cage. Subjects in group HC/L received the same treatments in the reverse order. A control group (HC/C) received equivalent experience of the training context but no presentations of the light. Fig. 5.6 shows the course of

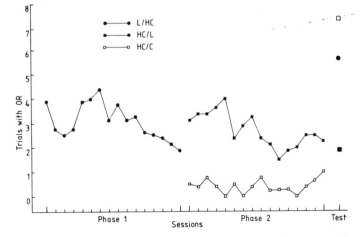

FIG. 5.6. Group mean trials per session on which an OR occurred for two phases of preexposure to a light and an habituation test. The two sections of group designation refer to the treatment given in the two preexposure phases. L: exposure to presentations of light; C: exposure to context alone: HC: remain in home cage. From Hall & Schachtman (1987).

habituation of the OR in the groups exposed to the light, along with the number of OR-like responses recorded on "dummy" trials for group HC/C. It also shows performance on a test session comprising 10 presentations of the light and given on the day following the end of preexposure. Group HC/L remained habituated; and, of central interest, the level of the OR was restored in group L/HC, that is, habituation appeared to have been forgotten over the retention interval. A further set of three groups was given identical preexposure treatments but then moved on to a test phase in which presentations of the light signaled food delivery. Fig. 5.7 shows the mean number of trials out of 10 per day on which subjects responded to the site of food delivery in the presence of the light. All groups showed conditioning by this measure but acquisition was less rapid in both groups of preexposed subjects. Latent inhibition was not diminished by the retention interval in group L/HC—indeed the effect was rather larger (although not reliably so) than that seen in group HC/L.

These results, then, allow a double dissociation of habituation and latent inhibition—some procedures will restore an habituated response while leaving latent inhibition intact; others attenuate latent inhibition but do not produce dishabituation.

Theoretical interpretations.   Wagner's (1976, 1981) associative account, with its assertion that habituation and latent inhibition both depend on the strength of a context-stimulus association, has difficulty in accommodating the findings described above. But they also create a problem for our own suggestion that habituation of the OR to a stimulus can be used as an index of the level of associability of that stimulus. Although we are as yet unsure of the full solution to this problem, the matter clearly requires some comment.

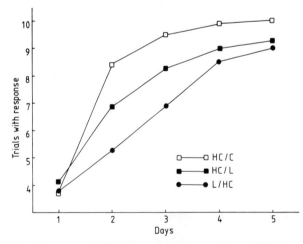

FIG. 5.7.   Group mean trials per conditioning session on which a response to the food magazine was recorded. Group designations as in Fig. 5.4. From Hall & Schachtman (1987).

Our tentative suggestion is that the likelihood of an OR might be determined not only by the specific state of habituation of the target stimulus but also by the extent to which the context in which it is presented is generally arousing. Habituation of the response would then reflect a decline in both the specific and the general process; but restoration of the response might be achieved, provided the tendency of the stimulus to evoke it still retains some strength, by an increase in the general level of arousal only (cf. the dual-process theory of Groves & Thompson, 1970). According to this account, the "dishabituation" produced by presenting the light in a novel context indicates not a change in the effectiveness of the light itself but the arousing effect of the context. It might plausibly be supposed that one of the effects of a long retention interval is to restore the arousing properties of a previously experienced context. If so, the restoration of the OR seen in these circumstances need not necessarily imply a change in the specific effectiveness of the light.

Evidence in favor of this dual-process interpretation comes from a recent unpublished study (again conducted in collaboration with Schachtman). Two groups of rats received 14 days of habituation training to the light by the end of which ORs were occurring on no more than 20% of trials. Both groups received a test session in which the light was presented in a different context. This context was familiar in that the animals had received 14 sessions of exposure to it. For one group (Group A-L/B in the table) these sessions followed habituation training whereas for the second group (Group B/A-L) these sessions preceded habituation training which itself immediately preceded the test. The design and results of the study are summarized in Table 5.1 which shows that the OR was *not* restored after the retention interval when exposure to the test context filled the interval. We can conclude that habituation of the specific response to the light does not necessarily wane with the passage of time. On the other hand, the effects of preexposure to the test context did not survive the 14-day interval during which the light was presented in another context. Subjects given this treatment (Group B/A-L) showed a restoration of the OR similar to that previously seen in subjects

TABLE 5.1
Design and Results of OR Experiment

	Stage 1	Stage 2	Test
Group B/A-L	B alone	Light in A 75% → 19%	Light in B 48%
Group A-L/B	Light in A 47% → 10%	B alone	Light in B 23%

Note: A and B represent different distinctive contexts. Subjects received 12 days of training in each of Stages 1 and 2 and a single test session. The light, when presented, occurred 10 times per session. Scores are percentage of trials on which OR occurred for the first and last sessions of Stages 1 and 2 and the test session.

transferred to an entirely novel context. We interpret this finding as suggesting that the arousing properties of the context will be reestablished over a retention interval and can boost the frequency of occurrence of a response that is otherwise unlikely to occur.

What remains to be explained is the fact that lost associability, as assessed by the latent inhibition procedure, is restored by a change of context, whereas the habituated OR is not (Hall & Channell, 1985b). We tentatively account for this discrepancy by noting that the conditioning phase of a latent inhibition procedure is a treatment that produces a change in the value of α whereas a simple habituation test does not. The habituation test reveals that a change of context does not itself restore α (dishabituation fails to occur if the changed context is familiar); the latent inhibition procedure shows that α is very rapidly restored by contextual change. Such an outcome can be predicted if it is allowed that a change of context causes changes in α to be determined solely or largely by events on the immediately preceding trial (i.e., if contextual change produced an increase in the value of γ in Equation 2). This interpretation is not implausible. It amounts to saying that an animal will still recognise an habituated stimulus when that stimulus is presented in a new context but will be prepared to change very quickly its assessment of that stimulus as being of no significance.

Conclusion

Exposure to a stimulus, either in isolation or followed by a reinforcer of consistent size, will cause that stimulus to lose effectiveness. With the addition of a relatively simple perceptual learning mechanism, orthodox associative learning theory finds itself able to accommodate these facts. Certain procedures (notably changes of context) can restore the lost effectiveness of a preexposed stimulus but do not appear to render the stimulus more effective than one that has not been preexposed. Thus our theory has no way of dealing with the observation that, an occasion, exposure to an object can facilitate later learning. We address this problem next.

IV.   INCREASES IN DISCRIMINABILITY

As we have already noted, rats given exposure to a pair of objects in their home cage show enhanced learning of a discrimination between these same objects. There is nothing in the theory proposed so far that allows us to anticipate this finding—both stimuli should lose associability during preexposure and the formation of the associations that underlie adequate discriminative performance should therefore be poor. We need to suppose, then, either that there is some feature of the procedure of these experiments that causes associability actually to increase as a result of preexposure or that some new (or additional) process, yet to be specified, is brought into play.

Increased Associability?

The most striking feature of the Gibson-Walk (1956) procedure is that exposure is given in the subject's home cage, ensuring a dramatic change of context when it comes to discrimination training. But although the theory proposed above allows that lost associability might be very quickly restored by a change of context it does not predict that preexposed subjects will outperform subjects for whom the test stimuli are novel.

It might be possible, however, to construct explanations for the positive transfer effect within the frameworks provided by other theories of changes in associability. Thus Wagner (1976, 1978) and Lubow et al. (e.g., Lubow, Rifkin, & Alek, 1976) might argue that the effectiveness of a stimulus can be enhanced by a change of context—that stimuli presented in a context in which they are unexpected might be particularly attention-getting. Admittedly, experiments on the context-specificity of latent inhibition using orthodox conditioning procedures have demonstrated only that latent inhibition is restricted to the context in which preexposure was given and have not found that a change of context can facilitate acquisition (Channell & Hall, 1983; Hall & Channell, 1985b; Lovibond et al., 1984). It remains possible, however, that a change of context from one Skinner box to another is much less salient than a change from the home cage to some conditioning apparatus. This possibility allows the argument that both procedures might raise associability but that only the latter is powerful enough to raise it above the level governed by a novel stimulus. Although there is no systematic evidence on this issue, the failure of Hall and Channell (1986) to demonstrate the basic context specificity of latent inhibition using the home cage as the context of preexposure in a taste aversion procedure, argues against this possibility. More critical perhaps is our recent demonstration (described below) that home-cage preexposure can, on occasion, retard subsequent learning in a different context. We conclude, therefore, that positive transfer after preexposure is not to be attributed to the symmetrical opposite of the process that is responsible for latent inhibition. We attribute latent inhibition to reduced associability. For positive transfer, some new mechanism is required.

Evidence for Changes of Discriminability

In discussing the beneficial effects of stimulus exposure, Hall (1980) identified two possible mechanisms. One was that the associability of the exposed stimuli might increase. The other was the possibility that stimuli presented during preexposure might in some way become more discriminable, from one another and from similar stimuli with which they might otherwise be confused. It is as if exposure to two shades of gray could render them effectively equivalent to black and white. The notion of associability change, by contrast, supposes that the attention governed by each gray stimulus will change but makes no suggestion that they might be less easily confused. If it is argued that the only change in associability produced by preexposure is a decline, then associability change cannot by itself explain the beneficial effects of preexposure when these occur. It remains possible, however, that preexposure causes both a loss in associability and an increase in discriminability and that the sort of transfer observed in an exposure learning study depends on the balance of these factors. There is some experimental evidence to support this contention.

Positive and negative transfer after home-cage exposure.   Channell and Hall (1981) found that simultaneous discrimination learning was facilitated by home-cage exposure but was retarded after equivalent exposure to the stimuli in the test apparatus. They speculated that the latter result was an example of latent inhibition (was a consequence of reduced associability) and that contextual change, by abolishing this effect, allowed some other (such as enhanced discriminability) to be observed. This study can be taken to show that even when stimuli have been rendered easily discriminable by preexposure, no advantage will be manifest if latent inhibition is profound. The experiment to be reported next was designed to examine the further implication that home-cage exposure should facilitate later learning only when the test problem is one that requires a discrimination between similar objects. When no such discrimination is required all that can be expected is some attenuation of latent inhibition.

In this study (conducted in collaboration with J. Harrison) three groups of rats received 40 days of preexposure. Two groups received exposure for 30 min per day to two plaques, one bearing horizontal and one vertical stripes (the stimuli used by Channell and Hall, 1981). For one group these stimuli were presented side by side on the end wall of a runway later to be used for discrimination training. A second group received equivalent exposure but with the stimuli being presented in the home cage. These animals also received half an hour's exposure to the runway (in the absence of the stimuli) each day. The third group was simply placed in the runway for half an hour each day. In the next stage of training all subjects were required to learn a presence/absence discrimination in the runway. On four trials each day one stimulus plaque (say horizontal) was present and food was given; on four trials there was neither stimulus nor food. Discrimination was assessed by scoring the number of days taken to reach a criterion requiring the response latency to be consistently longer on nonrewarded than on rewarded trials. The nonpreexposed group (with a mean days-to-criterion score of 4.5) formed the discrimination more readily than the preexposed groups, with the group experiencing a change of context (i.e., home-cage exposure) performing slightly better (mean score of 7.4) than the group preexposed in the apparatus (mean score of 8.9).

The poor performance of the group given exposure in the apparatus can be taken as an instance of latent inhibition. The performance of the home-cage group suggests that this effect is attenuated by a change in context but, in the absence of any requirement to discriminate between one stimulus plaque and the other, the subjects in this group showed no sign of positive transfer. It might be argued, however, that rather than supporting our interpretation, these results show merely that this successive, presence/absence discrimination procedure is less sensitive than the simultaneous procedures traditionally used in studies of these problems. Further stages of training allowed us to eliminate this possibility. Following discrimination training the animals were given a generalization test on which the other stimulus, not used in the presence/absence discrimination, was presented on 24 trials in extinction. The results (pooled times for the test expressed as a ratio of the mean score for positive trials on the last day of discrimination training) are shown in Fig. 5.8. This test revealed significantly less generalization in the two preexposed groups than in the control subjects for whom the test stimulus was novel. Thus in spite of the latent inhibition shown in initial acquisition, preexposed subjects showed good discrimination between the two preexposed stimuli. In a final test the original positive stimulus was presented again following the procedures used for the generalization test. Discrimination was again evident in the preexposed subjects (Fig. 5.8 shows a marked drop in the ratio scores for those groups) whereas control subjects continued to run only slowly, suggesting that for these subjects nonreinforced exposure to a different stimulus had generalized back to the original positive.

This experiment provides an empirical bridge between studies of latent inhibition and those concerned with so-called perceptual learning. The results from the presence-absence discrimination suggest that exposure to a stimulus will reduce the readiness with which it becomes associated with a reinforcer. The results of the test phase suggest that exposure also enables the stimulus to be better discriminated from other similar stimuli.

Enhanced discriminability of elementary stimuli after nonreinforced exposure.
The results just cited show that, in certain special circumstances, the enhanced discriminability produced by exposure can outweigh the effects of latent inhibi-

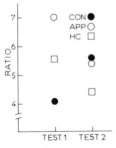

FIG. 5.8.   Group mean running speeds to a previously nonrewarded stimulus (Test 1) and to the stimulus previously associated with reward (Test 2) expressed as a ratio of terminal performance in rewarded training. Prior to rewarded training the Exp groups had received exposure to both stimuli either in the apparatus (App) or in the home (HC). Control subjects received no preexposure.

tion. It remains to establish the range of conditions in which changes in discriminability can play an important role. It may be that "perceptual differentiation,"
as it has been called (Hall & Channell, 1980) is not involved when the stimuli
are simple or "elementary." The learning theorist uses stimuli from different
modalities or chooses within a modality those that are in some sense elementary
(such as red and green keylights for a pigeon, sweet and acid tastes for a rat),
perhaps with the intention of eliminating perceptual learning effects. This restriction might justify the assertion that the processes of association, uncomplicat-
ed by perceptual effects are the prime concern and substance of the learning
theorist's experiments. If it were demonstrated, however, that even elementary
stimuli are subject to perceptual modification, this might force us to acknowledge
the difficulty (or even impossibility) of studying learning in a "pure" form.

The notion that perceptual differentiation might occur during exposure to even
simple stimuli is not novel (cf. Bitterman, Calvin, & Elam, 1953). But the notion
that changes in discriminability might be obscured by accompanying changes in
associability has implications for the conditions in which differentiation will show
itself. If changes in associability can be rendered inconsequential (for example,
by a change in context), animals should benefit from prior exposure to the stimuli subsequently used in a discrimination task. A change in context will help to
attenuate the effects of latent inhibition but the critical feature of the runway experiment just reported was that a discrimination was required. Even without a
contextual change, discriminative performance should be improved provided the
test does not require the acquisition of an association by the test stimulus. This
possibility was investigated in a recent unpublished experiment to be described
next.

Two groups of rats were trained using an appetitive-conditioning procedure.
One group (group B) of subjects was preexposed during six daily 1-hour sessions
to eight presentations of an auditory stimulus B (a tone or a clicker). The control
group (C) was simply placed in the conditioning chamber. All subjects then
received conditioning trials on which presentations of a novel auditory cue A (again
a tone or clicker) was followed by the delivery of three food pellets. Learning
was monitored by recording the development of the tendency to approach the
site of food delivery (to push upon a flap guarding the entrance to the food tray)
during the stimulus. As can be seen from Fig. 5.9, the groups did not differ in
the acquisition of flap-entry behavior in the presence of the A stimulus. Thus
in this procedure the detrimental effect of preexposure was avoided not by a change
of context but by using a novel stimulus during the acquisition phase. There followed three sessions assessing the extent of generalization to the remaining auditory cue, this being novel for group C and familiar for group B. Figure 5.9 shows
that preexposed subjects showed much less generalization of flap-entry behavior
than the group for which the test stimulus was novel—that is, preexposed subjects showed superior discrimination. We have observed essentially the pattern
of findings in a flavor-aversion paradigm (Honey & Hall, 1988a; also see Best

& Batson, 1977). These experiments demonstrate an enhancement of discriminability following stimulus preexposure using both stimuli and an apparatus to which the animal learning theorist is thoroughly accustomed. They imply that the role of perceptual effects in orthodox, supposedly simple, conditioning procedures may be more pervasive than has hitherto been assumed.

Mechanisms

To describe the enhancement of discriminability produced by stimulus exposure as "perceptual differentiation" does no more than restate the basic proposition. We need to try to specify the mechanism by which differentiation occurs. Unfortunately, there are few coherent hypotheses and even fewer data.

One suggestion put forward by Bateson and Chantrey (1972) attributes preexposure effects to the classificatory scheme induced by differing modes of presentation. Stimuli presented in close temporal and spatial contiguity will, they suggest, be "classified together." Stimuli occurring in different places and at different times will be "classified apart." Subsequent discriminative performance is held to be facilitated when the stimuli have been classified apart. Presenting stimuli in the home cage is thought to allow the subjects to inspect them sequentially and thus to promote classifying apart. Unfortunately, this formulation does not anticipate the finding, reported by Channell and Hall (1981), that preexposure to stimuli in the apparatus produced a retardation of discrimination learning even though the spatial layout of the stimuli during preexposure was much the same as that used for home-cage exposure. It remains possible that some unsuspected feature of exposure in the apparatus fostered a tendency to classify together and thus retarded discrimination. Accordingly, in a subsequent experiment (Hall &

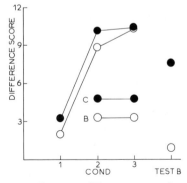

FIG. 5.9. Group mean flap-entry difference scores (responses during the CS-responses in a pre CS period) for subjects given preexposure to stimulus B and a control group given no preexposure. All subjects received three 10-s conditioning trials with the stimulus A on each of three sessions; and a single test session on which the 30-s B stimulus was presented on three occasions.

Channell, 1983) we devised a discrimination test that required the animals to classify the preexposed stimuli together. We reasoned that, for this task, preexposure in the home cage, which promotes classifying apart, should now hinder learning. Preexposure in the apparatus (which, on the basis of Channell & Hall's, 1981, finding must be supposed to promote classifying together) should now facilitate learning. We found, however, exactly the same pattern of results as was reported by Channell and Hall (1981) for an orthodox simultaneous discrimination test—home-cage exposure helped and exposure in the apparatus hindered later learning.

Although they rejected the specific theory proposed by Bateson and Chantrey (1972), Hall and Channell (1983) acknowledged the essential plausibility of the notion of classifying together. It seems very likely that animals would be able to learn that various aspects of a single but multifaceted object go together and should be treated as equivalent. We suggested, therefore, that during exposure to a complex object, the various "elementary stimuli" of which it is made up might become associated with each other. (That is, animals may not classify together the two stimulus plaques but may possibly classify together the various features of each one). The existence of such stimulus-stimulus associations might then facilitate subsequent discrimination learning. For instance, the formation of an association between just one of the aspects of the positive stimulus and food would permit the animal to choose correctly on a subsequent trial when it happened to notice some different aspects of the stimulus. This second aspect would not have a direct association with the representation of food but would be able to make contact with it by virtue of its direct association with the first aspect. It will be apparent that this interpretation of "perceptual" learning is one that attempts to reduce it to associative learning, in particular to the processes assumed to underlie sensory preconditioning or within-compound learning (cf. Rescorla & Durlach, 1981).

We are now rather more doubtful about the validity of this associative interpretation. Within-compound associations may well play an important role in many conditioning procedures but it seems unlikely that they are responsible for all the exposure learning effects discussed here. It is difficult to envisage, for instance, how the formation of within-compound associations during preexposure to the tone in the appetitive-conditioning experiment described above would allow the animal to discriminate more readily between the tone and the click. Indeed, one might imagine that such associations might result in more rather than less generalization in a group that had been preexposed to the tone. An association, formed during preexposure, between the distinctive elements and those elements that are common to both the tone and the click might actually enhance performance to the tone when it is tested following conditioning with the click (Rescorla, 1980).

Accordingly we choose, somewhat tentatively, to adopt the following working hypothesis: that the representations of the experimenter's "stimuli" become refined as a consequence of experience so that repeated presentations of a given object or event become increasingly capable of activating a more precise representation of that object or event. When they are first presented, the stimuli used in these experiments may be coded simply as being "an unusual sound" or "a striped object." But with repeated experience the coding will change to, for example, "a pure tone" or "an object bearing horizontal black and white stripes." Having coded the stimuli in this more precise way will enable the animal to discriminate these stimuli better from other novel tastes and other striped objects.

We may further speculate that the mechanism by which this change in the representation of the stimulus occurs will be subject to the same overall processing constraints that operate during conditioning. Thus conditioning is often assumed to be constrained by limitations on processing capacity (see, for example, Pearce & Hall, 1980). Similarly on first presentation, some of the elements of a novel stimulus will not be processed effectively and will consequently be at first absent from a representation of that stimulus. If it is assumed that those elements that are initially processed are precisely those elements from which there is substantial generalization, such as stimulus onset or a general increase in stimulation, then generalization will be extensive initially and will decline as those elements that are represented become familiar.

V. CONCLUSIONS AND IMPLICATIONS

In this final section we attempt to bring together the various theoretical notions outlined above and examine the implications of the resulting account of perceptual learning for theories of associative learning.

Interaction of Perceptual and Associative Processes

The theory of learning being proposed here is a hybrid incorporating both associative and nonassociative processes. It accepts that associations can be formed between the central representations of events but asserts also that these representations can themselves change.

First, repeated activation of a representation causes a loss of effectiveness so that the representation becomes less ready to enter into associations. The interaction between loss of associability and association formation has already been specified. Associability is lost as a stimulus comes fully to predict its consequences. Inconsistent presentation of a reinforcer serves to prevent or attenuate the loss.

Second, repeated presentation of a given environmental event will produce a change in the nature of the representation that is activated. Our working hypothesis is that initially only the most general features of the event are encoded but that with experience the encoding becomes more precise. We need now to say something about how this learning process interacts with the others we postulate. Again we have no very precise formulation to offer but we can rule out at least some possibilities. In an extreme form the notion of perceptual differentiation could be taken to imply that a quite different representation is activated on each presentation of a given event. If this were so, gradual changes in associative strength and associability could not occur over trials. We need to assume, therefore, that there is sufficient overlap between the representations activated on successive trials for the event to be identified as being essentially the same on the two trials. We are prepared to allow, however, that such generalization may not be complete and to accept the implication that the growth of associative strength and the decline of associability might be restricted by a failure to generalize fully from one trial to the next.

We consider next the implications of these ideas for learning theory generally. We have discussed elsewhere (Hall, Kaye, & Pearce, 1985) the way in which loss of associability can complicate the interpretation of experiments that try to use speed of learning as a measure of associative strength. We concentrate here, therefore, on the implications of the suggestion that the nature of central representations can change.

Implications

Experiments with compound stimuli.   Almost all the events used by experimenters as "stimuli" can be construed as being compounds of other stimuli. Here, however, we discuss studies using compounds deliberately constructed by the experimenter. The fact that the elements of such compounds are easily presented separately makes them amenable to analysis. And further, much in our current theoretical approach to Pavlovian learning has its origins in the study of compound stimuli (cf. Kamin, 1969). It has been usual to make the simplifying assumption (e.g., Rescorla & Wagner, 1972) that the elements of these compounds are perceived independently. Our account suggests, however, that a detailed specification of the components of the compound might emerge only with experience. This approach suggests new possible interpretations of established phenomena and we have space to mention a few of them here.

First, if the nature of the representation changes with experience it should be possible to detect changes in behavior over the course of conditioning that are not merely the product of the growth of associative strength. The results of experiments on "spontaneous configuring" (e.g., Bellingham & Gillette, 1981; Forbes & Holland, 1985) are compatible with this notion. Early in training the subjects respond readily to separately presented elements but with extended exposure to the compound they prove better able to discriminate the compound from its elements. Our account anticipates that such discrimination should be difficult in the early stages of training when the compound and the elements will be coded in much the same way. Only when the detailed nature of the compound has been encoded will a discrimination become possible.

An inability to discriminate the elements of a compound stimulus during initial presentations of that stimulus may also play a role in determining the outcome of experiments on nonreinforced preexposure. The left-hand panel of Fig. 5.10 summarizes the results of a recently completed study of taste-aversion learning in rats (Honey & Hall, 1988b). Subjects in group A received 4 days of preexposure on each of which they were allowed to consume 10 ml of flavor A (e.g., sucrose). Subjects in group W received water on these days. Both groups then received injections of LiCl. The figure shows that group W acquired the aversion readily whereas group A showed latent inhibition. A third group of subjects (AB) received preexposure to a compound stimulus (a mixture of sucrose and dilute HCl) before conditioning with one of the elements of the compound. In these animals conditioning proceeded relatively normally. An explanation for this attenuation of latent inhibition can be derived from our account of perceptual learning. If, during the initial trials of preexposure, animals encode the compound not as A plus B but as some undifferentiated whole (call it X) then on these trials the target element (A) will suffer little loss of associability as will be revealed when A is presented and conditioned alone.

Our interpretation of the attenuation of latent inhibition produced by exposing the target stimulus in compound with another has implications for overshadowing—the observation that reinforced presentations of an AB compound may endow A with less tendency to evoke the CR than the same number of training trials with A alone. In initial training with the compound, before perceptual differentiation has occurred, the representation activated will be of stimulus X. Effectively, therefore, compound training will allow fewer reinforced presentations of A than will the control procedure and on these grounds a relatively weak CR to stimulus A may be expected.

We do not put this forward as a complete account of overshadowing. The demonstration (e.g., Mackintosh & Reese, 1979; Revusky, 1971) of overshadow-

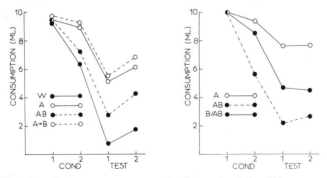

FIG. 5.10. Group mean amounts of a flavored solution (A) consumed during conditioning and on test trials (A presented alone) for groups preexposed to water (W), to the flavor (A), to the target flavor mixed with another (AB), or to serial presentations of A and B (A-B). In the right-hand panel, group B-AB received eight presentations of B alone before preexposure to the AB compound. After Honey & Hall (1988b).

ing with serial compound stimuli (i.e., with A preceding B) shows that the effect can occur with a procedure in which perceptual factors seem unlikely to be heavily involved (see below). Our suggestion serves to demonstrate, however, the important role that perceptual interactions are likely to play in helping to determine the outcome of many of our traditional experimental designs in which use is made of stimulus compounds.

Limitations of this analysis.   Our suggestion that serial presentation might reduce the role of perceptual effects makes clear the need to specify more precisely the conditions in which these effects are or are not important. We have experimental results relevant to three potentially relevant factors (Honey & Hall, 1988b). We begin with a comparison of serial and simultaneous compounds.

In our flavor-aversion study of latent inhibition we found that prior exposure to the simultaneous AB compound produced less latent inhibition to A than preexposure to A alone. This experiment also included a fourth group of subjects (A-B in Fig. 5.10). As the figure shows, only preexposure to the simultaneous compound (group AB) produced attenuation of latent inhibition. Animals preexposed to the serial compound showed perfectly normal latent inhibition. If our account of the attenuation seen in group AB is accepted then we must conclude that the perceptual processes it implies are not engaged by the serial procedure. It seems that studies using serial presentation of stimuli might allow the learning theorist to look at the interaction between elements in a compound when these are perceived independently.

Next, we have considered the possibility that experience of the elements of a compound outside the compound might aid perceptual differentiation. The right-hand panel of Fig. 5.10 presents the results of a further study of the attenuation of latent inhibition which used the same general procedures as that just described. Groups A and AB replicate the effect seen in our first experiment. The new condition (group B/AB) received two phases of preexposure. In the first they experienced eight nonreinforced presentations of stimulus B alone; in the second, four presentations of the simultaneous AB compound. Conditioning to A alone proceeded more slowly in group B/AB than in group AB—that is, the attenuation of latent inhibition produced by having B present during compound preexposure was itself attenuated when B had been preexposed. We conclude that prior exposure to B speeded the process of perceptual differentiation so that the subjects were able to identify stimulus A throughout compound preexposure. It may be noted that many studies of compound conditioning include a phase in which the subjects experience the elements of a compound independently.

The final factor to be considered concerns the nature of the stimuli. In these taste-aversion experiments the compound stimulus used (a mixture of sucrose and dilute acid) seems to the naive human observer to constitute a unique taste, the components of which are not immediately obvious. But other pairs of stimuli might not have this property. A compound in which the elements are drawn from different sensory modalities, for instance, might be differentiated from the outset. (See e.g., Brown, 1987; Riley, 1984, for a discussion of other possibly relevant factors.) We have recently investigated the possibility, again using the phenomenon of attenuation of latent inhibition as our touchstone, in an experiment using the conditioned suppression procedure. Three groups of rats received preexposure over 48 trials to presentation of a tone. One group (T) received just the tone; for a second group the tone (TL) was compounded with a bright light, for the third group (TC) the tone was compounded with a clicker. All groups then received conditioning trials (three per day) in which the tone alone was followed by shock. The acquisition of suppression is shown in Fig. 5.11. The group T learned slowly (i.e., showed latent inhibition) whereas the group TC learned readily. (Their acquisition was as rapid as that we have seen in other experiments in animals given no prior exposure.) We conclude that differentiation of the tone-clicker compound was sufficiently slow for little latent inhibition to accrue to the tone. In contrast, animals given a tone-light compound showed a full amount of latent inhibition, learning, if anything, even less readily than the tone-alone subjects. It may be added that the light is a perfectly effective stimulus, proving, in separate tests, to be just as salient as the clicker. Its failure to attenuate the effect of preexposure to the tone suggests to us that these stimuli from different modalities are differentiated, even in a simultaneous compound, right from the start. To the extent that previous experiments using compound stimuli have used events of this type, an interpretation that assumes that each element is treated independently may still be appropriate.

Conclusions.   In this final section we have done our best to play fair by traditional associative theory, emphasizing the circumstances in which perceptual differentiation effects may be disregarded. We should not overlook the fact, however, that many experiments using compounds have presented the elements simultaneously, have not given preexposure to the elements separately, and have

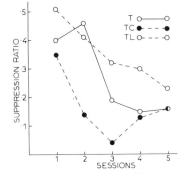

FIG. 5.11.   Group mean suppression ratios during tone-shock pairings for groups preexposed to the tone (T), to a compound of tone and clicker (TC), or to a compound of tone and light (TL).

used stimuli just as likely to interact as our tone and clicker. The results of these studies may need reinterpretation. More generally, it would be wrong to leave the reader with the impression that perceptual learning effects are awkward irrelevancies that get in the way of studying learning in a pure form and that can be avoided by an appropriate choice of stimuli and procedures. Rather, the argument of this chapter has been that perceptual learning is a basic form of learning, worthy of study in its own right and one that must be accommodated by any theory of learning with a claim to comprehensiveness. A theory of learning that concentrates solely on procedures in which perceptual learning plays little part may turn out to be internally satisfactory and self-consistent but will find itself unable to make contact with a wide range of phenomena that psychology is expected to explain.

ACKNOWLEDGMENTS

The experimental work described in this chapter was supported by grants from the United Kingdom Science and Engineering Research Council. We thank C. Bonardi, N. J. Mackintosh, P. Reed, and T. R. Schachtman for their comments on an earlier version of the chapter.

REFERENCES

Ayres, J. J. B., Moore, J. W., & Vigorito, M. (1984). Hall and Pearce negative transfer: Assessments in conditioned suppression and nictitating membrane conditioning experiments. *Animal Learning and Behavior, 12*, 428–438.

Bateson, P. P. G., & Chantrey, D. F. (1972). Retardation of discrimination learning in monkeys and chicks previously exposed to both stimuli. *Nature, 237*, 173–174.

Bellingham, W. P., & Gillette, K. (1981). Spontaneous configuring to a tone-light compound using appetitive training. *Learning and Motivation, 12*, 420–434.

Best, M. R., & Batson, J. D. (1977). Enhancing the expression of flavor neophobia: Some effects of the ingestion-illness contingency. *Journal of Experimental Psychology: Animal Behavior Processes, 3*, 132–143.

Bitterman, M. E., Calvin, A. D., & Elam, C. B. (1953). Perceptual differentiation in the course of nondifferential reinforcement. *Journal of Comparative and Physiological Psychology, 46*, 393–397.

Brown, M. F. (1987). Dissociation of stimulus compounds by pigeons. *Journal of Experimental Psychology: Animal Behavior Processes, 13*, 80–91.

Bouton, M. E., & Bolles, R. C. (1985). Contexts, event-memories, and extinction. In P. D. Balsam & A. Tomie (Eds.), *Context and learning* (pp. 133–166). Hillsdale, NJ: Lawrence Erlbaum Associates.

Channell, S., & Hall, G. (1981). Facilitation and retardation of discrimination learning after exposure to the stimuli. *Journal of Experimental Psychology: Animal Behavior Processes, 7*, 437–446.

Channell, S., & Hall, G. (1983). Contextual effects in latent inhibition with an appetitive conditioning procedure. *Animal Learning and Behavior, 11*, 67–74.

Couvillon, P. A., Tennant, W. A., & Bitterman, M. E. (1976). Intradimensional vs. extradimensional transfer in the discriminative learning of goldfish and pigeons. *Animal Learning and Behavior, 4,* 197–203.

Dodwell, P. C. (1961). Coding and learning in shape discrimination. *Psychological Review, 68,* 373–382.

Forbes, D. T., & Holland, P. C. (1985). Spontaneous configuring in conditioned flavor aversion. *Journal of Experimental Psychology: Animal Behavior Processes, 11,* 224–240.

Frey, P. W., & Sears, R. J. (1978). Model of conditioning incorporating the Rescorla-Wagner associative axiom, a dynamic attention process, and a catastrophe rule. *Psychological Review, 85,* 321–340.

Gibson, E. J. (1969). *Principles of perceptual learning and development.* New York: Appleton-Century-Crofts.

Gibson, E. J., & Walk, R. D. (1956). The effect of prolonged exposure to visually presented patterns on learning to discriminate them. *Journal of Comparative and Physiological Psychology, 49,* 239–242.

Groves, P. M., & Thompson, R. F. (1970). Habituation: A dual-process theory. *Psychological Review, 77,* 419–450.

Hall, G. (1974). Transfer effects produced by overtraining in the rat. *Journal of Comparative and Physiological Psychology, 87,* 938–944.

Hall, G. (1979). Exposure learning in young and adult laboratory rats. *Animal Behaviour, 27,* 586–591.

Hall, G. (1980). Exposure learning in animals. *Psychological Bulletin, 88,* 535–550.

Hall, G. (1983). *Behaviour: An introduction to psychology as a biological science.* London and New York: Academic Press.

Hall, G., & Channell, S. (1980). A search for perceptual differentiation produced by nondifferential reinforcement. *Quarterly Journal of Experimental Psychology, 32,* 185–195.

Hall, G., & Channell, S. (1983). Stimulus exposure and discrimination in rats: A test of a theory for the role of contextual factors. *Quarterly Journal of Experimental Psychology, 35B,* 135–147.

Hall, G., & Channell, S. (1985a). A comparison of intradimensional and extradimensional shift learning in pigeons. *Behavioural Processes, 10,* 285–295.

Hall, G., & Channell, S. (1985b). Differential effects of contextual change on latent inhibition and on the habituation of an orienting response. *Journal of Experimental Psychology: Animal Behavior Processes, 11,* 470–481.

Hall, G., & Channell, S. (1986). Context specificity of latent inhibition in taste aversion learning. *Quarterly Journal of Experimental Psychology, 38B,* 121–139.

Hall, G., Kaye, H., & Pearce, J. M. (1985). Attention and conditioned inhibition. In R. R. Miller & N. E. Spear (Eds.), *Information processing in animals: Conditioned inhibition* (pp. 185–207). Hillsdale, NJ: Lawrence Erlbaum Associates.

Hall, G., & Pearce, J. M. (1978). Transfer of learning across reinforcers: Appetitive discrimination learning between stimuli previously associated with shock. *Quarterly Journal of Experimental Psychology, 30,* 539–549.

Hall, G., & Pearce, J. M. (1979). Latent inhibition of a CS during CS–US pairings. *Journal of Experimental Psychology: Animal Behavior Processes, 5,* 31–42.

Hall, G., & Schachtman, T. R. (1987). Differential effects of a retention interval on latent inhibition and the habituation of an orienting response. *Animal Learning and Behavior, 15,* 76–82.

Holland, P. C. (1982). Interelement associations in serial compound conditioning. In M. L. Commons, R. J. Hernnstein, & A. R. Wagner (Eds.), *Quantitative analyses of behavior, Vol. III* (pp. 323–345). Cambridge, MA: Ballinger.

Honey, R. C., & Hall, G. (1988a). *Enhanced discriminability and reduced associability following flavor preexposure.* Manuscript submitted for publication.

Honey, R. C., & Hall, G. (1988b). Overshadowing and blocking procedures in latent inhibition. *Quarterly Journal of Experimental Psychology, 40B,* 163–186.

Kamin, L. J. (1969). Predictability, surprise, attention and conditioning. In R. A. Campbell, & R. M. Church (Eds.), *Punishment and aversive behavior* (pp. 279–296). New York: Appleton-Century-Crofts.

Kasprow, W. J., Schachtman, T. R., & Miller, R. A. (1985). Associability of a previously conditioned stimulus as a function of qualitative changes in the US. *Quarterly Journal of Experimental Psychology, 37B,* 33–48.

Kaye, H., & Pearce, J. M. (1984). The strength of the orienting response during Pavlovian conditioning. *Journal of Experimental Psychology: Animal Behavior Processes, 10,* 90–109.

Lashley, K. S. (1942). An examination of the continuity theory applied to discriminative learning. *Journal of General Psychology, 26,* 241–265.

Lashley, K. S., & Wade, M. &1946). The Pavlovial theory of generalization. *Psychological Review, 53,* 72–87.

Lawrence, D. H. (1949). Acquired distinctiveness of cues: I. Transfer between discriminations on the basis of familiarity with the stimulus. *Journal of Experimental Psychology, 39,* 770–784.

Lawrence, D. H. (1963). The nature of a stimulus: Some relationships between learning and perception. In S. Koch (Ed.), *Psychology: A study of a science, Vol. 5* (pp. 179–212). New York: McGraw-Hill.

Lovibond, P. F., Preston, G. C., & Mackintosh, N. J. (1984). Context specificity of conditioning, extinction, and latent inhibition. *Journal of Experimental Psychology: Animal Behavior Processes, 10,* 360–375.

Lubow, R. E. (1973). Latent inhibition. *Psychological Bulletin, 79,* 398–407.

Lubow, R. E., Rifkin, B., & Alek, M. (1976). The context effect: The relationship between stimulus preexposure and environmental preexposure determines subsequent learning. *Journal of Experimental Psychology: Animal Behavior Processes, 2,* 38–47.

Mackintosh, N. J. (1965). Selective attention in animal discrimination learning. *Psychological Bulletin, 64,* 124–150.

Mackintosh, N. J. (1969). Further analysis of the overtraining reversal effect. *Journal of Comparative and Physiological Psychology Monograph, 67,* No. 2, Part 2.

Mackintosh, N. J. (1974). *The psychology of animal learning.* London: Academic Press.

Mackintosh, N. J. (1975). A theory of attention: Variations in the associability of stimuli with reinforcement. *Psychological Review, 82,* 276–298.

Mackintosh, N. J., & Little, L. (1969). Intradimensional and extradimensional shift learning by pigeons. *Psychonomic Science, 14,* 5–6.

Mackintosh, N. J., & Reese, B. (1979). One-trial overshadowing. *Quarterly Journal of Experimental Psychology, 31,* 519–526.

Pearce, J. M., & Hall, G. (1980). A model for Pavlovian learning: Variations in the effectiveness of conditioned but not of unconditioned stimuli. *Psychological Review, 87,* 532–552.

Pearce, J. M., Kaye, H., & Hall, G. (1982). Predictive accuracy and stimulus associability: Development of a model for Pavlovian learning. In M. L. Commons, R. J. Herrnstein, & A. R. Wagner (Eds.), *Quantitative analyses of behavior Vol. III* (pp. 241–255). Cambridge, MA: Ballinger.

Rescorla, R. A. (1980). *Pavlovian second-order conditioning.* Hillsdale, NJ: Lawrence Erlbaum Associates.

Rescorla, R. A. (1985). Conditioned inhibition and facilitation. In R. R. Miller & N. E. Spear (Eds.), *Information processing in animals: Conditioned inhibition* (pp. 299–326). Hillsdale, NJ: Lawrence Erlbaum Associates.

Rescorla, R. A. (1986). Associative learning: Some consequences of contiguity. In N. M. Weinberger, J. L. McGaugh, & G. Lynch (Eds.), *Memory systems of the brain* (pp. 211–230). New York and London: The Guilford Press.

Rescorla, R. A., & Durlach, P. J. (1981). Within-event learning in Pavlovian conditioning. In N. E. Spear & R. R. Miller (Eds.), *Information processing in animals: Memory mechanisms* (pp. 81–111). Hillsdale, NJ: Lawrence Erlbaum Associates.

Rescorla, R. A., & Wagner, A. R. (1972). A theory of Pavlovian conditioning: Variations in the effectiveness of reinforcement and nonreinforcement. In A. H. Black & W. F. Prokasy (Eds.), *Classical conditioning II: Current research and theory* (pp. 64–99). New York: Appleton-Century-Crofts.

Revusky, S. (1971). The role of interference in association over a delay. In W. K. Honig & P. H. R. James (Eds.), *Animal memory* (pp. 155–213). New York: Academic Press.

Riley, D. A. (1984). Do pigeons decompose stimulus compounds? In H. L. Roitblat, T. G. Bever & H. S. Terrace (Eds.), *Animal cognition* (pp. 333–350). Hillsdale, NJ: Lawrence Erlbaum Associates.

Schachtman, T. R., Channell, S., & Hall, G. (1987). Effects of CS preexposure on inhibition of delay. *Animal Learning and Behavior, 15*, 301–311.

Siegel, S. (1967). Overtraining and transfer processes. *Journal of Comparative and Physiological Psychology, 64*, 471–477.

Sokolov, Y. N. (1963). *Perception and the conditioned reflex.* Oxford: Pergamon Press.

Spence, K. W. (1936). The nature of discrimination learning in animals. *Psychological Review, 43*, 427–449.

Sutherland, N. S. (1959). Stimulus analyzing mechanisms. In *Proceedings of a symposium on the mechanization of thought processes, Vol. 2* (pp. 575–609). London: Her Majesty's Stationery Office.

Sutherland, N. S., & Mackintosh, N. J. (1971). *Mechanisms of animal discrimination learning.* New York: Academic Press.

Taylor, C. (1964). *The explanation of behaviour.* London: Routledge and Kegan Paul.

Wagner, A. R. (1976). An information processing mechanism for self-generated or retrieval-generated depression in performance. In T. J. Tighe & R. N. Leaton (Eds.), *Habituation: Perspectives from child development, animal behavior, and neurophysiology* (pp. 95–128). Hillsdale, NJ: Lawrence Erlbaum Associates.

Wagner, A. R. (1978). Expectancies and the priming of STM. In S. H. Hulse, H. Fowler & W. K. Honig (Eds.), *Cognitive processes in animal behavior.* Hillsdale, NJ: Lawrence Erlbaum Associates.

Wagner, A. R. (1981). SOP: A model of automatic memory processing in animal behavior. In N. E. Spear & R. R. Miller (Eds.), *Information processing in animals: Memory mechanisms* (pp. 5–47). Hillsdale, NJ: Lawrence Erlbaum Associates.

6
Evolution of a structured connectionist model of Pavlovian conditioning (AESOP)

Allan R. Wagner
Susan E. Brandon
Yale University

Casual accounts of the conditioning process have been dominated since Pavlov by one or another conception of the notion of "substitution with pairing." It may be supposed that, as a result of prescribed juxtapositions of conditioned stimulus (CS) and unconditioned stimulus (US), the CS can come to act like a substitute for the US. Or, it may be supposed that as a result of certain conditions of practice of the unconditioned response (UR) in temporal relationship to the CS, the practiced behavior can come to be substituted for the original response to the CS. The notion is generally embraced by the reasoning that during conditioning an "association" or "connection" is strengthened between some functional "centers," i.e., between some CS representation and analogous US representation, or between a CS representation and UR process. Thus, it can be understood that when the CS representation is subsequently activated by the CS, the connecting link either affords activation of the US representation and, hence, activation of the UR process, or, affords activation of the UR process directly, so that the conditioned response (CR) occurs.

Any student of Pavlovian conditioning, of course, knows that such an account is, on the face of it, easy to discredit. In many, if not most, circumstances of Pavlovian conditioning, the CS does not appear to act like a substitute for the US and/or evoke a CR that mimics the practiced UR. The literature is filled with examples of the apparent inadequacy of a substitution notion of conditioning, examples of the sort that led Warner (1932) to his poetic summary, that "whatever response is grafted onto the CS, it is not snipped from the US." An influential study by Zener (1937) made it clear that the substitution notion did not fare well even in circumstances of salivary conditioning as employed by Pavlov. And, today, two of the most common preparations employed in investigations of Pavlovian conditioning, so-called autoshaping and the CER, are both notable for the manner in which the CR differs from the UR (e.g., Blanchard & Blanchard, 1969; Wasserman, Hunter, Gutowski, & Bader, 1975). Other functional dissimilarities add to the problem, e.g., the fact that the associative effects of pairing a neutral CS with a previously trained CS that might be considered a substitute for a US are quite different from the effects of pairing the neutral CS with the US itself, being prominantly "inhibitory" rather than "excitatory" (e.g., Konorski, 1948).

As a result, it is incumbent upon any modern theory of Pavlovian conditioning to distance itself in some fashion from a bald substitution account. For those theorists who have worked within what is today called a "connectionist" framework (Feldman & Ballard, 1982), i.e., within the general view that learning can be accounted for in terms of the modification of excitatory and/or inhibitory connections in a neural-network-like graph structure, it has been common to suggest that the problems with substitution theory could be solved by more insightful treatment of the representations that get connected. Consider, for example, Logan's (1977) "hybrid theory of conditioning." It begins familiarly enough, with the theoretical reasoning that a CS and a US each activates a representation that provokes behavioral responses, and that conditioning involves the development of an associative link whereby activation of the CS representation can activate a US representation. However, Logan explicitly denies that the US representation that can come to be activated by the CS is the same as the US representation activated by the US itself. Instead, he supposes that it is a different representation, which in the mentalistic language of the theory is referred to as an "anticipation of the US," rather than the "experience of the US." By this distinction Logan allows that the CR (that is, the "UR" to activation of the "anticipation-of-the-US" representation) need not be identical to the observed UR (that is, the UR to activation of the US representation), but might bear only some (unspecified) "family relationship to it."

Pearce and Hall (1980) similarly attempt to set their theoretical views apart from a substitution-with-pairing notion (refer to Chapter 5, this volume for a description of this theory). They begin with a conventional assertion, that "conditioning procedures result in the formation of an association between internal representation of the CS and US such that presentation of the CS becomes capable of producing activity appropriate to the occurrence of the US." However, they pointedly take leave of the substitution notion by asserting that the "activity appropriate to the occurrence of the US" that the CS becomes capable of producing is not the same as that produced by the US, but is rather that of a "US memory." Activation of a "US memory" representation is what is presumed to produce the CR.

Konorski (1967) made a related distinction. He supposed that the representation produced by any stimulus involves the activation of a series of "units" in order, as in a neuronal projection system, beginning with receptive units, followed by transit units, and eventually terminating with so-called gnostic units.

If it is assumed that units at several levels of the representational series are capable, when activated, of producing behavioral effects, then one would expect that the UR to its US would involve a complex of differentiated and/or interactive components. In comparison, Konorski assumed that a CS that has been paired with a US (and the full sequence of US-representational activity) will come only to activate a portion of the sequence appropriate to the US. Specifically, he assumed that only the highest level, gnostic units, of the US representation can be activated by a CS and only the activity of such units will, thus, be reflected in the CR. Konorski presented this reasoning in distinguishing between the direct experience of the *perception* of a stimulus and the associatively mediated experience of an *image* of the same stimulus. Were there not basis for the two being different (which he allowed that there might not always be in some afferent systems or in phylogenetically earlier animals), a CS would generally give rise to a hallucination of the US.

The goal of this chapter is to explicate the evolution of a theory of Pavlovian conditioning with which we have been associated that follows in the tradition of those conditioning theories (e.g., Konorski, 1948; Pavlov, 1927) which conceive of learning as involving a change in connections between presumed CS and US representations. It necessarily assumes obligation, like the treatments of Logan (1977), Pearce and Hall (1980) and Konorski (1967), to rationalize how the US representational activity that can come to be provoked by a CS is different from that which is provoked by the US itself. A core set of assumptions is contained in a model initially developed by Mazur and Wagner (1982), Donegan and Wagner (1987), Pfautz (1980), and Wagner (1981) that goes by the acronym, SOP (see below). The model is a detailed quantitative theory, shaped in part by the desideratum of being able to deduce the regularities of the Rescorla-Wagner equation (Rescorla & Wagner, 1972; Wagner & Rescorla, 1972), as discussed in Chapter 2, in most (but, pointedly, not all) relevant applications (see Mazur & Wagner, 1982). What we concentrate upon here, however, is its mechanistic features, that is, on how it attempts to capture, in abstract formulation, what might be entertained to be the basic episodic (i.e., real-time) processes responsible for the acquisition and performance of conditioned responding. SOP can, we think, be largely understood by appreciating how it calculates that a CS will in some ways become an effective substitute for a US, and in some ways not.

The working version of the theory that is the subject of our current research is referred to as AESOP. It portends an elaboration and extension of SOP, but has not yet been rendered in comparable quantitative terms. We will indicate the manner of challenge to SOP that leads us to think that some extension is necessary, and in final sections of the chapter, show how AESOP is designed to increase the scope and empirical adequacy of the theory. Suffice it to anticipate that the theoretical evolution that is most salient in AESOP, and that we emphasize here, is the richer conception of the stimulus representations involved in conditioning.

I. SOP

The acronym SOP was suggested in part by an apparent relationship between the model and the opponent-process theory of Solomon and Corbit (1974), especially as the latter has been construed by Schull (1979). Solomon and Corbit suggested that many phenomena involving hedonic stimuli could be understood by assuming that such stimuli produce not only a direct process (called α) in line with the prominent affective tone of the stimulus but also a "slave" reaction to the α process (called β) that is in opposition to the α process. Thus, for example, because the β process is slower to recruit and to dissipate than the α process, one can appreciate that a pleasant event might be followed by an unpleasant afterexperience. Schull proposed that many facts of conditioning involving aversive or appetitive USs might then be explained by assuming that one of the CRs that a CS may become capable of eliciting is the secondary, β, process but not the α process, initiated by a US. Our view was that it might be useful to expand upon these notions in two ways. That is, we supposed that (a) it might be useful to assume that unconditioned stimulus representation *generally* involves a sequence of a primary and a secondary component, i.e., beyond restriction to hedonic stimuli, and (b) that *all* conditioning effects (e.g., all conditioned response tendencies) are mediated by the "conditioning" of the secondary component in such sequence. There is a likeness of this view to the supposition of Konorski (1967) mentioned earlier, that in a cascade of representative activity produced by a US, it is only the final, gnostic, activity that is conditioned. What we suggested then, however, is that in such treatment it could not be assumed that the initial and secondary components are uniformly in opposition, as they are assumed to be in the more narrowly construed opponent-process theory. They might appear to be in some of their effects and not in others. SOP is a "sometimes-opponent-process" theory (Donegan & Wagner, 1987; Mazur & Wagner, 1982; Wagner, 1981).

SOP characterizes the representational activity that may be produced directly by a stimulus, or indirectly via associative connections, in terms of the state dynamics of stimulus nodes as depicted for a CS and for a US in Fig. 6.1a. A node is not an elemental theoretical unit but a functional grouping, within which one can distinguish different patterns of activity as a result of different conditions of stimulation. That is, each node is conceived of as consisting of a large but finite set of elements that can be variously distributed among the three states of inactivity (I), primary activity (A1) and secondary activity (A2). It is assumed that when a node is acted upon by the stimulus it represents, some proportion (p_1) of the elements in the I state will be promoted in each moment of stimulation to the A1 state, from which they will subsequently "decay" first to the A2 state and then back to inactivity. In contrast, it is assumed that when a node is acted upon via excitation propagated over associative connection(s), some proportion (p_2) of the elements in the I state will be promoted in each moment to the A2 state, from which they will also decay back to inactivity. Figure 6.1a summarizes these assumptions by way of appropriate state-transition diagrams within each node. SOP assumes that p_1 increases with increasing stimulus intensity and that p_2 increases with a measure of the summed products of the activity in connecting nodes and their relevant connection strengths, V_i. The momentary decay probabilities p_{d1} and p_{d2} can be viewed as reflecting suppressive (lateral inhibition-like) tendencies produced by concurrent activity in other nodes. The assumption is made that $p_{d1} > p_{d2}$.

SOP adopts the stochastic assumptions that it does as deliberate simplifications that allow determinant quantitative specification. Given the initial activity values for a node such that $p_I + p_{A1} + p_{A2} = 1.0$ and the parameters p_1, p_2, p_{d1}, and p_{d2}, one can specify the nodal activity states following any episode of stimulation. For example, the top diagram of Fig. 6.1b depicts the characteristic course of p_{A1} and p_{A2} following a single momentary presentation of a US to an inactive node. Likewise, the bottom diagram of Fig. 6.1b depicts the characteristic course of nodal activity in a US node following the activity of a CS with which the US has acquired excitatory connections. They illustrate the concrete embodiment of the theoretical principle that a stimulus will cause the node that it represents to take on a primary (A1) and secondary (A2) activity, in order, whereas an excitatory CS can affect a US node only by activating it to the secondary state.

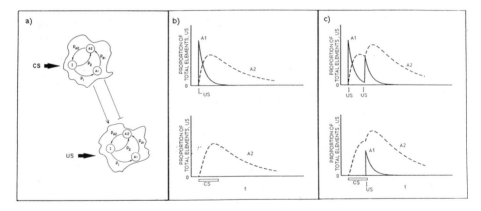

FIG. 6.1. (a) A depiction of two nodes in the memory system of SOP, one presumed to be directly activated by a CS and the other by a US in a Pavlovian conditioning situation. The connected circles within each node represent the three activity states in which nodal elements may momentarily reside, and the connecting paths represent the allowable state transitions. The two nodes are joined to suggest the manner of directional excitatory (pointing arrow) and inhibitory (stopped line) linkages that are assumed to be formed. (b) Representative simulations describing the proportions of elements in A1 and A2 over successive amounts of time following a punctate US (top graph) or an excitatory CS (bottom graph). (c) Simulation of the A1 and A2 processing when a US is added to the stimulation in the companion simulations of *b*.

This is the briefest of introductions to SOP so that the reader may prefer to consult Wagner (1981) or Mazur and Wagner (1982). However, the further features of SOP can be largely understood by appreciating how the theory speaks to three domains in which it may be asked whether the CS does or does not function as a substitute for the US. One domain concerns the character of responding observed in conditioning experiments. The second concerns the training conditions that produce excitatory versus inhibitory conditioning, and the third regards the refractory-like effects observed in studies of Pavlovian conditioning and habituation. These are described in the next sections.

The characteristics of response to the CS versus the US.

SOP assumes that the A1 and A2 process each has its own behavioral consequences. In some instances, this assumption is obviously invited by the nature of the unconditioned response to a stimulus, i.e., when some US produces a clear sequence of first one behavior and then another that would correspond to the theoretical processing sequence, A1 then A2. In other instances, the UR may not have salient descriptive discontinuities but may still be divisible into primary and secondary components on some functional basis. In conjunction with either case, it is expected that since an excitatory CS will not produce the full A1 and A2 activity in a US node but only the secondary, A2 activity, any CR that develops should not fully mimic the UR but should mimic the secondary component of the UR. SOP thus calculates that CSs will have a quite varied, but lawful, behavior-producing relationship to potential USs.

A striking example of a UR in which the A1 and A2 processes appear to be associated with notably antagonistic behaviors is in the common laboratory case of a naive rat subjected to a brief footshock. The immediate response is agitated hyperactivity (e.g., Blanchard & Blanchard, 1969; Blanchard, Dielman, & Blanchard, 1968; Bolles & Riley, 1973), which then, characteristically, is followed by a secondary, longer lasting hypoactivity or "freezing" response (Blanchard et al., 1968; Blanchard & Blanchard, 1969; Bolles & Collier, 1976; Bolles & Riley, 1973).[1] The notable fact is that the CR established to a CS paired with footshock consists of freezing, the secondary component of the UR, and not agi-

---

[1]The suggestion has been made that postshock freezing behavior in the rat is not a part of the UR to shock, but is rather a CR, conditioned to the environmental cues with which the shock was experienced (e.g., Fanselow, 1980). Support for this notion comes from the observation that postshock freezing is reduced when animals are removed from the shock environment and observed in a novel environment (Blanchard & Blanchard, 1969; Bolles & Collier, 1976; Fanselow, 1980). However, it is also the case that nonshocked animals may show less freezing in a novel environment that in a familiar environment (Blanchard et al., 1968). Furthermore, shocked animals show more freezing when placed in a novel context than do nonshocked animals (Bolles & Collier, 1976). Thus we remain comfortable with the assumption that postshock freezing is, at least in part, an unconditioned response in the rat.

tation, the primary component (Blanchard & Blanchard, 1969; Bolles & Collier, 1976; Fanselow, 1980; Fanselow & Baackes, 1982). The traditional Conditioned Emotional Response (CER) (Estes & Skinner, 1941) that has been so extensively used in investigation of Pavlovian conditioning presumably reflects such conditioned freezing.

Paletta and Wagner (1986) suggested that the relationship between CR and UR supposed by SOP was similarly exemplified in the case of conditioned activity changes produced with injection of morphine as the US. The well-known prominent response to morphine injection is sedation. One might thus be surprised by recent studies (e.g., Mucha, Volkovskis, & Kalant, 1981) that have administered morphine to rats in distinctive environments and observed that the environmental cues (CS) come to produce an activity change (CR) that is just the opposite, i.e., hyperactivity. But Paletta and Wagner (1986) pointed out that the initial sedation produced by morphine is likely to be followed by a period of hyperactivity (Babbini & Davis, 1972; Fog, 1969) and demonstrated in companion experiments that the conditioned response mimicked the secondary response to morphine.

Figure 6.2 depicts the data from both experiments. In the first, mean activity counts in a stabilimeter device were taken in successive observation periods, from 30 min preinjection to 24 hr postinjection, in relation either to a morphine injection (5mg/kg delivered sc) or a saline injection. The graph in the main body of Fig. 6.2 shows that there was little variation in the animals' activity on the different measurement occasions in the series following the saline injection. In contrast, the morphine injection produced an initial decrease in activity which was observed in the first 5 min after injection and was still prominent in the third postinjection measurement period beginning 60 min later. This sedation was followed by a marked hyperactivity, observed on the measure beginning 4 hr after injection, before behavior returned to the saline baseline. The second experiment showed that the CR that was produced by pairing morphine with the distinctive experimental environment mimicked the secondary, hyperactivity component of the biphasic UR. Here, rats were given ten daily injections of morphine sulfate (5 mg/kg) in the experimental chamber (M-E), the same injections in their home cage (M-HC), or only saline (S) in both environments. All three groups were then tested for their levels of activity in the experimental chamber following a saline injection, i.e., in the absence of morphine. The bar-graph insert of Fig. 6.2 displays the essential findings: The activity level for Group M-E, in which the environment had been associated with morphine, was substantially higher than that for Group M-HC, which had equal drug exposure but not in the test context, or Group S, which was drug naive. Siegel (e.g., 1979, 1981) has emphasized that the CR in studies like that of Paletta and Wagner, with pharmacological USs, will be "compensatory" to the prominent response to the US. This was certainly true in the Paletta and Wagner (1986) study. However, it is also true that the CR *mimicked* the secondary response to the drug, as anticipated by SOP. It remains

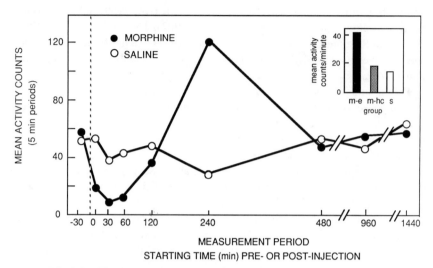

FIG. 6.2.   The line graph shows the temporal course of activity related to morphine or saline administration. Plotted are the mean activity counts during 5-min observation periods starting at 30 min prior to injection and ending at 24 hr post injection. The bar graph-insert shows mean activity counts during a saline test session for Group M-E, trained with morphine in the experimental environment; Group M-HC, which experienced the same morphine but in the home cage; and Group S, which received only saline in training. Drawn from Paletta & Wagner (1986).

to be seen whether the evidence for "conditioned compensatory responses" frequently observed with pharmacological USs will generally be found to be associated with a biphasic UR with a secondary component antagonistic to the prominent initial response.

In some cases, dissociable primary and secondary responses observed to a US may be complimentary rather than antagonistic. SOP again anticipates evidence that it is the secondary response which will be exhibited as the CR. Grau (1987) has suggested that this is in fact exemplified in findings involving the "analgesic" response to stimulation in the rat. For a period of time following an episode of footshock, the rat is less sensitive (hypoalgesic) to painful stimuli such as radiant heat applied to the tail (see, e.g., Chesher & Chan, 1977). Investigation of this unconditioned response has identified two components, an initial, short-duration hypoalgesia that is not modified by administration of the opiate antagonist, naloxone, and a secondary, more persistent hypoalgesia which is removed or reduced by naloxone (Lewis, Cannon, & Liebeskind, 1980; Mayer & Watkins, 1981). The initial, nonopioid component and secondary, opioid component of the analgesic response emerge sequentially (Drugan, Moye, & Maier, 1982; Grau, Hyson, Maier, Maddon, & Barchas, 1981) in the manner of A1 and A2. Of import for SOP, the analgesic response can be conditioned to environmental cues, and the form of the conditioned analgesia appears to be prominently opioid in nature, i.e., to be blocked by naloxone (Fanselow & Baackes, 1982; Fanselow & Bolles, 1979). Largely on the basis of observations such as these, Grau (1987) has suggested that the initial, short-duration nonopioid form of postshock analgesia in the rat can be identified with the A1 process, and the second, more persistent (and conditionable) opioid form with the A2 process. The point of the example here is that, according to SOP, the conditioned response to the CS can be identified with a secondary response to the US, even though there is no antagonism between the CR and the UR components or between the two UR components.

An important recent set of findings consistent with SOP comes from the neurobiological analyses of Pavlovian eyeblink conditioning in the rabbit (for review see Thompson, Clark, Donegan, Lavond, Lincoln, Madden, Mamounas, Mauk, McCormick, & Thompson, 1984). The UR in this preparation involves a blinking of the eye to a corneal airpuff or a paraorbital shock US, and the CR, when it develops to a CS such as a tone or light, is also an eyeblink. What is remarkable is that there appear to be two pathways contributing to the UR and that the CR is a result of conditioned activity in the one of these that would make the more delayed contribution. Thompson et al. (1984) have shown that the US affects the eyeblink UR through a relatively direct pathway and a relatively circuitous pathway. The relatively direct path consists of a monosynaptic (and dysynaptic) connection between the 5th sensory nucleus that receives input from the area of US application, and the 6th and 7th motor nuclei that control the eyeblink response. The relatively indirect path involves a sequence of brain stem and cerebellar structures between the same sensory nucleus and motor nuclei: there is a projection from that 5th nucleus to the inferior olive, where synapses are made with fibers that pass to the cerebellum, from which there is a return path via the red nucleus to the motor nuclei. Both the direct and indirect paths are engaged in the UR: Electrical stimulation in appropriate parts of either pathway produces an eyeblink response. There are a variety of observations that indicate that the CR is driven by the indirect (inferior olive, cerebellar, red nucleus) pathway. Most obvious is that if an animal is trained so that it gives a conditioned eyeblink response to a CS, lesions in this pathway remove the CR and make reacquisition impossible, while sparing the UR component that is generated through the direct path (Thompson et al., 1984). There is an apparent isomorphism between the neural circuitry for eyeblink conditioning in the rabbit and the abstract processes of SOP: The UR consists of two components, as a result of activity in both a shorter, more direct (A1) path and a longer, indirect (A2) path; the CR can be identified with activity of the components of the secondary UR circuit (A2). Wagner and Donegan (in press) have indicated reasons other than the form of the CR and UR for taking this apparent isomorphism seriously.

In summary, SOP describes the UR as biphasic and the CR as reflecting the secondary (sometimes opponent) rather than the primary component of the UR. In cases where the behavioral reflections of each component are antagonistic, such as with footshock and morphine USs (using activity as the dependent measure), it is easy to identify the separate components and observe the apparent relationships. In other instances, such as the analgesic response of a rat to footshock or the eyeblink response of a rabbit to an air puff delivered to the eye, the separate processing components have only recently been provisionally identified.

Excitatory versus inhibitory learning.

SOP presumes that a US provokes A1 and then A2 activity states in the relevant US node, whereas an excitatory CS can provoke only A2 activity in that same US node, as depicted in Fig. 6.1b. If a neutral CS were paired with the aforementioned excitatory CS it would presumably overlap with the same theoretical, A2, activity as it would if it were presented some time after the US itself. SOP, in its specific approach to excitatory and inhibitory learning, assumes that the learning that would accrue would be similar in those cases and different from that expected if the neutral CS is paired with the immediate, A1, consequence of a US. What follows is a brief description of the assumptions of SOP with reference to excitatory and inhibitory learning, and of some relevant investigations which support this assertion that two apparently dissimilar training paradigms— conditioned-inhibition training and backward US–CS pairing—can have similar consequences.

The model assumes that an increment in the *excitatory* link from one node to another occurs only in moments in which both nodes have elements in the A1 state, and that the size of the increment is proportional to a measure of the degree of joint, A1 activity. Stated more specifically, for the linkage from a CS node to a US node, it is assumed that the increment in excitatory strength (ΔV^+_{CS-SU}) in any moment is the product of $p_{A1,CS}$, the proportion of CS elements in the A1 state, times $p_{A1,US}$, the proportion of US elements in the A1 state (multiplied by an excitatory learning rate parameter, L^+). It is correspondingly assumed that an increment in *inhibitory* linkages from one node to another occurs only in moments in which the former node has elements in the A1 state, while the latter node has elements in the A2 state, and that the size of the increment is proportional to a measure of the degree of such joint activity. Stated more specifically, for the linkage from a CS node to a US node, it is assumed that the increment in inhibitory strength (ΔV^-_{CS-US}) in any moment is the product of $p_{A1,CS}$, the proportion of CS elements in the A1 state, times $p_{A2,US}$, the proportion of US elements in the A2 state (multiplied by an inhibitory learning rate parameter, L^-). At any moment and over any episode of time both kinds of conjoint activity may occur so that the net change in associative strength will be $\Delta V_{CS-US} = \Delta V^+_{CS-US} - \Delta V^-_{CS-US}$.

To illustrate the mechanisms of SOP regarding the formation of excitatory and inhibitory associations, Mazur and Wagner (1982) reported a series of simulations of SOP involving a variety of basic Pavlovian conditioning arrangements.

One instance of these is especially relevant to the present context and is reproduced in Fig. 6.3. The left column of graphs in panel *a* are representative simulations of a forward, trace-conditioning trial, in which a momentary CS precedes by some distance a momentary US. The right column of graphs in the same panel are representative simulations of a similar backward conditioning trial in which the CS follows the US. The top two graphs in each case describe the relevant activity dynamics of the CS and US nodes over time. The three lower graphs in each column trace, in order, the momentary excitatory conditioning, $\Delta V^+_{CS\text{-}US}$, the momentary inhibitory conditioning, $\Delta V^-_{CS\text{-}US}$, and the net momentary change in associative connection, $\Delta V_{CS\text{-}US}$, that result from the nodal activity in the two conditioning arrangements. In the case of the forward conditioning example, the values of $\Delta V^+_{CS\text{-}US}$ are greater than those of $\Delta V^-_{CS\text{-}US}$, consistent with the preferential overlap that is afforded the A1 activity of the CS node with the initial A1 activity of the US node versus the later occurring A2 activity of that node. In comparison, in the backward conditioning case, where $p_{A1,US}$ has largely decayed but $p_{A2,US}$ is substantial at the time of application of the CS, the succeeding increments in excitatory association, $\Delta V^+_{CS\text{-}US}$, are consistently less than the corresponding increments in inhibitory association, $\Delta V^-_{CS\text{-}US}$.[2] The result is that, whereas the algebraic consequence, $\Delta V_{CS\text{-}US}$, is uniformly positive in the forward conditioning case, it is uniformly negative in the backward conditioning case.

The overall associative outcomes of the two conditioning arrangements are obtained by summing the successive momentary values of $\Delta V_{CS\text{-}US}$ over the episodes depicted. Figure 6.3b summarizes the results of equivalent simulations with a range of CS-US relationships and indicates by the broken vertical lines where the examples of Figure 6.3a would fall in relationship to cases of greater or lesser asynchrony. As may be seen, all forward conditioning arrangements are expected to result in excitatory $V_{CS\text{-}US}$, with the magnitude of the excitatory learning decreasing exponentially as the CS–US interval increases. In contrast, the backward conditioning arrangements are expected to have *either* excitatory or inhibitory consequence depending upon the US–CS interval.

Until recently there has been considerable skepticism concerning the reality of any associative effects of backward, US–CS, pairings per se (see, e.g., Mackintosh, 1974) but it now seems clear that excitatory conditioning can result from sufficiently short intervals (e.g., Wagner & Terry, 1975) but that inhibitory learning is also a genuine outcome (e.g., Mahoney & Ayres, 1976; Maier, Rapaport, & Wheatley, 1976). An investigation by Larew (1986) is especially instructive

---

[2]A subtlety in the simulations described in Fig. 6.3 is that the learning rate parameter was taken to be greater for excitatory than for inhibitory learning (Mazur & Wagner, 1982). The perceptive reader will notice the differential weightings in the calculations of ΔV^+ versus ΔV^-, but they are of no significance to the argument presented here.

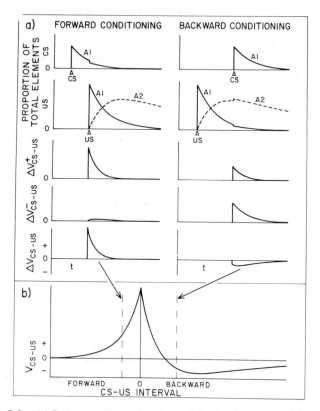

FIG. 6.3.   (a) Representative simulations of single trials of forward and backward conditioning. Displayed are the simulated patterns of activity in CS and US nodes (top two graphs in each column) and the simulated changes in $V^+_{CS\text{-}US}$, $V^-_{CS\text{-}US}$, and $V_{CS\text{-}US}$ (bottom three graphs in each column). (b) Predictions for $V_{CS\text{-}US}$ after one trial are shown for a range of forward and backward CS-US intervals. The broken vertical lines show where the two examples in a panel *a* fall on the abscissa. Reprinted from Mazur & Wagner (1982).

in that it asked, specifically, whether inhibitory learning occurs, as predicted by SOP in Fig. 6.3b, principally at intermediate US-CS intervals.

In one of several studies with similar outcomes, three groups of rats were given 25 widely distributed trials with a 2-sec footshock US followed by a 30-sec tone CS beginning either 1, 31, or 600 sec later. The associative consequences of these backward parings were subsequently evaluated via two assessment procedures, in comparison to a group that received only the US and no backward CS during training. One assessment involved a summation test. All subjects were given several forward pairings of a 30-sec light terminating with the US, and were then tested with the light alone versus the light in compound with the tone of interest while bar-pressing in a conventional CER situation. The top panel of Fig. 6.4 depicts the results for the four groups. What should be seen is that the addition of the tone somewhat decreased the conditioned suppression relative to that observed to the light alone in all groups, but that the effect was most substantial in the group trained with the intermediate, 31-sec US–CS interval, and was statistically reliable only in this case. The second, subsequent assessment procedure involved a retardation test. All subjects were given two sessions of equivalent forward pairings of the tone terminating with the US, during which the acquisition of conditioned suppression of the tone alone was measured. The bottom panel of Fig. 6.4 depicts the mean results from the same four groups over both test sessions. The notable difference was that the group originally trained with the 31-sec US–CS interval was retarded in developing conditioned suppression to the tone CS in comparison to the remaining groups which did not differ reliably. The Larew (1986) findings provide evidence of inhibitory learning as a consequence of backward US–CS pairings, and clear support for SOP's prediction of maximal inhibitory learning with intermediate US–CS intervals that should afford the most substantial preferential overlap of the A1 CS-nodal activity with the A2 US-nodal activity.

The technique that has been known since the reports of Pavlov (1927) to be effective in producing an inhibitory CS is the "conditioned inhibition" paradigm: Some CS, e.g. A, is reinforced by itself, while the CS of interest, e.g. X, is presented together with this otherwise reinforced stimulus without reinforcement, i.e., the contrast, A+, AX−, is arranged. As a consequence of such training,

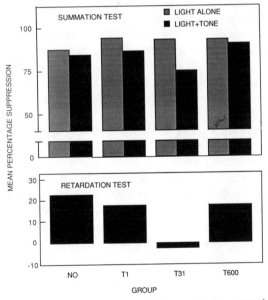

FIG. 6.4.   The top panel shows mean percentage suppression scores in a summation test for four groups trained with a tone CS at varying US–CS intervals (T1 with 1-sec, T31 with 31-sec, and T600 with 600-sec) or with no tone presentations (NO). The bottom graph shows mean percentage suppression scores to the tone in a retardation test for the same four groups. Drawn from Larew (1986).

the X cue can be expected to become effective in reducing the conditioned responding observed to another CS in a summation test, and to be retarded in acquiring
excitatory, CR-eliciting tendencies itself over a series of reinforced trials, just
as in the case of the Larew (1986) findings with a CS trained at an intermediate
backward interval with the US (Rescorla, 1969; Wagner & Rescorla, 1972).

A study by Savaadra reported by Wagner (1971) remains among the clearest
in indicating that the accrual of inhibition to a conditioned inhibitor depends on
its being paired with an excitatory CS or, as SOP would suppose, with conditioned activation of the US node to the A2 state. In this experiment, all subjects
received two cues A and B, differentially trained as excitatory CSs for the rabbit
conditioned eyeblink response. Cue A was presented and reinforced for 240 trials, while B was present and reinforced for only 8 trials. A third cue, C, to be
used in the test phase, was also highly trained in this phase. Following such training, a novel cue (X) was introduced in compound with either A or B for different
groups of rabbits, and the compound was nonreinforced, while the cue paired
with X continued to be presented alone and reinforced. The question was whether
X would become more inhibitory when trained with the stronger A cue as compared to the weaker B cue. This question was evaluated by returning the C cue,
and determining in a summation test the amount of reduction in conditioned
responding to C when in compound with X.

Figure 6.5 shows the data of interest from the test phase (involving 16 reinforced presentations of C and the compound CX for both groups). The two groups
responded at the same level to C alone. The addition of the X cue, however,
decreased this responding significantly more in the case of the group which had
previously experienced the nonreinforcement of X in compound with the relatively strong A cue than in the group which had experienced the nonreinforcement of X in compound with the relatively weak B cue. Inhibitory conditioning
appears to increase with the excitatory strength of the otherwise reinforced cue
with which the CS is paired.

The similarity of the inhibitory learning observed by Savaadra (Wagner, 1971)
to that observed by Larew (1986) is consistent with the assumptions of SOP regarding the nature of the representational activity that may be produced by an excitatory
CS versus the US with which it is associated. We would be remiss, however,
if we did not mention that an excitatory CS can appear, contrary to data such
as those of Savaadra, to confer excitatory effects on a neutral CS with which
it is paired. The phenomenon is, of course, "second-order conditioning" (Pavlov, 1927). Space allows us to say only that the careful investigation of this
phenomenon (e.g., Rashotte, 1981; Rescorla, 1980) suggests that it is accom-
plished, when it occurs, other than through induction of an excitatory link between the neutral CS and the US with which the excitatory CS had been trained.
A principle route, for example, is via an indirect associative link in which the
two CSs become associated (as SOP assumes they would), thereby allowing one
to access an associate of the other through a mediational bridge.

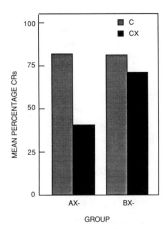

FIG. 6.5. Mean percentage conditioned responses in the evaluation of the conditioned inhibitory properties of X in two groups. For Group AX, X had been nonreinforced in compound with a relatively excitatory cue A, and for Group BX, X had been nonreinforced in compound with a less excitatory cue B. Drawn from Wagner (1971).

Refractory-like effects.

The stochastic assumptions of SOP concerning nodal dynamics make the A1 and A2 processes functional opponents in the sense that to the degree that a node is in the A2 state, it is less accessible for activation to the A1 state by appropriate stimulation. Figure 6.1b and 6.1c demonstrate the essential antagonism. That is, Fig. 6.1c presents identical simulations to those in Fig. 6.1b, but now including a target US presentation during the later phase of processing initiated by a US (top functions) or an excitatory CS (bottom functions). As may be seen, the target US does not in either case occasion the same level of A1 activity that it otherwise would (the A1 activity in the top function of Fig. 6.1b is the reference). The implications are that any behavioral consequences that are dependent upon A1 nodal activity being initiated by a US should potentially witness the kind of "refractory-like" effects which are depicted in Fig. 6.1c.

A major point of Fig. 6.1c is that a US and an excitatory CS have equivalent ability to confer a refractory-like effect on the processing of a subsequent US. This supposition has been central to our theorizing for some time (Wagner, 1976, 1978) and is believed to be supported by a considerable amount of prior research in our laboratory and other's. Here we will mention but some of the more obvious research examples, concerned with the predictable variation in the UR to a US and with the equally predictable variation in the excitatory, associative learning occasioned by a US.

Contemporaneous dissertations by Pfautz (1980) and Donegan (1981) demonstrated how the amplitude of rabbit eyeblink and gross body movement URs to a paraorbital shock US are diminished by either a shortly preceding instance of the same US or a preceding CS^+ with which the US has been paired. In the Pfautz (1980) study, USs were preceded by priming USs: rabbits were run in a single session with pairs of USs irregularly presented and separated by either .5, 2, or 16 sec. Figure 6.6a summarizes the major pattern of findings by showing the mean amplitude eyelid closure to a 5-mA target-US shock when that US was preceded by no shock (US), a 1-mA shock (US_1-US) 2-sec earlier or a 5-mA shock (US_5-US), also 2-sec earlier. Clearly, there was a decrement in responding to the target US when it was preceded by another shock, and this decrement was greater the higher the intensity of the priming US. In the Donegan (1981) study, rabbits were given discrimination training with auditory or visual CSs associated with US delivery (CS^+) or not (CS^-). Following the development of discriminative performance, test trials were arranged in which the UR was measured. Figure 6.6b depicts the mean amplitude eyelid closure with a 5-mA US, when that US was preceded by no CS (US), the CS^- (CS^--US), or the CS^+ (CS^+-US). As can be seen from this Figure, diminution of the UR was observed for those instances when the US was preceded by a CS^+ relative to CS^- and US-alone trials. The similarity of these results to those of Pfautz should be obvious.[3]

Another set of conceptually parallel studies was conducted by Terry (1976) and Savaadra (reported in Wagner, 1976), in this case demonstrating how the acquisition of a conditioned eyeblink response reinforced by a paraorbital shock US is diminished by either a shortly preceding instance of the same US or a preceding CS^+ with which the US has been paired. Terry (1976) trained rabbits with two CSs, one which was simply consistently reinforced by the presentation of a US, and a second which was similarly reinforced by a US but was also preceded 4 sec earlier by another, priming US. Figure 6.7a depicts the outcome of equivalent CS-alone test trials following the two training conditions. As is evident from this Figure, the percentage CRs was reliably less to a CS that was preceded by a US during training (US, CS-US) than to that which was not (CS–US). Savaadra (Wagner, 1976), using an experimental design which produces an effect we now refer to as "blocking" (Kamin, 1968), demonstrated a similar consequence with a previously trained CS^+. In this study, a novel cue (X) was reinforced in compound with either a stimulus that was highly trained as an excitatory CS (A), or an equivalent stimulus that was less trained (B). Following compound training, testing was administered so as to assess the level of conditioning that had accrued to X alone. As can be seen in Fig. 6.7b, responding to X was less frequent for the group which had had X trained in compound with A than for the group which had received X in compound with B.

---

[3]This brief synopsis cannot do justice to the findings of Donegan (1981) and Pfautz (1980), which did not ignore (as we do here) the behavior-generating, as well as the refractory-producing, effects of the priming stimuli. A fuller summary of the studies may be found in Wagner (1981).

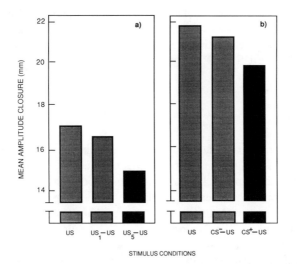

FIG. 6.6.   (a) Mean amplitude eyelid closure to a 5-mA shock US on trials when the designated target US was present in relative isolation (US),
was preceded by a 1-mA shock (US_1-US) or was preceded by a 5-mA
shock (US_5-US). (Drawn from Pfautz, 1980.) (b) Mean amplitude eyelid
closure to a 5-mA shock US on trials when the designated target US was
presented alone (US), was preceded by a CS^- (CS^--US), or was preceded
by a CS^+ (CS^+-US). Drawn from Donegan (1981).

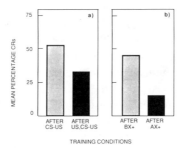

FIG. 6.7.   (a) Mean percentage conditioned responses to two CSs in a
test session, following CS-US pairings that were preceded by presentation of the same US(US,CS-US) or not (CS-US). Drawn from Terry (1976).
(b) Mean percentage conditioned responses to a cue X in a test session,
following training in which X was compounded with a highly excitatory
stimulus (AX+) or a less excitatory stimulus (BX+). Drawn from Wagner
(1976).

The similarity in the decremental effects of either a preceding instance of the same US or of a preceding excitatory CS is consistent with the assumption that both leave the US representation in a state other than that which would be initially provoked by the US. SOP denotes the state as A2.

II. CHALLENGES TO SOP

Although SOP is reasonably successful in accomplishing its aims, there are several classes of observations that make it clear that the model is, nonetheless, insufficient to meeting the general challenge that can be lodged against most stimulus-substitution notions. The essential problem lies in the simplifying assumption of SOP, that an experimental stimulus can be treated as identifiable with a *unitary* representation (node) in the memory system. This assumption leaves the theory vulnerable to observations in which there is some apparent dissociation among multiple "measures" of CS–US association so that it is theoretically embarrassing to hold that each reflects the acquired tendency of the CS to activate the same US node.

Divergence of response measures.

Suppose that there are two measurable CRs that come via CS-US pairings to be elicited by the same CS. According to SOP, both CRs would presumably reflect the tendency of the CS to activate the US node (to the A2 state) and should be stronger the more the conditions of training have increased the connection between the CS and US nodes (expressed in the associative value, V_{CS-US}). One might reasonably expect that one of the CRs would be a more or less sensitive measure of V_{CS-US} than the other, but with parametric variation in the conditions of training (e.g., variation in the number of trials, CS-US interval, US intensity, etc.) the two CRs should exhibit a concordance such that one measure could be expressed as a monotonic transform of the other. There should not be instances of so-called divergence of response measures over parametric variation in the conditions of training. However, there are data (e.g., Schneiderman, 1972; Vandercar & Schneiderman, 1967; Yehle, 1968) which appear to show that as the training conditions are made more effective for one CR measure, they are made less effective for another CR measure. For example, Vandercar and Schneiderman (1967) concurrently measured nictitating membrane responses and heart rate CRs in Pavlovian discrimination training with rabbits. Their data suggested that differential conditioned heart rate responding to reinforced and nonreinforced CSs was optimal when the CS–US interval was 2.25 sec, whereas differential conditioned nictitating membrane responding to the same stimuli was optimal when the CS-US interval was .75 sec.

Pharmacological and surgical manipulations

A second example should be seen as revealing the same problem. It is worthy of separate mention for arising in studies involving rather different experimental manipulations and for being recognizable as more or less interesting depending on companion information about the locus of the effects of the manipulations. Suppose again that there are two measurable CRs that come via CS-US pairings to be elicited by the CS, and it is assumed that both CRs reflect the acquired tendency of the CS to activate the same US node. It would be disturbing to this view if there were surgical and/or pharmacological treatments that would influence one CR measure and not the other, or, more generally, influence the two measures in different ways, unless the treatments had similar differential effects upon other measures involving those response systems. Each separable response measure can be expected to depend on different efferent mechanisms consequent to the US node, so that surgical and/or pharmacological treatments can be expected to influence one response measure differently than another by having effects at such loci. But such efferent effects should be evidenced in more general consequences; e.g., when tracing the pattern of the URs as well as CRs. There should not be instances of dissociation of response measures, *peculiar to the CR*, as a result of surgical or pharmacological treatment.

There are data (e.g., Buchanan & Powell, 1982; Powell, Hernandez, & Buchanan, 1985; Thompson et al., 1984) which have been purported to show that insult to one area of the nervous system or administration of a particular drug can selectively remove one CR without equivalently affecting another CR, and without companion differential effects on the general response systems involved. For example, systemic administration of muscarinic cholinergic antagonists, such as atropine and scopolomine, appear to interfere with acquisition of eyelid conditioning (Downs, Cardozo, Schneiderman, Yehle, Vandercar, & Zwilling, 1972; Kazis, Milligan, & Powell, 1973), while enhancing acquisition of conditioned bradycardia (Powell et al., 1985). In a study that has previously been mentioned, bilateral lesions of the dentate and interpositus nuclei of the cerebellum in the rabbit were found to prevent the acquisition of the NM/eyelid CR (Lincoln, McCormick, & Thompson, 1982), and to do so without impairing the motor response system as indicated with measures of the prominent initial eyeblink UR. It is significant, then, that the same lesion did not impair subjects' ability readily to acquire a conditioned heart rate deceleration to the same CS ineffective in eliciting conditioned eyeblinks (Thompson et al., 1986).

Modulation

A third example involves the potential dissociability of the tendency of a CS to *modulate* the conditioned responding occasioned by another CS from the tendency of the CS directly to excite or inhibit a characteristic CR. The distinction between the two tendencies has been vigorously made in recent studies (e.g., Bouton

& Bolles, 1985; Holland, 1985; Jenkins, 1985; Rescorla, 1985; Ross & Holland, 1981) on "occasion setting" in Pavlovian conditioning. A presumptive example of modulation is seen in a so-called feature-positive discrimination (where a compound CS, AX, is reinforced and one of the elements, X, is nonreinforced) when the animal responds to the compound AX and not to X, but also does not respond to A alone. In this case, it appears as though the "feature," A, is acting to facilitate the conditioned responding to X rather than to elicit such responding itself. In studies of this design and with the additional strategy of using qualitatively different CSs that are known to elicit CRs of characteristically different topography, Ross and Holland (1981) reported that the A cue appears to act *either* as a CR elicitor (increasing the likelihood of "its own" response on the occasion of AX versus X) or as a CR modulator (increasing the likelihood of the typical response to X on the occasions of AX versus X), depending upon the temporal arrangement of A to X in training: When A and X were coextensive, A behaved like a CR elicitor; when the onset and/or termination of A preceded that of X, A behaved like a CR modulator. The force of most of the literature on "occasion setting" that might further suggest that the modulating and eliciting characteristics acquired by a CS may be dissociable is clouded by the possibility that what is being observed is that CR elicitation can variously come under the control of isolable (e.g., A) or configural (e.g., A∩X) cues, as has otherwise been demonstrated (see e.g., Savaadra, 1975; Whitlow & Wagner, 1972). But the possibility must certainly be entertained that CS-US pairings can endow the CS with behavior-modulation tendencies that are theoretically separable from its CR-elicitation tendencies.

III. AESOP

The states of consciousness that accompany the activity of the [representations] . . . . have a two-fold aspect. In the first place, they are symbolic of occurrences in the environment . . . In the second place, they carry with them what is figuratively spoken of as a "tone" of pleasurable or painful feeling . . . . (C. Lloyd Morgan, 1894, pp. 186-187).

There is a rather well-understood, general way to approach the form of theoretical problem that has been exemplified in the preceding section. Put succinctly, one can acknowledge that representation of a US involves multiple US nodes that (a) code for dissociable components of the stimulus, (b) have differentiable behavioral consequences, and (c) can have their separate connections to CS nodes independently modified. Konorski (1967) included such reasoning in his final treatment of Pavlovian conditioning, and Mackintosh (1983) is (as usual) perceptive of its essence. As Mackintosh indicates, Konorski distinguished between the representation of the "emotional" attributes of any US and the representation of the remaining "sensory" attributes of the stimulus. He then assumed that CS-US pairings could lead to independent connections between the CS representations and the distinguishable US representations, according to separate parametric considerations, and as witnessed in characteristically different CRs. The association involving a CS and an emotive attribute was presumed to be reflected in the development of "preparatory CRs," generally being "diffuse" activity changes in keeping with the appetitive or aversive value of the US. The association involving a CS and the sensory attributes was presumed to be reflected in the development of "consummatory CRs," generally being "discrete" reflexes in keeping with the specific sensorium that is stimulated by the US.

It should be apparent how such an approach could, in principle, address the aforementioned problem of divergence of response measures, if the measures under consideration were from the different classes of preparatory versus consummatory responses, and if there were reason to suppose that variation in conditions of training (e.g., in CS-US interval) has dissimilar implications for associations involving the emotive versus sensory representations of the US. Konorski (1967) offered some speculations on this point. It should similarly be obvious that a given pharmacological or surgical manipulation could have differential impact upon one associative consequence versus the other, to influence the development and/or maintenance of preparatory CRs differently than consummatory CRs. Thompson et al. (1984) have suggested that such partitioning is just what may be seen in the neural circuit investigation we have mentioned. It is also reasonable to suppose that if this manner of distinction were useful, it might embrace some of the "occasion setting" findings on the modulation versus elicitation of CRs. It is well accepted that emotional Pavlovian conditioned response tendencies ("fear," "hope," etc.) modulate some kinds of unconditioned responses (see e.g., the extensive work of Davis, 1984, 1986, on modulation of the acoustic startle response), and acquired instrumental behaviors (see e.g., Rescorla & Solomon, 1967, in review of phenomena such as the CER). But there has been a notable reluctance seriously to entertain the notion that one (emotional-preparatory) Pavlovian response tendency might systematically modulate other (sensory-consummatory) Pavlovian CRs.

'AESOP' is the name of the current working model to which this reasoning has led us. It is a dual-representation version of SOP that supposes that stimulus coding involves theoretically separable "emotive" as well as "sensory" components, in line with the distinction made by Konorski (1967). AESOP is an "affective extension of SOP." It assumes that the presumably separable, sensory and emotional representations of a stimulus generally behave like separate nodes in SOP. That is, it assumes that each has an activity sequence of an A1 and A2 phase, in order, when initiated by the stimulus attributes that it unconditionally represents, and an activity of only A2, when initiated via associative connections by a conditioned stimulus. And it embraces all of the companion assumptions and implications of SOP that have been reviewed above, regarding the relationship of conditioned to unconditioned responding, excitatory versus inhibitory learning, and refractory-like effects, but now germane to each of the separate nodes.

The separability of the sensory and emotional nodes is expressed theoretically in two distinct ways. One way is in the assumption of orthogonality with stimulus variation. For example, one may assume that two USs are unlike in the sensory nodes that they activate but are alike in the emotive node that they activate (e.g., if they are applied to different receptive areas but are both "aversive"). The second is that the parameters of nodal activation and subsequent dynamics are free to be different in the two nodes concurrently activated by a stimulus. The most obvious instance of allowable difference is in the parameter of initial activation (the p_1 parameter of Fig. 6.1a). For example, whereas a typical Pavlovian US is likely to strongly activate both a sensory and emotional node, a typical Pavlovian CS may strongly activate a sensory node while only weakly activating an emotional node. Indeed, following this reasoning, we will generally ignore the emotional nodal activity generated by CSs, except as a consequence of conditioning. For reasons that are described in more detail below, AESOP also tentatively assumes that the time course of the A1 and A2 activity following nodal activation is more protracted (p_{d1} and p_{d2} in Fig. 6.1a, are smaller) in the case of emotional than sensory nodes. This difference should lead to corresponding differences in the persistence of the behaviors generated by emotional versus sensory nodal activity, and to differences in the CS-US interval function when assessed by CRs that presumably reflect the links that develop between a CS and the two classes of nodes.

In particular line with Konorski (1967) and in general sympathy with numerous "two-process" theorists (e.g., Mowrer, 1947; Rescorla & Solomon, 1967; Schlosberg, 1937; Thompson et al., 1986; Weinberger, 1982), we also assume that whereas the prominent behavioral consequence of conditioned (A2) activity of a sensory node is the elicitation of a discrete response, the prominent behavioral consequence of similar conditioned (A2) activity of an emotional node is the *diffuse modulation of behavior otherwise inititated*. The conditioned eyeblink response is presumed to typify the former, while the conditioned modulation of general activity (e.g., Bindra & Palfai, 1967), instrumental behavior (e.g., Rescorla & Solomon, 1967), and unconditioned reflexes (e.g., Davis, 1984) are presumed to exemplify the latter. Important to AESOP is the assumption that conditioned emotional activity can modulate discrete Pavlovian CRs (Konorski, 1967; Thompson et al., 1986) as well as other behaviors. A major challenge in developing a computational version of these notions will be in deciding how to characterize abstractly the locus and mechanism(s) of modulation. At the moment, we do not commit AESOP with respect to the numerous plausible alternatives (see e.g., Kandel, 1977; Konorski, 1967: Rescorla, 1985), except to insist that the modulation is by such route as to influence conditioned and unconditioned behavior. Fig. 6.8 attempts to capture the essence of AESOP as it may be contrasted with the conception of SOP depicted in Fig. 6.1a. The important message is that the activity of emotive US nodes (USϵ) need be separated from the activity of sensory US nodes (USσ), because they can come to have different associative connec-

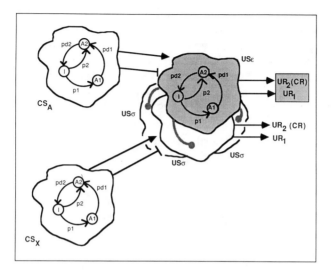

FIG. 6.8.   A depiction of nodes in the memory system of AESOP. Different here from the depiction of the nodes of SOP in Fig. 6.1a is the distinction between "sensory" and "emotive" US nodes labeled USσ and USε, respectively. See text for description of the characteristic differences.

tions with experimental CSs, can produce different URs and CRs, and interact such that emotive nodes can modulate the activity of sensory nodes.

Application to CS-US interval functions

AESOP is designed to allow for certain differences in CS-US interval functions for the behavioral measures that reflect conditioning involving the sensory versus the emotive aspects of a stimulus. In the preceding sketch of AESOP, it was indicated that whereas it is assumed that the presumably separable, sensory and emotional representations of a US each generally behaves like a node in SOP, the dynamic parameters (p_{d1} and p_{d2}) that govern the time course of the A1 and A2 phases of nodal activity are different in the two cases. Specifically, AESOP assumes that the decay parameters are smaller in the case of emotional as compared to sensory nodes, so that, following nodal activation, the A1 phase is more persistent and the A2 phase is both slower to recruit and more persistent. This has interesting implications for both "forward" and "backward" conditioning, but especially for the latter.

Figure 6.9 shows the results of simulations of backward conditioning with a punctate US followed by a punctate CS, that may be compared to those of Fig. 6.2. Panel *a* reproduces the same A1 activity course of the CS, and the same A1 and A2 activity courses of the US as depicted in Fig. 6.2, which were based on values of $p_{d1} = .1$ and $p_{d2} = .02$ in each case. It then adds a further set of

A1 and A2 processes, indicated to be initiated by the US, and identified with substantially lower decay rates, specifically, with $p_{d1} = .02$ and $p_{d2} = .004$ (but maintaining the relationship $p_{d1} = 5p_{d2}$). AESOP supposes that this more persistant US-nodal activity is characteristic of emotive versus sensory nodes, and the nodal activity has been thus labeled. The differential consequences for associative learning are depicted in panel *b*. The function now labeled 'USσ' is identical to the backward portion of the US-CS interval function in Fig. 6.2, showing the same initial excitatory learning, followed by inhibitory learning at an intermediate interval, prior to eventual absence of associative effect. In comparison it may be seen that whereas the function labeled 'USϵ' evidences the same *pat-*

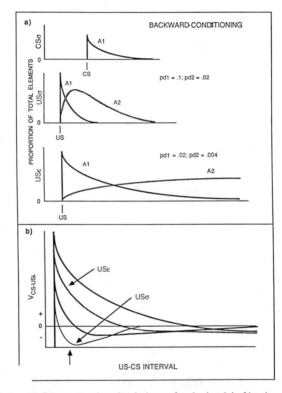

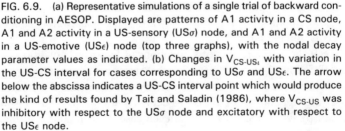

FIG. 6.9.   (a) Representative simulations of a single trial of backward conditioning in AESOP. Displayed are patterns of A1 activity in a CS node, A1 and A2 activity in a US-sensory (USσ) node, and A1 and A2 activity in a US-emotive (USϵ) node (top three graphs), with the nodal decay parameter values as indicated. (b) Changes in V_{CS-US_i} with variation in the US-CS interval for cases corresponding to USσ and USϵ. The arrow below the abscissa indicates a US-CS interval point which would produce the kind of results found by Tait and Saladin (1986), where V_{CS-US} was inhibitory with respect to the USσ node and excitatory with respect to the USϵ node.

tern, it is markedly displaced in time, so that at the point marked by the arrow on the abscissa, V_{CS-US_o} is near maximally negative while V_{CS-US_ϵ} is very substantially positive. The unlabeled functions represent similar simulations with intermediate or more extreme US decay values to emphasize the regularity of the predicted shift in backward conditioning effects as p_{d1} and p_{d2} are made smaller.

AESOP thus leads to the rather unique prediction that, with separate assessment of associations reflecting the emotive and sensory characteristics of a US, the appropriate choice of US-CS interval may yield indices of CS-US associations that are inhibitory in terms of one measure and excitatory in terms of another. Tait and Saladin (1986) have provided data that appear to show just such an effect. After training rabbits with a single backward US-CS interval (where the US was a 100-msec paraorbital shock, the CS was a 1000-msec tone, and the US-CS interval was 500 msec), the behavioral properties of the CS were assessed in two independent ways: in a conditioned punishment test, measuring the tendency of the CS to suppress on-going drinking behavior when administered in a lick-contingent fashion (a presumptive measure of fear conditioning), and in an eyeblink acquisition test, assessing the effect of the backward pairings to influence development of the eyeblink response over a series of forward, CS-US conditioning trials (a common "savings" measure of the association reflected in the eyeblink CR). The results are shown in Fig. 6.10. The observation was, that in relationship to the performance of comparison groups that had been exposed to either forward CS-US pairings, the CS alone, the US alone, or no stimulation, the performance of the group trained with the backward interval showed the CS to be excitatory on the fear measure (i.e., the CS suppressed drinking, similarly to the case of the forward pairings) and inhibitory on the eyeblink measure (i.e., acquisition of the eyeblink response was impaired). This is precisely the kind of reflection of divergence of response measures that AESOP is calculated to address. The US–CS interval employed presumably caused the CS nodal activity to overlap preferentially with A1 activity of the slower-to-decay emotional US node, causing excitatory learning, but preferentially with A2 activity of the faster-to-decay sensory US node, concurrently causing inhibitory learning. A candidate point is marked by the arrow on the US–CS interval of Fig. 6.9b.

The Tait and Saladin findings are, we think, of major importance. They deserve to be replicated and systematically extended. AESOP offers the clear prediction that the relationship between the two measures of conditioned suppression and eyeblink conditioning will systematically change as depicted in Fig. 6.9b, with increasing US–CS intervals. At sufficiently short intervals and with appropriately sensitive tests (e.g., Wagner & Terry, 1975), both the eyeblink and fear measures should be excitatory; at longer intervals, including those used by Tait and Saladin, the fear measure should be excitatory while the eyeblink measure is inhibitory; at still longer intervals the fear measure should be more inhibitory than the eyeblink measure, which will more quickly of the two return to neutrality.

The presumed differences in the nodal dynamics of emotional versus sensory

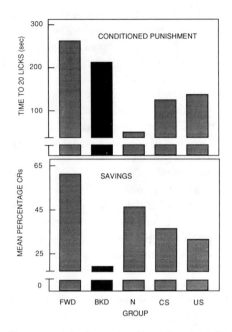

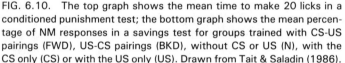

FIG. 6.10.   The top graph shows the mean time to make 20 licks in a
conditioned punishment test; the bottom graph shows the mean percentage of NM responses in a savings test for groups trained with CS-US
pairings (FWD), US-CS pairings (BKD), without CS or US (N), with the
CS only (CS) or with the US only (US). Drawn from Tait & Saladin (1986).

representations do not have such rich implications for differences in the CS–US
interval functions over the range of *forward intervals*. What they do lead to,
without further assumptions, is the expectation of greater net excitatory learning
over all forward intervals in the case of emotive as compared to sensory conditioning. If the A1 activity of emotional nodes is slower to decay and hence the
A2 activity is slower to recruit, it would be expected that any CS that has its
A1 trace decaying over these times (as is presumed for those CSs that terminate
with or before the US) would acquire relatively greater advantage of excitatory
versus inhibitory learning and hence greater net associative strength. This provides a rationalization for the well-known fact emphasized by Konorski (1967),
that measures of "preparatory" conditioning, such as the CER (e.g., Kamin,
1965), reveal substantial excitatory learning over CS–US intervals much longer
than those that are effective for discrete "consummatory" responses such as the
eyeblink (e.g., Smith, Coleman, & Gormezano, 1969).

On the other hand, the theory does not obviously anticipate other potential
differences in the nature of the forward CS–US interval function for associations
involving emotional versus sensory US nodes, e.g., the notion of Konorski (1967)
that while consummatory CRs are better acquired with short CS–US intervals,
preparatory CRs are better acquired with longer intervals. It should be recog-

nized that the empirical data on this point remain unclear. For example, Ross (1961), using human subjects, found that potentiation of the unconditioned eyeblink response by an aversively trained CS was substantial only following CS-shock intervals that were considerably *longer* (2 to 10-sec) than the 0.5-sec interval that would have been optimal for eyeblink conditioning. On the other hand, in another example, Davitz, Mason, and Mowrer (1957) found that conditioned freezing in rats trained with CS–US intervals varying between 0 and 600 sec, was simply greater the *shorter* the CS–US interval.

The shape of the forward CS–US function predicted by SOP (and AESOP), in fact, varies with several characteristics of training beyond what can be described here. Thus, for example, while Fig. 6.3 shows the predictions following a single trace-conditioning trial to be a monitonically decreasing function with increasing CS–US intervals, Mazur and Wagner (1982) show, via like simulations, the predictions following a delayed conditioning trial (where the CS continues until the time of the US) to be a nonmonotonic function, with a maximum at some intermediate CS duration close to the US. And they allow how multiple-trial procedures might be expected to impose a secondary sharpening on the function via temporal discrimination and stimulus-competition effects. Some of these complications may have differential influences on conditioning involving the sensory versus emotive US representation. But to a first approximation, AESOP does not expect there to be any difference in such characteristics as the overall shape of the forward CS–US interval function or the interval of maximum conditioning as a result of the differences that are supposed in the dynamics of emotive and sensory nodes. It will be important further to evaluate how the empirical forward CS–US interval functions differ.

Application to modulation

AESOP assumes that whereas conditioned (A2) activity of sensory and emotive nodes may both be evident in the elicitation of conditioned responses, a prominent behavioral consequence of conditioned activity of an emotive node is (also) the diffuse *modulation of behavior otherwise initiated*. The possibility can thus be entertained that some of the evidence concerning "occasion setting" could be attributable to the fact that a CS that controls the activation of an emotive US node can have a modulatory influence on the response elicited by a CS associated with a sensory US node. That is to say, in a feature positive (AX+, X−) discrimination, where A is a relatively long cue which precedes the X cue, it is quite possible that the differential responding to AX versus X reflects the tendency of A to potentiate or modulate the CR to X rather than produce the response itself. This is consistent with the previously mentioned observation of Ross and Holland (1981) that in some circumstances, A increases the likelihood of the response characteristically evoked by X rather than producing a response typically evoked by A.

We have recently sought to evaluate the theoretical usefulness of conceiving of occasion setting occurring in this way, via the interaction of separate US nodes representing the emotive and sensory characteristics of Pavlovian USs, as outlined in AESOP. Variations upon the rabbit eyeblink conditioning situation that has frequently been used to advantage in our laboratory (e.g., Donegan, 1981; Pfautz & Wagner, 1976; Savaadra, 1975; Terry & Wagner, 1975; Wagner & Terry, 1975) appeared ideally suited to this research. The conditioned eyeblink response is a prototypical discrete CR, under the tight control of CSs that are closely timed to the US (e.g., Smith et al., 1969), but the same paraorbital shock US as employed in the conditioning of this response produces a variety of other conditioned behaviors in the rabbit, such as heart-rate changes (e.g., Powell et al., 1985; Schneiderman, 1972; Schneiderman, Smith, Smith, & Gormezano, 1966) that are often taken to be reflective of the class of diffuse emotional response tendencies. And, most pointedly, the results of neurobiological and pharmacological investigations with this preparation, such as those we have mentioned, have led Thompson and his colleagues (Thompson et al., 1986) to the tentative inference that the conditioned eyeblink response may be modulated by fear responses conditioned to situational stimuli. However, whereas there are some examples of discriminated conditioned eyeblink responding in the rabbit that would invite description as involving "occasion setting" (e.g., Gormezano & Kehoe, 1983; Kehoe, Marshall-Goodell, & Gormezano, 1987; Kehoe & Morrow, 1984; Terry & Wagner, 1975), there were no reasonably direct demonstrations in the literature that the conditioned eyeblink response is subject to modulation by experimentally isolable contextual stimuli that might be entertained also to control separable conditioned emotional response tendencies. Our investigations of these possibilities have only begun, but data collected thus far in several unpublished experiments are strongly encouraging.

Experiment 1 was intended as both an initial exploration of the robustness of "occasion-setting" within the eyeblink situation and the reasonableness of the modulation interpretation. Eight rabbits were first given partial reinforcement training with a conventional, brief CS (a 1050-msec light or vibrotactual stimulus, designated "X") overlapping and terminating with a 50-msec paraorbital shock US on half of the occasions. This phase of training also involved two manipulable "contextual" stimuli which were a 30-sec, 3500-Hz tone and a 30-sec broad-spectrum noise, designated "A" or "B" in counterbalanced fashion. These were presented in a pseudorandom sequence, separated by 90-sec interstimulus intervals. The conventional CS, X, was programmed to occur (with equal likelihood) either 7, 12, 17, 22, or 27 sec into the A and B contextual stimuli, and was consistently reinforced in the A context and nonreinforced in the B context. Had the A and B stimuli been conventional CSs coextensive with the X cue, we would have expected on the basis of prior investigations (e.g., Wagner, Logan, Haberlandt, & Price, 1968) that the subjects would have learned to respond discriminatively on AX versus BX trials as a result of excitatory and inhibitory tendencies accruing to the positive (A) and negative (B) features. In this case, however, we could assume that the temporal relationship between the contexts and the US were considerably beyond the bounds generally believed to be effective for eyeblink conditioning (e.g., Smith et al., 1969) while still within the realm of intervals that would produce "fear" conditioning (e.g., Rescorla & Solomon, 1967; Wagner & Larew, 1985).

With daily training sessions of 288 total A(X+) and B(X−) trials, there were reliably greater conditioned eyeblink responses to X in the former as compared to the latter trials on the third day of training and following. The left panel of Fig. 6.11 exemplifies the effects observed by presenting the mean amplitude of the eyeblink CR recorded to X in the two contexts from a final test session that followed six training sessions, and in which X was consistently presented in the midpoint of presentations of A or B; i.e., 17 sec after stimulus onset.

It is important to the modulation notion that in neither this nor any earlier session was there any observed tendency for A or B alone to elicit the eyeblink response. It is, however, possible that there was differential conditioned responding to the specific A(X) and B(X) stimuli as a result of associative learning involving stimulus patterns or configurations (e.g., Hull, 1943; Whitlow & Wagner, 1972) unique to the occasions. Thus, it was also important to assess whether or not the apparent modulation produced by A and B would generalize to another, highly discriminable, conventional CS with which the contexts had not been trained. For this purpose, following the development of differential responding to A(X) and B(X), another CS, Y (the aforementioned 1050-msec cue not used as X for individual subjects) was partially reinforced in the absence of either A or B, but then was tested in the two contexts. The right panel of Fig. 6.11 depicts the results taken from the same test session as those in the left panel. The amplitude of the eyeblink CR elicited by Y was reliably greater when evaluated in context A rather than alone, and was reliably less when evaluated in context B rather than alone.

The differential conditioned eyeblink responding in the A and B contexts in Experiment 1 appears to represent the kind of modulation proposed by AESOP insomuch as the responding did not appear to be directly elicited by A versus B, and was not peculiar to the training configuration A(X) versus B(X), but was seen when a separately trained cue (Y) was tested in their presence. One cannot tell from these data, however, whether or not the *development* of the modulation tendencies was dependent upon the differential reinforcement of X (or some similar, eyeblink-eliciting stimulus) in the two contexts during training, where A and B provided consistent prediction of occasions for the reinforcement and nonreinforcement of X. Such dependence has generally been emphasized in the occasion-setting literature (e.g., Holland, 1983; Rescorla, 1985), whereas the simpler alternative is that the contexts need only have been associated with differential schedules of the aversive US sufficient to be differentially "fear" producing. To evaluate the sufficiency of the latter alternative, Experiment 2 was conducted.

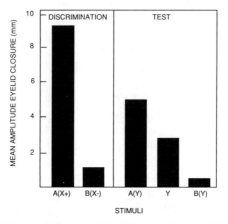

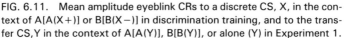

FIG. 6.11.   Mean amplitude eyeblink CRs to a discrete CS, X, in the context of A[A(X+)] or B[B(X−)] in discrimination training, and to the transfer CS, Y in the context of A[A(Y)], B[B(Y)], or alone (Y) in Experiment 1.

This experiment was identical to Experiment 1, except as noted, including eight subjects and the same counterbalanced stimuli. In this case, X was omitted, so that the subjects received discrimination training with one context, A(+), regularly including a US at the same positions as in Experiment 1, but otherwise unsignaled, and the other context, B(-), not including US occurrence. Y was again partially reinforced in isolation as in Experiment 1, but this training was begun prior to the A(+)/B(−) experience and then was interspersed with the context discrimination training. The final test session was similar to that in Experiment 1, with the novel presentation of Y within the A and B contexts as well as the presentation of Y alone. Figure 6.12 summarizes the findings. The left panel displays the mean amplitude eyelid closures observed at the points in the two contexts equivalent to the scheduled occasions for X in Experiment 1, and for Y in the same session. It makes the obvious point that the contexts alone, at the moments measured, did not produce any eyeblink responses. The right panel displays the mean amplitude eyeblink responses to Y under the several test conditions. The greater response to Y in the A context than alone or than in the B context was highly reliable. There was less responding to Y in the B context than alone, but this difference was not statistically significant.

Experiments 1 and 2 are clear in showing that a contextual stimulus that has been paired with application of an aversive paraorbital shock US will potentiate the conditioned eyeblink CR to a brief CS that has otherwise been paired with the same US. Because the temporal relationship between the contextual stimulus and the US was unlike those that are generally taken to be necessary for developing an association that will cause a CS to elicit an eyeblink CR in this preparation (e.g., Smith et al., 1969), and because there was no detectable tendency for the contexts alone to produce eyelid closure, we are encouraged to think that the contexts acquired a modulating tendency (that might be mediated by association with an emotive representation of the US) that is separate from any eyeblink CR-eliciting tendency (that might be mediated by association with a sensory representation of the US). It is possible, however, to view the same data as challenging our usual assumptions about the effective temporal relationships for eyeblink conditioning, and as suggesting that the compound tests were sensitive in revealing a conventional association between the context and the US (i.e., similar to that between the brief CS and the US) to a degree that the tests of conditioned responding to the context alone were not. In effect, one could conclude that the strength of the context-US association was subthreshold for response elicitation, but substantial. Experiments 3 and 4 were appropriate next steps in an attempt to resolve these competing interpretations (which are of the essence of the abstract issue involving unitary versus multiple US nodes).

If the contextual stimuli of Experiments 1 and 2 were effective by virtue of the control which they exercised over an emotional representation (fear) of the aversive US, then one might expect to observe a potentiation of the eyeblink UR to the US just as there was potentiation of the eyeblink CR to the CS. The potentiation of unconditioned defensive reflexes by a stimulus previously paired with an aversive US is exceedingly well known and has become, arguably, the most useful "measure" of fear in various theoretical and practical contexts (e.g., Davis, 1984, 1986). And potentiation of the eyeblink UR has specifically been used (in humans) in studies of fear conditioning (e.g., Ross, 1961).

These facts become especially interesting in the context of attempts to distinguish between associative *modulation* and associative *combination*, because the most prominent effect of associative combination is a decrease in the amplitude of the UR when a US is preceded by an effective CS. The phenomenon has been

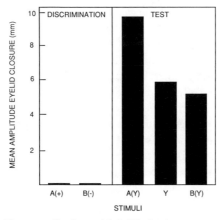

FIG. 6.12.   Mean amplitude eyeblink CRs in the context of A[A(+)] or B[B(−)] in discrimination training, and to the CS, Y, in the context of A[A(Y)], B[B(Y)], or alone (Y) in Experiment 2.

termed the "conditioned diminution of the UR" (Kimble & Ost, 1961) and has been studied in our laboratory (Donegan, 1981), as described earlier, as an instance of associatively generated refractory-like effects. That is, we have understood it in terms of the A2 process generated by the CS precluding the full A1 activity being generated by a US, as exemplified in the top graph of Fig. 6.1c. There is one complication. In the eyeblink conditioning situation, in which both A1 and A2 activity of the US node (we need now say 'sensory node') are assumed to generate eyeblink responses (to different degrees), the measured eyeblink response at the time of the US is, in fact, facilitated at *low* US intensities when preceded by a conventional CS+ as compared to when alone (Donegan, 1981). But the contrasting expectations are relatively clear: If the contextual stimulus in Experiments 1 and 2 were effective in potentiating the CR by virtue of associative summation, it should be expected concomitantly to diminish the unconditioned eyeblink response to the paraorbital-shock US at moderate to strong intensities, as observed in other instances and as shown in Fig. 6.6b; alternatively, if the contextual stimulus were effective in potentiating the CR by virtue of modulation, mediated by separable conditioned emotional processes, it should be expected to potentiate the unconditioned eyeblink response over these same intensities (up to some ceiling, of course).

These contrasting predictions were tested in a third experiment conducted in our laboratory, in collaboration with Joan Bombace and William Falls. We used exactly the same training protocol as in the previous experiment: eight rabbits were run with two contextual stimuli, A and B, and separately trained Y cue. But rather than examine the modulation of CRs to Y in the context of A or B, we looked at the effect of A and B on the unconditioned responding to paraorbital shocks at three levels of shock intensity, 1.5, 3.0, and 4.5 mA. Performance in the test session is shown in Fig. 6.13. The amplitude of the URs increased as expected with increasing shock intensity. And, as predicted by AESOP, stimulus A facilitated the UR at each level of shock intensity: i.e., UR amplitude was reliably greater in the context of A than of B at all three intensities. The somewhat greater response to the US in B than alone was not statistically significant, but might suggest either some generalization of the modulation effect that accrued to A, or perhaps more likely, an unconditioned response-facilitation effect (see, e.g., Ison & Leonard, 1971; Weisz & LoTurco, 1988).

AESOP specifically suggests that the kind of UR modulation seen in Experiment 3 should be quite general, so as to apply to defensive URs provoked by stimuli other than the US involved in acquisition of the modulating tendency. The UR modulation by fearful CSs that has been most studied is the potentiation of the acoustically elicited startle response (e.g. Davis, 1984, 1986). We anticipated that if the contextual stimulus used in the preceding modulation studies were effective in potentiating the eyeblink CR and UR by virtue of engendering a conditioned emotional reaction, then they should be similarly effective in potentiating a startle response to an adequate stimulus. This prediction was the focus of

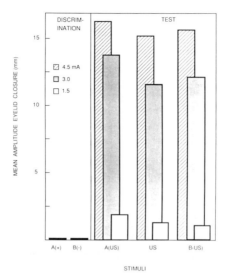

FIG. 6.13.   Mean amplitude eyeblink responses in the context of A[A(+)]
or B[B(−)] in discrimination training, and mean amplitude eyeblink URs
in the context of A[A(US)], B[B(US)], or alone (US) across three levels
of US intensity in Experiment 3.

Experiment 4. Following the test session just described, the same rabbits were
retrained and then subjected to a test similar to that of Experiment 3 but with
a brief startle-eliciting stimulus as the probe stimulus. The stimulus was a 50-msec,
$3.4 \times 10^4 \mathrm{N/m^2}$ airpuff directed to the left ear at a point 3 cm exterior to the auditory canal. The startle reaction was measured via EMG activity recorded from
surface electrodes placed above the *trapezius, pars cervicallis* muscle of the neck.
Figure 6.14 summarizes the findings in a manner similar to the eyeblink findings
in the preceding studies. There was negligible EMG activity recorded to the A
and B contexts alone. But there was reliable facilitation of the startle response
to the air puff by A relative to that seen in the presence of B or to the air puff alone.

There has been an abundance of recent suggestions (e.g., Bouton & Bolles,
1985; Holland, 1985; Jenkins, 1985; Rescorla, 1985) to the effect that one Pavlovian CS may act, not directly to elicit a characteristic CR, but rather somehow
to "enable", "gate", or "set the occasion" for the eliciting tendency of another
CS. Such surely appears to have been exemplified in Experiments 1 and 2 in
which the A and B contextual stimuli controlled different amplitudes of conditioned eyeblink response to the discrete X and Y CSs. There are numerous ways
in which such gating-like effects could be brought about, and, indeed, it appears
most likely that different mechanisms have been involved in different reported
instances. For example, Holland (1983, 1985), in an appetitive, activity-
conditioning situation with rats has generally observed that the occasion-setter

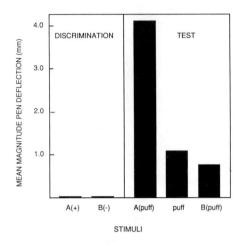

FIG. 6.14. Mean amplitude pen deflection for EMG-response to an air-puff startle stimulus, delivered to the ear, in the context of A[A(+)] or B[B(−)] in discrimination training, and in the context of A [A(puff)], B[B(puff)], or alone (puff) in Experiment 4.

has influence only on the response to a specific CS with which it has been trained, i.e., does not show the kind of transfer of control from CS_X to CS_Y observed in Experiment 1. As is often acknowledged (e.g., Jenkins, 1985), such specific effect could as well be described as indicating that the subjects resolved the discrimination problem by forming controlling associations to a configural cue (e.g., Whitlow & Wagner, 1972).

The sense of the several observations in Experiments 1 through 4 is that the gating observed in the situation under investigation was notably different. The A and B contextual stimuli came to control not only different amplitudes of the conditioned eyeblink response to a discrete CS, but also of the unconditioned eyeblink response to the paraorbital, training US, and of the unconditioned startle response to an unrelated, air puff stimulus to the ear. Much more research will be required in order to characterize fully the acquisition and expression of the modulation observed. But the general distinction included in AESOP of the separability of emotive and sensory US nodes, with the former having modulatory effects that includes influence upon the latter, appears well-grounded.

IV. CONCLUDING COMMENTS

A substitution view of Pavlovian conditioning, whether it be that the CS comes to have an acquired equivalence to the US or that the response to the CS comes to have an acquired quivalence to the UR, instantiates what Bolles (1975) has called the ''correspondence assumption.'' In either its S-S or S-R form it involves the reasoning that conditioning leads to connections between theoretical representations and/or processes that correspond rather simply to the stimuli and/or behaviors of training. What is remarkable is not that such reasoning would be judged lacking (Bolles, 1975), for such has been the informed judgment since the early systematic investigations of conditioning (e.g., Warner, 1932; Zener, 1937). What is remarkable is that few serious alternatives have been developed and comparatively evaluated, so that in casual accounts commentators often fall back on the substitution (correspondence) reasoning.

Modern studies of animal learning have granted considerable attention to Pavlovian conditioning. But one could argue that the research has been instigated less by an interest in explaining the essential features of Pavlovian conditioning, per se, than by the perceived advantages that such conditioning presents for addressing some of the fundamental, transituational issues of associative learning. For example, Kamin (1969), Rescorla (1969), and Wagner (1969) focused on studies from two conditioning preparations, eyeblink conditioning in the rabbit and the conditioned emotional response in the rat, for what they might reveal about how associative learning comes, more-or-less generally, to reflect the relative validity of available cues. The situations can be well controlled. And, Kamin, Rescorla, and Wagner could simply suppose that the well-mannered observed tendency for a CS followed by paraorbital shock to produce eyelid closure, or the similar tendency for a CS followed by footshock to cause freezing, was a monotonic reflection of CS–US association. From the available data, theorists such as Wagner and Rescorla (1972), Mackintosh (1975), and Pearce and Hall (1980) could proceed to the construction and evaluation of the kinds of contrasting proposals concerning associative learning that are described in Chapters 2 and 5.

It is another thing to ask why the measure of association involving the eyelid CR should be a closure that resembles the prominent topography of the UR, whereas the measure of association involving the CER should correspond to a decrease in activity quite opposite to the agitated immediate UR. Likewise, although the eyelid CR and the CER both show sensitivity to the contingency that is arranged between CS and US, as well as to the relative validity of the available CSs (e.g., Kamin, 1969; Rescorla, 1969; Wagner, 1969), one must question the adequacy of our understanding of these effects if our theories do not explain how a given temporal relationship between CS and US can have opposite associative consequences on one measure versus the other (Tait & Saladin, 1986). SOP was developed (Donegan & Wagner, 1987; Mazur & Wagner, 1982; Pfautz, 1980; Wagner, 1981) in an attempt to address certain of the essential features of Pavlovian conditioning, features that have here been organized around the observed character of conditioned and unconditioned responding, the occasions for excitatory and inhibitory learning and apparent refractory-like effects of CSs and

USs. The extension to AESOP was deemed necessary to address certain additional features of Pavlovian conditioning that we have here organized around the divergence of response measures and phenomena of CR modulation.

SOP and AESOP are connectionist models. Theories of Pavlovian conditioning have rarely been offered in any other terms. Even when interpretations have been otherwise couched, a connectionist structure is usually transparent. Wagner (1976, 1978), for example, presented an information processing theory centered around the presumed operating characteristics of short-term memory, but also pointed out how its assumptions and predictions were isomorphic to those of a connectionist network (see also Pfautz & Wagner, 1976). The connectionist theme in theories of Pavlovian conditioning is noteworthy in so much as one of the more profound changes that has occurred in theories of cognition over the past decade has been a shift in interest from rule-based symbol-manipulation formalisms congruent with a serial computer to connectionist conceptualizations involving massively interconnected, neuron-like elements in parallel computation (see Hinton & Anderson, 1981; Rumelhardt & McClelland, 1986). Many authors (e.g., Gluck & Bower, 1988; Sutton & Barto, 1981) have thus suggested that conditioning propositions should find useful integration into network models of more complex phenomena, the use of the delta rule of Rescorla and Wagner (1972) being a good example. If this is so, then it should be appreciated that a thrust of the present chapter is that there is need to recognize the structural givens in the network within which connections are modified. This is one of the messages of SOP in the manner in which it attempts to lend understanding to what is and is not consistent in the relationship that obtains between CRs and URs. It is an even more obvious message of AESOP in its assumption that one class of nodes modulates another in an asymmetric relationship. We think this message is worth taking away, even if the particular provisional models prove mistaken.

The Man and the Lion

A Man and a Lion traveled together through the forest. They soon began to boast of their respective superiority to each other in strength and prowess. As they were disputing, they passed a statue, carved in stone, which represented ''A Lion strangled by a Man.'' The traveler pointed to it and said: ''See there! How strong we are, and how we prevail over even the king of beasts.'' The Lion replied: ''This statue was made by one of you men. If we Lions knew how to erect statues, you would see the man placed under the paw of the Lion.''
One story is good till another is told.
(attributed to Aesop by Sir Roger L'Estrange, Kt., in *Fables of Aesop*, 1704.

ACKNOWLEDGMENTS

The research reported here and preparation of the chapter were supported in part by National Science Foundation Grants BNS80-23399 and BNS-8709680 to

Allan R. Wagner and a MacArthur Foundation Postdoctoral Fellowship to Susan E. Brandon.

REFERENCES

Babbini, M., & Davis, W. M. (1972). Time-dose relationships for locomotor activity effects of morphine after acute or repeated treatment. *British Journal of Pharmacology, 46*, 213–224.

Bindra, D., & Palfai, T. (1967). Nature of positive and negative incentive-motivational effects on general activity. *Journal of Comparative and Physiological Psychology, 63*, 288–297.

Blanchard, R. J., & Blanchard, D. C. (1969). Crouching as an index of fear. *Journal of Comparative and Physiological Psychology, 67*, 370–375.

Blanchard, R. J., Dielman, T. E., & Blanchard, D. C. (1968). Prolonged aftereffects of a single foot shock. *Psychonomic Science, 10*, 327–328.

Bolles, R. C. (1975). Learning, motivation, and cognition. In W. K. Estes (Ed.), *Handbook of learning and cognitive processes* (Vol. 1). Hillsdale, NJ: Lawrence Erlbaum Associates.

Bolles, R. C., & Collier, A. C. (1976). The effect of predictive cues on freezing in rats. *Animal Learning & Behavior, 4*, 6–8.

Bolles, R. C., & Riley, A. L. (1973). Freezing as an avoidance response: Another look at the operant-respondent distinction. *Learning and Motivation, 4*, 268–275.

Bouton, M. E., & Bolles, R. C. (1985). Contexts, event memories, and extinction. In P. D. Balsam & A. Tomie (Eds.), *Context and learning* (pp. 133–166). Hillsdale, NJ: Lawrence Erlbaum Associates.

Buchanan, S. L., & Powell, D. A. (1982). Cingulate cortex: Its role in Pavlovian conditioning. *Journal of Comparative and Physiological Psychology, 95*, 755–774.

Chesher, G. B., & Chan, B. (1977). Footshock induced analgesia in mice: Its reversal by naloxone and cross tolerance with morphine. *Life Sciences, 21*, 1569–1574.

Davis, M. (1984). The mammalian startle response. In R. C. Eaton (Ed.), *Neural mechanisms of startle behavior* (pp. 287–351). New York: Plenum Press.

Davis, M. (1986). Pharmacological and anatomical analysis of fear conditioning using the potentiated startle paradigm. *Behavioral Neuroscience, 100*, 808–818.

Davitz, J. R., Mason, D. J., & Mowrer, O. H. (1957). Conditioning of fear: A function of the delay of reinforcement. *American Journal of Psychology, 70*, 69–74.

Donegan, N. H. (1981). Priming-produced facilitation or diminution of responding to a Pavlovian unconditioned stimulus. *Journal of Experimental Psychology: Animal Behavior Processes, 7*, 295–312.

Donegan, N. H., & Wagner, A. R. (1987). Conditioned diminution and facilitation of the UR: A sometimes opponent-process interpretation. In I. Gormezano, W. F. Prokasy, & R. F. Thompson (Eds.), *Classical conditioning III* (pp. 339–369). Hillsdale, NJ: Lawrence Erlbaum Associates.

Downs, D., Cardozo, C., Schneiderman, N., Yehle, A. R., VanderCar, D. H., & Zwilling, G. (1972). Central effects of atropine upon aversive classical conditioning in rabbits. *Psychopharmacologia, 23*, 319–333.

Drugan, R. C., Moye, T. B., & Maier, S. F. (1982). Opioid and nonopioid forms of stress-induced analgesia: Some environmental determinants and characteristics. *Behavioral and Neural Biology, 35*, 251–264.

Estes, W. K., & Skinner, B. F. (1941). Some quantitative properties of anxiety. *Journal of Experimental Psychology, 29*, 390–400.

Fanselow, M. E. (1980). Conditional and unconditional components of post-shock freezing. *Pavlovian Journal of Biological Science, 15*, 177–182.

Fanselow, M. E., & Baackes, M. P. (1982). Conditioned fear-induced opiate analgesia on the formalin test: Evidence for two aversive motivational systems. *Learning and Motivation, 13*, 200–221.

Fanselow, M. S., & Bolles, R. C. (1979). Naloxone and shock-elicited freezing in the rat. *Journal of Comparative and Physiological Psychology, 93*, 736–744.

Feldman, J. A., & Ballard, D. H. (1982). Connectionist models and their properties. *Cognitive Science, 6*, 205–254.

Fog, R. (1969). Behavioral effects in rats of morphine and amphetamine and of a combination of the two drugs. *Psychopharmacologia, 16*, 305–312.

Gluck, M. A., & Bower, G. H. (1988). From conditioning to category learning: An adaptive network model. *Journal of Experimental Psychology: General, 117*, 227–247.

Gormezano, I., & Kehoe, E. J. (1983). Associative transfer in classical conditioning to serial compounds. In M. L. Commons, R. J. Herrnstein, & A. R. Wagner, (Eds.), *Quantitative analyses of behavior: Vol. 3. Acquisition* (pp. 297–322). Cambridge, MA: Ballinger.

Grau, J. W. (1987). The central representation of an aversive event maintains opioid and nonopioid forms of analgesia. *Behavioral Neuroscience, 101*, (2), 272–288.

Grau, J. W., Hyson, R. L., Maier, S. F., Maddon, J., & Barchas, J. D. (1981). Long-term stress-induced analgesia and activation of the opiate system. *Science, 213*, 1409–1411.

Hinton, G. E., & Anderson, J. A. (1981). *Parallel models of associative memory.* Hillsdale, NJ: Lawrence Erlbaum Associates.

Holland, P. C. (1983). Occasion-setting in Pavlovian feature positive discriminations. In M. L. Commons, R. J. Herrnstein, & A. R. Wagner (Eds.), *Quantitative analyses of behavior: Discrimination processes, 4*, 182–206.

Holland, P. C. (1985). The nature of conditioned inhibition in serial and simultaneous feature negative discriminations. In R. R. Miller & N. E. Spear (Eds.), *Information processing in animals: Conditioned inhibition* (pp. 267–297). Hillsdale, NJ: Lawrence Erlbaum Associates.

Hull, C. L. (1943). *Principles of behavior.* New York: Appleton-Century-Crofts.

Ison, J. R., & Leonard, D. W. (1971). Effects of auditory stimuli on the amplitude of the nictitating membrane reflex of the rabbit (Oryctolagus Cuniculus). *Journal of Comparative and Physiological Psychology, 75*, 157–164.

Jenkins, H. M. (1985). Conditioned inhibition of key pecking in the pigeon. In R. R. Miller & N. E. Spear (Eds.), *Information processing in animals: Conditioned inhibition* (pp. 327–353). Hillsdale, NJ: Lawrence Erlbaum Associates.

Kamin, L. J. (1965). Temporal and intensity characteristics of the conditioned stimulus. In W. Prokasy (Ed.), *Classical conditioning* (pp. 118–147). New York: Appleton-Century-Crofts.

Kamin, L. J. (1968). Attention-like processes in classical conditioning. In M. R. Jones (Ed.), *Miami symposium on the prediction of behavior: Aversive stimulation.* Florida: University of Miami Press.

Kamin, L. J. (1969). Selective association and conditioning. In N. J. Mackintosh & W. K. Honig (Eds.), *Fundamental issues in associative learning.* Halifax, Nova Scotia: Dalhousie.

Kandel, E. R. (1977). A cell-biological approach to learning. *Society for Neuroscience,* Bethesda, MD.

Kazis, E., Milligan, W. L., & Powell, D. A. (1973). Autonomic-somatic relationships: Blockade of heart rate and corneo-retinal potential responses. *Journal of Comparative and Physiological Psychology, 84*, 98–110.

Kehoe, E. J., Marshall-Goodell, B., Gormezano, I. (1987). Differential conditioning of the rabbit's nictitating membrane response to serial compound stimuli. *Journal of Experimental Psychology: Animal Behavior Processes, 13*, 17–30.

Kehoe, E. J., & Morrow, L. D. (1984). Temporal dynamics of the rabbit's nictitating membrane response in serial compound conditioned stimuli. *Journal of Experimental Psychology: Animal Behavior Processes, 10*, 205–220.

Kimble, G. A., & Ost, J. W. P. (1961). A conditioned inhibitory process in eyelid conditioning. *Journal of Experimental Psychology, 61*, 150–156.

Konorski, J. (1948). *Conditioned reflexes and neuron organization.* Cambridge, England: Cambridge University Press.

Konorski, J. (1967). *Integrative activity of the brain.* Chicago: University of Chicago Press.

Larew, M. B. (1986). *Inhibitory learning in Pavlovian backward conditioning procedures involving a small number of US–CS trials.* Unpublished doctoral dissertation, Yale University.

L'Estrange, Sir R. L. Kt. (1704). *Fables of Aesop and other eminent mythologists, with morals and reflections.* Fourth edition, printed for R. Sare, A. & J. Churchil, D. Brown, T. Goodwin, M. Wotton, J. Nicholson, G. Sawbridge, B. Tooke & G. Strahan: London.

Lewis, J. W., Cannon, J. T., & Liebeskind, J. C. (1980). Involvement of central muscarinic cholinergic mechanisms in opioid stress analgesia. *Brain Research, 270,* 289–293.

Lincoln, J. S., McCormick, D. A., & Thompson, R. F. (1982). Ipsilateral cerebellar lesions prevent learning of the classically conditioned nictitating membrane/eyelid response. *Brain Research, 242,* 190–193.

Logan, F. A. (1977). Hybrid theory of classical conditioning. In G. Bower (Ed.), *The psychology of learning and motivation.* New York: Academic Press.

Mackintosh, N. J. (1974). *The psychology of animal learning.* New York: Academic Press.

Mackintosh, N. J. (1975). A theory of attention: Variations in the associability of stimuli with reinforcement. *Psychological Review, 82,* 276–298.

Mackintosh, N. J. (1983). *Conditioning and associative learning.* New York: Oxford University Press.

Mahoney, W. J., & Ayres, J. J. B. (1976). One-trial simultaneous and backward fear conditioning as reflected in conditioned suppression of licking in rats. *Animal Learning & Behavior, 4,* 357–362.

Maier, S. P., Rapaport, P., & Wheatley, K. L. (1976). Conditioned inhibition and the UCS–CS interval. *Animal Learning & Behavior, 4,* 217–220.

Mayer, D. J., & Watkins, L. R. (1981). The role of endorphins in endogenous pain control systems. In H. M. Emrich (Ed.), *Modern problems of pharmacopsychiatry: The role of endorphins in neuropsychiatry.* (pp. 68–96). Basel S. Karger.

Mazur, J. E., & Wagner, A. R. (1982). An episodic model of associative learning. In M. Commons, R. Herrnstein, & A. R. Wagner (Eds.), *Quantitative analyses of behavior: Acquisition* (Vol. 3, pp. 3–39). Cambridge, MA: Ballinger.

Morgan, C. L. (1894). *Introduction to comparative psychology.* London: Walter Scott, Ltd.

Mowrer, O. H. (1947). On the dual nature of learning—A reinterpretation of "conditioning" and "problem-solving." *Harvard Educational Review, 17,* 102–148.

Mucha, R. F., Volkovskis, C., & Kalant, H. (1981). Conditioned increases in locomotor activity produced with morphine as an unconditioned stimulus, and the relation of conditioning to acute morphine effect and tolerance. *Journal of Comparative and Physiological Psychology, 96,* 351–362.

Paletta, M. S., & Wagner, A. R. (1986). Development of context-specific tolerance to morphine: support for a dual-process interpretation. *Behavioral Neuroscience, 100,* 611–623.

Pavlov, I. P. (1927). *Conditioned reflexes.* Oxford: Oxford University Press.

Pearce, J. M., & Hall, G. (1980). A model for Pavlovian learning: Variations in the effectiveness of conditioned but not of unconditioned stimuli. *Psychological Review, 87,* 532–552.

Pfautz, P. L. (1980). *Unconditioned facilitation and diminution of the unconditioned response.* Unpublished doctoral dissertation, Yale University.

Pfautz, P. L., & Wagner, A. R. (1976). Transient variations in responding to Pavlovian conditioned stimuli have implications for mechanisms of "priming." *Animal Learning and Behavior, 4,* 107–112.

Powell, D. A., Hernandez, L., & Buchanan, S. L. (1985). Intraseptal scopolamine has differential effects on Pavlovian eyeblink and heart rate conditioning. *Behavioral Neuroscience, 99,* 75–87.

Rashotte, M. E. (1981). Second-order autoshaping: Contributions to the research and theory of Pavlovian reinforcement by conditioned stimuli. In C. M. Locurto, H. S. Terrace, & J. Gibbon (Eds.), *Autoshaping and conditioning theory* (pp. 139–180). New York: Academic Press.

Rescorla, R. A. (1969). Conditioned inhibition of fear. In N. J. Mackintosh & W. K. Honig (Eds.), *Fundamental issues in associative learning.* Halifax: Dalhousie University Press.

Rescorla, R. A. (1980). *Pavlovian second-order conditioning.* Hillsdale, NJ: Lawrence Erlbaum Associates.

Rescorla, R. A. (1985). Inhibition and facilitation. In R. R. Miller & N. E. Spear (Eds.), *Information processing in animals: Conditioned inhibition* (pp. 299–326). Hillsdale, NJ: Lawrence Erlbaum Associates.

Rescorla, R. A., & Solomon, R. L. (1967). Two-process learning theory: Relationships between Pavlovian conditioning and instrumental learning. *Psychological Review, 74*, 151–182.

Rescorla, R. A., & Wagner, A. R. (1972). A theory of Pavlovian conditioning: Variations in the effectiveness of reinforcement and nonreinforcement. In A. H. Black & W. F. Prokasky (Eds.), *Classical conditioning II* (pp. 64–99). New York: Appleton-Century-Crofts.

Ross, L. E. (1961). Conditioned fear as a function of the CS–US and probe stimulus interval. *Journal of Experimental Psychology, 61*, 265-273.

Ross, R. T., & Holland, P. C. (1981). Conditioning of simultaneous and serial feature positive discriminations. *Animal Learning and Behavior, 9*, 293-303.

Rumelhardt, D. E., & McClelland, J. E. (1986). *Parallel distributed processing: Exploration in the microstructure of cognition, Vol. 1: Foundations.* Cambridge, MA: Bradford Books/MIT Press.

Saavadra, M. A. (1975). Pavlovian compound conditioning in the rabbit. *Learning and Motivation, 6*, 314-326.

Schlosberg, H. (1937). The relationship between success and the laws of conditioning. *Psychological Review, 44*, 379-394.

Schneiderman, N. (1972). Response system divergencies in aversive classical conditioning. In A. H. Black & W. F. Prokasy (Eds.), *Classical conditioning II: Current theory and research.* New York: Appleton-Century-Crofts.

Schneiderman, N., Smith, M. C., Smith, A. C., & Gormezano, I. (1966). Heart-rate classical conditioning in rabbits. *Psychonomic Science, 6*, 241-242.

Schull, J. (1979). A conditioned opponent theory of Pavlovian conditioning and habituation. In G. H. Bower (Ed.), *The psychology of learning and motivation* (Vol. 13). New York: Academic Press.

Siegel, S. (1979). The role of conditioning in drug tolerance. In J. D. Keehn (Ed.), *Psychopathology in animals: Research applications* (pp. 143–168). New York: Academic Press.

Siegel, S. (1981). Classical conditioning, drug tolerance, and drug dependence. In Y. Israel, F. B. Sloser, H. Kalant, R. E. Popham, W. Schmidt, & R. G. Smart (Eds.), *Research advances in alcohol and drug abuse* (Vol. 7, pp. 207–246). New York: Plenum.

Smith, M. C., Coleman, S. R., & Gormezano, I. (1969). Classical conditioning of the rabbit's nictitating membrane response at backward, simultaneous, and forward CS–US intervals. *Journal of Comparative and Physiological Psychology, 69*, 226-231.

Solomon, R. L., & Corbit, J. D. (1974). An opponent-process theory of motivation. *Psychological Review, 81*, 119-145.

Sutton, R. S., & Barto, A. G. (1981). Toward a modern theory of adaptive networks: Expectation and prediction. *Psychological Review, 88*, 135-170.

Tait, R. W., & Saladin, M. E. (1986). Concurrent development of excitatory and inhibitory associations during backward conditioning. *Animal Learning and Behavior, 14*, 133-137.

Terry, W. S. (1976). The effects of priming US representation in short-term memory on Pavlovian conditioning. *Journal of Experimental Psychology: Animal Behavior Processes, 2*, 354-370.

Terry, W. S., & Wagner, A. R. (1975). Short-term memory for "surprising" versus "expected" unconditioned stimuli in Pavlovian conditioning. *Journal of Experimental Psychology: Animal Behavior Processes, 1*, 122-133.

Thompson, R. F., Clark, G. A., Donegan, N. H., Lavond, D. G., Lincoln, J. S., Madden, J., Mamounas, L. A., Mauk, M. D., McCormick, D. A., & Thompson, J. K. (1984). Neuronal substrates of learning and memory: A "multiple-trace" view. In G. Lynch, J. L. McGaugh, & N. M. Weinberger (Eds.), *Neurobiology of learning and memory* (pp. 137-164). New York: The Guilford Press.

Thompson, R. F., Donegan, N. H., Clark, G. A., Lavond, D. G., Lincoln, J. S., Madden, J., Mamounas, L. A., Mauk, M. D., & McCormick, D. A. (1986). Neuronal substrates of discrete, defensive conditioned reflexes, conditioned fear states, and their interactions in the rabbit. In I. Gormezano, W. F. Prokasy, & R. F. Thompson (Eds.), *Classical conditioning III* (pp. 371-399). Hillsdale, NJ: Lawrence Erlbaum Associates.

Vandercar, D. H., & Schneiderman, N. (1967). Interstimulus interval functions in different response systems during classical discrimination conditioning of rabbits. *Psychonomic Science, 9*, 9–10.

Wagner, A. R. (1969). Stimulus validity and stimulus selection in associative learning. In N. J. Mackintosh & W. K. Honig (Eds.), *Fundamental issues in associative learning* (pp. 90–122). Halifax, Nova Scotia: Dalhousie.

Wagner, A. R. (1971). Elementary associations. In H. H. Kendler & J. T. Spence (Eds.), *Essays in neobehaviorism: A memorial volume to Kenneth W. Spence* (pp. 187–213.). New York: Appleton-Century-Crofts.

Wagner, A. R. (1976). Priming in STM: An information-processing mechanism for self-generated or retrieval-generated depression in performance. In T. J. Tighe & R. N. Leaton (Eds.), *Habituation: Perspectives from child development, animal behavior, and neurophysiology* (pp. 95–128). Hillsdale, NJ: Lawrence Erlbaum Associates.

Wagner, A. R. (1978). Expectancies and the priming of STM. In S. H. Hulse, H. Fowler, & W. K. Honig (Eds.), *Cognitive aspects of animal behavior* (pp. 177–209). Hillsdale, NJ: Lawrence Erlbaum Associates.

Wagner, A. R. (1981). SOP: A model of automatic memory processing in animal behavior. In N. E. Spear & R. R. Miller (Eds.), *Information processing in animals: Memory mechanisms* (pp. 5–47). Hillsdale, NJ: Lawrence Erlbaum Associates.

Wagner, A. R., & Donegan, N. H. (in press). Some relationships between a computational model (SOP) and an essential neural circuit for Pavlovian (rabbit eyeblink) conditioning. In R. D. Hawkins & G. H. Bower (Eds.), *The psychology of learning and motivation, Vol. 22: Computational models of learning in simple neural systems*. Orlando: Academic Press.

Wagner, A. R., & Larew, M. B. (1985). Opponent processes and Pavlovian inhibition. In R. R. Miller & N. E. Spear (Eds.), *Information processing in animals: Conditioned inhibition* (pp. 233–265). Hillsdale, NJ: Lawrence Erlbaum Associates.

Wagner, A. R., Logan, F. A., Haberlandt, K., & Price, T. (1968). Stimulus selection in animal discrimination learning. *Journal of Experimental Psychology, 76*, 171–180.

Wagner, A. R., & Rescorla, R. A. (1972). Inhibition in Pavlovian conditioning: Application of theory. In R. A. Boakes & M. S. Halliday (Eds.), *Inhibition and learning* (pp. 301–336). London: Academic Press.

Wagner, A. R., & Terry, W. S. (1975). Backward conditioning to a CS following an expected vs. a surprising UCS. *Animal Learning & Behavior, 3*, 370–374.

Warner, L. H. (1932). An experimental search for the "conditioned response." *Journal of Genetic Psychology, 41*, 91–115.

Wasserman, E. A., Hunter, N. B., Gutowski, K. A., & Bader, S. A. (1975). Autoshaping chicks with heat reinforcement: The role of stimulus-reinforcer and response-reinforcer relations. *Journal of Experimental Psychology: Animal Behavior Processes, 1*, 30–38.

Weinberger, N. M. (1982). Effects of conditioned arousal on the auditory system. In A. L. Beckman (Ed.), *The neural basis of behavior* (pp. 63–91). New York: Spectrum.

Weisz, D. J., & LoTurco, J. J. (1988). Reflex facilitation of the nictitating membrane response remains after cerebellar lesions. *Behavioral Neuroscience, 102*, 203–209.

Whitlow, J. W., & Wagner, A. R. (1972). Negative patterning in classical conditioning: summation of response tendencies to isolable and configural components. *Psychonomic Science, 27*, 299–301.

Yehle, A. L. (1968). Divergent response systems in rabbit conditioning. *Journal of Experimental Psychology, 77*, 468–473.

Zener, K. (1937). The significance of behavior accompanying conditioned salivary secretion for theories of the conditioned response. *American Journal of Psychology, 50*, 384–403.

7 Sign-Tracking: The Search for Reward

Arthur Tomie
William Brooks
Barbara Zito
Rutgers University

I. INTRODUCTION

We have recently discovered that animals tend to approach and contact stimuli predictive of reward when such stimuli are highly localized in space. The phenomenon is called "sign-tracking" because the animals move about so as to be in close physical proximity to the signal. Not all stimuli that signal reward are amenable to approach and contact. In many procedures, signals for reward (i.e., Pavlovian CSs and instrumental discriminative stimuli) are diffuse and not highly localized in space. Examples of such signals are auditory stimuli emanating from a speaker panel or visual stimuli (e.g., chamber illumination) provided by the illumination of a diffuse array of houselights. On the other hand, there are instances where the locus of the reward signal is discrete and highly circumscribed, as in the case of illuminating a 1-inch diameter circular disk or inserting a retractable operant lever. It is this type of reward signal that concerns us here. In this chapter, we discuss the behavioral consequences of localizing signals for reward as well as the implications of the observations derived from this research for a number of phenomena in animal learning.

The approach and contact behaviors elicited by localized signals for reward were first reported by Brown and Jenkins in 1968. Prior to the publication of their work, the effects of cue localization were largely unappreciated. Brown and Jenkins labeled the approach and contact behavior "autoshaping" because the pigeons appeared to "shape" themselves to perform a prototypic free-operant response (i.e., pecking of a response key). It is now clear that autoshaping is something of a misnomer. This effect of cue localization is more accurately described by the term "sign-tracking" (cf. Hearst & Jenkins, 1974) which points to the signal-directed nature of the behaviors elicited by the localized cue. Autoshaping is the most thoroughly investigated exemplar of sign-tracking behavior, and, consequently, much of this chapter focuses on the keylight directed behavior of the pigeon.

There are a number of excellent reviews of the autoshaping literature. The earliest review was the influential monograph of Hearst & Jenkins (1974) which, in particular, details the similarities between autoshaping and "feature effects" in instrumental discrimination learning. The review paper by Schwartz and Gamzu (1977) explores the possibility that autoshaping may mediate behavioral contrast. Several excellent reviews of the sign-tracking literature have appeared more recently (Buzsaki, 1982; Davis & Hurwitz, 1977; Dickinson & Boakes, 1979); moreover, there is now an excellent book relating autoshaping to conditioning theory (Locurto, Terrace, & Gibbon, 1981).

The Brown and Jenkins Experiment

We begin with a description of the original work performed by Brown and Jenkins (1968) and a review of the context in which that work was done. Brown and Jenkins noted that the acquisition of Pavlovian CRs is derived from a positive correlation or contingency between a signal (CS) and a biologically significant event (US); whereas, instrumental responses develop from the contingency between the instrumental response and the biologically significant event (i.e., reinforcing stimulus). The reinforcing stimulus, may, therefore, foster the acquisition of Pavlovian CRs, particularly when the reinforcing stimulus is presented in a manner such that it is reliably signaled by a distinctive stimulus. In instrumental discrimination learning procedures, the reinforcer is contingent upon the performance of the instrumental response in the presence of a discriminative stimulus. It follows, therefore, that the discriminative stimulus will be positively correlated with the reinforcer and, as a Pavlovian CS, it will elicit CR topographies which may affect the performance of the instrumental response.

Because Pavlovian CRs were traditionally viewed as autonomically mediated, reflexive, and involuntary (cf. Kimble, 1961; Konorski & Miller, 1937, Mowrer, 1947; Schlosberg, 1937; Skinner, 1938; Turner & Solomon, 1962) the role of the Pavlovian CR was seen as primarily motivational (Hull, 1943; Miller, 1941; Mowrer, 1960; Rescorla & Solomon, 1967; Schlosberg, 1937). That is, the Pavlovian CR was largely seen as an emotional response (such as fear) which affected the subject's tendency to perform the instrumental behavior. Pavlovian CRs were not thought of as complex peripheral motor responses mediated by the skeletal-motor musculature. We should note that there are instances where Pavlovian procedures have been successfully employed in the conditioning of certain discrete skeletal responses (cf. patellar reflex conditioning in humans (Schlosberg, 1928) and paw flexion conditioning in humans (Konorski & Szwejsowska, 1956). These are more accurately described as simple reflexive motor performances, which are less complex than the skeletal sign-tracking CR discussed in this chapter.

As noted by Brown and Jenkins much of the literature on instrumental discrimination learning has been derived from procedures wherein the instrumental behavior was food reinforced pecking of a response key by a pigeon and the discriminative stimulus was the illumination of the response key by a distinctive stimulus (such as a red color). The pecking of the response key was widely regarded as an instrumental behavior (governed by its consequences), moreover, the contingency between the illumination of the keylight with a red color and the presentation of the food reinforcer was widely regarded as unrelated to the acquisition or maintenance of the keypecking response. Brown and Jenkins (1968) questioned this presumption. They asked if the development of keypecking to the illuminated keylight was attributable to the Pavlovian relationship between the illumination of the keylight and the presentation of food.

In their experiment, Brown and Jenkins placed pigeons trained to feed from a food magazine into a standard operant conditioning chamber for pigeons. In such an apparatus the response key is a 1-inch diameter translucent circular disk which is illuminated by the operation of a rear mounted stimulus projector bulb. The subjects were then exposed to 160 conditioning trials. Each trial consisted of 8 sec of keylight illumination followed by 4 sec of access to a food magazine filled with mixed pigeon grain. Trials were separated by a mean intertrial interval (ITI) of 60 sec. Presentation of the food magazine occurred on each trial regardless of the occurrence of keypecking. Keypecking while the key was illuminated resulted in the immediate termination of the keylight and the presentation of 4 sec of access to food. Keypecking during the intertrial interval delayed the onset of the subsequent trial by 60 sec. Surprisingly, pigeons began to peck at the illuminated key even though they were not required to do so to obtain food (i.e., there was no instrumental contingency between the pigeon's keypecking response and the presentation of the food).

The discovery of this phenomenon, which Brown and Jenkins labeled "autoshaping" (because the pigeons appear to "shape" themselves to keypeck), was extremely important. Obviously, if the keypecking behavior was truly Pavlovian, then Brown and Jenkins have identified a new type of Pavlovian CR, a signal-directed behavior whose topography consists of complex skeletal motor responses heretofore considered conditionable only by instrumental procedures. This, in turn, suggests that Pavlovian CRs may affect the performance of instrumental responses in ways not previously considered.

This is not to say that Brown and Jenkins felt that instrumental factors played no role in autoshaping. They felt that the emergence of the first keypeck was unlikely due to instrumental learning; however, keypecks beyond this point were considered to be at least partially influenced by the resulting temporal contiguity between keypecking and food delivery. The role of instrumental processes in autoshaping (the acquisition of keypecking) and automaintenance (asymptotic key-pecking performance) are discussed in more detail later.

The Keylight-Food Relationship.

Temporal Contiguity Between Keylight and Food.   Obviously, the Pavlovian interpretation of autoshaping specifies that the keypecking CR will be dependent upon the manner in which the keylight and food are presented. Brown and Jenkins observed substantial autoshaping only in groups of pigeons that received forward pairings of keylight illumination and food presentation. Little, if any, keypecking was observed in groups that received keylight illumination only (CS only), food presentation only (US only), backward pairings (US followed by CS) or forward pairings of an unilluminated key (key was illuminated during the ITI) and the presentation of food. They concluded that keypecking develops only when key illumination is temporally contiguous and antecedent to the delivery of food.

Contingency Between Keylight and Food.   Brown and Jenkins (1968) demonstrated that autoshaping was attributable to the temporally contiguous illumination of the response key and the presentation of food, in that order. Shortly thereafter, other researchers began to study the effects of varying the contingency between these two elements, while holding constant the number of CS–US pairings. The role of CS–US contingency in the acquisition of autoshaping was first investigated by Gamzu and Williams (1973). Gamzu and Williams gave pigeons 8.6 sec trials of keylight (mean ITI = 30 sec) with the probability of grain delivery set at 0.03 during each second of the keylight interval and at 0.0 during the ITI (differential contingency condition). When the pigeon's schedule was altered such that grain delivery as equally probable (.03) during the ITI as during a trial (nondifferential contingency condition), keypecking was extinguished. When the original differential CS–US contingency was restored, the pigeons reacquired the autoshaping CR. In summary, they found that the rate of keypecking during the CS periods was directly related to the degree of contingency between the illumination of the key (CS) and the presentation of grain (US); moreover, keypecking was not maintained, despite frequent CS–US pairings, when food was equally likely to occur in the absence of the keylight.

Instrumental Interpretations of Autoshaping

Autoshaping is clearly dependent upon a positive contingency between the illumination of the keylight and the presentation of food. This is consistent with a Pavlovian interpretation of the phenomenon. It does not, however, eliminate the possibility that the pigeons acquired keypecking "superstitiously." That is, from an instrumental learning perspective, one might argue that the delivery of food following (although not dependent upon) the occurrence of a keypeck would lead to the acquisition of keypecking (cf. Herrnstein & Morse, 1957; Skinner, 1948). This type of adventitious reinforcement of keypecking cannot account for the occurrence of the first keypeck; however, it does provide a plausible instrumental account of keypecking thereafter.

Concern over the possibility of superstitious conditioning was explicitly acknowledged by Brown and Jenkins (1968), and was systematically evaluated by Williams and Williams (1969). In their experiment, keypecking during the keylight CS resulted in the omission of the food US. If the pigeon did not keypeck during the keylight CS, then the food US was presented. The application of this omission contingency precludes the possibility of close temporal contiguity between keypecking and food presentation, and therefore, reduces the plausibility that the acquisition of keypecking would be attributable to instrumental factors (i.e., superstition). Williams and Williams (1969) found that despite eliminating keypeck-food pairings, keypecking was reliably acquired in all 13 subjects. This result indicates that the development of signal directed behavior is not dependent upon a response-reinforcer relation (intended or otherwise) and discredits this type of instrumental interpretation of autoshaping.

The Generality of Autoshaping

Research into the phenomena of autoshaping has, in a number of ways, extended far beyond the initial studies of Brown and Jenkins (1968). Variations of the Brown and Jenkins procedure have been used in studies on pigeons employing a wide range of stimuli and reinforcers (cf. Jenkins & Moore, 1973; Woodruff & Williams, 1976). Autoshaping of the pecking response has been observed using food US in other avian species, including the domestic chick (McCracken & Mazula, cited in Wasserman, 1981) and the bobwhite quail (Gardner, 1969). Moreover, in domestic chicks, signal-directed pecking has been elicited by pairing key illumination with heat US (Wasserman, Hunter, Gutowski, & Bader, 1975). On the other hand; Powell, Kelly, and Santisteban (1975) have failed to observe autoshaping in two species of crow (common crow and fish crow) and Wilson (1978) observed autoshaping of pecking but little automaintenance in three species of corvids (carrion crow, rook, and jay).

Approach and contact of localized visual stimuli paired with food has been observed in several cold-blooded species, including goldfish (Brandon & Bitterman, 1979; Woodard & Bitterman, 1974), tilapia fish (Squire, 1969), and monitor lizards (Loop, 1976). The form of the contact with the CS often resembles components of the species' feeding behavior.

There are numerous reports of sign-tracking in the rat. The usual procedure consists of inserting a lever into the chamber just prior to the delivery of food (Atnip, 1977; Cleland & Davey, 1983; Davey & Cleland, 1982; Locurto, Terrace, & Gibbon, 1976; Mowrer & Hull, 1974; Stiers & Silberberg, 1974). The rats approach and contact the lever with the mouth (licking and gnawing) or forepaws (touching). With varying degrees of success, other types of CSs and USs have also been employed in autoshaping procedures with rats (cf. Peterson, Ackil, Frommer, & Hearst, 1972; Timberlake & Grant, 1975). Sign-tracking has also been observed with guinea pigs, who approach and contact a lever paired with food (Poling & Poling, 1978), with cats, who approach and contact a small loudspeaker paired with food (Grastyan & Vereczkei, 1974), and with dogs, who approach and orient toward but do not contact a light panel that signals food (Jenkins, Barrera, Ireland, & Woodside, 1978; Pavlov, 1934; Wasserman, 1978; Zener, 1937).

Autoshaping has also been observed in primates. Illumination of a light paired with presentation of food produces approach and contact behavior in rhesus monkeys (Likey, 1974; Sidman & Fletcher, 1968) and in squirrel monkeys (Gamzu & Schwam, 1974; Schwam & Gamzu, 1975). Finally, there are a number of demonstrations of approach and contact behavior in adult humans (Pithers, 1985; Wilcove & Miller, 1974) and human children (Ragain, Anson & Sperber, 1976; Zeiler, 1972).

II. THE ROLE OF THE CONDITIONED STIMULUS

Autoshaping has been observed using a number of different conditioned stimuli. The CSs that have generally been found to be most effective in eliciting sign-tracking behavior are those that are highly localized in space.

Spatial Localization of the CS

To what extent is the acquisition and maintenance of sign-tracking behavior dependent upon the spatial localization of the CS? In a study using pigeons, Wasserman (1973a) found that eliminating the houselight from the autoshaping procedure reduced the speed of acquisition of and the asymptotic level of keypecking to a keylight paired with food presentation. Similar effects have been reported by Hearst (1975). Wasserman argued that key illumination is more highly localized (though probably less salient) in a chamber illuminated by a houselight because reflected key illumination is readily detected throughout a dark chamber. Apparently, reducing the extent to which the keylight CS is spatially localized reduces the pigeon's tendency to approach and contact this stimulus.

The effects of localizing the visual display used as the CS may be more directly evaluated by manipulating the size of the stimulus display. Sperling and Perkins (1979) reported that the number of trials to the first keypeck was less when the CS was illumination of the keylight by four elements arranged in a compact array (.40 cm from the center of the key to the center of each element) as compared to when the four elements ere arranged in a dispersed array (.70 cm from the center of the key to the center of each element). However, they reported that the size of the stimulus display had no reliable effect upon rate of keypecking thereafter. Holland (1980) found that rats approach and contact a highly localized light source (a single lamp bulb) to a greater degree than a partially localized light source (a tubular incandescent lamp). Moreover, a nonlocalized light source (four spaced tubular incandescent lamps) elicited little sign-tracking behavior.

Is sign tracking observed with auditory signals for food? It appears that the CS contact component of the approach and contact CR is largely eliminated when auditory stimuli are employed as CSs. Bilbrey and Winokur (1973) have reported that CS contact behavior does not occur when grain presentation is preceded by a tone presented either from a speaker separate from the response key or from a speaker mounted behind the response key. Steinhauer, Davol, and Lee (1977) have reported that reliable key contact behavior in pigeons can be induced by delivering the tone CS through a speaker mounted behind the response key. This is effective only when the pigeons were first given extensive magazine training wherein the tone was presented through a speaker in the food magazine when the grain was available.

Jenkins (1973) has shown that pigeons will approach (i.e., move toward the side of the chamber on which the speaker is mounted) and make pecking motions toward the key (which was directly in front of the speaker); however, Jenkins noted that the amount of CS contact behavior observed with the tone in this study was much less than that seen when the speakers were replaced with keylights. A number of other reported attempts to elicit sign-tracking behavior in rats using auditory CSs have been altogether unsuccessful (Cleland & Davey, 1983; Harrison, 1979). In the Cleland and Davey study, clickers and lights were directly compared. They found that auditory stimuli elicited only CS orientation, whereas, visual stimuli elicited CS orientation and CS approach behavior. Clearly, studies using auditory CSs have produced less clear-cut evidence of sign-tracking behavior, and, in all cases where the effectiveness of auditory CSs is directly compared to visual CSs, visual stimuli were clearly far superior in eliciting approach and contact CRs.

Proximity of the Keylight and the Hopper

In the autoshaping apparatus, the keylight is normally situated within a few inches of the food magazine aperture (i.e., food hopper). How is autoshaping affected by the physical proximity or spatial contiguity of the keylight and the food hopper? Can the approach to the CS be partially explained by this arrangement? A number of experimenters have physically isolated the keylight from the vicinity of the food hopper. Jenkins (1973) placed two keylights 3 feet from either side of the food hopper. He reported that pigeons will approach and contact only the keylight which reliably preceded grain delivery. Jenkins (1973) reported a similar result when auditory stimuli were presented through speakers physically removed from the vicinity of the food hopper. It appears, therefore, that the

the sign-tracking CR is truly CS directed and not merely an approach response to the food hopper aperture.

This point is made in a particularly effective fashion in studies which systematically manipulate keylight location. Smith (1970) employed the center key of a three key array to train pigeons in a typical autoshaping procedure. The subjects were then given autoshaping trials with the same visual stimulus projected on one of the two remaining response keys. Smith observed that all of the pigeons moved away from the vicinity of the center key and pecked the illuminated side key on it's first presentation. This indicates that the pigeon will track the visual CS even when it changes location between trials. Skinner (1971), provides an even more compelling example of a pigeon tracking a moving signal of impending reward. In this case, the procedure consisted of a light moving from right to left behind a translucent wall in the pigeon's chamber. When the light reached the left edge of the plastic panel, the food dispenser at the right side of the chamber was operated. Just as in the previous demonstrations of tracking, the pigeons pecked at the light as it coursed along. They continued to peck at the moving light even though this behavior brought them farther away from the food magazine and had absolutely no effect on food delivery.

A pigeon tracking a visual CS so as to move away from the vicinity of the food hopper may reduce feeding time or miss the delivery of food altogether. That is, the food hopper may be raised for its scheduled duration of access and then be lowered, before the pigeon can return from the vicinity of the keylight. In the previously mentioned experiment by Jenkins (1973) in which keylights were 3 feet removed from the food magazine, pigeons continued to keypeck even though, as a consequence, the time available for eating was reduced by approximately 50%. In many instances, the pigeon's tracking behavior resulted in the effective omission of the opportunity to eat. The pigeons continued, nevertheless, to track the CS. This result is consistent with the observations of Williams and Williams (1969), who previously showed that autoshaping is not effectively eliminated by the omission contingency. On the other hand, there is some evidence that the effectiveness of omission procedures in autoshaping in the pigeon is affected by the proximity of the keylight to the food hopper. Peden, Browne, and Hearst (1977) showed that when the keylight and the food hopper were close together an explicit omission contingency was less effective than when they were far apart (separated by 2 feet).

The effects of proximity of the signal to the food magazine have also been studied in autoshaping in rats. Holland (1980) found that when the CS was located farther away from the food magazine, rats displayed more magazine directed behaviors (i.e., rearing, magazine contact behavior, etc.); moreover, when the CS was located near the food magazine, less magazine directed and more CS directed behavior was observed. Similar effects have been reported by Karpicke (1978).

Generalization Between Keylight and Hopper Light

During the autoshaping trial the illumination of the keylight is followed by the presentation of the food hopper. Coextensive with the raising of the food hopper is the illumination of the hopper aperture with a food hopper light. The food hopper light is, therefore, perfectly correlated with the availability of food, and should become a discriminative stimulus for pecking at the grain in the hopper. Because the keylight and the hopper light are both localized visual stimuli, the pecking elicited by the keylight may be viewed, at least in part, as a stimulus generalization effect. That is, the pigeon may learn to peck for grain in the presence of the food hopper light (i.e., the food hopper light is a discriminative stimulus for the instrumental response of pecking for food) and generalize this pecking response to the keylight.

There is substantial evidence that such generalization effects do occur. For example, Gilbert (1973) made the food hopper light less predictive of the presence of food by removing the shield below the keylight. This shield normally prevents the food hopper from being illuminated by the keylight, and, therefore, Gilbert's procedure made food hopper illumination a less valid discriminative stimulus for pecking (because the food hopper was not illuminated when grain was not present). He found that the acquisition of autoshaping was retarded by this manipulation and attributed this effect to the loss of discriminative control of pecking by the hopper light, which, in turn, should reduce generalization of pecking to the keylight.

Fisher and Catania (1977) employed a two-key (red and green) autoshaping procedure. They noted that the first keypeck (and the majority of them thereafter) occurred to the key whose color matched that of the food hopper light. Similar effects have been reported by Davol, Steinhauer, and Lee (1977) and Ettinger, Finch and McSweeney (1978). Likewise, Sperling, Perkins, and Duncan (1977) found that the first autoshaping keypeck was to the keylight color which was the same as the hopper light; moreover, this effect was observed even when the illumination of the matching key color was negatively related to the presentation of food (i.e., negative automaintenance procedure).

Davol, Steinhauer, and Lee (1977) trained pigeons to feed from the food hopper in an illuminated chamber. They reported that autoshaping is observed under these conditions, however, when the food hopper light was also eliminated, then autoshaping was not acquired. Comparable effects have been reported by Ettinger et al. (1978). They exposed pigeons to an autoshaping procedure in the presence or absence of food hopper illumination. They found that pigeons did not peck a lighted key when the food hopper was not illuminated, but they did reliably peck the key when the food hopper was illuminated.

These studies clearly demonstrate that the initiation of keypecking in autoshaping studies with pigeons is at least partially explained by the phenomenon of stimulus generalization (pecking in the presence of the hopper light generalizes to the keylight). This is important for several reasons. Recall that the instrumental interpretation of autoshaping (superstitious or adventitious reinforcement of keypecking by food reward) failed to account for the occurrence of the first keypeck. The type of analysis put forth here suggests that instrumental analyses are not altogether unable to provide an explanation of the origins of that first keypeck. It should be noted, however, that the generalization hypothesis is not an adequate account of autoshaping. There are numerous control conditions included in autoshaping studies which provide for both food hopper and keylight illumination (i.e., random presentations of keylight CS and food hopper US) which have failed to produce autoshaping. Moreover, there are numerous demonstrations of autoshaping and sign-tracking where the stimulus generalization interpretation simply cannot apply. For example, a number of researchers have demonstrated approach to signals other than keylights (cf. Jenkins, 1973; Timberlake & Grant, 1975; see also Steinhauer et al., 1977), while still others have demonstrated approach to keylights where the presentation of the US is not accompanied by the illumination of a localized visual stimulus (cf. Peterson et al., 1972; Wasserman, 1973b; Woodruff and Williams, 1976).

Effects of Trial Duration and Trial Spacing

The duration of the keylight CS has profound effects upon autoshaping. Baldock (1974) compared CS durations from 4 to 32 sec (the ITI remained the same) and looked for differences in the speed of acquisition of autoshaping. He found that when the intertrial interval (ITI) was held constant, acquisition rate was inversely related to CS duration (i.e., the longer the duration of the CS the more slowly the keypecking CR was acquired).

Terrace, Gibbon, Farrell, and Baldock (1975), showed that when keylight CS duration was held constant, increases in the duration of the ITI facilitated keypeck acquisition. In their experiment 12 groups of magazine trained pigeons were exposed to autoshaping sessions consisting of one of twelve different variable ITIs (ranging from 5 to 400 sec). For all the pigeons, the trials consisted of 10 sec of green keylight followed by access to the food magazine. Terrace et al. observed better autoshaping with longer ITIs. They found that the duration of the ITI was not only inversely related to the number of trials to the first keypeck but also directly varied with the terminal response rate and probability of making at least one peck during a trial. The profound effect of temporal spacing of trials upon the speed of acquisition of autoshaping has also been reported by other investigators (Gibbon, Baldock, Locurto, Gold, & Terrace, 1977; Gibbon, Locurto & Terrace, 1975; Perkins, Beavers, Hancock, Hemmendinger, Hemmendinger, & Ricci, 1975; Jenkins, Barnes, & Barrera, 1981).

These data indicate that the duration of the keylight CS and the duration of the intertrial interval have opposite effects upon autoshaping. A number of investigators (cf. Gibbon & Balsam, 1981; Jenkins et al., 1981) have observed that the proportion of the total session time which is devoted to the presentation of the autoshaping CS is highly predictive of CR performance. Gibbon and Balsam (1981) have proposed that each presentation of the food US increases the associative strength of all stimuli present (including background stimuli) in direct and inverse proportion to their salience and duration, respectively. The shorter duration keylight accrues association with food more rapidly than does the background. Autoshaping is elicited when the associative strength of the keylight relative to the associative strength of the background exceeds some threshold value. Their model (Scalar Expectancy Theory) provides a formal approach for deriving estimates of associative strength; moreover, it uncouples, to some extent, those factors that determine CS–US association from those that determine performance of the CR. This is an important distinction (see Chapter 2 by Durlach and Chapter 3 by Miller and Matzel) which is discussed in greater detail at the end of that chapter. Another important issue addressed by the model is the role of contextual stimuli in autoshaping. As seen in a later section, the acquisition of autoshaping is profoundly affected by the pairing of contextual stimuli with food.

III. THE ROLE OF THE UNCONDITIONED STIMULUS

In Pavlovian conditioning the UR (unconditioned response) elicited by the US is often a major determinant of the topography of the CR. It is the similarity of the CR and the UR which promulgates the notion that the CS comes to substitute for the US (i.e., "stimulus substitution theory"). Although many such CRs are highly reflexive and/or autonomically mediated (e.g., salivary conditioning, eyeblink conditioning, GSR), there are numerous examples of Pavlovian conditioning in which complex behavioral sequences that are components of the UR are conditioned to predictive stimuli (Rackham, 1971; Thompson & Sturm, 1965).

Pavlovian conditioning of complex skeletal motor sequences does not typically result in approach and contact with the CS as is seen in autoshaping. Are the similarities between CR and UR observed in the conditioning of complex skeletal CRs also observed in autoshaping? There is considerable evidence that such is the case (i.e., the nature of the US used in autoshaping studies determines, to a large extent, the topography of the CR elicited; see Chapter 6 by Wagner and Brandon). Consider, for example, the results of an experiment performed by Jenkins and Moore (1973). They noted that the topography of the pigeon's autoshaping CR differed when water (as opposed to food) was used as the US. Moreover, the differences in topography were clearly related to the US employed. Water deprived pigeons approached and contacted the keylight CS (which predicted the presentation of the water US). The form of the autoshaping CR resembled the pigeon's drinking behavior. That is, the pigeons were observed to approach the keylight and make contact with slight opening and closing movements of the beak coordinated with licking and swallowing movements. Food deprived pigeons, on the other hand, contacted the keylight CS (which predicted the presentation of the food US) in a manner which resembled the pigeon's eating behavior. That is, the pigeons were observed to approach the keylight and make contact with a sudden ballistic thrust of the slightly open beak.

Further experiments by Jenkins and Moore (1973) indicate that this effect was attributable to the nature of the US rather than to the subject's deprivation state. In order to assess the effects of the deprivation state, Jenkins and Moore deprived the pigeons of both food and water. The pigeons were then given autoshaping training with food serving as the US for the initial sessions and water serving as the US for later sessions. Pictures of the pigeon's keypecks showed that the form of the autoshaping CR varied with the changes in the US. Similar types of observations have been reported by Davey and Cleland (1982), who noted that rats bite levers whose insertion predicts solid food and lick levers whose insertion predicts liquid food. These effects were also found to be independent of the animal's deprivation condition.

The relationship between the topography of the CR and the topography of the UR has also been explored by Peterson et al. (1972) using positively reinforcing intracranial stimulation of the lateral hypothalamus as a US. In their experiment one group of rats was presented with trials of a 15 sec insertion of one of two retractable illuminated levers. Insertion of one of the two levers was always followed by the presentation of food whereas insertion of the second lever was uncorrelated with food delivery. A second group was exposed to the same contingencies except that the food US was replaced with intracranial stimulation. The behaviors elicited by the US included sniffing, postural adjustments, and exploratory behavior. All animals in both groups were food deprived and had stimulating electrodes implanted in the lateral hypothalamus. They observed that the topography of the autoshaping CR elicited by the lever paired with food was licking and gnawing whereas the topography of the autoshaping CR elicited by the lever paired with intracranial stimulation was the same type of sniffing, pawing, and exploratory behavior that generally results from hypothalamic stimulation. These results are similar to those reported by Jenkins and Moore (1973) in that the topography of the CR is closely related to the topography of the UR.

The results reported by Peterson et al. (1972) indicate that even when the UR does not include the complex skeletal motor behaviors involved in approaching and contacting the US, the CS comes to elicit approach and contact behaviors. This indicates that the approach and contact component of the CR is not dependent upon the elicitation of such behaviors by the US. This conclusion is supported by the results of a number of other studies that do not employ brain stimulation as US. For example, when water is used as the US and manipulations are employed to eliminate the approach and contact behaviors normally observed during drinking, approach and contact to a keylight CS is still observed. Woodruff and Williams (1976) implanted a cannula into an adult pigeon's beak, through which they were able to deliver a water US such that the pigeon was not required to make any consumatory approach response. The delivery of water in this manner, typically evoked swallowing and mumbling movements from experimentally naive pigeons. In contrast, the autoshaping CR that was acquired was more elaborate. While noncontingent presentations of water and the keylight failed to elicit anything more than swallowing and mumbling, pigeons in the positive contingency group exhibited keylight directed responses such as bobbing, rooting and pecking, in addition to the behaviors elicited by the injection of water. It appears, therefore, that the approach and contact component of the UR is not necessary for the development of the approach and contact CR.

One question that arises from procedures that eliminate the approach component of the UR is the role of the subject's preexperimental history with the US. That is, the adult pigeon has previously learned to approach and contact water. The approach and contact CR may, therefore, reflect this aspect of the subject's previous experience with the US. To determine the role of this type of previous experience with the US, Woodruff and Starr (1978) placed 3–4 day-old chicks in an autoshaping experiment, where force feeding of food and water was the method of delivery of the USs. The chicks had been force fed in this manner throughout their rearing. Observations of the chick's behavior revealed that even without any history of consummatory approach responding, subjects given trials of a keylight paired with reward, develop US appropriate signal directed responding. Pecking at the keylight CSs was not acquired by chicks presented water or food in a random or negatively contingent fashion. Interestingly, when the chicks were given autoshaping trials using sand as the US, Woodruff and Starr did not record any autoshaping to the keylight. This suggests that the role of the CS in autoshaping may be to release patterns of behavior biologically organized and predetermined for the US. There is considerable evidence that appetitive-consummatory motor patterns can exist in a "preformed" state in the neural circuitry of the brainstem and their expression is dependent upon the presence of appropriate external stimulation (cf. Bullock, 1961; Glickman & Schiff, 1967; Valenstein, 1969). Woodruff and Williams (1976) argue that the form of the autoshaping response is accounted for by the notion of "learned release."

The "learned release" hypothesis may provide a framework for understanding the results of autoshaping studies which purport to demonstrate that the topography of the CR is not necessarily related to the topography of the UR. There are a number of demonstrations of sign-tracking which clearly show that the behaviors elicited by localized visual CSs are not those elicited by the US. For example, Wasserman (1973b) exposed 3-day-old chicks to an 8 sec keylight (CS) followed by 4 sec of heat (US). He found that the chicks developed approach, snuggling, and pecking behaviors directed toward the keylight. Wasserman noted that the heat lamp US elicited unenergetic and undirected postures and movements, and concluded that the topography of the UR was not predictive of the topography of the CR. These data may be consistent with a "learned release" interpretation of autoshaping. Hogan (1974) has reported that snuggling and pecking are part of the normal heat seeking repertoire of chicks in the natural environment.

"Learned release" may also account for the results of an experiment reported by Rachlin (1969) who observed approach and contact to a keylight CS which predicted shock termination (US). Autoshaping was not observed when the illumination of the key was not predictive of shock termination. The autoshaping CR elicited by the illumination of the key was keypecking and wing-flapping, neither of which was reported as a component of the UR. These data may be taken as consistent with the "learned release" hypothesis because both pecking and wing-flapping are components of the pigeon's normal pattern of aggressive behavior. Interestingly, when key illumination is paired with the presentation of shock, pigeons move away from the vicinity of the keylight (Dunham, Mariner, & Adams, 1969; Green, 1978; Green & Rachlin, 1977; Schwartz, 1973; Wesp, Lattal, & Poling, 1977).

Do the attributes of the CS play a role in "learned release"? That is, do all CS's release the same sequence for a particular US? Timberlake and Grant (1975) found that when the presentation of food (US) was predicted by the insertion of another rat, the topography of the rat's CR was orientation toward the CS rat, approach toward the CS rat, and social contact (paw, groom, crawl over, sniff, etc.) directed toward the US rat. When food was signaled by the insertion of a wooden block the topography of the CS was orientation toward the wooden block CS, without appreciable approach or social contact. Timberlake and Grant argued that the rat is a social forager and the food US elicits a variety of social feeding behaviors. The components of the UR that will be released depends on the nature of the CS. In this case, the rat CS releases primarily social contact, whereas, the wooden block CS does not. Previously we have seen that smaller visually localized CSs elicit gnawing and feeding behaviors (cf. Cleland & Davey, 1983, Peterson et al., 1972; Locurto et al., 1976).

Because all species do not exhibit the same behavioral repertoire in the presence of a particular US, Timberlake and Grant would predict that there will be cross-species variations in the topography of the autoshaping CR that develops with a particular US. This may account for many of the failures to produce autoshaping when procedures that reliably elicit signal directed responding in one species are implemented in another species. For example, the use of an illuminated key as a signal for grain readily results in keylight directed pecking behavior in pigeons but not in crows (Powell et al., 1975). Crows are capable of instrumental keypecking behavior for grain reward, although this response rapidly waned when grain was presented independently of keypecking (Powell & Kelly, 1976). Presumably, these differences in the acquisition and maintenance of autoshaping reflect cross-species differences in the degree to which grain elicits pecking behavior. Crows are preferentially meat eaters and naturally display a tearing response to food. This type of UR is presumably less compatible with keypecking than is the pigeon's natural feeding behavior.

Studies that vary the US and its method of delivery are important for several reasons. They demonstrate that the US is often an important determinant of the topography of the autoshaping CR. They also indicate that the approach and contact behaviors which normally form an important part of the consummatory behavior elicited by appetitive USs are not necessary for the development of the approach and contact components of the autoshaping CR. The data are consistent with the "learned release" hypothesis (Woodruff & Williams, 1976) which states that the US elicits a highly organized, biologically predetermined set of behaviors which come to be elicited by the CS. It would be inappropriate to conclude that the role played by the localized visual CS is that of a target. It appears that the CR observed in autoshaping with a particular US is that subset of those behaviors elicited by the US which are also appropriate to the nature of the CS (Timberlake & Grant, 1975; also Timberlake and Lucas, 1989).

IV.   INSTRUMENTAL FACTORS IN AUTOSHAPING

Pigeons have been extensively employed as experimental subjects in studies of instrumental performance using free-operant procedures. The prototypic free-operant response employed has been the pecking of a response key. This response has typically been reinforced by the presentation of grain. Because the likelihood of keypeck responding increases when the response is followed by temporally contiguous presentation of grain, it seems plausible that the autoshaping keypeck CR may be affected by the grain US instrumentally. That is, the acquisition of autoshaping may be influenced by the instrumental reward relation between keypecking and food.

As noted earlier, Williams and Williams (1969) eliminated the possibility that the autoshaping keypeck CR would be followed closely in time by the presentation of grain by employing an omission contingency (i.e., presentation of grain was contingent upon the nonoccurrence of keypecking). They observed that the keypecking CR was acquired despite the negative relationship between keypecking and food. Although this study demonstrates that the acquisition of autoshaping is not wholly due to superstitious instrumental conditioning, it does not imply that instrumental factors play no role in autoshaping. Williams and Williams (1969) observed that the omission contingency had an effect on autoshaping. It reduced the level of keypecking below that observed when the subjects were given autoshaping trials without the omission contingency.

Williams and Williams (1969) asked if the pigeon's keypecking CR was completely insensitive to it's outcome by comparing autoshaping to two simultaneously illuminated signals for food (green and red keylight). While both keys were illuminated for 6 sec, pecks at one of the keys (omission key) resulted in the termination of illumination of both keylights and the cancellation of the programmed access to grain. In contrast, pecks at the second keylight (irrevelant key) had no programmed consequences. Williams and Williams observed that pigeons pecked on the irrelevant key rather than the omission key. They concluded that the autoshaping CR is affected by instrumental factors.

Note that the results of this experiment are inconsistent with a secondary reinforcement interpretation of autoshaping (see also Hursh, Navarick, and Fantino, 1974, for a possible example of secondary reinforcement effects in autoshaping). This type of instrumental conditioning analysis of autoshaping presumes that stimuli paired with food reward (i.e., keylight termination) acquire response strengthening properties. The argument that keypecking is strengthened by keylight termination leads to the prediction that keypecking would not develop to the irrelevant key, where keypecking has no programmed consequences.

Instrumental conditioning is profoundly affected by the interval between the occurrence of the response and the presentation of the reinforcer. The longer the delay the less effective the reinforcer. Deich and Wasserman (1977) placed an omission contingency during the first or the second half of an 8 sec keylight trial. Operant conditioning of keypecking would presumably be more successful with shorter delays between keypecking and food (i.e., when the omission contingency was in effect during the first half of the autoshaping trial). The results were consistent with such an operant conditioning interpretation. Similar effects of delaying reinforcement in autoshaping have been reported by Locurto et al. (1976) who placed rats in a chamber where the insertion of a lever CS was followed 15 sec later by retraction of the lever and the presentation of food (US). Each time the rats contacted the lever, the food US was delayed by 2.5 sec for one group and 10 sec for another. Yoked controls in this experiment were groups of rats matched for the delay of the food. The results of this study were consistent with those of previous experiments in that fewer lever contacts were recorded for the animals that experienced the response dependant delay in comparison to their matched yoked controls. This effect was also demonstrated to be dependent on the magnitude of the delay as the animals that experienced the 10 sec delays responded less than did the rats in the 2.5 sec delay group. Clearly, appetitive instrumental factors can have a significant effect on autoshaping.

The effects of aversive instrumental factors in autoshaping has been less thoroughly evaluated, likely because the majority of autoshaping procedures utilize appetitive USs. Appetitively maintained instrumental responses, however, can be weakened by the response contingent application of negatively reinforcing stimuli (e.g., electric shock). Punishment procedures have been shown to be effective in suppressing autoshaping. Wesp et al. (1977) exposed magazine trained pigeons to the typical autoshaping paradigm of 8 sec keylight trials followed by 4 sec access to grain. All keypecks (during either the CS or during the intertrial interval) were followed by the application of shock. The results indicated the pigeon's keypecking was reliably suppressed relative to yoked controls that received a similar number of shocks in a response independent fashion.

The conclusion supported by the studies cited above is that the autoshaping CR, though largely derived from the Pavlovian relationship between CS and US, is nevertheless, reliably and systematically affected by a number of CR–reinforcer manipulations known to affect the strength of instrumental behaviors.

Note that in the aforementioned studies the effects of instrumental relations are seen only on the maintenance of keypecking (i.e., automaintenance) and not on the acquisition of keypecking (i.e., autoshaping). The differential effectiveness of instrumental manipulations has been related to differences in the topography of the autoshaping keypeck early during autoshaping as compared to later during automaintenance. Schwartz and Williams (1972a) reported that the distribution of keypeck durations observed during autoshaping was of short duration (less than 20 msec), whereas, keypeck duration during automaintenance was often two to five times longer. When the omission contingency was subsequently introduced, they observed that only the long duration keypecks were eliminated by the instrumental contingency (i.e., the short duration keypecks persisted). They note that the keypecks observed during free-operant procedures (e.g., fixed-interval schedules, fixed ratio schedules) were typically of long duration and, moreover, that the distribution of keypeck durations was altered by differential reinforcement of long duration keypecks but not by differential reinforcement of short duration keypecks. They concluded that there are two different types of keypecks observed during autoshaping in the pigeon: Short duration keypecks elicited by stimuli paired with food (i.e., Pavlovian keypecks) appear early during autoshaping and persist during omission training, whereas, long duration keypecks maintained by food reward (i.e., operant keypecks) appear later during automaintenance and are eliminated by the omission contingency.

The conclusion supported by the studies cited above is that the maintenance of the keypecking CR is reliably and systematically affected by a number of keypeck–food manipulations that are known to affect the strength of a wide range of instrumental behaviors. Perhaps the initial approach and contact CR is derived solely from the Pavlovian relationship between key illumination and food, but, clearly, subsequent responding is not. The occurrence of the keypecking CR, followed closely in time by the presentation of food, allows for the possibility of "superstitious" instrumental strengthening of the keypecking CR. Apparently, such superstitious conditioning of keypecking does occur, and affects maintenance of keypecking to a considerable extent. However, it must be noted that while the involvement of instrumental factors in the maintenance of the keypecking CR is obviously considerable, there is less evidence that the initiation of approach and contact is derived from instrumental considerations.

How might the law of effect (i.e., strengthening of responses by their consequences) account for the initiation of keypecking? As noted earlier, there is some evidence that autoshaping is derived, in part, from the generalization of instrumental grain pecking in the presence of the hopper light to the pecking of the key-light. While possibly relevant to the traditional autoshaping procedure, this type of approach cannot account for the numerous instances of autoshaping and sign-tracking observed using other procedures.

Much of this discussion of autoshaping presumes that it is reasonable to dichotomize Pavlovian and instrumental learning processes. The tone of this analysis reflects the axiomatic tenets of traditional two-factor theory which, by legislative fiat, segregated behavior into nonoverlapping sets (Williams, 1981). It was this climate and *Zeitgeist* into which autoshaping was born (Terrace, 1981), and, accordingly, much of the work we have reviewed reflects the inertia of this orientation. Because of the incisive and rigorous experimental analysis applied to autoshaping, it no longer seems reasonable to distinguish between operants and respondents as distinct classes of behavior conditionable by different types of contingencies. Clearly, the distinction will never again appear to be as clear-cut. Even more clearly, the past fruits of that labor now seem tainted. It is not surprising that contemporary approaches to conditioning and learning now emphasize the biconditional determinants of learned behavior (Wasserman, 1981; Williams, 1981) and the biological and comparative-evolutionary determinants of response evocation (Buzsaki, 1982; Wasserman, 1981). Autoshaping was the catalyst of this change.

V.   EFFECTS OF CS–US CONTINGENCY

Positive CS–US Contingency

As noted earlier, the approach and contact CR observed with pigeons is seen only when there is a positive contingency between the illumination of the keylight and the presentation of food (cf. Gamzu & Williams, 1971). There are a number of different ways that the manipulation of CS–US contingency has been shown to affect autoshaping. For example, Hearst and Jenkins (1974) used a two-key apparatus in which the illumination of one key was positively correlated with food, whereas, the illumination of the alternative key was randomly related to food. They observed that pigeons began to peck only at the key that signaled the delivery of food.

This type of manipulation of CS–US contingency provides a demonstration that subjects are sensitive to differences in contingencies presented concurrently and that they will approach and contact the CS most predictive of the US.

Negative CS–US Contingency

Positive CS–US contingency elicits approach and contact behavior. On the other hand, no keypecking behavior is observed to be elicited by a negative CS–US contingency (Gamzu & Williams, 1973). The negative CS–US contingency is not, however, without effect. Wasserman, Franklin and Hearst (1974) recorded the pigeon's position in the operant chamber relative to the keylight CS. In their study, the illuminated keylight randomly alternated between the left and right keys of a three key array (located on one wall of the experimental chamber). For one group of pigeons there was a positive contingency (CS–US explicitly paired) between the illumination of the keylight and the presentation of grain, whereas, for the second group there was a negative contingency (CS–US explicitly unpaired) and for the third group there was a zero contingency (CS–US random). Wasserman et al. (1974) observed that the positive contingency elicited approach (pigeons occupied the keylight side of the operant chamber) and contact behavior (i.e., keypecking), while the negative contingency elicited withdrawal from the vicinity of the keylight.

It is now well documented that procedures that provide for negative correlations between localized visual CS and appetitive US produce withdrawal from the vicinity of the CS (cf. Bottjer, 1982; Hearst, Bottjer, & Walker, 1980; Hearst & Franklin, 1977; Kaplan & Hearst, 1985). The withdrawal from keylight CR is important because it provides for ongoing (i.e., trial-by-trial) assessment of Pavlovian inhibitory conditioning (as opposed to the use of postconditioning assays for inhibition). Moreover, it provides one of the few instances where the topography of the inhibitory CR is clearly specified (as opposed to the widely adopted convention of characterizing inhibition by the diminution of the excitatory CR).

The effects of negative keylight-food contingency have also been evaluated using traditional tests for inhibition. For example, Wasserman and Molina (1975) trained pigeons with an explicitly unpaired procedure then compared acquisition of autoshaping to the same or to a novel CS in a paired procedure (i.e., retardation test for inhibition). That is, pigeons were given 7 daily sessions in which the illumination of the keylight was isolated from the presentation of the food magazine by a minimum of 40 sec. On day 8, all of the pigeons received autoshaping trials. For half of the pigeons the autoshaping CS was novel, whereas, for the other half of the pigeons the autoshaping CS was the same keylight used in the explicitly unpaired procedure. Comparison of the number of trials to the first keypeck revealed that initiation of keypecking was slower to the explicitly unpaired keylight stimulus than to the novel one. Because an inhibitory CS should be retarded in being converted into an excitatory stimulus, this type of result is obviously consistent with the hypothesis that the explicitly unpaired CS is inhibitory.

Zero CS–US Contingency

Wasserman et al. (1974) evaluated the effects of positive, negative, and zero contingency on approach/withdrawal behavior, using Gamzu and Williams' (1973) method of altering the US probabilities during the trial and the ITI. Three separate groups were formed by having the probability generator sampled during the keylight trial for the positive contingency, during the ITI for the negative contingency and in both intervals for the zero contingency. They found, as previously reported in their first experiment, that the positive contingency group approached and contacted the keylight CS while the negative contingency group withdrew from the vicinity of the keylight CS. They also observed that the zero contingency treatment yielded neither approach nor withdrawal from the keylight. The results are consistent with the notion that the approach and withdrawal behaviors reflect excitatory and inhibitory CR topographies, respectively, and that the zero contingency treatment provides an appropriate pseudoconditioning control procedure.

The zero CS–US contingency elicits neither approach nor withdrawal from the vicinity of the CS. It does, however, interfere with subsequent autoshaping. Mackintosh (1973) has reported that pigeons exposed to random presentations of green key CS and food US were subsequently profoundly retarded in the acquisition of autoshaping, requiring many more pairings of the green key and the food to establish reliable keypecking. Mackintosh's observations have been replicated by Tomie, Murphy, Fath, and Jackson (1980) and are consistent with the observations of other investigators (cf. Bilbrey & Winokur, 1973). Moreover, Gamzu and Williams (1971, 1973) have reported that prior exposure to zero contingency between keylight and food subsequently suppressed asymptotic levels of keypecking during automaintenance.

Similar types of interference effects have been reported by Wasserman et al. (1974) using the approach/withdrawal measures. They reported that the pigeons receiving either zero or negative contingency treatment were subsequently retarded in approaching the keylight when the keylight was presented so as to be predictive of food. The retarding effects of zero contingency pretraining are not unique to autoshaping, having previously been reported in a number of other Pavlovian conditioning procedures (cf. Baker & Mackintosh, 1977; Kremer, 1971; Rescorla, 1968).

Retardation.   Hall and Honig (1974) have reported a similar type of retardation effect using a somewhat different procedure. In their experiment, pigeons were administered response-independent food reinforcement in the presence of diffuse green and red houselights. For one group of subjects, the presentation of food was correlated with the color of the houselight such that reinforcers were presented in only one component of a two-component multiple schedule, while, for the other group, the reinforcers were presented in an uncorrelated manner (i.e., food was presented in both components equally often). The subjects were subsequently tested for the acquisition of autoshaping in the presence of a neutral white houselight. They observed that the acquisition of keypecking to the autoshaping CS was substantially retarded following the prolonged experience with uncorrelated houselight CS–food US presentations.

The pattern of results reported by Hall and Honig (1974) is important, for it indicates that the interference engendered by uncorrelated CS–US pretraining is *not specific* to the pretraining CS. Tomie (1976b, 1981) has replicated this type of effect and has noted that the physical characteristics of the randomly presented pretraining CS have no systematic effect on the magnitude of the subsequently observed retardation. That is, whether the randomly presented pretraining CS is a diffuse auditory stimulus (e.g., tone) or a localized visual stimulus (e.g., red light projected onto the response key), the subsequent effects of such pretraining upon the acquisition of autoshaping are virtually identical.

Context Effects and Autoshaping. Tomie (1976a, 1976b, 1981) has argued that the deleterious effects of such pretraining procedures may reflect blocking of conditioning to the autoshaping CS by the prior conditioning of contextual stimuli which are present during the autoshaping phase. That is, during pretraining the unsignaled USs are paired with the situational stimuli of the experimental context. Contemporary theoretical views of Pavlovian conditioning (cf. Rescorla & Wagner, 1972) suggest that contextual stimuli should become excitatory as a result of such pretraining. What effect might this excitatory context exert upon autoshaping? Kamin (1969) has shown that the conditioning of a novel CS is retarded if such conditioning is conducted in the presence of another CS which has already been conditioned. Tomie has argued that because the contextual stimuli are present and probably conditioned during pretraining as a result of their repeated pairings with the food US, and, moreover, because they are also present and compounded with the keylight CS during autoshaping, the context may exert a blocking influence during the test. Moreover, such an effect of the context would be expected following any pretraining procedure which provided for unpredictable presentations of food.

Tomie has shown that the deleterious effects of such pretraining procedures are specific to the pretraining context. That is, gross alterations of the contextual stimuli between pretraining and testing (for the acquisition of autoshaping) alleviates the retarding effects of "Learned Laziness" pretraining (Balsam & Schwartz, 1981; Rescorla, Durlach, & Grau, 1985; Tomie, 1981), "Learned Irrelevance" pretraining (Tomie et al., 1980), and "General Inattentiveness" pretraining (Tomie, 1976a, 1976b). Tomie (1976b, 1981) and Balsam and Schwartz (1981) has also shown that the retardation of autoshaping in the excitatory context can be attenuated by extinguishing the context prior to testing for autoshaping. That is, nonreinforced exposure to the context between pretraining with unpredictable presentations of food and testing for autoshaping attenuates the retardation effect.

What is the topography of the CR elicited when a hungry pigeon is placed in a context associated with the presentation of food? Balsam (1984, 1985) and Rescorla et al. (1985) have reported that there is an increase in activity (as measured by number of closure of microswitch operated floor panels or by observer's rating of videotape, respectively) during that part of the daily session which precedes the presentation of food. The topography of the activity CR is idiosyncratic (i.e., varies markedly from subject to subject) but is usually described as head bobbing often accompanied by moving back and forth in front of the food hopper. The activity CR resembles "interim responses" elicited from the pigeon by periodic presentations of response-independent food (Staddon & Simmelhag, 1971).

Several lines of evidence suggest that the context quickly becomes a signal for food. Balsam and Schwartz (1981) have reported that the speed of acquisition of autoshaping is negatively related to the number of presentations of the food hopper which precedes autoshaping. They found that acquisition of keypecking was reliably retarded by fewer than 10 feedings prior to the initiation of autoshaping. Rescorla et al. (1985) have observed reliable increases in activity conditioned to context (i.e., observed prior to the delivery of food) by the fourth session of training. These data suggest that the pigeon rapidly learns to associate the presentation of food with the experimental setting.

How does the association between the context and food affect autoshaping? Balsam (1985) has found, in both ring doves and pigeons, a negative between-subjects correlation between activity level conditioned to context and the speed of acquisition of autoshaping, indicating that subjects that exhibit strong activity CRs are retarded in acquiring the keypecking CR. There are two fundamentally different ways that the context–food association may engender interference with autoshaping. It may affect the *learning* of the keylight–food association (cf. Rescorla & Wagner's [1972], linear-operator model). This suggests that the association between context and food (established during pretraining with unpredictable US presentations) may interfere with the subsequent learning of the keylight–food association. In this view, autoshaping is not observed because the pigeon does not associate key illumination with food. On the other hand, Gibbon and Balsam's (1981) Scalar Expectancy Theory proposes that the context–food association affects the *performances* of the autoshaping CR, but not the learning of the keylight–food association. In this view, autoshaping is not observed until the ratio of the keylight–food association relative to the context–food association exceeds threshold.

The view that context affects learning of the keylight–food association is supported by experiments which compare directly automaintenance in contexts which had been conditioned to different degrees. Grau and Rescorla (1984) reported that the performance of the previously established autoshaping CR is largely unaffected by the test context. Similar effects have been reported by Durlach (1983). On the other hand, there are a number of studies whose results support the notion that context–food association modulates the performance of the keypecking CR. For example, Lindbloom and Jenkins (1981) observed that intertrial USs had a detrimental effect on automaintenance. Specifically, once autoshaping had been established, adding USs during the ITI produced a profound response decrement; yet when all USs were subsequently deleted, responding recovered to near its previous level. These data suggest that the performance of autoshaping cannot be entirely determined by the keylight–food association.

VI. THEORETICAL IMPLICATIONS OF AUTOSHAPING

Distinctions Between Operants and Respondents

Autoshaping was unexpected. Traditional views of Pavlovian conditioning did not suggest that we should concern ourselves with the effects of localizing the CS. Even more unexpected than the nature of the CS was the topography of the elicited CR. No phenomenon has done more to lay to rest the notion that Pavlovian CRs and instrumental behaviors are fundamentally different types of behaviors controlled by different associative relations. We should not underestimate the importance of this revelation. The longstanding commitment to traditional distinctions between respondents and operants was so strong that earlier reports of pigeons displaying complex skeletal CRs to signals for food were not readily accepted as exemplars of Pavlovian conditioning.

In 1964, Longo, Klempay, and Bitterman reported that pigeons' activity was conditioned to stimuli predictive of food. These researchers compared the anticipatory activity of two groups of pigeons during the presence of either a 1 or 10 sec buzzer that had previously been paired with food delivery. When the pigeons were later exposed to a 40 sec test trial of the buzzer CS alone, they observed, in both groups, an increase in anticipatory movements above baseline levels. They noted that the complex skeletal responses might be Pavlovian. On the other hand, they noted that the greater conditioning in the 10 sec group was inconsistent with the well documented relation in the Pavlovian literature of superior conditioning with shorter interstimulus intervals. They also noted that the 10 sec buzzer provided more opportunity for superstitious conditioning. Unfortunately, their study did not include controls (i.e., omission training procedures) to evaluate for possible adventitious reinforcement of superstitious behaviors. Somewhat later, using similar procedures, Slivka and Bitterman (1966) exposed groups of pigeons to either partial reinforcement or continuous reinforcement procedures. The CS in their study was a change in the food magazine light. They noted that the partial reinforcement manipulation did not reduce the amount of anticipatory responding and that this result was consistent with a Pavlovian rather than an instrumental interpretation of the phenomenon.

Kimble (1964) published a critical comment on the first paper. He objected strenuously to the conclusion that perhaps complex skeletal behaviors could be conditioned by Pavlovian procedures. For the most part, his objections were based on the notion that Pavlovian CRs and instrumental responses were distinctive and nonoverlapping behavioral sets, separable on the basis of topography (cf. Kimble, 1961). According to this view, Pavlovian CRs were exclusively reflexive and involuntary, while instrumental behaviors were performances mediated exclusively by the peripheral skeletal musculature. Kimble argued that it was premature to accept the notion that anticipatory skeletal behaviors could be conditioned by Pavlovian procedures until all possible interpretations based on instrumental factors had been conclusively ruled out.

This type of distinction between Pavlovian and instrumental CRs was widely cherished. There were, moreover, profound implications of this view. Because peripheral skeletal responses were thought to be modified only by instrumental factors, the possible range of effects of Pavlovian CRs on instrumental performance were necessarily limited. They were seen largely as motivational modulators (cf. Hull, 1943; Mowrer, 1947; Rescorla & Solomon, 1967). That is, Pavlovian CRs were thought to affect instrumental behavior by modulating the motivation or incentive to perform the response.

The phenomenon of autoshaping suggests that Pavlovian CRs may affect the measurement of instrumental performance in another important way. Because they may closely resemble the topography of instrumental behaviors, the occurrence of sign-tracking CRs may inflate estimates of the strength of discriminated operants. Obviously, for this reason, the discovery of autoshaping could not be easily dismissed or overlooked. After all, here was a Pavlovian procedure that elicited a response that was virtually indistinguishable from the prototypic free-operant response extensively studied in pigeons. We shall see that autoshaping has played a substantial role in discriminated operant procedures. We shall also see how an appreciation of its effects has modified the way that we view a number of instrumental learning phenomena.

Autoshaping and Feature Effects

Jenkins and Sainsbury (1969, 1970) have reported that the speed of acquisition of instrumental discrimination learning is dramatically affected by whether the distinctive feature (i.e., stimulus that differentiates the positive and negative discriminative stimuli from one another) is arranged so as to be presented on the positive trial as opposed to the negative trial. If the feature (for example, a black dot) appears on the pigeon's response key only on the positive (S+) trials, the pigeons learn the discrimination and cease responding on S− trials. On the other hand, if the distinctive feature appears only on the negative (S−) trials, pigeons learn the discrimination much more slowly, if at all.

The feature effect in instrumental discrimination learning has been extensively characterized (cf. Farthing, 1971; Furrow & LoLordo, 1975; Sainsbury, 1971). The phenomenon appears to be attributable to sign-tracking. Subjects placed on feature positive discriminations begin to peck directly at the distinctive feature on the S+ display before they begin to eliminate responding to the S− display. On the other hand, in the feature negative case, subjects direct keypecks away from the distinctive feature and toward the part of the S− display which is common to the S+. In both cases, subjects track the signal which is most highly correlated with the presentation of food reward. In the feature positive case this facilitates the acquisition of the discrimination, whereas, in the feature negative case it has the opposite effect.

Autoshaping and Behavioral Contrast

Behavioral contrast was initially reported by Reynolds (1961) who evaluated the rate at which pigeons peck an illuminated disk of light during a MULT VI 3 min/VI 3 min schedule of food reward. During each of the successively presented components of the MULT schedule the response key was illuminated by a distinctive keylight color (i.e., the keylight alternated between red and green). Reynolds found that the pigeon responded at a comparable rate during the two components of the nondifferential MULT schedule. When he subsequently altered the situation so that one of the keylights now signaled an extinction schedule (i.e., MULT VI 3 min/EXT schedule), Reynolds observed that the response rate during the unaltered VI 3 min component increased markedly, even though the rate of reinforcement during that component was unchanged.

Schwartz and Gamzu (1977) have proposed an autoshaping account of behavioral contrast. They note that during the differential MULT schedule the keylight discriminative stimuli are differentially paired with food reward. Such differential pairings of keylight CS and food US would be expected to produce signal-directed keypecking behavior (i.e., autoshaping) in the pigeons. Their additivity theory of behavioral contrast proposes that the increase in keypecking observed during the VI 3 min component of the differential MULT schedule beyond the level previously observed during the nondifferential MULT schedule reflects the summation of Pavlovian keypecks on the baseline rate of instrumental keypecking.

This interpretation is supported by several lines of evidence. As noted earlier, Schwartz and Williams (1972b) have reported that keypecks observed during the acquisition of autoshaping are of briefer duration (less than 20 msec) than are keypecks observed during automaintenance. Moreover, only the longer duration keypecks are eliminated by the omission contingency. This suggests that instrumental and Pavlovian keypecks may be differentiated on the basis of keypeck duration. An analysis of keypeck durations observed during nondifferential and different MULT schedules reveals that there is an increase in the frequency of short duration keypecks during differential MULT schedule procedures (Schwartz, 1977). Further support is provided by the results of behavioral contrast studies which separate the locus of the discriminative stimulus from the locus of the response manipulandum. For example, Keller (1974) utilized one key of a two key apparatus to signal the component of the MULT schedule in effect. The second key was constantly illuminated and served as the keypeck manipulandum. He observed no pecking of the signal key during the nondifferential MULT schedule but pecking of the signal key increased during differential MULT schedule procedures. Moreover, the sum of the rates of pecking on both keys was greater than the rate of pecking on the manipulandum key during the nondifferential MULT schedule phase.

The notion that autoshaping accounts for behavioral contrast suggests that behavioral contrast should be observed only under conditions which promote autoshaping. The procedures employed in the vast majority of behavioral contrast studies include precisely those conditions which would foster autoshaping (i.e., use of a localized visual CS projected onto the response manipulandum). Is behavioral contrast in pigeons observed in other types of free-operant procedures? Schwartz (1972) and Hearst and Gormley (1976) have reported that behavioral contrast in pigeons is not observed when the discriminative stimuli are not projected upon the response key. Moreover, Westbrook (1973) and Hemmes (1973) have reported that pigeons show behavioral contrast when the operant is keypecking but not when the operant is foot pressing of a bar or treadle. Is behavioral contrast observed in other types of free-operant MULT schedule procedures that do not use pigeons as subjects? Freeman (1971) using rats bar-pressing for food reward failed to observe behavioral contrast in the unaltered VI component when the other component was changed to EXT. He observed instead that the response rate decreased in both the VI and EXT components (i.e., negative induction effect). Pear and Wilkie (1971) and Bernheim and Williams (1967) using rats in bar-pressing and running wheel situations, respectively, reported that behavioral contrast is observed in only some of their subjects, and, certainly not to the degree reported with pigeons. (See also Guttman, Sutterer, & Brush, 1975). In summary, it appears that to a large extent the occurrence of behavioral contrast is dependent upon the conditions known to produce autoshaping.

It should be noted, however, that autoshaping does not provide a complete account of behavioral contrast. There are a number of manipulations which reliably produce behavioral contrast which do not enhance the predictive value of the keylight signal present during the unaltered component. For example, Terrace (1968) has shown that changing the VI schedule to a DRL (differential reinforcement of low rates of responding) schedule produces behavioral contrast even though there was, by explicit arrangement, no reduction in the rate of reinforcement in the altered component. Brethower and Reynolds (1962) have shown that adding brief electric shock punishment to the reward schedule reduces the response rate during the punished component of the MULT schedule but does not affect the density of rewards earned. An increase in responding in the unaltered component of the MULT schedule was observed, nevertheless.

Distinctions Between Learning and Performance

It is interesting that the modulating effects of context on the acquisition of Pavlovian CRs were most readily studied by researchers of autoshaping. Moreover, it is interesting that the distinctions between learning and performance effects were most compelling to researchers of autoshaping. Why has this relatively new type of Pavlovian conditioning procedure served as the vehicle for these types of developments? Why have such developments, which have broad significance for all forms of Pavlovian conditioning, awaited the discovery of autoshaping? Apparently, autoshaping brings sharply into focus the different ways that Pavlovian CSs may affect one another.

That is, in large part, attributable to the selective dissociation of autoshaping. Autoshaping differs from other types of Pavlovian conditioning procedures in that only particular types of CSs may be successfully employed. Because other types of CSs (i.e., nonlocalized cues) express their association with food in topographies other than keypecking, the effects of other CSs upon the learning and/or performance of autoshaping may be more readily evaluated. In other Pavlovian conditioning procedures, the CR is not as readily related to a particular CS. Therefore, discerning the effects of other CSs upon the learning and/or performance of CRs elicited by a particular CS is more difficult. Indeed, it is likely that the CS-directed nature of the autoshaping CR has encouraged a far more sophisticated analysis of context-cue interactions and learning vs. performance distinctions than would have otherwise been possible.

REFERENCES

Atnip, G. W. (1977). Stimulus- and response-reinforcer contingencies in autoshaping, operant, classical, and omission training procedures in rats. *Journal of the Experimental Analysis of Behavior, 28*, 59–69.

Baker, A. G., & Mackintosh, N. J. (1977). Excitatory and inhibition conditioning following uncorrelated presentations of CS and UCS. *Animal Learning and Behavior, 5*, 315–319.

Baldock, M. D. (1974). *Trial and intertrial interval durations in the acquisition of autoshaped key pecking.* Paper presented at the meetings of the Eastern Psychological Association. Philadelphia.

Balsam, P. D. (1984). Bring the background to the foreground: The role of contextual cues in autoshaping. In M. Commons, R. Herrnstein & A. R. Wagner (Eds.), *Quantitative analyses of behavior: Volume 3: Acquisition.* Cambridge, Mass: Ballinger.

Balsam, P. D. (1985). The functions of context in learning and performance. In P. D. Balsam & A. Tomie (Eds.), *Context and learning.* Hillsdale, NJ: Lawrence Erlbaum Associates.

Balsam, P. D., & Schwartz, A. L. (1981). Rapid contextual conditioning in autoshaping. *Journal of Experimental Psychology: Animal Behavior Processes, 1*, 382–393.

Bernheim, J. W., & Williams, D. R. (1967). Time-dependent contrast effects in a multiple schedule of food reinforcement. *Journal of the Experimental Analysis of Behavior, 10*, 243–249.

Bilbrey, J., & Winokur, S. (1973). Controls for and constraints on auto-shaping. *Journal of the Experimental Analysis of Behavior, 20*, 323–332.

Bottjer, S. W. (1982). Conditioned approach and withdrawal behavior in pigeons: Effects of a novel extraneous stimulus during acquisition and extinction. *Learning and Motivation, 13*, 44–67.

Brandon, S. F., & Bitterman, M. E. (1979). Analysis of autoshaping in goldfish. *Animal Learning and Behavior, 7*, 57–62.

Brethower, D. M., & Reynolds, G. S. (1962). A facilitative effect of punishment on unpunished behavior. *Journal of the Experimental Analysis of Behavior, 5*, 191–199.

Brown, P. L., & Jenkins, H. M. (1968). Auto-shaping of the pigeon' key-peck. *Journal of the Experimental Analysis of Behavior, 11*, 1–8.

Bullock, H. T. (1961). Origins of patterned nervous discharge. *Behaviour, 17*, 48–60.

Buzsaki, G. (1982). The "where is it?" reflex: Autoshaping and the orienting response. *Journal of the Experimental Analysis of Behavior, 37*, 461–484.

Cleland, G. G., & Davey, G. C. L. (1983). Autoshaping in the rat: The effects of localizable visual and auditory signals for food. *Journal of the Experimental Analysis of Behavior, 40*, 47–56.

Davey, G. C., & Cleland, G. C. (1982). Topography of signal-centered behavior: Effects of deprivation state and reinforcer type. *Journal of the Experimental Analysis of Behavior, 38*, 291–304.

Davis, H., & Hurwitz, H. M. B. (Eds.). (1977). *Operant-Pavlovian interactions*. Hillsdale, NJ: Lawrence Erlbaum Associates.

Davol, G. H., Steinhauer, G. D., & Lee, A. (1977). The role of the preliminary magazine training in the acquisition of the autoshaped key peck. *Journal of the Experimental Analysis of Behavior, 28*, 99–106.

Deich, J. D., & Wasserman, E. A. (1977). Rate and temporal pattern of key pecking under autoshaping and omission schedules of reinforcement. *Journal of the Experimental Analysis of Behavior, 27*, 399–405.

Dickinson, A., & Boakes, R. A. (1979). *Mechanisms of learning and motivation: A memorial volume to Jerzy Konorski*. Hillsdale, NJ: Lawrence Earlbaum Associates.

Dunham, P. J., Mariner, A., & Adams, H. (1969). Enhancement of off key-pecking by on-key punishment. *Journal of the Experimental Analysis of Behavior, 12*, 789–797.

Durlach, P. J. (1983). Effect of signaling intertrial unconditioned stimuli in autoshaping. *Journal of Experimental Psychology: Animal Behavior Processes, 9*, 374–389.

Ettinger, R. H., Finch, M. D., & McSweeney, F. K. (1978). The role of generalization in the acquisition of autoshaped keypecking in pigeons. *Bulletin of the Psychonomic Society, 12*, 235–238.

Farthing, G. W. (1971). Discrimination of compound stimuli involving the presence or absence of a distinctive visual feature. *Journal of the Experimental Analysis of Behavior, 16*, 327–336.

Fisher, M. A., & Catania, A. C. (1977). Autoshaping: Relation of feeder colour to choice of key colour. *Bulletin of the Psychonomic Society, 9*, 439–442.

Freeman, B. J. (1971). Behavioral contrast: Reinforcement frequency or response suppression? *Psychological Bulletin, 75*, 347–356.

Furrow, D. R., & LoLordo, V. M. (1975). Stimulus control in a discrimination based on a distinctive feature. *Journal of the Experimental Analysis of Behavior, 23*, 217–222.

Gamzu, E., & Schwam, E. (1974). Autoshaping and automaintenance of a key-press response in squirrel monkeys. *Journal of Experimental Analysis of Behavior, 21*, 361–371.

Gamzu, E., & Williams, D. R. (1971). Classical conditioning of a complex skeletal response. *Science, 171*, 923–925.

Gamzu, E., & Williams, D. R. (1973). Associative factors underlying the pigeon's key pecking in autoshaping procedures. *Journal of the Experimental Analysis of Behavior, 19*, 225–232.

Gardner, W. M. (1969). Auto-shaping in bobwhite quail. *Journal of the Experimental Analysis of Behavior, 12*, 279–281.

Gibbon, J., Baldock, M. D., Locurto, C., Gold, L., & Terrace, H. S. (1977). Trial and intertrial durations in autoshaping. *Journal of Experimental Psychology: Animal Behavior Processes, 3*, 264–284.

Gibbon, J., & Balsam, P. (1981). Spreading association in time. In C. M. Locurto, H. S. Terrace, & J. Gibbon (Eds.), *Autoshaping and Conditioning Theory*. New York: Academic Press.

Gibbon, J., Locurto, C. M., & Terrace, H. S. (1975). Signal-food contingency and signal frequency in a continuous trials auto-shaping paradigm. *Animal Learning and Behavior, 3*, 317–324.

Gilbert, R. M. (1973). Keypecking in an imperfect environment for autoshaping. *Bulletin of the Psychonomic Society, 2*, 10–12.

Glickman, S. E., & Schiff, B. A. (1967). A biological theory of reinforcement. *Psychological Review, 74*, 81–109.

Grastyan, E., & Vereczkei, L. (1974). Effects of spatial separation of the conditioned signal from the reinforcement: A demonstration of the conditioned character of the orienting response or the orientational character of conditioning. *Behavioral Biology, 10*, 121–146.

Grau, J. W., & Rescorla, R. A. (1984). Role of context in autoshaping. *Journal of Experimental Psychology: Animal Behavior Processes, 10*, 324–332.

Green, L. (1978). Are there two classes of classically-conditioned responses? *Pavlovian Journal of Biological Science, 13*, 154–162.

Green, L., & Rachlin, H. (1977). On the directionality of key pecking during signals for appetitive and aversive events. *Learning and Motivation, 8*, 551–568.

Guttman, A., Sutterer, J. R., & Brush, F. R. (1975). Positive and negative behavioral contrast in the rat. *Journal of the Experimental Analysis of Behavior, 23*, 377–383.

Hall, G., & Honig, W. K. (1974). Stimulus control after extradimensional training in pigeons: A comparison of response contingent and noncontingent training procedures. *Journal of Comparative and Physiological Psychology, 87*, 945–952.

Harrison, J. M. (1979). The control of responding by sounds: Unusual effect of reinforcement. *Journal of the Experimental Analysis of Behavior, 32*, 167–181.

Hearst, E. (1975). Pavlovian conditioning and directed movements. In G. H. Bower (Ed.), *The Psychology of learning and motivation* (Vol. 9). New York: Academic Press.

Hearst, E., Bottjer, S. W., & Walker, E. (1980). Conditioned approach-withdrawal behavior and some signal-food relations in pigeons. *Bulletin of the Psychonomic Society, 16*, 183–186.

Hearst, E., & Franklin, S. R. (1977). Positive and negative relations between a signal and food: Approach-withdrawal behavior to the signal. *Journal of Experimental Psychology: Animal Behavior Processes, 3*, 37–52.

Hearst, E., & Gormley, D. (1976). Some tests of the additivity (autoshaping) theory of behavioral contrast. *Animal Learning and Behavior, 4*, 145–150.

Hearst, E., & Jenkins, H. M. (1974). Sign tracking: The stimulus-reinforcer relation and directed action. *Monograph of the Psychonomic Society*, Austin, Texas.

Hemmes, N. S. (1973). Behavioral contrast in pigeons depends upon the operant. *Journal of Comparative and Physiological Psychology, 85*, 171–178.

Herrnstein, R. J., & Morse, W. H. (1957). Some effects of response-independent positive reinforcement on maintained operant behavior. *Journal of Comparative and Physiological Psychology, 50*, 461–467.

Hogan, J. A. (1974). Responses in Pavlovian conditioning studies. *Science, 186*, 156–157.

Holland, P. C. (1980). Influence of visual conditioned stimulus characteristics on the form of Pavlovian appetitive conditioned responding in rats. *Journal of Experimental Psychology: Animal Behavior Processes, 6*, 81–97.

Hull, C. L. (1943). *Principles of behavior*. New York: Appleton-Century-Crofts.

Hursh, S. R., Navarick, D. J., & Fantino, E. (1974). Automaintenance: The role of reinforcement. *Journal of the Experimental Analysis of Behavior, 21*, 117–124.

Jenkins, H. M. (1973). Effects of the stimulus-reinforcer relation on selected and unselected responses. In R. A. Hinde & J. Stevenson-Hinde (Eds.), *Constraints on learning*. New York: Academic Press.

Jenkins, H. M., Barnes, R. A., & Barrera, F. J. (1981). Why autoshaping depends on trial spacing. In C. M. Locurto, H. S. Terrace, & J. Gibbon (Eds.), *Autoshaping and conditioning theory*. New York: Academic Press.

Jenkins, H. M. Barrera, F. J., Ireland, C., & Woodside, B. (1978). Signal-centered action patterns of dogs in appetitive classical conditioning. *Learning and Motivation, 9*, 272–296.

Jenkins, H. M., & Moore, B. R. (1973). The form of the autoshaped response with food or water reinforcers. *Journal of the Experimental Analysis of Behavior, 20*, 163–181.

Jenkins, H. M. & Sainsbury, R. S. (1969). The development of stimulus control through differential reinforcement. In N. J. Mackintosh & W. K. Honig (Eds.), *Fundemental issues in associative learning*. Halifax: Dalhousie University Press.

Jenkins, H. M. & Sainsbury, R. S. (1970). Discrimination learning with the distinctive feature on positive or negative trials. In D. Mostofsky (Ed.), *Attention: Contemporary theory and analysis*. New York: Appleton-Century-Crofts.

Kamin, L. J. (1969). Predictability, surprise, attention and conditioning. In B. A. Campbell & R. M. Church (Eds.), *Punishment and aversive behavior*. New York: Appleton-Century-Crofts.

Kaplan, P. S., & Hearst, E. (1985). Contextual control and excitatory versus inhibitory learning: Studies of extinction, reinstatement, and interference. In P. D. Balsam & A. Tomie (Eds.), *Context and learning*. Hillsdale, NJ: Lawrence Erlbaum Associates.

Karpicke, J. (1978). Directed approach responses and positive conditioned suppression in the rat. *Animal Learning and Behavior, 6*, 216–224.

Keller, K. (1974). The role of elicited responding in behavioral contrast. *Journal of the Experimental Analysis of Behavior*, *21*, 249–257.

Kimble, G. A. (1961). *Hilgard and Marquis' conditioning and learning* (2nd ed.). New York: Appleton-Century-Crofts.

Kimble, G. A. (1964). Comment on Longo, Klempay, and Bitterman. *Psychonomic Science*, *1*, 40.

Konorski, J., & Miller, S. (1937). On two types of conditioned reflex. *Journal of Genetic Psychology*, *16*, 264–272.

Konorski, J., & Szwejkowska, G. (1956). Reciprocal transformations of heterogeneous conditioned reflexes. *Acta Biologicae Experimentalis*, *18*, 142–165.

Kremer, E. F. (1971). Truly random and traditional control procedures in CER conditioning in the rat. *Journal of Comparative and Physiological Psychology*, *76*, 441–448.

Likey, D. G. (1974). Autoshaping in the rhesus monkey. *Animal Learning and Behavior*, *2*, 203–206.

Lindbloom, L. L., & Jenkins, H. M. (1981). Responses eliminated by noncontingent or negatively contingent reinforcement recover in extinction. *Journal of Experimental Psychology: Animal Behavior Processes*, *7*, 175–190.

Locurto, C., Terrace, H. S., & Gibbon, J. (1976). Autoshaping, random control and omission training in the rat. *Journal of the Experimental Analysis of Behavior*, *26*, 451–462.

Locurto, C., Terrace, H. S., & Gibbon, J. (Eds.). (1981). *Autoshaping and conditioning theory*. New York: Academic Press.

Longo, N., Klempay, S., & Bitterman, M. E. (1964). Classical appetitive conditioning in the pigeon. *Psychonomic Science*, *1*, 19–23.

Loop, M. S. (1976). Auto-shaping—A simple technique for teaching a lizard to perform a visual discrimination task. *Copeia*, *3*, 574–576.

Mackintosh, N. J. (1973). Stimulus selection: Learning to ignore stimuli that predict no change in reinforcement. In R. A. Hinde and J. S. Hinde (Eds.), *Constraints on learning* (pp. 75–100). New York: Academic Press.

Miller, N. E. (1941). An experimental investigation of acquired drives. *Psychological Bulletin*, *38*, 534–535.

Mowrer, O. H. (1947). On the dual nature of learning—A reinterpretation of "conditioning" and "problem-solving." *Harvard Educational Review*, *17*, 102–148.

Mowrer O. H. (1960). *Learning theory and behavior*. New York: Wiley.

Mowrer, J. S., & Hull, J. H. (1974). Autoshaping and instrumental learning in the rat. *Journal of Comparative and Physiological Psychology*, *86*(4), 724–729.

Pavlov, I. P. (1934). An attempt at a physiological interpretation of obsessional neurosis and paranoia. *Journal of Mental Science*, *80*, 187–197.

Pear, J. J., & Wilkie, D. M. (1971). Contrast and induction in rats on multiple schedules. *Journal of the Experimental Analysis of Behavior*, *15*, 289–296.

Peden, B. F., Browne, M. P., & Hearst, E. (1977). Persistent approaches to a signal for food despite food omission for approaching. *Journal of Experimental Psychology: Animal Behavior Processes*, *3*, 377–399.

Perkins, C. C. Jr., Beavers, W. O., Hancock, R. A., Jr., Hemmendinger, P. C., Hemmendinger, D., & Ricci, J. A. (1975). Some variables affecting rate of key pecking during response-independent procedures (autoshaping). *Journal of the Experimental Analysis of Behavior*, *24*, 59–72.

Peterson, G. B., Ackil, J. E., Frommer, G. P., & Hearst, E. S. (1972). Conditioned approach and contact behavior toward signals for food or brain-stimulation reinforcement. *Science*, *177*, 1009–1011.

Pithers, R. T. (1985). The roles of event contingencies and reinforcement in human autoshaping and omission responding. *Learning and Motivation*, *16*, 210–237.

Poling, A., & Poling, T. (1978). Automaintenance in guinea pigs: Effects of feeding regimen and omission training. *Journal of the Experimental Analysis of Behavior*, *30*, 37–46.

Powell, R. W., & Kelly, W. (1976). Responding under positive and negative response contingencies in pigeons and crows. *Journal of Experimental Analysis of Behavior*, *25*, 219–225.

Powell, R. W., Kelly, W., & Santisteban, D. (1975). Response-independent reinforcement in the crow: Failure to obtain autoshaping or positive automaintenance. *Bulletin of the Psychonomic Society, 6*(5), 513–516.

Rachlin, H. (1969). Autoshaping of key pecking in pigeons with negative reinforcement. *Journal of the Experimental Analysis of Behavior, 12,* 521–531,

Rackham, D. (1971). *Conditioning of the pigeon's courtship and aggressive behavior.* Unpublished Master's thesis. Dalhousie University.

Regain, R. D., Anson, J. E., & Sperber, R. D. (1976). Autoshaping and maintenance of a lever press response in mentally retarded children. *The Psychological Record, 26,* 105–109.

Rescorla, R. A. (1968). Probability of shock in the presence and absence of CS in fear conditioning. *Journal of Comparative and Physiological Psychology, 66,* 1–5.

Rescorla, R. A., Durlach, P. J., & Grau, J. W. (1985). Contextual learning in Pavlovian conditioning. In P. D. Balsam & A. Tomie (Eds.), *Context and Learning.* Hillsdale, NJ: Lawrence Erlbaum Associates.

Rescorla, R. A., & Solomon, R. L. (1967). Two-process learning theory; Relationships between Pavlovian conditioning and instrumental learning. *Psychological Review, 74,* 151–182.

Rescorla, R. A., & Wagner, A. R. (1972). A theory of Pavlovian conditioning: Variations in the effectiveness of reinforcement and nonreinforcement. In A. H. Black & W. F. Prokasy (Eds.), *Classical conditioning II: Current theory and research.* New York: Appleton-Century-Crofts.

Reynolds, G. S. (1961). Behavioral contrast. *Journal of the Experimental Analysis of Behavior, 4,* 57–74.

Sainsbury, R. S. (1971). Effect of proximity of elements on the feature-positive effect. *Journal of the Experimental Analysis of Behavior, 16,* 315–326.

Schlosberg, H. (1928). A study of the conditioned patellar reflex. *Journal of Experimental Psychology, 11,* 468–494.

Schlosberg, H. (1937). The relationship between success and the laws of conditioning. *Psychological Review, 44,* 379–394.

Schwam, E., & Gamzu, E. (1975). Constraints on autoshaping in the squirrel monkey: Stimulus and resonse factors. *Bulletin of the Psychonomic Society, 5*(5), 369–372.

Schwartz, B. (1972). The role of positive conditioned reinforcement in the maintenance of key pecking which prevents delivery of primary reinforcements. *Psychonomic Science, 28,* 277–278.

Schwartz, B. (1973). Maintenance of keypecking in pigeons by a food avoidance but not a shock avoidance contingency. *Animal Learning and Behavior, 1,* 164–166.

Schwartz, B. (1977). Studies of operant and reflexive key pecks in the pigeon. *Journal of the Experimental Analysis of Behvior, 27,* 301–314.

Schwartz, B., & Gamzu, E. (1977). Pavlovian control of operant behavior. An analysis of autoshaping and its implications for operant conditioning. In W. K. Honig & J. E. R. Staddon (Eds.), *Handbook of operant behavior.* Englewood Cliffs, NJ: Prentice-Hall.

Schwartz, B., & Williams, D. R. (1972a). Two different kinds of key peck in the pigeon: Some properties of responses maintained by negative and positive response-reinforcer contingencies. *Journal of the Experimental Analysis of Behavior, 18,* 201–216.

Schwartz, B., & Williams, D. R. (1972b). The role of the response-reinforcer contingency in negative auto-maintenance. *Journal of the Experimental Analysis of Behavior, 71,* 351–357.

Sidman, M., & Fletcher, F. G. (1968). A demonstration of auto-shaping with monkeys. *Journal of the Experimental Analysis of Behavior, 11,* 307–309.

Skinner, B. F. (1938). *The behavior of organisms: An experimental analysis.* New York: Appleton-Century-Crofts.

Skinner, B. F. (1948). "Superstition" in the pigeon. *Journal of Experimental Psychology, 38,* 168–172.

Skinner, B. F. (1971). Technical comment on auto-shaping. *Science, 173,* 752.

Slivka, R. M., & Bitterman, M. E. (1966). Classical appetitive conditioning in the pigeon: Partial reinforcement. *Psychonomic Science, 4,* 181–183.

Smith, S. G. (1970). Auto-shaping: A three key technique. *The Psychological Record, 20,* 343–345.

Sperling, S. E., & Perkins, M. E. (1979). Autoshaping with common and distinctive stimulus elements, compact and dispersed arrays. *Journal of the Experimental Analysis of Behavior, 31*, 383–394.

Sperling, S. E., Perkins, M. E., & Duncan, H. J. (1977). Stimulus generalization from feeder to response key in the acquisition of autoshaped responding. *Journal of the Experimental Analysis of Behavior, 27*, 469–478.

Squire, L. H. (1969). Autoshaping key responses with fish. *Psychonomic Science, 17*, 3.

Steinhauer, G. D., Davol, G. H. & Lee, A. (1977). A procedure for autoshaping the pigeon's key peck to an auditory stimulus. *Journal of the Experimental Analysis of Behavior, 28*, 97–98.

Staddon, J. E. R., & Simmelhag, V. L. (1971). The "Superstition experiment": A reexamination of its implications for the principles of adaptive behavior. *Psychological Review, 78*, 3–43.

Stiers, M., & Silberberg, A. (1974). Lever-contact responses in rats: Automaintenance with and without a negative response-reinforcer dependency. *Journal of the Experimental Analysis of Behavior, 22*, 497–506.

Terrace, H. S. (1968). Discrimination learning, the peak shift and behavioral contrast. *Journal of the Experimental Analysis of Behavior, 11*, 727–741.

Terrace, H. S. (1981). Introduction: Autoshaping and two-factor learning theory. In C. M. Locurto, H. S. Terrace, & J. Gibbon (Eds.), *Autoshaping and conditioning theory*. New York: Academic Press.

Terrace, H. S., Gibbon, J., Farrell, L., & Baldock, M. D. (1975). Temporal factors influencing the acquisition of an autoshaped key peck. *Animal Learning and Behavior, 3*, 53–62.

Thompsom, T., & Sturm, T. (1965). Classical conditioning of aggressive display in siamese fighting fish. *Journal of the Experimental Analysis of Behavior, 8*, 397–403.

Timberlake, W., & Grant, D. L. (1975). Auto-shaping in rats to the presentation of another rat predicting food. *Science, 190*, 690–692.

Timberlake, W., & Lucas, G. A. (1989). Behavior systems and learning: From misbehavior to general principles. In S. B. Klein & R. R. Mowrer (Eds.), *Contemporary learning theories: Instrumental conditioning theory and the impact of biological constraints on learning*. Hillsdale, NJ: Lawrence Erlbaum Associates.

Tomie, A. (1976a). Retardation of autoshaping: Control by contextual stimuli. *Science, 192*, 1244–1245.

Tomie, A. (1976b). Interference with autoshaping by prior context conditioning. *Journal of Experimental Psychology: Animal Behavior Processes, 2*, 323–334.

Tomie, A. (1981). Effect of unpredictable food on the subsequent acquisition of autoshaping: Analysis of the context-blocking hypothesis. In C. M. Locurto, H. S. Terrace & J. Gibbon (Eds.), *Autoshaping and conditioning theory*. New York: Academic Press.

Tomie, A., Murphy, A. L., Fath, S., & Jackson, R. L. (1980). Retardation of autoshaping following pretraining with unpredictable food: Effects of changing the context between pretraining and testing. *Learning and Motivation, 11*, 117–134.

Turner, L. H., & Solomon, R. L. (1962). Human traumatic avoidance learning: Theory and experiments on the operant-respondent distinction and failures to learn. *Psychological Monographs, 76*, (40, Whole No. 559)

Valenstein, E. S. (1969). Behavior elicited by hypothalamic stimulation: A prepotency hypothesis. *Brain, Behavior and Evolution, 2*, 295–316.

Wasserman, E. A. (1973a). The effect of redundant contextual stimuli and autoshaping the pigeon's keypeck. *Animal Learning and Behavior, 181*, 875–877.

Wasserman, E. A. (1973b). Pavlovian conditioning with heat reinforcement produces stimulus-directed pecking in chicks. *Science, 181*, 875–877.

Wasserman, E. A. (1978). The relationship between motor and secretory behaviors in classical appetitive conditioning. *Pavlovian Journal of Biological Science, 13*, 182–186.

Wasserman, E. A. (1981). Response evocation in autoshaping: Contributions of cognitive and comparative-evolutionary analyses to an understanding of directed action. In C. M. Locurto, H. S. Terrace & J. Gibbon (Eds.), *Autoshaping and conditioning theory*. New York: Academic Press.

Wasserman, E., Franklin, S., & Hearst, E. (1974). Pavlovian appetitive contingencies and approach vs. withdrawal to conditioned stimuli in pigeons. *Journal of Comparative and Physiological Psychology, 86*, 616–627.

Wasserman, E. A., Hunter, N. B., Gutowski, K. A., & Bader, S. A. (1975). Autoshaping chick with heat reinforcement: The role of stimulus-reinforcer and response-reinforcer relations. *Journal of Experimental Psychology: Animal Behavior Processes, 1*, 158–169.

Wasserman, E. A., & Molina, E. J. (1975). Explicitly unpaired key light and food presentations: Interference with subsequent auto-shaped key pecking in pigeons. *Journal of Experimental Psychology: Animal Behavior Processes, 104*(1), 30–38.

Wesp, R. K., Lattal, K. A., & Poling, A. D. (1977). Punishment of Autoshaped key-peck responses of pigeons. *Journal of the Experimental Analysis of Behavior, 27*, 407–418.

Westbrook, R. F. (1973). Failure to obtain positive contrast when pigeons press a bar. *Journal of the Experimental Analysis of Behavior, 20*, 499–510.

Wilcove, W. G., & Miller, J. C. (1974). CS–UCS presentations and a lever: Human autoshaping. *Journal of Experimental Psychology, 103*, 868–877.

Williams, D. R. (1981). Biconditional behavior: Conditioning without constraint. In C. M. Locurto, H. S. Terrace, & J. Gibbon (Eds.), *Autoshaping and conditioning theory*. New York: Academic Press.

Williams, D. R., & Williams, H. (1969). Auotmaintenance in the pigeon: Sustained pecking despite contingent non-reinforcement. *Journal of the Experimental Analysis of Behavior, 12*, 511–520.

Wilson, B. (1978). *Autoshaping in pigeons and corvids*. Unpublished doctoral dissertation, The University of Sussex.

Woodard, W. T., & Bitterman, M. E. (1974). Autoshaping in the goldfish. *Behavior Research Methods and Instrumentation, 6*, 409–410.

Woodruff, G., & Starr, D. (1978). Autoshaping of initial feeding and drinking reactions in newly hatched chicks. *Animal Learning & Behavior, 6*, 265–272.

Woodruff, G., & Williams, D. R. (1976). The associative relation underlying autoshaping in the pigeon. *Journal of the Experimental Analysis of Behavior, 26*, 1–13.

Zeiler, M. D. (1972). Superstitious behavior in children: An experimental analysis. *Advances in Child Development and Behavior, 7*, 1–29.

Zener, K. (1937). The significance of behavior accompanying conditioned salivary secretion for theories of the conditioned response. *American Journal of Psychology, 50*, 384–403.

II CURRENT STATUS OF TRADITIONAL LEARNING THEORY

8
The Case for a Return to a Two-Factor Theory of Avoidance: The Failure of Non-Fear Interpretations

Donald J. Levis
State University of New York at Binghamton

> *Show me a man who is not a slave. One is a slave to lust, another to greed, another to ambition, and all men are slaves to fear (Seneca,* Epistulae and Lucilium, *Epis. 22.11)*
>
> *Fear of danger is ten thousand times more terrifying than danger itself. (Daniel Defoe,* Robinson Crusoe, *p. 161)*

I. INTRODUCTION

Perhaps no other psychological motive has played such a dominant role in shaping the past, present, and future destiny of the human race than the emotion of fear. Fear provided the motivation for our ancestors to band together in groups, to develop weapons for protection, and to create superstitions to explain the unknown. Fear has played a major role in the struggle for human survival and in the facilitation of human death—in the creation of war and in the need to seek peace. Fear can motivate success and produce failure; make a hero out of a coward and make a strong person weak; generate wealth and create poverty; foster control and facilitate compromise. Fear often modifies rational objectives with irrational solutions, such as providing the major deterrent to prevent nuclear war, while at the same time providing the major motive to build even more destructive weapons. It is unlikely the human race would have survived and developed without the motivational effects of fear; yet ironically, because of fear, civilization is now in danger of extinction.

What is fear, how is it learned, what variables maintain and control it, and what procedures remove it? Although ancient scholars like Empedocles and Hippocrates studied the link between emotions and personalities, the impact of emotions on human behavior and thought has largely been scientifically ignored throughout most of our history (Freud, 1938). Perhaps because such an acknowledgment is painful, the dominant theme that humans are governed by rational thoughts and motives still persists. This attitude exists today despite the growing emotional problems plaguing society reflected in the areas of mental health, drug addiction, unwanted pregnancies, discrimination, divorces, and in failures of interpersonal communication. At a time when human problems cry out for solution, contemporary learning theory is moving away from an interest in motivational issues to an emphasis on cognitive variables. Unfortunately, the study of cognitive processes in the normal and psychopathological human are conducted and interpreted as if such processes were operating in a vacuum devoid of any emotional input and direction. In fact, the emphasis on interpreting behavior cognitively has become so strong in recent years that human cognitive attributes are ascribed to infrahumans including the laboratory rat, fish, and even the cockroach (e.g., Seligman, 1975).

One purpose of this chapter is to generate a renewed interest in the scientific study of how the emotional system interacts with behavior and with cognitive processes. To achieve this objective, the present review centers on a major theoretical contribution to the area first outlined by O. H. Mowrer in 1947. This theory, which addresses the relationship between fear and avoidance behavior, is referred to as two-factor or two-process theory of avoidance. Although Mowrer (1960a, 1960b) creatively revised and extended his 1947 version to encompass all learning, the interest here remains with the earlier version which focuses on avoidance.

Not only has Mowrer's theory of avoidance withstood the test of time, but the conceptualization of fear as a drive stimulus, a notion borrowed from Hull (1943), has not only played a significant role in the understanding of avoidance behavior (McAllister & McAllister, 1971) but has also led to the development of other drive-motivational theories. Examples of these include the study of self-punitive (masochistic-like) behavior (Brown, 1965; Mowrer, 1950), conflict behavior (Miller, 1959), frustration and anger (Amsel, 1958, 1962, 1971; Brown & Farber, 1951), the human drives for money, power, and prestige (Brown, 1961), and the study of human psychopathological behavior including its acquisition (Dollard & Miller, 1950; Levis, 1985), maintenance (Levis & Boyd, 1979; Stampfl & Levis, 1969), and treatment (Stampfl, 1970; Stampfl & Levis, 1967; Wolpe, 1958).

Despite the substantial theoretical and empirical contributions of each of the above motivational approaches, the literature of the last 20 years has produced a series of attacks designed to reduce the influence of these positions, especially that of Mowrer's. The sources of these criticisms can be divided into three camps: (1) those who maintain constructs like *fear* are not needed (e.g., Herrnstein, 1969); (2) those who want to replace the construct *fear* with a cognitive construct (e.g., Seligman & Johnston, 1973), and (3) those who still use the term *fear* but emphasize the organism's inherited or instinctual characteristics (e.g., Bolles, 1970; Seligman, 1971).

As this chapter unfolds it will be argued that most of the attacks on Mowrer's theory are unfounded and unsupported, reflecting in many cases a misrepresentation of the position. It should also become apparent that alternative theories which attempt to remove the concept of fear are not only conceptually and empirically inadequate but suffer in predictive power. It should be made clear at this point that I do not focus on those theories that offer a contrasting position to that of Mowrer's but keep intact the S–R motivational component (see Brown, 1961; Denny, 1971; McAllister & McAllister, 1971). These, as well as the other S–R motivational theories are also being challenged and, for purpose of convenience, are lumped together under the heading of *fear theory*.

II.   THE HULL–SPENCE TRADITION

What is believed to be at stake here has more to do with issues of philosophy of science and theory construction than it does with the merits of a particular point in a particular theory. Fear theory represents an outgrowth of a philosophy of science of neo-behaviorism illustrated by the Hull–Spence contributions of the 40s and 50s (see Hilgard & Bower, 1966). Neo-behaviorism like the earlier radical behaviorism strove to move the young field of psychology away from the study of consciousness to the study of behavior which was *public* rather than *private* and nonconfirmable. An identity was made with the natural sciences through an emphasis on objectivism, measurement, and verification. Following the lead of evolutionary theory, the laws of behavior were believed to be reflected across the phylogenetic spectrum. It then followed that much could be learned about the complex human by studying infrahuman behavior, thereby isolating the laws of behavior more readily. This assumption gave behaviorism a sense of purpose and relevance.

The neo-behaviorists went beyond the earlier Watsonian behaviorist's simple S–R connections to concepts which were labeled intervening variables or hypothetical constructs. The purpose of each construct was to summarize into one concept the impact of a variety of experimental findings believed to reflect the same process, and/or to suggest the presence of an influencing variable which defied direct measurement. The real genius of the Hull–Spence approach was the ability to integrate such constructs into a format that directly led to testable assumptions and the development of general laws of behavior. They achieved this objective by operationally defining each construct with a definitional structure which was orthogonal to the dependent measure used to assess the degree of learning. Such a strategy greatly enhanced the predictive power of their theory by removing surplus meaning concepts and untestable mentalistic terms. Yet, their neo-behavioral approach, like the radical behaviorism of the past, viewed any behavior under consideration as starting with a measurable stimulus and ending with a measurable response, independent of whether the behavior is overt (as in running or talking) or covert (as in imagining or feeling).

The importance of operationalizing procedures, removing surplus meaning concepts, and defining constructs by an independent input and output definitional structure was highlighted in the historical debates between the Hull–Spence and Tolman positions. For example, Hull operationally defined the construct of hunger drive by the amount of time food was deprived. He also determined that drive could be independently assessed by measuring increases in the organism's motor activity level. By developing a functional relationship between the deprivation level and the level of activity, the researcher could independently assess the presence of the construct, quantify it, and establish its role on learning a particular task. In fact, the power of this procedural strategy has not been fully recognized or implemented. For example, by empirically establishing rules to equate a given level of activity to a given state of drive, the researcher, in principle, could determine on a *subject by subject* basis the degree of drive present prior to introducing the learning task. Such a strategy would not only insure that the boundary conditions of the theory have been met, but greatly reduce the degree of error variance associated with individual differences. Such an enhanced definitional precision would clearly facilitate the development of precise empirical statements, the fostering of differential predictions, and the determination of the merits of a given position. In the same vein, a look through the window of history suggests that theoretical constructs should only be introduced when the data compellingly requires the inclusion of such a concept, or when the addition of the construct significantly increases both explanatory and predictive power.

Tolman (1932), on the other hand, introduced theoretical constructs like expectancy, cognitions, and purpose which failed specification by independent procedural and measurement criteria. Theories of this kind, which tend to dominate the learning field today, provide ample room for the theorist to provide a variety of post-hoc explanations which protect the theory from disconfirmation. As Osgood (1953) appropriately concluded:

> Tolman has shown a magnificent lack of concern over the details of behaving. Having cognitions and demands; appropriate behaviors just appear spontaneously . . . this lack of concern has certain advantages chiefly that the important phenomenon of response equivalence can be accepted without explanation. It also has a serious disadvantage from the standpoint of theory, namely, that there is a gap in the inferential sequence which makes detailed predictions impossible. . . . (p. 391)

Unfortunately, the lessons of the past were not learned. Many became disillusioned by the inability of the general theories to resolve the issues of the time and attributed this failure to neo-behaviorism. Skinner's (1950) suggestion that the field should return to the philosophy of radical behaviorism gained significant support in the 50s, 60s, and 70s. However, Skinner's approach could not fill the void for a field that correctly recognized much earlier that psychology had advanced beyond the stage of radical behaviorism. The positive contributions of neo-behaviorism were soon forgotten and a decreased interest in theory emerged. The animal learning field's research interest became myopic and static which resulted in a loss of a sense of importance, relevance, and leadership.

Current attempts to fill this void reflect a parasitic desire to enhance the value of animal learning studies by borrowing from the independent movements in cognitive and genetic psychology while ignoring the historical advances made by neo-behaviorism. This strategy insures that the field of animal learning will continue to retain its *third world* status. Neo-behaviorism rose to power precisely because it represented a way of conceptualizing psychology as a science that provided rules and assumptions which facilitated the field's growth. A central feature of this movement is the assumption that the basic laws of behavior are reflected across the phylogenetic scale, can be more readily determined in a laboratory setting using a less complex organism, and will be of value in understanding the behavior of the human species.

The position is taken here that if the field of animal learning is to survive and regain its ability to advance knowledge about behavior, it must return to the earlier philosophical premises which enhanced its ability to build and flourish. The effects of rejecting, or more precisely not learning, the guiding scientific philosophy behind the behavioral movement can clearly be seen today in a field that is being inundated by a lack of scientific rigor, by numerous surplus meaning concepts, and by largely untestable theoretical positions that fail to provide differential predictions.

The issue confronting the field today is not whether genetics or cognitive behavior play a role in determining behavior. Rather, the issue is whether these constructs can be shown to enhance predictive power and not readily be explained by more parsimonious interpretations. Watson (1919) was interested in behavior labeled cognitive as was Hull and as early as 1930 and 1931; Spence, a key leader in the neo-behavioral movement, used the term "cognitive" in the title of his 1966 paper. What Spence realized was that the objective study of behavior had developed to the point where some such cognitive concepts were essential if systematic progress in theory construction were to go forward. Similarly, Mowrer concluded in 1960a:

> Indeed, it is perhaps not too much to say that we have reached a point at which, if consciousness were not itself experienced, we would have to invent some such equivalent construct to take its place. Behaviorism was thus no idle "detour" or meaningless aberration. It was instead a new foundation which had to be laid before a sounder total psychology could be constructed. (p. 7)

The neo-behaviorist's renewed interest in cognitive phenomena in no way suggested the abandonment of the S–R framework or the basic objective of behaviorism to develop a science of psychology free of nontestable constructs and terms. Unfortunately, rather than build on the foundation of behaviorism, the wave of interest in cognitive issues, which gained momentum in the 1960s and is ongoing today, has resulted, in many cases, in an abandonment of the tenets of behaviorism. As Amsel and Rashotte (1984) observed:

> The "animal learning establishment" and "the old stimulus-response paradigm" have been attacked by a succession of "born-again" cognitivists (e.g., Bolles, 1975; Dickinson, 1980; Honig, 1978) who advocate changes in learning theory that are generally less parsimonious, more mentalistic, and more structuralist. (p. 11)

And as Skinner (1984) concluded:

> Cognitive psychology is frequently presented as a revolt against behaviorism, but it is not a revolt; it is a retreat. Everyday English is full of terms derived from ancient explanations of human behavior. We spoke that language when we were young. When we went out into the world and became psychologists, we learned to speak in other ways but made mistakes for which we were punished. But now we can relax. Cognitive psychology is Old Home Week. We are back among friends speaking the language we spoke when we were growing up. We can talk about love and will and ideas and memories and feelings and states of mind, and no one will ask us what we mean; no one will raise an eyebrow. (pp. 949–950)

Thus, for the behaviorists the onslaught of cognitive terms and theories that have become the "vogue of the day" represents a retreat to older times. Few cognitive theories have advanced the field in the way Watson, Hull, and Spence did when addressing such issues. Rather, the cognitive movement has been absorbed by a host of terms and theories that have little or no operational specificity and have yielded few differential predictions. When applied to the field of animal learning, the cognitive movement attempts to interpret data that already is more parsimoniously explained by existing behavioral theories. Yet the trend persists and is accompanied more by a sense of profundity and relevancy that a genuine desire to provide a deeper understanding of the issues at hand.

This movement toward cognitive and genetic interpretations has also impregnated the field of avoidance learning which represents an area of profound theoretical and applied interest. It is this area, more than any other, that provides the battleground for determining whether the study of learned affect will regain its theoretical and empirical influence. Today, as in the past, findings in this area raise certain critical theoretical issues in need of resolution. It is important that these issues be clearly understood and formally addressed theoretically if our knowledge of this area is to advance.

III. THE AVOIDANCE PARADOX—THE NEED FOR A CONSTRUCT

In the early 40s the empirical findings that animals could learn a response that prevented the presentation of shock did not appear to be theoretically important. The fact that avoidance responses were learned seemed to reflect everyday experience. After all, does not a child after touching a hot stove learn to avoid it? The explanation of this behavior seemed clear; the child keeps away from the stove so it won't get burned. In the same vein, the rat responds to the CS in order to avoid the electrical stimulation (Hilgard & Marquis, 1940). However, this causal, common sense interpretation did not sit well with the behaviorist who strove to rid psychology of teleological concepts. For example, Schoenfeld (1950) asked the critical question. How can the nonoccurrence of an unconditioned stimulus (shock) act as a reinforcement?

It soon became apparent that the area of avoidance responding was more problematic for the field of learning than was first realized. The above paradox of how the response was strengthened needed an answer. In the appetitive learning situation, the acquisition of the response requires the presence of the reinforcing UCS (e.g., food) and usually requires a number of such training trials before the response is learned. Furthermore, once the UCS or reinforcement is removed, unlearning or extinction takes place. In avoidance learning the acquisition of the response occurs in the absence of the UCS, a condition repeatedly shown to produce *extinction*, not acquisition.

The puzzle became even more complex when the issue was raised as to how the animal made its *first* avoidance response. Prior to the occurrence of the first response, the animal was never exposed to the contingency that an avoidance response terminated the CS and prevented the occurrence of shock. A simple random occurrence explanation for the first response seemed unlikely given the finding that rats could learn the response within one to three CS–UCS pairings. Finally, it was unclear how the removal of the UCS following the learning of the response continued to produce an acquisition and maintenance function (faster response latencies and continued responding) which was then followed at some point by an extinction function (slower response latencies and no responding).

IV. TWO-FACTOR THEORY OF AVOIDANCE— AN OVERVIEW

Although other theorists (e.g., Miller, 1948; Sheffield, 1948) made significant contributions to resolving the paradoxes, it was Mowrer's (1947) rather simple, yet ingenious theoretical solution that attracted the most attention. Although influenced considerably by Hull's (1943) theory of behavior, Mowrer did not believe avoidance learning could be explained adequately by appealing solely to the laws of instrumental learning nor did he feel that Pavlov's (1927) principles of classical conditioning were able to handle the findings. Rather, Mowrer (1939) sided with Freud's (1936) interpretation of avoidance behavior. Freud concluded that human symptoms of psychopathology were essentially learned avoidance behaviors enacted by the patient to remove *danger* signals linked to the patient's unconscious (avoided memory). The aversive cues eliciting symptom behavior were considered to be generalized cues associated with earlier traumatic learning situations. From Freud's analysis it was clear that symptoms which developed later in life were not necessarily enacted at the time of the traumatic learning. This observation suggested to Mowrer that two types of learning were involved in avoidance behavior, not one as argued by Hull or by Pavlov. Thus, he combined the laws of classical conditioning and the laws of instrumental learning into one theory producing his two-factor position.

Active Avoidance Learning

Mowrer, as well as others (e.g., Miller, 1948, 1951) realized that to adequately resolve the existing avoidance paradoxes, the explanations required the introduction of a theoretical construct which reflected some process going on within the organism. Mowrer concluded that the process was emotional and involved the autonomic nervous system. He reasoned what the animal first learns is to become afraid. Fear learning, Mowrer's first factor, results simply from the pairing of a CS with an aversive UCS, such as electric shock. The occurrence of shock produces an unconditioned response (UCR), which represents a noxious event. Through a procedure of classical conditioning, via the principle of contiguity, fear becomes associated or conditioned to the CS (see Gormezano & Kehoe, 1981). Once conditioned, the CS is now capable of eliciting the emotional response in the absence of the UCS. Following in the tradition of Hull, fear was viewed as a drive stimulus and, as such, its presence acts as a motivator and its removal serves as a reinforcer.

To explain the occurrence of the first avoidance response, Mowrer drew upon the motivational attributes of fear. Following the conditioning of fear to the CS, its presentation activates the organism which, in turn, increases the probability that the animal will engage in the desired response. Once the avoidance response occurs, it is followed by the termination of the CS and a corresponding reduction in the presence of fear stimuli. This reduction in drive provides the necessary reinforcement for strengthening the avoidance behavior. Repeated avoidance responses are continually reinforced as long as drive stimuli are reduced following the occurrence of the response. Thus, the laws of trial and error or instrumental learning are enacted to account for the second factor of Mowrer's two-factor theory, the avoidance behavior.

It is important to recognize that the animal does not avoid to prevent the presentation of shock (an expectancy position) but rather to *escape* the aversive properties of the CS. Mowrer was unhappy with the term *avoidance* which he argued confused the situation because of its added surplus meaning. He preferred the more descriptively correct term *escape* from the CS.

It should also be recognized that while acquisition is occurring, so is the concurrent process of extinction. Each avoidance trial provides an extinction trial since the CS occurs in the absence of the UCS presentation. To explain how the animal continues to learn before the effects of extinction are observed, one has to remember that the experimental arrangement permits the animal's response to determine the length of the CS presentation on each trial. Observation reveals that once avoidance responding occurs, animals will respond faster and faster to the point that CS onset elicits the response. The shorter the latency to respond, the less CS exposure occurs which, in turn, minimizes the effects of extinction. As discussed later, that part of the CS interval that is not exposed, in principle, maintains its fear eliciting properties until it is exposed (conservation of anxiety hypothesis). Thus, as long as short latency avoidance responses occur, extinction to the CS is held to a minimum. With more trials, the shorter part of the CS interval will undergo an extinction effect to the point that longer CS exposures are needed to elicit sufficient fear to drive the response. At some point, the latency to respond will get longer and longer, eventually resulting in complete CS exposure and subsequent extinction.

Passive Avoidance Learning

The introduction of the fear construct not only permitted the resolution of the avoidance paradoxes but also facilitated the development of the theory to include passive avoidance learning. *Passive* refers to the notion that learning is defined by the nonoccurrence of a particular response determined by the experimenter following the use of a punishment procedure. The avoidance may involve a particular place or a designated response and in principle may involve a very active process. Mowrer (1960a, p. 32) concluded that in both active and passive avoidance learning, fear conditioning is involved, and in both instances a way of behaving is found which eliminates or controls the fear level. In theory, the main distinction between the two learning situations is the type of stimuli to which fear gets conditioned. In passive avoidance learning, these stimuli primarily are produced by the behavior or response which the experimenter desires to prevent. In active avoidance learning, the fear-arousing stimuli primarily are not response produced but are extrinsic rather then intrinsic, independently produced rather than response-dependent. But, as Mowrer noted, in both cases there is avoidance and in both cases there is punishment. He then concluded the underlying laws for producing both behaviors are identical.

Finally, it is important to recognize that Mowrer (1960a, p. 33) conceptualized active avoidance, like passive avoidance, as representing a *conflict* situation. While the pitting of two opposing drives in passive avoidance learning is clear when the animal is punished for approaching food, the competing drives in active avoidance learning is less so. Mowrer reasoned that there is always some inertia against movement and in active avoidance there is an attempt being made to coerce, or drive, an organism to do something, as opposed to preventing it from doing something. As I argue later when Mowrer's theory is extended, the conflict between responding and nonresponding can become strong in active avoidance learning, especially when apparatuses are used that increase the probability that nonresponding will be reinforced.

Initial Attempts to Eliminate Fear

As stated earlier, a theoretical explanation should strive to be as parsimonious as possible. Upon the introduction of Mowrer's theory, critics, in the best tradition of science, sought to provide alternative hypotheses which could explain the data without the need of a construct. Thus, attempts were made to provide an explanation of avoidance learning by solely appealing to the laws of classical conditioning or solely to the laws of trial and error learning.

It could be argued by appealing to the Pavlovian principles of classical conditioning, that flight from the shock compartment is a reflexive reaction (UCR) to the shock (UCS) which then becomes connected to the CS (see Bolles, 1969, 1971). Such an interpretation does not require the construct fear. Unfortunately, this analysis falls short in many areas. It does not provide an adequate explanation for passive avoidance learning or for studies where an escape response is not permitted during the fear conditioning trials (Brown & Jacobs, 1949; McAllister & McAllister, 1971). Furthermore, freezing or immobility can be just as easily demonstrated to follow shock presentation as flight. As is outlined shortly, by extending fear theory, rules can be provided for when flight or freezing will be the more dominant response.

On the other hand, Schoenfeld (1950) argued that the avoidance response is primarily an escape response (agreeing with Mowrer), reinforced not by fear reduction (disagreeing with Mowrer), but primarily by the termination of secondary noxious stimuli. The attempt being made here is to get around the need for a motivational variable by arguing that from pairing a CS with shock, the CS acquires an aversive property, thereby *in its own right* becoming a conditioned or secondary aversive stimulus (see Dinsmoor, 1950, 1954; Sidman & Boren, 1957). Unfortunately, the radical behaviorist's attempt to eliminate the *fear* problem by using a descriptive label like *aversive* begs the key issue. Mowrer's theory takes the next logical step and answers the question of how the stimuli becomes aversive. The failure to take this step leaves the radical behaviorist with the illogical conclusion that if the CS becomes aversive *in its own right* it should be avoided by an animal not previously conditioned (Mowrer, 1960a, p. 50). The radical behaviorists clearly did not intend this conclusion but by leaving the reactions of the organism out of the picture when discussing S–R connections, the end result frequently leads to such an absurdity, as well as greatly reduced predictive power. From this reviewer's perspective, it is clear that a choice needs to be made as to whether the organism's reactions to the CS is motivational or cognitive. As discussed later, Herrnstein (1969), in his attempt to keep radical behaviorism intact by attacking the motivational variable of fear, forced himself, unwittingly, into a theory of avoidance that justly deserves the term "cognitive."

V. TWO-FACTOR THEORY: A CLARIFICATION
AND EXTENSION

Two-factor theory was the subject of considerable research activity in the 50s, which resulted in the confirmation of many of the theory's key predictions. As a result, the theory became the dominant position in the avoidance area (Brown & Farber, 1968; Mowrer, 1960a). However, a growing dissatisfaction with fear theory developed in the late 60s which continues to the present time (e.g., Herrnstein, 1969; Seligman & Johnston, 1973). Besides issues of data and theory, other reasons are believed to have contributed to the model's eventual decline. For one thing, Mowrer lost interest in the animal learning field following the publication of his two volumes in 1960. This resulted in the removal of a key champion of the theory. For another, a crisis in the animal learning field as a whole was developing. The infusion of a host of new Ph.D programs, the proliferation of research papers, and the cry for relevance, especially from granting agencies, altered the reinforcement schedule for the basic research scientists. Courses in philosophy of science, history and systems, and in theories of learning were dropped from graduate curriculum. A corresponding loss of student interest in animal learning developed along with an increased interest in more applied fields of psychology. It appeared as if the abandonment of the general theories of behavior, together with the promise they held and the exciting research controversies they created, resulted in a void in the animal learning field which has yet to be fully filled.

The demand by society for psychology to provide quick solutions to complex social problems also forced many animal psychologists out of the area into more fundable fields. The classical theoretical issues of the field seemed to lose their importance. Many saw the growing interest in the cognitive field as a way to fill the void in animal learning. Thus, the drive to stamp out the *old* animal theories with a *new* cognitive language took hold and the "cognitive bandwagon" effect Skinner (1984) talked about became the dominant theme.

Nevertheless, whether fear-theory is to remain a viable influence must rest on the merits of the position and on whether the existing criticisms have leveled a mortal blow. Equally important is the question as to whether an alternative theory exists to replace fear-theory, which not only encompass the area covered by fear-theory but generates a greater number of supported differential predictions. A theory shouldn't die or fade away unless it is replaced by an even better theory.

From this reviewer's perspective, the existing criticisms of fear-theory are easily handled by the model and no existing alternative theory even comes close to generating the predictions and empirical support. If this opinion is accurate, it then becomes even more puzzling why a large segment of the field shares the opposite opinion. Although some reasons for the attacks on fear-theory have already been listed, it became clear from reviewing the literature to prepare this chapter, that a lot of the blame must be shared by fear-theorists themselves. As is illustrated later, fear-theorists own attempts to address criticisms have added to the existing confusion (e.g., Rescorla & Solomon, 1967; Solomon & Wynne, 1954). Although Mowrer provided the basic outline of the theory, a consistent effort has not been made to delineate and explain the details of the theory in a formal systematic manner. Much of the confusion in the avoidance area could have been eliminated if this had been done earlier. Rather than simply addressing the existing criticism which was my original intent, it became clear that the power of fear-theory can be better illustrated by providing a more detailed statement. Emphasis is placed on making a number of logical extensions that either have been overlooked, ignored, or do not appear in one place. The merits of the existing criticism can then be evaluated against precise predictions generated from the theory. One apparent byproduct of this endeavor is that two-factor theory makes a number of predictions that have, as yet, not been fully tested.

Fear Acquisition

The typical answer by fear-theorists to the question of how fear or emotional conditioning is learned is to appeal to the principles of Pavlovian classical conditioning. Thus, the frequently stated position is that fear learning occurs through the principle of contiguity, the pairing of a *neutral* stimulus with a noxious event. It is understood that the noxious event can represent a UCS or a previously conditioned aversive CS. Although correct as stated, it may provide more theoretical clarity if the answer given to the question were as follows: fear learning occurs whenever the presentation of a noxious event (UCS) produces a UCR in the organism. Since the presentation of a noxious event is always preceded at some point by nonnoxious stimuli, the focus changes from the issue of how fear is learned, to how fear is *maintained* to a given stimulus situation. This is believed to be the critical issue.

The first implication of this rewording is that in most cases some fear learning always occurs when a noxious event occurs. Keep in mind that Pavlovian principles also state that fear is unlearned to a stimulus situation when the presence of the conditioned stimulus situation occurs in the absence of the noxious event. Thus, whether or not fear will be maintained to the CS complex is dependent upon *the degree of stimulus change* that occurs following the offset of the UCS or noxious event. Other conditioning variables like the intensity and duration of the CS and UCS will play their expected roles. It should also be kept in mind that even if the environmental stimuli preceding and following a noxious event remain unchanged, internal cues can be altered by both the onset and offset of the noxious event. This analysis highlights the position that learning (excitation) and unlearning (inhibition) are concurrently involved during the acquisition phase of an experiment with CS exposure and CS change playing a critical role in determining whether fear is maintained and whether an instrumental response can be reinforced.

The CS Complex

In theory, all stimuli, both internal and external, that immediately precede the onset of the UCS are potentially conditionable. From this analysis, there is no one CS but a complex set of stimuli that are initially conditioned. It should be understood that the differential maintenance of fear to various stimuli compromising the complex is a separate issue and that not all elements within the complex necessarily have the same level of fear associated with them. Such variables as intensity, saliency, discriminability, repeatability, and latent inhibition all play a role in resolving this issue. Given the above statement, it is no wonder that critics of two-factor theory have argued that fear theory has difficulty specifying the CS (Herrnstein, 1969; Seligman & Johnston, 1973).

The criticism of the lack of CS specificity from this reviewer's point of view is less a theoretical issue and more a measurement problem that affects all theories. Pavlov (1927, p. 38) was one of the first to recognize the complexities of this issue. Noting this inherent difficulty, Pavlov outlined the problems associated with decoding the contributing elements of even a single element of the complex like a tone or light. He concluded that the number of potentially effective stimuli is extended almost indefinitely. In discussing the same topic, Hull (1943) devoted a whole chapter (chapter 13) to the issue of what is the CS. He begins with a simple example of a dog being conditioned to salivate to a buzzer paired with food. In Hull's words:

> Among the many additional components of the conditioned stimulus (S) not ordinarily mentioned are: the fact that the animal's two ears receive the buzzer vibrations with different intensity or in different phase, depending on (1) the direction of the bell from the dog's head and (2) the orientation of the head at the moment; the pressure of the dog's feet against the table top upon which it stands; the pressure of each of the three or four restraining bands upon the skin receptors of the dog's neck, thighs, etc.; the biting of a number of insects which may be hidden in the dog's hair; the contact of the capsule over the fistula; the pressure of the muzzle against the dog's head; the pressure of the rubber tube in the dog's mouth; the odor of the rubber from which the tube is made, . . . ; the infinite number and variety of proprioceptive impulses originating in the several parts of the other muscles of the animal's body as they are employed in the maintenance of the postures taken from moment to moment; the too little understood stimulations associated with the bodily state resulting from food, water, and sexual privation, rectum and bladder pressure, etc.; and finally, the perseverative traces of all the multitude of stimuli recently acting, whether the stimulus energy is continuing to act at the moment or not. *The conditioned stimulus in the experiment under consideration includes all of the immensely complicated stimulus elements here enumerated and many more besides;* nevertheless this list, incomplete as it is, should aid the reader somewhat in overcoming the misleading suggestion of singularity and simplicity otherwise likely to be conveyed by the S of the symbol $S^H R$. (pp. 205–206)

From the above, it should be clear that Pavlov and Hull, as well as other major learning theorists (see Hilgard & Bower, 1966), viewed the specification of the CS as representing an incredibly complex problem. This problem is not particular to avoidance learning although it does present a more intricate learning situation than the relatively simpler classical conditioning paradigm discussed by Pavlov and Hull.

Nevertheless, a number of statements can be made as to what stimuli are potentially conditionable in avoidance learning. First, the CS complex can incorporate other external cues, in addition to the warning stimuli, such as apparatus cues, room cues, handling cues, etc. Second, the CS complex can also include cues produced by the organism, like muscle movements or other response produced cues (Schoenfeld, 1950) or even internal cues associated with a given drive state (e.g., hunger cues, heart palpitations). Finally, as Hull noted, the stimulus traces from each of these different sets of cues may also play an important role in eliciting a conditioned response.

Although the assumption that conditioning involves a complex set of stimuli is not disputed, theorists frequently fall into the trap of only considering the designated externally presented CS as the CS conditioned when interpreting their data. This oversimplification has led to many questionable conclusions and possible misinterpretation of results.

Transfer of Conditioned Fear

The transfer of conditioned fear from a given CS complex to another is facilitated by at least two separate principles: contiguity and stimulus similarity. For example, in the case of stimulus similarity, the more similar the CS is to the transfer stimulus the greater the degree of transfer. Direct pairing of the two stimuli, if similar, is not required, a process referred to as stimulus generalization. For example, if a 4 KHz tone is conditioned to elicit fear, the introduction of an 8 KHz tone should also elicit fear although to a somewhat lesser degree. If a light is introduced, fear from the onset of the tone may not transfer because of stimulus dissimilarity. If, however, the light is paired with the tone (contiguity) transfer can take place via higher order conditioning. But the transfer of fear also occurs across the CS–UCS interval and the same principles as noted above are believed to be operating. From the classical conditioning literature it appears that direct conditioning to the CS from the UCS occurs for the rat around .5 sec prior to UCS onset. If a 10-sec CS–UCS interval is used, the question then becomes how does the fear transfer back to the onset of the CS. One could take the position that the total CS is directly conditioned by the UCS but this becomes problematic for certain kinds of data (see Dubin & Levis, 1973; Levis & Dubin, 1973; Levis & Stampfl, 1972). Rather, it seems more reasonable to argue that fear transfers across the CS–UCS interval on the basis of the combined principles of contiguity and stimulus similarity resulting in a temporal gradient of stimulus generalization. That is to say, if direct conditioning occurs around a half a second to a tone CS, then since the next second of tone before that period involves a similar stimulus, fear will generalize from the half second to the full second. The process of generalization will continue across the CS–UCS interval in an orderly decreasing manner since 10 sec of tone is more dissimilar to half a second of tone than is five sec of tone. Although Mowrer's position is not dependent upon accepting the above rationale, a decreasing gradient of fear across the CS interval is hypothesized and is important in understanding issues related to avoidance response latencies.

It is also argued that the greater the stimulus change that occurs prior to the onset of the UCS when compared to the stimulus situations following the offset of the UCS, the greater the transfer of fear across the CS–UCS interval and the greater the maintenance of fear to the CS. It is the *relative stimulus change* that is important and not the absolute intensity of the CS complex (Logan, 1954; Perkins, 1953).

The Roles of CS and UCS Onset and Offset

According to two-factor theory, the onset of the UCS results in drive induction while the offset of the UCS results in drive reduction. The same roles are basically ascribed to conditioned stimuli except the role of CS offset is in need of further clarification. Mowrer argued that the resulting drive reduction following CS offset provides the necessary reinforcement for strengthening the avoidance response. This concept of drive reduction as a reinforcer is the critical feature of Mowrer's theory which allowed him to resolve the avoidance paradox of how such responding is learned. Ironically, it is the issue of drive reduction that has been most criticized by contemporary theorists. In describing Mowrer's theory the statement is often made that CS offset reinforces the avoidance response. Although basically correct, the statement represents an extrapolation from the theory and not a precise statement of the underlying principle. The principle used by Mowrer is more correctly phrased as follows: CS offset results in a reduction in aversiveness which produces a reinforcing state of affairs capable of strengthening any behavior correlated with the reduction. What is frequently overlooked is that *CS offset may strengthen* any behavior *correlated with its reduction including a response incompatible with avoidance learning* (McAllister & McAllister, 1971).

An additional statement is needed to help clarify the issue of the speed of fear reduction and the total amount of per trial reinforcement. The amount of acquired fear reduction that can occur on a given trial is believed to be dependent on two factors: (1) the amount of fear elicited by the CS on that trial, and (2) the degree of relative stimulus change following CS offset. The greater the stimulus change from the stimulus situation immediately preceding UCS onset to the stimulus situation following offset of the CS, the greater the reduction in aversiveness.

The magnitude of the reinforcement effect for a particular instrumental response on a given trial will depend on the following three factors: (1) the amount of fear reduction; (2) the previous strength of the reinforced response; and (3) the strength of incompatible response tendencies. Given a constant per trial reduction in drive, the resulting reinforcement effect will produce greater strengthening of the response earlier in training and will produce less strengthening with respect to the magnitude of the response as learning approaches asymptote. Thus, at asymptote, little fear reduction is needed to strengthen the response and, in the same vein, little fear is needed to drive the response. In the Hullian tradition, the resulting behavior is a function of the habit strength of the reinforced response minus the habit strength of the incompatible responses.

Therefore, it is possible to arrange the situation so that the offset of the experimenter's manipulated CS (e.g., a tone) leads to a strong reinforcement effect and the same CS element results in a weak reinforcement effect. This can be achieved by correlating the offset of the tone with a change in the rest of the CS complex (e.g., apparatus cues) as opposed to keeping the remaining CS complex constant proceeding and following the response. I refer to the former situation as differentiated and the latter undifferentiated. Figure 8.1 depicts a hypothetical fear reduction gradient under two different experimental situations while the fear activation level is held constant. Notice that in the undifferentiated condition the fear level is reduced at a slower rate, weakening the temporal correlation between the response and the maximum level of reinforcement, which is also less than that obtained in the differentiated stimulus situation. The figure also illustrates that less fear reduction is needed to maintain responding as learning progresses. However, it should be recognized that the fear level elicited by the CS onset would be differentially reduced in the undifferentiated condition because of the generalized extinction effects from the apparatus fear cues that did not change following a response.

Response Characteristics

According to Mowrer, the fear response involves the direct conditioning of the autonomic nervous system. Therefore, these responses can be indirectly assessed through autonomic indices like skin conductance or behavioral correlates of autonomic responding such as urination, defecation, or increased skeletal activity. The strength of fear can also be indirectly assessed by monitoring the reinforced instrumental response such as the trials to an acquisition criterion, the latency of the response, and trials to extinction, or by using transfer tests (e.g., CER). Caution should be maintained since each of these indices of fear are indirect measures in that other response systems may interact within an inhibitory or facilitatory manner.

Fear reduction, if sufficient, should be capable of reinforcing any instrumental response in the organism's repertoire. However, in comparing different

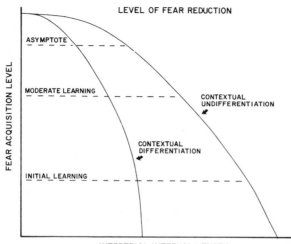

FIG. 8.1.   A hypothetical gradient of fear reduction following avoidance responding using an apparatus with differentiated and undifferentiated contextual (apparatus) cues preceding and following a response. The gradient illustrates the theoretical assumption that the rate of fear reduction is affected by the contextual environment. The graph also illustrates that the magnitude of fear reduction required to reinforce a response changes as a function of previous reinforced trials (learning).

response systems it is important to take into consideration the differences in response topography such as the effortfulness of the response, the strength of incompatible response tendencies, and the amount of fear reduction needed to equate reinforcement effects. One should also hold constant the relative degree of stimulus change following a response.

Fear Maintenance and Extinction

Holding conditioning trials constant, fear maintenance to the CS complex is inversely related to the degree of exposure to the CS complex. On the other hand, extinction of fear to the CS complex is directly related to the degree of CS exposure including any generalization of extinction effects. Per trial fear maintenance and extinction is dependent upon the response latency of the instrumental response and on the degree to which the response removes the conditioned CS complex. Mowrer (1960a) did not specify whether fear extinction in discrete-trial avoidance learning is a function of an interaction of per trial CS exposure and number of extinction trials or simply, as the reviewer suspects, the total amount of CS exposure which is independent of the number of trials. Fatigue resulting from the repeated occurrence of the instrumental response may also be a factor in fear extinction but only in the sense that it results in more CS exposure via longer response latencies or incompatible responses.

Another misunderstood point is that nowhere in two-factor theory does Mowrer make a statement that a one-to-one correspondence exists between the extinction of the instrumental response and the extinction of the fear response. The theory does state that if fear or drive is absent, the instrumental response will not be emitted but the converse does not necessarily hold. For a well-learned avoidance response to extinguish, all that is required is that the fear level elicited on that trial be below the threshold level required to elicit the response (as in Hull's theory). Therefore, a degree of residual fear most likely will be present depending on the criterion of extinction imposed, the response characteristic in question, and the existing strength of incompatible response tendencies.

VI. PREDICTIONS AND SUPPORTING EVIDENCE FOR TWO-FACTORY THEORY

At the core of Mowrer's theory is the concept that fear functions as a generalized drive in the manner in which Hull conceptualized hunger, thirst, and sex. There is general agreement that for a construct to be classified as a drive or motivational variable, three conditions must be met (Brown & Farber, 1968):

1. its onset must be shown to serve as a punisher;
2. its presence must be demonstrated to produce an activating or energizing effect in the organism; and
3. its offset must be demonstrated to be reinforcing.

Support for Motivational Interpretation

Secondary Punisher.   There is little question in the literature that the onset of a conditioned aversive CS can function as a punisher. A large number of studies using humans subjects have demonstrated that words like "wrong" or "bad" can function as secondary punishers (e.g., Levis & Warehime, 1971; Thorndike, 1935). An equally large body of infrahuman studies have demonstrated that the onset of an aversive CS can produce punishment-like effects on temporally antecedent responses (Barlow, 1952; Dyal & Goodman, 1966; Evans, 1962; Hake & Azrin, 1965; Kaye, Cox, Bosack, & Anderson, 1965; Mowrer & Aiken, 1954; Seligman, 1966). As Brown and Farber (1968) concluded: "In sum, therefore, there appears to be little reason for doubting that stimuli previously associated with aversive events function as secondary punishers" (p. 108).

Energizing Effects.   Support for the second criterion that the presence of an aversively conditioned CS produces an energizing or activating effect in the organism has been both indirect and direct. Many anecdotal examples exist at the human level where in the presence of a strong fear stimulus, superhuman feats of strength or flight have been reported. Laboratory evidence demonstrating extreme resistance to extinction of avoidance responding (Levis & Boyd, 1979), the reinforcing effects of fear reduction (Kalish, 1954), and establishing spatial gradients of fear motivated avoidance (Brown, 1948; Bugelski & Miller, 1938) are very consistent with the contention that fear produces energizing effects.

More direct evidence emanates from studies that attempt to measure the energizing capacity of the CS by the augmentation of unlearned reactions such as the startle reflex. Brown, Kalish, and Farber (1951) and Meryman (1952, 1953) have been successful in this endeavor (also see Champion, 1964; Ross, 1961; Spence & Runquist, 1958). Kurtz and Siegal (1966) have argued that the startle response may be a result of direct conditioning of skeletal response, a possibility, but one that does not eliminate the additional presence of a motivational effect. Wagner (1963) has shown that the startle response can be augmented by other aversive events which are hard to interpret from the viewpoint that particular skeletal responses are conditioned.

Other lines of evidence supporting this proposition also exist. Bull and Overmier (1968) demonstrated that a CS separately paired with shock and then introduced during ongoing avoidance responding produced a facilitatory effect on the responding. A similar facilitory effect can be found following CS termination when a short delay CS or a trace CS is used (Kamano, 1970). Finally, Malloy and Levis (1988) found that the force of a human avoidance response as measured by squeezing a hand dynamometer reliably discriminated between CS conditions assumed to differ in fear strength. They also reported a difference in the magnitude of the skin conductance response at a point where fear theory would predict differential levels of activation.

Turning to a related issue, Mowrer specifically stated that fear is initially elicited by the *onset* of the UCS. A Hullian interpretation on the other hand, argued that the *offset* of the UCS (drive reduction) reinforces fear. In a clever series of studies to test this prediction, Mowrer found that the data confirmed his contention that UCS onset was the critical factor which supported the need for two-factors (Mowrer & Lamoreaux, 1946; Mowrer & Solomon, 1954; Mowrer & Viek, 1948).

Reinforcing Properties of CS Termination

The assumption that the offset of an aversive CS results in a reinforcing state of affairs is central to Mowrer's position and to fear theory. The first empirical question is whether an organism will learn to escape from stimuli associated with an aversive UCS. Overwhelming evidence exists that the probability of an instrumental response will increase if the response in question results in the termination of an aversively conditioned stimulus. In fact, a wide variety of responses have been demonstrated to increase following CS termination (Brown & Jacobs,

1949; Goldstein, 1960; Hoffman & Fleshler, 1962; Kalish, 1954; Ley, 1965; McAllister & McAllister, 1964, 1971; Miller, 1948). On the other hand, if the external CS complex is not terminated, learning of an avoidance response will not occur or will be greatly retarded as is the case when the avoidance response only reduces the frequency of shock (Herrnstein & Hineline, 1966; Sidman, 1953a, 1953b). In concluding their review, Brown and Farber (1968) noted that only a few experiments exist where an organism failed to escape a CS and these can be attributed to an insufficient number of fear-conditioning trials (Desiderato, 1964), to a weak UCS (Anderson & Johnson, 1966; Annau & Kamin, 1961; Goldstein, 1960) or to competing responses fostered by a strong UCS (McAllister & McAllister, 1971).

If fear theory is correct about CS offset producing a reinforcing state of affairs via a reduction in the presence of aversive stimuli, then the critical test becomes one of demonstrating that a previously conditioned aversive CS can provide the reinforcement for the learning of a *new response*. Miller's (1948) experiment was the first to demonstrate this point. He conditioned rats to escape a box previously associated with shock. Following this training, the escape route was blocked, which could only be unblocked by the rat turning a wheel. The only source of drive present were the conditioned fear cues since the UCS had been discontinued. Over 50% of the rats learned to turn the wheel to open a door which permitted an escape to the "safe" (nonfear cue) side. In a related demonstration, Brown and Jacobs (1949) were concerned that Miller's study might have involved the emotion of "frustration" since the first escape response learned was blocked. They then replicated the Miller results without allowing the animals to initially escape before the wheel turning task. McAllister and McAllister (1962, 1964, 1965, 1971; McAllister, McAllister, Brooks, & Goldman, 1972) regularly employ a two-stage procedure in their work in which they separate conditioning trials from the instrumental avoidance learning trials. In the first stage, classical fear conditioning trials are administered by pairing the box cues with a shock, UCS. Following this phase, the UCS is discontinued and the animal is permitted to escape the shock box by running or jumping into a "safe," nonshocked box. It is difficult to interpret the learning of the escape or avoidance response by appealing to the direct conditioning of the response or to some other construct besides fear. It is no wonder that critics of fear theory have frequently failed to cite the extensive contributions of the McAllisters.

VII. AVOIDANCE RESPONDING IN THE PRESENCE OF AN EXTERNAL WARNING STIMULUS

As noted in the proceeding section, avoidance responding is not dependent on the previous learning of an escape response to the UCS nor does it occur without an adequate stimulus change being correlated with the response. Further, the rate and magnitude of the reinforcement effect depends on the relative degree of stimulus change which follows a response. Stimulus change, in turn, can be manipulated at least two ways: (1) by changing the apparatus or situational cues following a response; or (2) by adding a number of distinctive cues to the experimenter designated CS. Keeping these points in mind, fear theory is now in a position to make a number of predictions which should eliminate some confusion over a variety of paradoxical findings.

Differentiated Apparatus Cues

The one-way avoidance apparatus provides an ideal situation for altering the apparatus cue preceding and following a response. The color or illumination of the box, the floor surface, and the dimension of the box can be altered between the shock and nonshock compartments. If these cues are changed following a response, the situation between the shock and nonshock compartment can be described as highly differentiated. If the apparatus cues are not changed, the situation can be described as relatively undifferentiated. A comparison between these situations clearly confirms the stimulus change hypothesis that animals will learn the one-way avoidance responses faster and resist extinction longer if the apparatus cues are different (Denny & Adelman, 1955; Denny, Koons, & Mason, 1959; Denny & Weisman, 1964; Franchina, Bush, Kash, Troen, & Young, 1973; Knapp, 1965).

McAllister and McAllister (1962), who were the first to highlight the importance of the apparatus cues, reported that the addition of an externally introduced CS (an increase in illumination) reliably enhanced performance over an apparatus CS, alone condition. However, in an experiment reported by Levis, Bouska, Eron, and McIlhon (1970), using a differentiated one-way apparatus, the addition of two externally manipulated cues (tone plus flashing lights) did not lead to an enhancement of performance when compared to a one-cue condition (tone or lights). But these investigators did report that resistance to extinction was enhanced if the two cues were ordered serially (S1 followed by S2).

Differentiated one-way avoidance responding is quickly learned with the average number of UCS presentations being around 3 to 4 shock trials. A reasonable number of these animals learn following the administration of only one shock trial. Levis (1971a) reported that one-trial-a-day avoidance training in a differentiated, one-way apparatus also produces fast acquisition of the response (an average of 3.6 shock trials) and did not reliably differ on six acquisition indices when compared to a massed-trial procedure in which the same number of trials were conducted in a single day. If properly arranged, human avoidance learning can also be demonstrated to produce rapid avoidance learning (Levis, 1971b; Levis & Levine, 1972; Levis & Warehime, 1971).

Undifferentiated Apparatus Cues

The converse is also true for the stimulus change hypothesis. That is to say, as the relative difference between the conditioned stimulus situation preceding and following a response is decreased, so is the ability of the CS complex to function as a discrimination stimulus for drive induction and drive reduction. The standard shuttlebox bar-press, and wheel-turning apparatuses are examples of experimental settings where the apparatus cues are undifferentiated preceding and following a response. The theory predicts that the same externally manipulated CS (e.g., a tone) presented in an undifferentiated apparatus as opposed to a differentiated apparatus will lead to less drive induction and produce smaller reinforcement effects. This in turn should lead to slower acquisition of the avoidance response, slower generalization of response latencies from the point of the UCS onset to CS onset, and poorer avoidance maintenance and resistance to extinction. Furthermore, because the point of maximum reinforcement effect following CS offset is delayed by the presence of the remaining part of the CS complex (apparatus cues), the probability will increase that incompatible response will be reinforced (see Fig. 8.1). If the rate of fear reduction following a response is diminished, the correlation between the response and fear reduction will become weaker. If at the point of maximum fear reduction the animal is engaging in an incompatible response (e.g., freezing), this response in turn will be reinforced. Further, a similar effect will occur on those trials in which the animal fails to respond adding to the development of incompatible response tendencies. The theory states that CS offset leads to fear reduction independent of what the animal behavior is. A failure to avoid can also lead to the learning of incompatible responses in a differentiated apparatus. However, in the latter situation, the reinforcement effects are weaker upon a failure to avoid that when a response occurs since the response is followed by a greater stimulus change. In addition, incompatible responses may occur because the animal learns to develop postural responses to reduce the intensity effects of the UCS (Bracewell & Black, 1974). Finally, one needs to take into consideration the response topography of the avoidance response. If it is high on the family habit hierarchy of responses (see Hull, 1943) like running is for the rat, then less of a magnitude of reinforcement effect is needed to strengthen the response. However, if the topography is rarely engaged in, like pressing a bar or turning a wheel, a greater reinforcement effect is needed to elevate the strength of that response over the strength of incompatible response tendencies. If a difficult response topography is used for the avoidance response, learning may never occur using the standard procedures.

These predictions have indeed been born out by the literature. The use of undifferentiated apparatuses has resulted in poorer avoidance learning, as well as complete failures to learn (Anderson & Nakamura, 1964; Feldman & Bremmer, 1963; Fitzgerald & Brown, 1965; Meyer, Cho, & Wesemann, 1960; Mowrer, 1940; Theios & Dunaway, 1964). For example, Meyer et al. (1960) reported considerable difficulty in establishing even low levels of responding in the bar press situation, while Fitzgerald and Brown, using a wheel turning situation, reported that no group's performance exceeded 42% avoidance on any day. The standard shuttlebox situation also results in poorer learning when compared to a one-way situation but is somewhat better than that obtained for bar-press and wheel-turning response. In our laboratory employing a shuttlebox about 35% of the rats failed to meet a learning criterion of 10 consecutive avoidances within 150 training trials. This finding is consistent with Brush (1966) who reported that 28% of his animals failed to make three consecutive shuttlebox avoidances.

Another way to extend the delay of reinforcement effect is for the experimenter to delay terminating the external CS following a response. If the delay of the CS termination was long enough and an undifferentiated apparatus were used, avoidance learning would cease to occur. Kamin (1956, 1957a, 1957b, 1957c) conducted a series of experiments in a shuttlebox apparatus investigating the effects of CS termination. He reported, that the best learning occurred in the immediate CS terminated condition with progressively poorer performance with longer delays. Although he interpreted his data from a different perspective, the results are very consistent with fear-theory predictions. Fear-theory would also predict differential effects for the delay of CS termination when the apparatus cues are undifferentiated, or why a differentiated apparatus leads to less freezing than an undifferentiated one. To the author's knowledge this prediction has yet to be tested.

Response Characteristics

As already noted, the topography of the response needs to be taken in consideration when analyzing avoidance behavior. Because rats fail at times to learn response topographies other than running or jumping, and because incompatible responses like freezing are readily observed, Bolles (1970, 1971) argued that only "species specific defense reactions" will be readily established as avoidance responses. According to this position, if one of these species-specific defense reactions coincides with the requirement for an avoidance response, the response will be selected, in large part because the other defense reactions will be punished. However, if the avoidance response requirement does not elicit a species-specific defense reaction, learning will not occur. Bolles considers the dominant species-specific defense reaction to a stimulus like electric shock to be either mobility in the form of flight or immobility in the form of freezing.

A two-factor theory would clearly disagree with the thrust of this analysis. It is difficult to understand from Bolles' position why a flight response in a one-way apparatus readily occurs when the stimulus situation is differentiated and the same response is retarded when the apparatus cues are undifferentiated, or why a differentiated apparatus leads to less freezing than an undifferentiated apparatus. For Bolles' position to be scientifically meritorious, the rules for when and under what conditions a given species-specific response will be elicited need to be clearly specified.

On the other hand, fear theory maintains that fear reduction, because it is a reinforcer, should be capable of strengthening any response in the animal repertoire. Just as Skinner (1962) demonstrated with positive reinforcement that animals can learn a variety of responses, including playing ping-pong, so should, in principle, this same effect occur when fear reduction serves as the reinforcement. One only has to listen to the variety of anecdotal experiences shared by experimenters who conduct aversive experiments to become sensitive to the fact that animals will learn all sorts of responses to avoid shock, which alters the experimental arrangement. For example, if the box dimensions are too narrow, animals will learn to bridge their feet against the wall of the apparatus to keep off the aversive grid floor. They will also jump out of the apparatus if given a chance, the ultimate avoidance response (see McAllister, McAllister, & Benton, 1983) or as this writer once observed (Levis, 1966a) cling to a light bulb at the top of the apparatus by holding onto the bulb by its teeth. Most experimenters are aware that when they develop a new apparatus, they must make it foolproof from a variety of unwanted avoidance behaviors.

All that is necessary for the learning of any avoidance response is to arrange the situation so the response can occur and insure that it is properly reinforced. For example, the poor performance in the shuttle situation can be easily rectified by creating a situation where the apparatus cues are differentiated following a response like in the one-way situation. Stampfl, aware of importance that the CS complex plays in avoidance learning, developed in 1959 (personal observation) a shuttlebox that incorporated the critical features of the one-way apparatus, yet required the same shuttling behavior. The key feature of this apparatus involved the covering of the grid floor with a solid floor before the onset of the CS and following its offset. This was achieved by modifying a standard shuttlebox with two independent sliding floors. Thus, during the intertrial interval both solid floors were in place covering the grid floor. With the onset of the external CS (e.g., a tone), the floor of the compartment on which the rat resided would be removed exposing the grid floor. The rat would then respond by running to the second compartment which consisted of a solid floor and the absence of the CS. Following a response the solid floor would be returned to the compartment the rat left. After an intertrial interval the procedure was again repeated. Thus, the animal always ran from a CS present grid-floor condition to a solid-floor CS absent condition. Shuttlebox acquisition was as quick or almost as quick as that obtained for a one-directional response as reported by those who used the Stampfl-box design (Boyd & Levis, 1979; Kostanek & Sawrey, 1965; Modaresi, 1975). Although Stampfl essentially only changed one apparatus cue (the floor surface), he reasoned that this was the most ''salient'' cue since shock was administered through the grid floor. Unpublished data from the author's laboratory support the contention that the change in floor surface was indeed the most salient cue when compared to a tone CS and changes in the illumination of the apparatus walls. A pseudo-conditioning control group indicated little or no responding to the pull of the floor, per se.

Previous theoretical attempts to account for the discrepancies between avoidance learning in a differentiated one-way apparatus versus an undifferentiated shuttle-box or bar-press apparatus have focused on differences in response topographies (Bolles, 1967), response conflict (Theios, Lynch, & Lowe, 1966) or task difficulty (Isaacson & Olton, 1967; Weitzman, 1966). McAllister and McAllister (1971) were two of the few experimenters who emphasized the differences in the stimulus context. The evidence supports the stimulus change hypothesis and suggests that other more difficult, nonspecies specific response topographies should, in principle, also be quickly learned. However, fear reduction does not have the degree of stimulus control that, for example, food reward has, so it may be necessary to build up the strength of a given response with positive reward prior to introducing avoidance conditioning. The stronger the to-be-conditioned response in the family hierarchy of responses, the less effect competing response tendencies will have (see the transfer study of Leonard, Tafeen, & Fey, 1972).

A final note to consider under this section is that the stimulus change hypothesis is a *relative change hypothesis* in the manner suggested by the Perkins-Logan stimulus-intensity-dynamism hypothesis (Logan 1954; Perkins, 1953). From this analysis it is immaterial whether the CS involves the addition or removal of a given CS component. Supporting evidence for this position in the avoidance area is provided in a series of studies by Levis (1971c, also see Miller & Levis, 1971).

The UCS Intensity Paradox

Interestingly, one-way avoidance learning is facilitated by an increase in shock intensity (Moyer & Korn, 1966; Theios, et al., 1966) while an inverse relationship between the intensity of shock and avoidance performance is typically found in undifferentiated apparatuses like the shuttlebox (Levine, 1966; McAllister, McAllister, & Douglass, 1971; Moyer & Korn, 1964; Theios et al., 1966). This paradox does provide a problem for two-factor theory which predicts a direct relationship between the intensity of fear conditioning and UCS intensity. It also predicts a direct relationship between the intensity of conditioned fear and the strength of any instrumental response reinforced by fear reduction. But as already discussed, the undifferentiated apparatus situation leads to the reinforcement of incompatible instrumental response tendencies. Strong shocks, especially in the initial acquisition phase where few avoidances occur, should provide a greater accumulated reinforcement effect for nonresponding, producing the noted inverse relationship (see McAllister et al., 1971). As expected, a differentiated shuttlebox situation removes the inverse relationship between shock intensity and avoidance performance (Boyd & Levis, 1979; Levis & Boyd, 1973; Modaresi, 1975).

Intertrial Interval

It has been established in discrete-trial studies that avoidance responding tends to be facilitated by the use of a long intertrial interval (Brush, 1962; Denny & Weisman, 1964; Weisman & Litner, 1971). According to the present analysis of fear theory, the length of the intertrial interval should play less of a role when the apparatus cues are differentiated. In the differentiated apparatus setting, fear reduction is believed to occur rapidly because of the greater degree of stimulus change. However, in the undifferentiated apparatus setting, reinforcement effects are delayed and, as noted earlier, can lead to the reinforcement of incompatible responses. In this setting, the longer intertrial interval length would permit the apparatus fear cues to undergo a greater extinction effect which in turn should weaken the strength of any incompatible responses that have developed on a given trial (see McAllister et al., 1983). The same analysis would apply to the situation where classical fear conditioning trials are administered before avoidance responding is permitted. In fact, it would be predicted that shorter intertrial intervals between CS–UCS presentations during fear conditioning trials would reduce the acquisition rate of subsequence avoidance or escape from fear responses.

In an attempt to explain intertrial interval responding, Mowrer and Lamoreaux (1951) suggested that these responses simply reflect the ongoing process of discrimination learning involved in a conditioning procedure. Such a notion implies that the intertrial responses are generalized avoidance responses elicited by the fear associated to the background cues of the undifferentiated apparatus. This hypothesis was supported by Levis (1971d) who found that intertrial responses that occurred in a standard shuttlebox situation covaried with the degree of CS complexity. As the complexity of the CS increased, the rate of intertrial responding decreased, while the absolute level of avoidance responding appeared to be relatively independent of the absolute level of intertrial responding. It would also follow from the position that if intertrial responses are generalized conditioned responses rather than random spontaneous responses, then avoidance learners should produce more intertrial responses when compared to nonlearners. Further, the development of intertrial responses should not occur when the CS and UCS are not contingently paired. Support for both these predictions was obtained in the Levis (1971d) experiment. Finally, if intertrial responses are generalized responses, they should occur earlier in training and show a decrease as avoidance performance improves and the discrimination of the CS becomes well established. This tends to be the general finding in the literature (Black & Carlson, 1959; Brush, 1957; Church, Brush, & Solomon, 1956; Kamin, 1954; Thompson, Sachson, & Higgins, 1969).

The Use of Incompatible Responses as an Index of Fear

It is well recognized that incompatible responses like freezing can occur during the course of avoidance acquisition as they do in cases of appetitive learning. Whether or not immobility or freezing responses are innate reactions to the elicitation of fear (Bolles, 1971; Weiss, Krieckhaus, & Conte, 1968) or are reinforced because they reduce the painful effects of shock (Lawry, Lupo, Overmier, Koche-var, Hollis, & Anderson, 1978; Marlin, Berk, & Miller, 1978), fear theory suggests they should be reinforced if correlated with CS termination. Therefore, such incompatible responses, as is the case with active avoidance, can be used as an index of fear (Blanchard & Blanchard, 1969). In the same vein, the CER procedure has been commonly used to assess the fear properties to the CS. It will be recalled that in the CER paradigm, a previously fear conditioned CS is superimposed on an ongoing appetitive operant response like bar pressing for food. Fear is assessed by the degree of suppression of bar press performance in the presence of the feared conditioned CS.

Because fear is considered to have an activating effect on the organism, it is not initially clear why the CER procedure would produce suppression of responding. Although accelerated responding to the CS in the context of this paradigm has been reported (Brimer & Kamin, 1963; Henderson, 1964; Strouthes & Hamilton, 1959; Valenstein, 1959), nonresponding in the presence of the CS appears to be the more dominant response tendency. The previous analysis of the effects of CS offset during classical fear conditioning trials would suggest that immobility would be the dominant response prior to the transfer test. It would also follow that the suppression effects during the transfer test could be mitigated or even result in facilitation if a very weak shock is used during fear conditioning trials or the fear conditioning trials are administered in a different environment than involved during CER testing (Dexter & Merrill, 1969).

The activation hypothesis is no way limited by a suppression finding. Mowrer viewed fear as an emotional response elicited by the autonomic nervous system. In theory, it is the autonomic system that is first activated which is then transferred to the skeletal system. The question then became one of determining what responses are reflecting the activating properties of fear. Autonomic measures of fear should clearly be affected by the presentation of a fear CS and readily have been shown to be so affected (e.g., Peterson & Levis, 1985; Levis & Smith, 1987). The skeletal system should also be activated and supporting evidence has already been cited. In the case of a suppression or freezing response both autonomic and skeletal signs of activation (e.g., trembling) should be present.

VIII. AVOIDANCE RESPONDING IN THE ABSENCE OF AN EXTERNAL WARNING STIMULUS

Two procedures have been developed which suggest that avoidance responding can be demonstrated to occur in the absence of an external warning stimulus. The first procedure involves the use of a trace conditioning procedure. The trace procedure differs from the standardly used delayed avoidance procedure in that the CS is presented only for a brief period (1 or 2 sec). For example, if a 10-sec CS–UCS interval is used in a delayed procedure, the CS remains on until a response occurs. However, when a trace procedure is employed, the CS comes on, say for 2 sec and then goes off. CS offset is followed by 8 sec of "no CS" which is followed by shock. In both procedures, the UCS will not be presented on a trial where a response occurs within the 10-sec period signaled by the onset of the CS. The second procedure, referred to as free-operant avoidance learning, or Sidman avoidance, eliminates completely the use of the externally presented CS. Rats will learn to press the bar in the absence of an external warning stimulus, which has the effect of postponing shock or reducing the frequency of shock presentation.

Critics have argued that the demonstration of avoidance responding in the absence of an identifiable external warning signal is problematic for fear theory (e.g., Herrnstein, 1969). The major point of this argument assumes that the termination of an external warning stimulus is a necessary condition for the reinforcement of an avoidance response. As noted in the earlier discussion of what stimuli are conditioned, the assumption that the only CS eliciting fear is the external warning stimulus manipulated by the experimenter is not only naive, but contrary to what has already been firmly established in the literature (e.g., McAllister & McAllister, 1962). Thus, we again see an advancement of an argument whose premise misrepresents fear-theory. Nevertheless, fear-theory does maintain that avoidance behavior is elicited by fear stimuli and reinforced by a reduction in the presence of fear stimuli. Therefore the theory has a responsibility to identify the stimuli involved.

In reviewing the trace conditioning avoidance literature, it should be established from the start that long nonsignal periods (greater than 20 sec) following the trace signal has been shown to produce very little avoidance in both a one-way apparatus (Warner, 1932) and in a two-way shuttle situation (Kamin, 1954). The best results are obtained when the total interval prior to shock onset is from 5 to 10 sec. Mowrer and Lamoreaux (1951) were the first to demonstrate that a trace procedure produced considerably more intertrial responding than the delayed CS procedure. They argued that this increase in intertrial responding from a trace procedure was expected because shock was delivered in the presence of stimuli very similar to the stimuli present in the intertrial interval. This in turn would increase the generalization of fear during the nonshock periods and produce more *spontaneous* intertrial responding. The typically used delayed CS procedure would facilitate the discrimination between situation safe and situation noxious resulting in fewer intertrial responses. Not only was this prediction confirmed by others (e.g., Bolles, Stokes, & Younger, 1966; Kamin, 1954) but Kamin (1954) reported that the rate of intertrial responding under some trace conditions was so high that the occurrence of the avoidance response might be spurious and could be attributed to the spontaneous rate of intertrial responses. In either case, two-factor theory has little difficulty handling the results of trace conditioning by appealing to the trace of the CS, temporally conditioned cues and the context cues as providing the stimulus for eliciting responding in the no-signal period prior to shock onset. A response in turn, is reinforced by a reduction to some extent in each of these cue categories. It should be noted that although the response may help eliminate or reduce the stimulus traces cues, trace stimuli decrease in intensity as a function of exposure time from the offset of the CS (Hull, 1943). Thus fear theory would make the following prediction:

1. delayed CS presentation procedure should produce faster avoidance acquisition and fewer intertrial responding than a trace procedure;

2. the shorter the "no-stimulus" period is in trace procedure the better the avoidance learning;

3. shorter "no stimulus" periods should produce less intertrial responding;

4. better avoidance learning should occur when a response to the external CS used in a trace procedure results in the termination of the "warning" stimulus than when the warning stimulus remains a fixed duration whether a response occurs before its offset or not.

Although some of these predictions have yet to be fully tested, the existing data are supportive.

Turning to the Sidman procedure, the problem of isolating the CS or establishing a Pavlovian component becomes more difficult. The free operant procedure differs from the delayed and trace conditioning procedures in at least four important ways: (1) no external warning stimulus is presented by the experimenter; (2) the procedure is continuous during a session rather than broken up into trials; (3) shock is brief and inescapable being set at a fixed duration; and (4) the response does not prevent the occurrence of shock but rather just postpones it for a fixed duration (e.g., 10 sec). In the original Sidman (1953a, 1953b) procedure, shock was delivered at a fixed schedule (e.g. 10 sec) if there were no intervening responses. Thus the procedure can be divided into two temporal features as Sidman suggested. The first interval is referred to as the "shock-shock interval" and reflects the interval between shocks if there is no response. The second interval is labeled the "response-shock interval" and reflects the interval between a response and a shock, again if there are no intervening responses (see Sidman, 1966).

Before discussing the Sidman procedure, it should be recalled that learning a bar press avoidance rarely occurs when an external stimulus is presented and a delayed conditioning procedure is used (Meyer, Cho, & Wesemann, 1960). It was argued earlier, that although an avoidance response will terminate the external warning stimulus, most of the CS complex (apparatus cues including grid floor) is still present following a response. Although fear would be expected to be reduced during the no-shock intertrial interval, the rate of reduction would, in theory, be slowed by the presence of the apparatus fear-cues. This in turn would most likely lead to strengthening responses incompatible with active responding as is the case in the CER paradigm. It would also follow that the bar press escape response would be quickly learned, and occur rapidly after UCS onsets. The fast response time associated with the bar press escape response would reduce the aversive consequence of shock considerably when contrasted to the shuttle situation.

Now if we return to an analysis of the procedure it becomes clear that the shock-shock interval is much shorter than that typically used in discrete trial avoidance procedures. This decrease in the shock-shock interval would keep the fear level high preventing much reduction or extinction from the passage of time. Because of the high fear level there should be a corresponding increase in activity level. This increase in activity level should, in turn, increase the probability that the bar will be pressed. It should be noted that this is the same rationale Mowrer and Lamoreaux applied when predicting increased intertrial responding with a trace conditioning procedure. It would then follow, given the contingency of the Sidman procedure, that the response produced cues associated with bar press responding would function as a discriminative stimulus to predict shock-free time. As the response-shock interval became longer, greater fear reduction would occur to the apparatus cues resulting in an increase probability that the bar press response will be reinforced since it is occurring in the presence of fear reduction.

The foregoing analysis, which is essentially the same as that suggested by Anger (1963), would lead to the prediction confirmed by Sidman (1953b) that the bar press responding should increase as the response-shock interval is made longer than the shock-shock interval (also see Weisman & Litner, 1971). It would also follow that as training increases, the proportion of shocks successfully avoided increases, as is the case with avoidance responding in extinction. Further, bar press responding should, in turn, decrease, which is exactly what Sidman (1966) reported.

Herrnstein and Hineline (1966) modified the Sidman procedure by introducing two randomly programmed shock procedures, one resulting in a high density level of shock presentation and one resulting in a lower density of shock. A response in this situation simply changes the shock schedule from a high density to a low density schedule. In this situation, a response reduces shock frequency but not for a fixed time as with the standard Sidman procedure. Thus, it was possible that the next shock following a response could occur within 2 sec or 20 seconds. They reported some rats still learned to avoid.

Although Herrnstein (1969) strongly argued that the Herrnstein and Hineline data dealt a strong blow to two-factor theory, the reality of the situation is that the above logic still holds. The only new prediction added by fear theory is that the Herrnstein and Hineline procedure when compared to the Sidman procedure would greatly retard the acquisition (because shock could immediately follow a response, punishing it) leading to either no learning or requiring extensive training (hundreds of presses) for the longer response-shock period to reinforce responding. Herrnstein and Hineline confirmed this expectation since it took not hundreds but thousands of responses and thousands of shocks before regular responding was obtained for those animals that learned.

As Mackintosh (1974, pp. 324–325) noted, when discussing Herrnstein and Hineline's experiment, free-operant avoidance schedules do not produce random distribution of responses in time and that those temporal distributions of responding observed, suggest that the subject's behavior is affected by changes in the momentary probability of shock in the manner required by an Anger-type analysis (also see Rescorla, 1968 for additional support). In closing, Pear, Moody, and Persinger (1972) reported the interesting observation that some responses recorded in the bar press situation are bites on the lever which appear to be directly elicited by shock. It is quite possible that the Sidman procedure not only elicits fear but also frustration which could augment the above interpretation.

IX. THE RELATIONSHIP BETWEEN AUTONOMIC CONDITIONING AND AVOIDANCE BEHAVIOR

Mowrer (1947) adapted the historical contention (Konorski & Miller, 1937; Schlosberg, 1937; Skinner, 1935) that classical (fear) conditioning involves the *direct* conditioning of visceral responses which are governed by the peripheral autonomic nervous system. Although the weight of evidence supports the earlier contention that the autonomic system can mediate instrumental learning (Rescorla & Solomon, 1967), the classical issue as to whether it is a necessary condition is still open to debate. Although space limitations preclude a detailed discussion of this topic area, the reader is referred to the Rescorla and Solomon (1967) article which provides a more comprehensive review.

Given Rescorla and Solomon's excellent defense of fear theory's original position, it is surprising that they chose to advance the notion that what concomitance exists between autonomic responses and instrumental behavior is due to mediation by a common central state. From this position they suggested that concurrent measurements of autonomic and instrumental behavior is not the optimal experimental strategy but rather an irrelevant one. They then concluded that ". . . the essential postulate of two-process theory will then be that manipulation of Pavlovian conditioning procedures should have important effects upon instrumental behavior" (p. 170).

Given our current state of knowledge, it is the reviewer's opinion that the adoption of a central state hypothesis is premature, as well as scientifically limiting. As Mowrer (1960a, pp. 202–203) correctly concluded, much has yet to be learned about interworking between the divisions of the autonomic nervous system. As the young field of psychophysiology develops, more refined differential predictions from two-factor theory should forthcoming (see Holzman & Levis, in press; Levis & Smith, 1987; Malloy & Levis, in press; Peterson & Levis, 1985).

The following predictions would stem from the theory as presented here:

1. An autonomic correlate should precede the occurrence of an avoidance response.

2. The magnitude of this correlate should increase with the acquisition of the instrumental response holding CS exposure constant.

3. As avoidance learning progresses, response magnitude of the correlate should undergo a reduction (less fear is needed to drive the response) but still be present.

4. The greater the degree of unextinguished CS exposure on a given trial, the more intense the autonomic reaction.

5. The faster and greater the degree of stimulus change following the offset of the CS, the faster and the greater will be the corresponding reduction in the autonomic correlates.

6. Avoidance extinction should result in a progressive decrease in the magnitude of responding as indexed by the amount of CS exposure, and

7. residual fear as indexed by an autonomic response is to be expected following the initial extinction of the avoidance response and will remain unless further complete CS exposure trials are given.

This latter prediction is based on the assumption that most avoidance response cease to occur not when complete fear extinction occurs but only when the fear level needed to elicit that response is below threshold (see Hull, 1943, pp. 322–348).

X. AVOIDANCE MAINTENANCE AND EXTINCTION

Perhaps more than any other issue covered, the present topic of avoidance maintenance and extinction has produced the most criticism of two-factor theory. In words of Seligman and Johnston (1973): "Even the more flexible versions [of fear theory], however, cannot be reconciled with the great resistance to extinction of avoidance and the concomitant absence of fear" (p. 69). Unfortunately, considerable theoretical and empirical confusion exists in this area stimulated both by fear-theorists and by critics of fear-theory. *It is hard to find an area in psychology where a time-honored theory is so quickly abandoned, by so many, primarily on the basis of casual observations which have been accepted as fact, in lieu of any attempt to provide systematic and direct measurement.* Data are provided that support the contention that many of these nonscientific observations when subjected to direct measurement are inaccurate. Finally, it should become apparent that one of the strongest areas of fear-theory is its position on avoidance maintenance and extinction.

Avoidance Maintenance in Extinction

A frequently stated misconception is the belief that laboratory avoidance is a remarkably persistent behavior. In the words of Seligman and Johnston (1973):

"Animals will commonly respond for hundred of trials without receiving a shock" (p. 77). Yet, even a cursory review of the avoidance literature will reveal that trials to extinction in a differentiated apparatus averages less than 100 and in an undifferentiated apparatus less than 50. As Mackintosh (1974) correctly concluded, there are recorded cases of extreme avoidance persistence, "but these seem to be the exception rather than the rule" (p. 347).

Part of the above misconception can be attributed to the frequent citation of those few studies that do report highly persistent behavior (e.g., Solomon, Kamin, & Wynne, 1953); part to the selectively reporting of data (Seligman & Campbell, 1965); and part to the observation that human clinical symptoms (avoidance behaviors) persist in the absence of any real danger for years. In fact, it was precisely because of this laboratory finding of infrequent avoidance persistence that fear interpretations of psychopathology were vulnerable to criticism. Fortunately, recent evidence at the infrahuman level (e.g., Levis & Boyd, 1979; McAllister, McAllister, Scoles, & Hampton, 1986; Stampfl, 1987) and the human level (Malloy & Levis, in press) indicates that extreme resistance to extinction can be reliably obtained.

Variables Enhancing Resistance to Extinction

Procedurally, extinction is defined as the presentation of the CS in the absence of the UCS. Bolles, Moot, and Grossen (1971) reported that the above traditionally defined extinction procedure resulted in a less rapid loss of avoidance than procedures in which shocks are presented independent of subject's behavior. However, if the avoidance-shock contingency is kept intact and shock is presented intermittently in extinction following the failure to respond, resistance to extinction is greatly enhanced (Denny & Dmitruk, 1967; McAllister et al., 1986). As noted earlier, other acquisition variables like UCS intensity effects and task difficulty clearly play a role in extinction as does the presence of differentiated or undifferentiated apparatus cues.

The Principles of Conservation of Anxiety and Partial Irreversibility

Solomon and Wynne (1954), in discussing two previously conducted studies (Solomon et al., 1953; Solomon & Wynne, 1953) which demonstrated extreme resistance to extinction, noted three important observations that required explanation. First, the avoidance latencies of their dogs shortened considerably with training with response latencies between 1 and 4 sec being common (they used a 10-sec CS–UCS interval). Second, they noted that overt signs of anxiety disappeared with training and seemed nonexistent in extinction when short-latency responses occurred. Third, if a dog happened to produce a long-latency response on a particular extinction trial, they observed the reappearance of behavioral signs of fear on that trial and the return of short latency responses for the next few trials. (It should be noted that their observations about the presence or absence of fear were not based on any objective measurement procedure.)

The above observations stimulated Solomon and Wynne (1954) to advance their well-known conservation of anxiety hypothesis. To account for the observation that overt signs of anxiety rapidly disappeared during training with the occurrence of short latency avoidance responses, they postulated that the latency to respond for the avoidance response was faster than that required for the fear reaction. Therefore, without fear elicitation and subsequent fear reduction, the habit strength of the avoidance response was weakened, resulting in longer latency responses. The resulting longer CS exposure, in turn, provided sufficient time for the elicitation of the fear response. Once fear reoccurred its reduction strengthened the avoidance habit which, in turn, produced faster response latencies on subsequent trials. The conservation part of the hypothesis referred to the notion that fear to the unexposed part of the CS will be protected from extinction because of nonexposure, a requirement for extinction.

Although the conservation of anxiety hypothesis provided an extension of two-factor theory to account for the varying avoidance response latencies noted during extinction and for the maintenance of avoiding responding, Solomon and Wynne felt compelled to introduce yet another principle, that of partial irreversibility. They used the latter principle to explain the extreme resistance to extinction they obtained. They attributed the failure of some of their dogs to extinguish to the intense, traumatic shock used in their experiments. The principle of partial irreversibility is predicated on the position that a very intense pain-fear reaction to a given CS complex will result in a *permanent* fear reaction.

Unfortunately, the combined principles of conservation of anxiety and partial irreversibility, as stated, raise more questions for fear-theory than they solve. For one thing, if a short CS exposure does not provide sufficient time for the fear response to occur, how can the avoidance response be elicited? A fear position requires that fear stimuli be present to elicit avoidance behavior. For another, the principle of partial irreversibility suggests a functional autonomy position for avoidance responding which violates the laws of Pavlovian extinction.

The above dilemma, concerning the presence of fear to a short CS exposure is one which is easily resolved. As suggested earlier, fear must be present for an avoidance response to occur but with extended training only a fractional level of fear is needed to elicit a response and such small levels of fear may not be visually observable. As far as the partially irreversibility hypothesis is concerned, this hypothesis is rejected unless stronger, more direct evidence is presented. The counter position taken is that Solomon's dogs would have eventually extinguished if a sufficient number of trials were conducted (see Levis & Boyd, 1979). Surprisingly, Solomon never compared the effects of a moderate UCS with his traumatic shock level. When the appropriate study was conducted in Solomon's laboratory by Brush (1957), shock intensity was not found to be the key variable in producing resistance to extinction. Rather the key variable appears to be related to the use of a very noisy drop-gate which both added to the CS complex and blocked intertrial responses (see Church et al., 1956).

Conservation of Anxiety Hypothesis Reinterpreted and Extended

Clearly, the conservation of anxiety hypothesis is a key concept in fear theory's explanation of changes in the avoidance response topography and in explaining avoidance maintenance during extinction. Realizing the importance of this contribution, Stampfl argued that infrahuman avoidance (see Levis, 1966b, Levis & Boyd, 1979) as well as human symptom maintenance (Levis, 1985; Stampfl & Levis, 1967, 1969, 1973) could be more readily explained by developing and extending the conservation of anxiety hypothesis. He reasoned that if short-latency avoidance responses conserved the fear to longer CS exposures by preventing their exposure, then the process of conservation could be maximized even further by reducing the generalization of extinction effects from a short CS exposure to a long CS exposure. To achieve this objective, Stampfl suggested the dividing of the CS–UCS interval into distinctive CS components and ordering them serially (e.g., tone followed by flashing lights). Once short-latency avoidance responses to the first component in the CS chain (S_1), were regularly obtained, the second cue (S_2), in the chain would not be exposed. Because the S_2 component is highly dissimilar to the S_1 component, any extinction effects that generalize from the S_1 exposure would have minimum effects on the dissimilar S_2 component. The greater the reduction in generalization of extinction from the early part of the CS–UCS interval to the later portions, the greater the amount of anxiety that would be conserved to the components closer to UCS onset.

However, fear to the S_1 component will eventually extinguish producing longer avoidance response latencies until the S_2 component is exposed. At this point, the fear level changes from a relatively low to a high state because of the greater fear level conserved to the S_2 component. The S_2 component because of its higher fear level can now function as a second order conditioning stimulus capable of reconditioning the fear level to the S_1 component (see Rescorla, 1980). The reconditioning effect $(S_1\text{-}S_2)$ should result in the return of short-latency responses to the S_1 component. Theoretically, as long as sufficient fear remains to the S_2 component (the interval closest to the end of the CS–UCS interval), the reconditioning effect should continue to repeat itself. However, each reconditioning trial will result in less strengthening as more exposure occurs to the S_2 component. The overall effect will result in the avoidance latencies going back and forth in a kind of see-saw manner like that illustrated in Fig. 8.2. Stampfl (Stampfl, 1970, 1987; Stampfl & Levis, 1967, 1969) has extended this position to explain the long-term maintenance of human psychological symptoms, which are believed to result from a series of encoded conditioning effects stored in memory and ordered sequentially in terms of their accessibility and aversive loading.

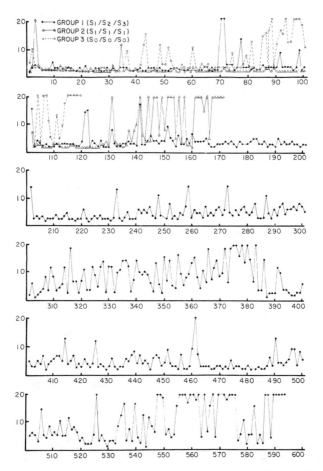

FIG. 8.2. Trial by trial avoidance response latencies in extinction are plot-ted for three different rats from the Levis and Boyd (1979) study. The subjects selected were the best responders in each group. Group 1 sub-jects were exposed to a three component serial CS; Group 2 subjects to a single component CS; and Group 3 subjects to only the apparatus cues. The total CS–UCS interval was 18 sec with each serial component being 6 sec in duration. The purpose of this graph is to illustrate the Conserva-tion of Anxiety Hypothesis.

Considerable support for the serial CS hypothesis has been obtained. When serial CS cues are compared to nonserial CS procedures at the infrahuman level, the serial CS procedures have been shown to enhance resistance to extinction in both differentiated (Boyd & Levis, 1976; Kostanek & Sawrey, 1965: Levis, 1966a, 1966b; Levis et al., 1970; Levis & Boyd, 1979) and undifferentiated, apparatuses (Levis, 1970; Levis & Dubin, 1973; Levis & Stampfl, 1972; Oliverio, 1967). Extreme resistance to extinction has been reported in each of the cited studies using a differentiated apparatus and in human subjects (Malloy & Levis, in press). A serial compound procedure (S_1/S_1S_2) has been shown to enhance the effects over a straight serial procedure (S_1S_2) as has the addition of a third component (Levis, 1970; Levis et al., 1970; Levis & Stampfl, 1972). The effect is not dependent upon the duration of a given component (Levis & Dubin, 1973; Levis & Stampfl, 1972) or on the increased number of stimulus onsets or offsets resulting from the use of the procedure (Levis & Boyd, 1979; Levis & Stampfl, 1972; Malloy & Levis, in press). In addition, support for the operation of the principle of anxiety conservation using a nonserial procedure has been obtained (Delude & Carlson, 1964; Weinberger, 1965) as well as the enhancement of this principle through the use of a serial CS (Levis & Boyd, 1979; Levis & Stampfl, 1972; Molloy & Levis, in press). The establishment of short-latency responses to the S1 component is considerably enhanced when a differentiated apparatus is used (Levis et al., 1970) or when the similarity between components is increased (Dubin & Levis, 1973; also see Kehoe, 1982).

Response Prevention

One of the key assumptions of two-factor theory is that avoidance responding is dependent on the presence of fear eliciting stimuli. Therefore, if fear to the CS is completely extinguished independently of avoidance extinction, the reintroduction of the CS should not elicit responding. This prediction can be demonstrated by blocking a previously conditioned avoidance response from occurring and presenting CS alone trials (fear extinction trials) which, in turn, are followed by reintroducing an opportunity to respond. Studies using this response prevention procedure have repeatedly demonstrated the facilitation of avoidance extinction (e.g., Baum, 1966, 1969, 1970; Berman & Katsev, 1972; Monti & Smith, 1976).

However, Page (1955) and Coulter, Riccio, and Page (1969) have challenged the hypothesis that the decrement in avoidance strength following response prevention results from extinction of conditioned fear via CS exposure. Rather, they argue that the avoidance decrement occurs because the animals learn a competing response, usually crouching and freezing, to cope with the fear. This seems to the reviewer to be a rather curious conclusion since the position negates the laws of Pavlovian extinction. Rather, fear theory would predict both processes are going on and if sufficient CS exposure is given both instrumental response patterns will extinguish. Shipley, Mock, and Levis (1971) tested the competing response hypothesis directly. Rather than relying on casual observation to determine the occurrence of incompatible responses, they measured movement responses directly during the prevention period, during the CS period, and during the intertrial interval. Holding the experimentally manipulated CS constant during the prevention phase and providing controls for the difference in the apparatus cues following CS offset and for differences in transport cues, they compared a response prevention procedure with a response delayed procedure in which the animals were permitted to respond after receiving a fixed duration of CS exposure. The two-factor theory would predict comparable results whether a response occurs or not as long as the exposure to the CS complex was comparable. Their data support the contention that with repeated CS alone trials a decrease in response strength occurs to both the avoidance response and to the incompatible responses. They further demonstrated that on avoidance trials the activity level of the animal increased both following the onset of the CS and following a response to the non-shocked compartment. The delayed and response prevention procedures yielded comparable results in avoidance extinction. Fear extinction was found to occur in direct proportion to the total amount of CS exposure, irrespective of the subject's activity level, number of trials, or the instrumental contingencies involved. These results, and that of others (Bersh & Paytner, 1972; Wilson, 1973), are in complete agreement with a two-factor fear interpretation.

Total CS Exposure

The position adopted here is that *total CS exposure, not trials to avoidance extinction,* should be used as an index to assess the degree of fear extinction. This argument is based on the premise that trials to extinction of the avoidance response can be influenced by other variables such as the learning of incompatible response tendencies, the associative strength of the avoidance behavior, and the contingency that the subject controls the per trial amount of CS exposure by the latency of the response. Shipley (1974) using a classical conditioning procedure followed by a CER transfer test, confirmed that fear extinction was a direct function of total amount of CS exposure and independent of per trial CS exposure or any interaction effects.

The above findings are central to dispelling the concern that fear has to have extinguished when avoidance behavior continues over many trials. For example, Seligman and Johnston (1973) noted that one of Solomon's dogs responded after meeting an acquisition criterion for over 500 trials (490 trials prior to the reintroduction of shock) without showing any signs of extinction while others were still making short-latency responses when stopped after 200 extinction trials. They quoted Annau and Kamin (1961) who reported that rats exposed to a classical fear-conditioning procedure extinguished within 40 trails following high levels of shock. Because of this disparity in trials to extinction, Seligman and Johnston concluded that fear to the CS had extinguished in the Solomon studies long before the avoidance responding was terminated. However, a different picture emerges when one addresses the issue of total CS exposure. Assuming the average response latency for Solomon's dogs was around 2 sec, total CS exposure for the animal that responded for around 500 trials would be 1000 sec. Total CS exposure for complete extinction in the Annau and Kamin study was 2400 sec. Contrary to Seligman and Johnston's argument, it does not follow that fear had extinguished. The use of total CS exposure, as opposed to trials to extinction, also corrects a number of other misconceptions in the literature such as those generated by the study of Kamin, Brimer, and Black (1963).

Residual Fear

A number of studies (e.g., Riccio & Silvestri, 1973) have reported that following the extinction of an avoidance response, the CS has been found to still be capable of eliciting fear as indexed by a CER or passive avoidance testing procedure. Although the finding of residual fear to the CS has been suggested as being problematic for fear theory (Riccio & Silvestri, 1973), fear-theory would expect, as already noted, that in most cases some residual fear should be present unless a lot of CS exposure is given. Each instrumental response has a different threshold level and for extinction of that response to occur all that is required is for the fear level to drop below the necessary level required to elicit the response. Passive avoidance and the CER procedures are considered to be more sensitive indices of fear and should require a lower threshold level for detecting the presence of fear. The issue of residual fear will only become problematic for fear theory if the strength of residual fear can be shown to reinforce the learning of a new response with a higher threshold value than that required for the avoidance response. To my knowledge this has not been demonstrated (see Callen, McAllister, & McAllister, 1984).

Safety-Signal Hypothesis

Mowrer (1960a), in reformulating his two-factor theory, hypothesized that fear reduction following the offset of an aversive CS or UCS can be conditioned to antecedent stimuli, just as fear induction following shock onset can be. If an externally presented ''safety'' signal and/or response produced cues are correlated with (signal) the offset of a noxious event, they can acquire positive secondary value (Mowrer's constructs of hope and relief). The presentation of a stimulus specifically associated with the omission of an expected shock has been shown to depress the rate of avoidance responding (Bull & Overmier, 1968; Grossen & Bolles, 1968; LoLordo, 1967; Rescorla & LoLordo, 1965; Weisman & Litner, 1969). Following Mowrer's lead, Bolles (1970) has proposed that CS termination combined with the feedback from the avoidance response-produced stimuli serve as safety signals since they are paired with no shock (also see Denny & Weisman, 1964). Once such safety signals have been established to be operating, it may be argued (see Gray, 1975) that they provide a source of positive reinforcement to maintain avoidance responding in the absence of fear. As Seligman and Johnston (1973) noted, for this state of affairs to occur it must be maintained that stimuli paired with no-shock can retain their positive reinforcing safety properties long after motivating fear has extinguished. This has yet to be conclusively demonstrated and were it so determined this would not markedly alter two-factor theory. The finding that safety signals can function as positive second-ary stimuli is consistent with a fear reduction position but to suggest they are capable of reinforcing an avoidance response in the absence of fear is not.

Asymptotic Avoidance Performance

Seligman and Johnston (1973) developed their cognitive theory of avoidance large-ly because of their belief that fear is not the motivator of sustained avoidance. Although they acknowledged that a fear construct is needed to explain avoidance acquisition, once the response is well learned they maintain fear extinguishes prior to avoidance extinction. They then suggest that the avoidance response continues because the animal *expects* the absence of a response will be followed by shock. Extinction occurs only when the animal's expectancy changes to one that says the absence of a response will not be followed by shock. As is the case with all existing cognitive theories of avoidance, the rules for how the cognitive variable undergo a change or when the change will occur remains unspecified (see Levis, 1976).

Herrnstein's (1969) theory of avoidance, which Mackintosh (1974, p. 330) suggests is perhaps "masquerading as an expectancy theory" also has difficulty interpreting sustained avoidance responding (see Seligman & Johnston, 1973). In addition, Hernnstein's analysis is unable to account for the observed temporal distributions of responding in unsignaled free-operant experiments as well as ac-counting for response topography findings with signaled avoidance. In the same vein, the use of a safety-signal hypothesis to account for sustained avoidance is problematic as previously outlined and has equal difficulty in accounting for response prevention data.

Fear theory, on the other hand, is consistent in its interpretation that fear is eliciting asymptotic avoidance behavior. But because of the accrued associative strength developed at the point of asymptotic performance only a fractional amount of fear is needed to trigger and reinforce the avoidance response. But because extinction is an ongoing process during avoidance, short latency asymptotic response should periodically weaken, producing longer exposure to the CS, which in turn increases the magnitude of reward and associative strength. This should result in the return of short latency response (conservation of anxiety hypothesis) with the process being repeated until complete extinction occurs. To my knowledge, no other nonfear theory can satisfactorily explain the differences in response latencies that not only occur in extinction but in acquisition (see Levis, 1970; Levis & Dubin, 1973; Levis & Stampfl, 1972).

Support for the Presence of Fear

The Seligman and Johnston theory of avoidance is predicated on their unsystematic observation that fear does not appear to be present during sustained avoidance responding. Although they do predict that fear, as indexed by autonomic responses and conditioned emotional responding (CER), will not be present to the short-duration CS during asymptotic responding, they chose to develop their theory before testing the merits of this key assumption. Levis and Boyd (1979, Exp. 2) directly tested this proposition by conditioning rats to reach an asymptotic criterion of 50 consecutive, short-latency responses. Fear to the short duration CS would not be expected by Seligman and Johnston to be present after this extended training period is completed. Using a CER procedure and controlling for CS duration, Levis and Boyd found substantial suppression of appetitive responding to the CS indicating the presence of fear. In the same vein, a study conducted by Malloy and Levis (in press) showed substantial autonomic responding in human subjects after hundreds of short-latency avoidance trials. These results strongly suggest the basic premise of the Seligman and Johnston theory is in error (also Starr & Mineka, 1977).

Seligman and Johnston's theory suggests that in the development of an expectancy a response will not be followed by the CS, and may produce either a gradual or a quick change from responding to nonresponding. Fear theory, on the other hand, predicts a gradual change in response latencies throughout the course of extinction, as previously described. Levis and Boyd (1979, Exp. 1), after establishing extreme resistance to extinction of an avoidance response using a serial CS procedure plotted the response latency during extinction and found, as suspected from fear-theory, a gradual decrease in latency to respond. They also noted that all animals extinguished, but if the experiment had been stopped after 200 trials, one might have erroneously concluded, as did Solomon and Wynne, that some subjects would never stop responding. *The data support the long established contention that given sufficient time and CS exposure, extinction is inevitable.* Boyd and Levis (1976) reported additional data that a fear gradient is operating in extinction which decreases in magnitude as the distance from the point of UCS onset increases. Given the existing empirical evidence there is little reason to suggest that fear is not present during asymptotic avoidance and there are a lot of reasons for rejecting alternative interpretations.

XI. SUMMARY

At this point it should be clear that Hernnstein's (1969) often quoted contention that two-factor theory has "passed over a line into irrefutable doctrine" (p. 67), is not only an assertion whose basis is obscure as concluded by Mackintosh (1974, p. 323) but is completely contrary to the established predictive power of the theory. It should also be clear that the current trend to abandon fear theory is not only premature, but misguided. The existing alternative viewpoints are mainly founded on untested premises which are largely based on unscientific observation. In addition, they are lacking in predictive power. Two-factory theory has the distinct advantage of covering a wide range of data, explaining numerous paradoxes and having most of its major assumptions strongly supported on empirical grounds. A key factor in the theory's predictive power is the introduction of a construct that can be defined and assessed independently of monitoring the instrumental avoidance behavior. The advantage of using autonomic measures as a fear indicator, especially in human research, is reason enough for refraining from adopting a central state hypothesis of integration. The call to measure and plot avoidance latency distributions as well as to directly assess the development of incompatible responses should go far in the quest to strengthen or weaken the premises of the theory outlined in this chapter.

Despite the established theoretical power of two-factor theory, the model should not be uncritically accepted. The current downfall and existing misinterpretation of the theory stem is, in part, due to the fear-theorist's complacency. The theory needs to be continually developed and expanded, integrating new data and generating new predictions. Well-conceptualized criticism is an important factor in testing the limits and growth potential of any theory. In this vein, creative and scholarly attempts to restate fear-theory in a manner that makes it consistent with expectancy theory, as Mackintosh (1974) has so eloquently done, should be avoided. Such a strategy glosses over critical differences between theories and leads to a lack of interest in generating differential predictions. The differences not similarities between opposing viewpoints stimulates the advancement of new knowledge. In this regard, fear theory has not outlived its usefulness; its value is not historical but contemporary; it can not be so arbitrarily dismissed by less encompassing and poorly supported alternative viewpoints; and its ongoing development appears to hold a bright and productive future.

XII.   EPILOGUE

My interest in two-factor theory rests largely in the theoretical extension of this model by Thomas G. Stampfl to the area of psychopathology. Stampfl, drawing upon his extensive experience with child and adult psychopathology, coupled with his knowledge of animal experimentation, bridged the gap between the two disciplines. Using established infrahuman principles, he delineated the variables responsible for acquiring, maintaining, and treating human symptoms. This approach referred to as Implosive (Flooding) Therapy (Stampfl, 1966, 1970; Stampfl & Levis, 1967, 1969, 1976) represents a bridge between Pavlov and Freud (Levis & Stampfl, 1969). The strength of the model resides in its ability to conceptualize both complex human cognitive concepts (e.g., thoughts, images, and memories) and behavioral data from an S–R learning framework.

Over 20 years of experience in using the implosive technique in the treatment of severe human psychopathology, has me convinced of the importance of a conditioning interpretation. The memory reactivation component of the implosive technique has resulted in the uncovering of a series of traumatic conditioning events in most patients which are directly related to the reported clinical symptoms. The more traumatic memories seem to have been encoded intact as suggested by the recovery of detailed contextual stimuli and by their intense emotional loading. The content of the avoided memories primarily reflect emotional experiences in childhood involving extensive psychological, physical and/or sexual abuse incorporating a variety of emotional conflicts. The manner in which these memories become reactivated appears to be incredibly similar across patients suggesting that a very lawful S–R process is involved in their decoding (see Spear, 1978). Experience dictates that cognitive interpretations, self-understanding, or coping strategies play little or no role in modifying or eliminating the level of affective conditioning involved. One only has to be exposed to some of this clinical material to become convinced of its importance in the maintenance as well as the removal of psychopathological behavior.

If the learning field is ever going to make substantial contributions in resolving human psychological suffering, the answer will not result from an emphasis on understanding cognitive development per se. Rather what is required is a better understanding of the principles of emotional conditioning and how they interact with internal cognitive processes. In particular, the largely neglected field of conflict, as well as the areas of avoidance, motivation, and punishment, need to be readdressed with a renewed sense of importance and purpose. It is the hope that this chapter will in some small way help to rekindle this interest.

REFERENCES

Amsel, A. (1958) The role of frustrative nonreward in noncontinuous reward situations. *Psychological Bulletin, 55*, 102–119.

Amsel, A. (1962). Frustrative nonreward in partial reinforcement and discrimination learning: Some recent history and a theoretical extension. *Psychological Review, 69*, 306–328.

Amsel, A. (1971). Frustration, persistence, and remission. In H. D. Kimmel (Ed.), *Experimental psychopathology*. New York: Academic Press.

Amsel, A., & Rashotte, M. E. (1984). *Mechanisms of adaptive behavior: Clark L. Hull's theoretical papers with commentary*. New York: Columbia University Press.

Anderson, D. C., & Johnson, L. (1966). Conditioned fear as a function of US intensity under conditions of drive constancy. *Psychonomic Science, 5*, 443–444.

Anderson, N. H., & Nakamura, C. Y. (1964). Avoidance decrement in avoidance conditioning. *Journal of Comparative and Physiological Psychology, 57*, 196–204.

Anger, D. (1963). The role of temporal discriminations in the reinforcement of Sidman avoidance behavior. *Journal of Experimental Analysis of Behavior, 6*, 477–506.

Annau, Z., & Kamin, L. J. (1961). The conditioned emotional response as a function of intensity of the US. *Journal of Comparative and Physiological Psychology, 54*, 428–430.

Barlow, J. A. (1952). Secondary motivation through classical conditioning: One trial nonmotor learning in the white rat. *American Psychology, 7*, 273.

Baum, M. (1966). Rapid extinction of an avoidance response following a period of response prevention in the avoidance apparatus. *Psychological Reports, 18*, 59–64.

Baum, M. (1969). Extinction of an avoidance response following response prevention: Some parametric investigations. *Canadian Journal of Psychology*, *23*, 1–10.

Baum, M. (1970). Extinction of avoidance responding through response prevention (flooding). *Psychological Bulletin*, *74*, 276–284.

Berman, J. S., & Katsev, R. D. (1972). Factors involved in the rapid elimination of avoidance behavior. *Behaviour Research and Therapy*, *10*, 247–256.

Bersh, P. J., & Paynter, W. Jr. (1972). Pavlovian extinction in rats during avoidance response prevention. *Journal of Comparative and Physiological Psychology*, *78*, 255–259.

Black, A. H., & Carlson, N. J. (1959). Traumatic avoidance learning: A note on intertrial-interval responding. *Journal of Comparative and Physiological Psychology*, *52*, 759–760.

Blanchard, R. J., & Blachard, D. C. (1969). Passive and active reactions to fear-eliciting stimuli. *Journal of Comparative and Physiological Psychology*, *68*, 129–135.

Bolles, R. C. (1967). *Theory of motivation*. New York: Harper & Row.

Bolles, R. C. (1969). Avoidance and escape learning: Simultaneous acquisition of different responses. *Journal of Comparative and Physiological Psychology*, *68*, 355–358.

Bolles, R. C. (1970). Species-specific defense reactions and avoidance learning. *Psychological Review*, *77*, 32–48.

Bolles, R. C. (1971). Species-specific defense reactions. In F. R. Brush (Ed.), *Aversive conditioning and learning* (pp. 183–233). New York: Academic Press.

Bolles, R. C., Moot, S. A., & Grossen, N. E. (1971). The extinction of shuttlebox avoidance. *Learning and Motivation*, *2*, 324–333.

Bolles, R. C., Stokes, L. W., & Younger, M. S. (1966). Does CS termination reinforce avoidance behavior? *Journal of Comparative and Physiological Psychology*, *62*, 204–207.

Boyd, T. L., & Levis, D. J. (1976). The effects of single-component extinction of a three-component serial CS on resistance to extinction of the conditioned avoidance response. *Learning and Motivation*, *7*, 517–531.

Boyd, T. L., & Levis, D. J. (1979). The interactive effects of shuttlebox situational cues and shock intensity. *The American Journal of Psychology*, *92*, 125–128.

Bracewell, R. J., & Black, A. H. (1974). The effects of restraint and noncontingent pre-shock on subsequent escape learning in the rat. *Learning and Motivation*, *5*, 33–69.

Brimer, C. J., & Kamin, L. J. (1963). Disinhibition, habituation, sensitization, and the conditional emotional response. *Journal of Comparative and Physiological Psychology*, *56*, 508–516.

Brown, J. S. (1948). Gradients of approach and avoidance responses and their relation to level of motivation. *Journal of Comparative and Physiological Psychology*, *41*, 450–465.

Brown, J. S. (1961). *The motivation of behavior*. New York: McGraw-Hill.

Brown, J. S. (1965). A behavioral analysis of masochism. *Journal of Experimental Research in Personality*, *1*, 5–70.

Brown, J. S., & Farber, I. E. (1951). Emotions conceptualized as intervening variables with suggestions toward a theory of frustration. *Psychological Bulletin*, *48*, 465–495.

Brown, J. S., & Farber, I. E. (1968). Secondary motivational systems. *Annual Review of Psychology*, *19*, 99–134.

Brown, J. S., & Jacobs, A. (1949). The role of fear in the motivation and acquisition of responses. *Journal of Experimental Psychology*, *39*, 747–759.

Brown, J. S., Kalish, H. I., & Farber, I. E. (1951). Conditioned fear as revealed by magnitude of startle response to an auditory stimulus. *Journal of Experimental Psychology*, *41*, 317–328.

Brush, F. R. (1957). The effect of shock intensity on the acquisition and extinction of an avoidance response in dogs. *Journal of Comparative and Physiological Psychology*, *50*, 547–552.

Brush, F. R. (1962). The effects of intertrial interval on avoidance learning in the rat. *Journal of Comparative and Physiological Psychology*, *55*, 888–892.

Brush, F. R. (1966). On the differences between animals that learn and do not learn to avoid electric shock. *Psychonomic Science*, *5*, 123–124.

Bugelski, R., & Miller, N. E. (1938). A spatial gradient in the strength of avoidance responses. *Journal of Experimental Psychology*, *23*, 494–505.

Bull, J. A., III, & Overmier, J. B. (1968). Additive and subtractive properties of excitation and inhibition. *Journal of Comparative and Physiological Psychology*, *66*, 511–514.

Callen, E. J., McAllister, W. R., & McAllister, D. E. (1984). Investigations of the reinstatement of extinguished fear. *Learning and Motivation*, *15*, 302–320.

Champion, R. A. (1964). The latency of the conditioned fear-response. *American Journal of Psychology*, *77*, 75–83.

Church, R. M., Brush, F. R., & Solomon, R. L. (1956). Traumatic avoidance learning: The effects of CS–US interval with a delayed-conditioning procedure in a free responding situation. *Journal of Comparative and Physiological Psychology*, *49*, 301–308.

Coulter, X., Riccio, D. C., & Page, H. A. (1969). Effects of blocking on instrumental avoidance response: Facilitated extinction but persistence of "fear." *Journal of Comparative and Physiological Psychology*, *68*, 377–381.

Delude, L. A., & Carlson, N. J. (1964). A test of the conversation of anxiety and partial irreversibility hypothesis. *Canadian Journal of Psychology*, *18*, 15–22.

Denny, M. R. (1971). Relaxation theory and experiments. In F. R. Brush (Ed.), *Aversive conditioning and learning*. New York: Academic Press.

Denny, M. R., & Adelman, H. M. (1955). Elicitation theory: I. Analysis of two typical learning situations. *Psychological Review*, *62*, 290–296.

Denny, M. R., & Dmitruk, V. M. (1967). Effect of punishing a single failure to avoid. *Journal of Comparative and Physiological Psychology*, *63*, 277–281.

Denny, M. R., Koons, P. B., & Mason, J. E. (1959). Extinction of avoidance as a function of the escape situation. *Journal of Comparative and Physiological Psychology*, *52*, 212–214.

Denny, M. R., & Weisman, R. E. (1964). Avoidance behavior as a function of length of nonshock confinement. *Journal of Comparative and Physiological Psychology*, *59*, 252–257.

Desiderato, O. (1964). Generalization of acquired fear as a function of CS intensity and number of acquisition trials. *Journal of Experimental Psychology*, *67*, 41–47.

Dexter, W. R., & Merrill, H. K. (1969). Role of contextual discrimination in fear conditioning. *Journal of Comparative and Physiological Psychology*, *69*, 677–681.

Dinsmoor, J. A. (1950). A quantitative comparison of the discriminative and reinforcing functions of a stimulus. *Journal of Experimental Psychology*, *41*, 458–47.

Dinsmoor, J. A. (1954). Punishment: I. The avoidance hypothesis. *Psychological Review*, *61*, 34–36.

Dollard, J., & Miller, N. E. (1950). *Personality and psychotherapy*. New York: McGraw-Hill.

Dubin, W. J., & Levis, D. J. (1973). Influence of similarity of components of a serial CS on conditioned fear in the rat. *Journal of Comparative and Physiological Psychology*, *85*, 304–312.

Dyal, J. A., & Goodman, E. D. (1966). Fear conditioning as a function of CS duration during acquisition and suppression tests. *Psychonomic Science*, *4*, 249–250.

Evans, W. O. (1962). Producing either positive or negative tendencies to a stimulus associated with shock. *Journal of Experimental Analysis of Behavior*, *5*, 335–337.

Feldman, R. S., & Bremmer, F. J. (1963). A method for rapid conditioning of stable avoidance bar pressing behavior. *Journal of Experimental Analysis of Behavior*, *6*, 393–394.

Fitzgerald, R. D., & Brown, J. S. (1965). Variables affecting avoidance conditioning in free-responding and discrete-trial situations. *Psychological Reports*, *17*, 835–843.

Franchina, J. J., Bush, M. E., Kash, J. S., Troen, D. M., & Young, R. L. (1973). Similarity between shock and safe areas during acquisition, transfer, and extinction of escape behavior in rats. *Journal of Comparative and Physiological Psychology*, *84*, 216–224.

Freud, S. (1936). *The problem of anxiety* (pp. 85–92). (Trans. by H. A. Bunker.) New York: Psychoanalytical Quarterly Press and W. W. Norton.

Freud, S. (1938). The psychopathology of everyday life. In *The basic writings of Sigmund Freud*. New York: Random House.

Goldstein, M. L. (1960). Acquired drive strength as a joint function of shock intensity and number of acquisition trials. *Journal of Experimental Psychology, 60,* 349–358.

Gormezano, I., & Kehoe, E. J. (1981). Classical conditioning and the law of contiguity. In P. Harzem & M. D. Zeiler (Eds.), *Advances in analysis of behaviour, Vol. 2. Predictability, correlation, and contiguity.* New York: Wiley.

Gray, J. A. (1975). *Elements of a two-process theory of learning.* New York: Academic Press.

Grossen, N. E., & Bolles, R. C. (1968). Effects of classical conditioned "fear signal" and "safety signal" on nondiscriminated avoidance behavior. *Psychonomic Science, 11,* 321–322.

Hake, D. F., & Azrin, N. H. (1965). Conditioned punishment. *Journal of Experimental Analysis of Behavior, 8,* 279–293.

Henderson, N. D. (1964). A species difference in conditioned emotional response. *Psychological Reports, 15,* 579–585.

Herrnstein, R. (1969). Method and theory in the study of avoidance. *Psychological Review, 76,* 49–69.

Herrnstein, R. J., & Hineline, P. N. (1966). Negative reinforcement as shock frequency reduction. *Journal of the Experimental Analysis of Behavior, 9,* 421–430.

Hilgard, E. R., & Bower, G. H. (1966). *Theories of learning.* New York: Appleton-Century-Crofts.

Hilgard, E. R., & Marquis, P. G. (1940). *Conditioning and learning.* New York: Appleton-Century.

Hoffman, H. S., & Flesher, M. (1962). The course of emotionality in the development of avoidance. *Journal of Experimental Psychology, 64,* 288–294.

Holzman, A. D., & Levis, D. J. (in press). The effects of the number of stimulus modalities included in a fear-eliciting imagery scene on reported imagery clarity, scene repetition, and sympathetic (fear) arousal. *Cognitive Therapy and Research.*

Hull, C. L. (1930). Simple trials and error learning: A study in psychological theory. *Psychological Review, 37,* 241–256.

Hull, C. L. (1931). Goal attraction and directing ideas conceived as habit phenomena. *Psychological Review, 38,* 487–506.

Hull, C. L. (1943). *Principles of behavior.* New York: Appleton-Century-Crofts.

Isaacson, R. I., & Olton, D. S. (1967). Further comments: Nonincremental avoidance behavior. *Psychonomic Science, 9,* 445–446.

Kalish, H. I. (1954). Strength of fear as a function of the number of acquisition and extinction trials. *Journal of Experimental Psychology, 47,* 1–9.

Kamano, D. K. (1970). Types of Pavlovian conditioning procedures used in establishing CS+ and their effect upon avoidance behavior. *Psychonomic Science, 18,* 63–64.

Kamin, L. J. (1954) Traumatic avoidance learning: The effects of CS–US interval with a trace-conditioning procedure. *Journal of Comparative and Physiological Psychology, 47,* 65–72.

Kamin, L. J. (1956). The effects of termination of the CS and avoidance of the US on avoidance learning. *Journal of Comparative and Physiological Psychology, 47,* 65–72.

Kamin, L. J. (1957a). The effects of termination of the CS and the avoidance of the US on avoidance learning: An extension. *Canadian Journal of Psychology, 11,* 48–56.

Kamin, L. J. (1957b). The gradient of delay of secondary reward in avoidance learning. *Journal of Comparative and Physiological Psychology, 50,* 445–449.

Kamin, L. J. (1957c). The delay of secondary reward gradient in avoidance learning tested on avoidance trials only. *Journal of Comparative and Physiological Psychology, 50,* 450–456.

Kamin, L. J., Brimer, C. J., & Black, A. H. (1963). Conditioned suppression as a monitor of fear of the CS in the course of avoidance training. *Journal of Comparative and Physiological Psychology, 56,* 497–501.

Kaye, H., Cox, J., Bosack, T., & Anderson, K. (1965). Primary and secondary punishment of toe sucking in the infant rhesus monkey. *Psychonomic Science, 2,* 73–74.

Kehoe, E. J. (1982). Conditioning with serial compound stimuli: Theoretical and empirical issues. *Experimental Animal Behaviour, 1,* 30–65.

Knapp, R. K. (1965). Acquisition and extinction of avoidance with similar and different shock and escape situations. *Journal of Comparative and Physiological Psychology, 60,* 272–273.

Konorski, J., & Miller, S. (1937). On two types of conditioned reflex. *Journal of Genetic Psychology, 16*, 246–272.

Kostanek, D. J., & Sawrey, J. M. (1965). Acquisition and extinction of shuttlebox avoidance with complex stimuli. *Psychonomic Science, 3*, 369–370.

Kurtz, K. H., & Siegal, A. (1966). Conditioned fear and magnitude of startle response: A replication and extension. *Journal of Comparative and Physiological Psychology, 62*, 8–14.

Lawry, J. A., Lupo, V., Overmier, J. J., Kochevar, J., Hollis, K. H., & Anderson, D. C. (1978). *Animal learning and behavior, 6*, 141–154.

Leonard, D. W., Tafeen, S. O., & Fey, S. G. (1972). The transfer of one-way and handled-shuttle pretraining to standard-shuttle avoidance learning. *Learning and Motivation, 3*, 59–72.

Levine, S. (1966). UCS intensity and avoidance learning. *Journal of Experimental Psychology, 71*, 163–164.

Levis, D. J. (1966a). Implosive therapy, Part II: The subhuman analogue, the strategy, and the technique. In S. E. Armitage (Ed.), *Behavioral modification techniques in the treatment of emotional disorders*. Battle Creek, Michigan: V.A. Hospital Publications, pp. 22–37.

Levis, D. J. (1966b). Effects of serial CS presentation and other characteristics of the CS on the conditioned avoidance response. *Psychological Reports, 18*, 755–766.

Levis, D. J. (1970). Serial CS presentation and the shuttlebox avoidance conditioning: A further look at the tendency to delay responding. *Psychonomic Science, 20*, 145–147.

Levis, D. J. (1971a). One-trial-a-day avoidance learning. *Behavioral Research Methods and Instrumentation, 3*, 65–67.

Levis, D. J. (1971b). Effects of serial CS presentation on a finger-withdrawal avoidance response to shock. *Journal of Experimental Psychology, 87*, 71–77.

Levis, D. J. (1971c). Short- and long-term auditory history and stimulus control in the rat. *Journal of Comparative and Physiological Psychology, 74*, 298–314.

Levis, D. J. (1971d). The effects of CS complexity on intertrial responding in shuttlebox avoidance conditioning. *American Journal of Psychology, 84*, 555–564.

Levis, D. J. (1976). Learned helplessness: A reply and an alternative S–R interpretation. *Journal of Experimental Psychology: General, 10*, 47–65.

Levis, D. J. (1985). Implosive theory: A comprehensive extension of conditioning theory of fear/anxiety to psychopathology. In S. Reiss & R. R. Bootzin (Eds.), *Theoretical issues in behavior therapy*. New York: Academic Press.

Levis, D. J., Bouska, S., Eron, J., & McIlhon, M. (1970). Serial CS presentations and one-way avoidance conditioning: A noticeable lack of delayed responding. *Psychonomic Science, 20*, 147–149.

Levis, D. J., & Boyd, T. L. (1973). Effects of shock intensity on avoidance responding in a shuttlebox to serial CS procedures. *Psychonomic Bulletin, 1*, 304–306.

Levis, D. J., & Boyd, T. L. (1979). Symptom maintenance: An infrahuman analysis and extension of the conservation of anxiety principle. *Journal of Abnormal Psychology, 88*, 107–120.

Levis, D. J., & Dubin, W. J. (1973). Some parameters affecting shuttle-box avoidance responding with rats receiving serially presented conditioned stimuli. *Journal of Comparative and Physiological Psychology, 82*, 328–344.

Levis, D. J., & Levine, H. S. (1972). Escape maintenance under serial and simultaneous compound presentation of separately established conditioned stimuli. *Journal of Experimental Psychology, 95*, 451–452.

Levis, D. J., & Smith, J. E. (1987). Getting individual differences in autonomic reactivity to work *for* instead of *against* you: Determining the dominant "psychological" stress channel on the basis of a "biological" stress test. *Psychophysiology, 24*, 346–352.

Levis, D. J., & Stampfl, T. G. (1969). Implosive therapy: A bridge between Pavlov and Freud? *Association for Advancement of Behavior Therapy, Newsletter, 4*(2), 8–10.

Levis, D. J., & Stampfl, T. G. (1972). Effects of serial CS presentations on shuttlebox avoidance responding. *Learning and Motivation, 3*, 73–90.

Levis, D. J., & Warehime, R. G. (1971). The effects of primary and secondary aversive motivation on finger-withdrawal reaction time responses. *Journal of Experimental Psychology, 89,* 126–131.

Ley, R. (1965). Effects of food and water deprivation on the performance of a response motivated by acquired fear. *Journal of Experimental Psychology, 69,* 583–589.

Logan, F. A. (1954). A note on stimulus intensity dynamism. *Psychological Review, 61,* 77–80.

LoLordo, V. M. (1967). Similarity of conditioned fear responses based upon different aversive events. *Journal of Comparative and Physiological Psychology, 64,* 154–158.

Mackintosh, N. J. (1974). *The psychology of animal learning.* New York: Academic Press.

Malloy, P., & Levis, D. J. (1988). A laboratory demonstration of persistent human avoidance. *Behavior Therapy.*

Marlin, N. C., Berk, A. M., & Miller, R. R. (1978). Modification and avoidance of unmodifiable and unavoidable footshock. *Bulletin of Psychonomic Society, 11,* 203–205.

McAllister, W. R., & McAllister, D. E. (1962). Role of the CS and of apparatus cues in the measurement of acquired fear. *Psychological Reports, 11,* 749–756.

McAllister, D. E., & McAllister, W. R. (1964). Second-order conditioning of fear. *Psychonomic Science, 1,* 383–384.

McAllister, W. R., & McAllister, D. E. (1965). Variables influencing the conditioning and the measurement of acquired fear. In W. F. Prokasy (Ed.), *Classical conditioning: A symposium.* New York Appleton-Century-Crofts.

McAllister, W. R., & McAllister, D. E. (1971). Behavioral measurement of conditioned fear. In F. R. Brush (Ed.), *Aversive conditioning and learning.* New York: Academic Press.

McAllister, W. R., McAllister, D. E., & Benton, M. M. (1983). Measurement of fear of the conditioned stimulus and of situational cues at several stages of two-way avoidance learning. *Learning and Motivation, 14,* 92–106.

McAllister, D. E., McAllister, W. R., Brooks, C. I., & Goldman, J. A. (1972). Magnitude and shift of reward in instrumental aversive learning in rats. *Journal of Comparative and Physiological Psychology, 80,* 490–501.

McAllister, W. R., McAllister, D. E., & Douglass, W. K. (1971). The inverse relationship between shock intensity and shuttle-box avoidance learning in rats: A reinforcement explanation. *Journal of Comparative and Physiological Psychology, 74,* 426–433.

McAllister, W. R., McAllister, D. E., Scoles, M. T., & Hampton, S. R. (1986). Persistence of fear-reducing behavior: Relevance for the conditioning theory of neurosis. *Journal of Abnormal Psychology, 95,* 365–372.

Meryman, J. J. (1952). *Magnitude of startle response as a function of hunger and fear.* Unpublished master's thesis, State University of Iowa.

Meryman, J. J. (1953). *The magnitude of an unconditioned GSR as a function of fear conditioned at a long CS–UCS interval.* Unpublished doctoral dissertation, State University of Iowa.

Meyer, D. R., Cho, D., & Wesemann, A. F. (1960). On problems of conditioning discriminated lever-press avoidance responses. *Psychological Review, 67,* 224–228.

Miller, B. V., & Levis, D. J. (1971). The effects of long-term auditory exposure upon the behavioral preference of rats for auditory stimuli. *Journal of Developmental Psychology, 5,* 178.

Miller, N. E. (1948). Studies of fear as an acquirable drive: I. Fear as motivation and fear-reduction as reinforcement in the learning of a new response. *Journal of Experimental Psychology, 38,* 89–101.

Miller, N. E. (1951). Learnable drives and rewards. In S. S. Stevens (Ed.), *Handbook of experimental psychology.* New York: Wiley.

Miller, N. E. (1959). Liberalization of basic S–R concepts: Extensions to conflict behavior, motivation and social learning. In S. Koch (Ed.), *Psychology: A study of a science, II.* New York: McGraw-Hill.

Modaresi, H. A. (1975). One-way characteristic performance of rats under two-way signaled avoidance conditions. *Learning and Motivation, 6,* 484–497.

Monti, P. M., & Smith, N. F. (1976). Residual fear of the conditioned stimulus as a function of response prevention after avoidance or classical defensive conditioning in the rat. *Journal of Experimental Psychology: General, 105,* 148–162.

Mowrer, O. H. (1939). A stimulus-response analysis of anxiety and its role as a reinforcing agent. *Psychological Review*, *46*, 553–565.

Mowrer, O. H. (1940). Anxiety-reduction and learning. *Journal of Experimental Psychology*, *27*, 497–516.

Mowrer, O. H. (1947). On the dual nature of learning—A re-interpretation of "conditioning" and "problem-solving." *Harvard Educational Review*, *17*, 102–148.

Mowrer, O. H. (1950). Pain, punishment, guilt, and anxiety. In P. H. Hoch & J. Zubin (Eds.), *Anxiety* (pp. 27–40). New York: Grune & Stratton.

Mowrer, O. H. (1960a). *Learning theory and behavior*. New York: Wiley.

Mowrer, O. H. (1960b). *Learning theory and the symbolic processes*. New York: Wiley.

Mowrer, O. H., & Aiken, E. G. (1954). Contiguity vs. drive-reduction in conditioned fear: Temporal variations in conditioned and unconditioned stimulus. *American Journal of Psychology*, *67*, 26–38.

Mowrer, O. H., & Lamoreaux, R. R. (1946). Fear as an intervening variable in avoidance conditioning. *Journal of Comparative and Physiological Psychology*, *39*, 29–50.

Mowrer, O. H., & Lamoreaux, R. R. (1951). Conditioning and conditionality (discrimination). *Psychological Review*, *58*, 196–212.

Mowrer, O. H., & Solomon, L. N. (1954). Contiguity vs. drive-reduction in conditioned fear: The proximity and abruptness of drive-reduction. *American Journal of Psychology*, *67*, 15–25.

Mowrer, O. H., & Viek, P. (1948). An experimental analogue of fear from a sense of helplessness. *Journal of Abnormal and Social Psychology*, *83*, 193–20.

Moyer, K. E., & Korn, J. H. (1964). Effects of UCS intensity on the acquisition and extinction of an avoidance response. *Journal of Experimental Psychology*, *67*, 352–359.

Moyer, K. E., & Korn, J. H. (1966). Effects of UCS intensity on the acquisition and extinction of a one-way avoidance response. *Psychonomic Science*, *4*, 121–122.

Oliverio, A. (1967). Effects of different conditioning schedules based on visual and acoustic conditioned stimulus on avoidance learning of two strains of mice. *Journal of Psychology*, *65*, 131–139.

Osgood, C. E. (1953). *Method and theory in experimental psychology*. New York: Oxford University Press.

Page, H. A. (1955). The facilitation of experimental extinction by response prevention as a function of the acquisition of a new response. *Journal of Comparative and Physiological Psychology*, *48*, 14–16.

Pavlov, I. P. (1927). *Conditioned reflexes*, London: Oxford University Press.

Pear, J. J., Moody, J. E., & Persinger, M. A. (1972). Lever attacking by rats during free-operant avoidance. *Journal of the Experimental Analysis of Behavior*, *18*, 517–523.

Perkins, C. C., Jr. (1953). The relation between conditioned stimulus intensity and response strength. *Journal of Experimental Psychology*, *46*, 225–231.

Peterson, D. A., & Levis, D. J. (1985). The assessment of bodily injury fears via the behavioral avoidance slide-test. *Behavioral Assessment*, *7*, 173–184.

Rescorla, R. A. (1968). Pavlovian conditioned fear in Sidman avoidance learning. *Journal of Comparative and Physiological Psychology*, *65*, 55–60.

Rescorla, R. A. (1980). *Pavlovian second-order conditioning: Studies in associative learning*. Hillsdale, NJ: Lawrence Erlbaum Associates.

Rescorla, R. A., & LoLordo, V. M. (1965). Inhibition of avoidance behavior. *Journal of Comparative and Physiological Psychology*, *59*, 406–412.

Rescorla, R. A., & Solomon, R. L. (1967). Two-process learning theory: Relationships between Pavlovian conditioning and instrumental learning. *Psychological Review*, *74*, 151–182.

Riccio, D., & Silvestri, R. (1973). Extinction of avoidance behavior and the problem of residual fear. *Behavior Research and Therapy*, *11*, 1–9.

Ross, L. E. (1961). Conditioned fear as a function of CS–UCS and probe stimulus intervals. *Journal of Experimental Psychology*, *61*, 265–273.

Schoenfeld, W. N. (1950). An experimental approach to anxiety, escape and avoidance behavior. In P. H. Hoch & J. Zubin (Eds.), *Anxiety*. New York: Grune and Stratton.

Schlosberg, H. (1937). The relationship between success and the laws of conditioning. *Psychological Review, 44*, 379–394.

Seligman, M. E. P. (1966). CS redundancy and secondary punishment. *Journal of Experimental Psychology, 72*, 546–550.

Seligman, M. E. P. (1971). Phobias and preparedness. *Behavior Therapy, 2*, 307–321.

Seligman, M. E. P. (1975). *Helplessness: On depression, development and death*. San Francisco: W. H. Freeman.

Seligman, M. E. P., & Campbell, B. A. (1965). Effect of intensity and duration of punishment on extinction of an avoidance response. *Journal of Comparative and Physiological Psychology, 59*, 295–297.

Seligman, M. E. P., & Johnston, J. C. (1973). A cognitive theory of avoidance learning. In F. J. McGuigan & D. B. Lumsden (Eds.), *Contemporary approaches to conditioning and learning*. Washington, DC: V. H. Winston.

Sheffield, F. D. (1948). Avoidance training and the contiguity principle. *Journal of Comparative and Physiological Psychology, 47*, 97–100.

Shipley, R. H. (1974). Extinction of conditioned fear in rats as a function of several parameters of CS exposure. *Journal of Comparative and Physiological Psychology, 87*, 699–707.

Shipley, R. H., Mock, L. A., & Levis, D. J. (1971). Effects of several response prevention procedures on activity, avoidance responding, and conditioned fear in rats. *Journal of Comparative and Physiological Psychology, 77*, 256–270.

Sidman, M. (1953a). Avoidance conditioning with brief shock and no exteroceptive warning signal. *Science, 118*, 157–158.

Sidman, M. (1953b). Two temporal parameters of the maintenance of avoidance behavior by the white rat. *Journal of Comparative and Physiological Psychology, 46*, 253–261.

Sidman, M. (1966). Avoidance behavior. In W. K. Honig (Ed.), *Operant behavior: Areas of research and application*. New York: Appleton-Century-Crofts.

Sidman, M., & Boren, J. J. (1957). A comparison of two types of warning stimulus in an avoidance situation. *Journal of Comparative and Physiological Psychology, 50*, 282–287.

Skinner, B. F. (1935). Two types of conditioned reflex and a pseudo type. *Journal of Genetic Psychology, 12*, 66–77.

Skinner, B. F. (1950). Are theories of learning necessary? *Psychological Review, 57*, 193–216.

Skinner, B. F. (1962). Two "synthetic social relations." *Journal of the Experimental Analysis of Behavior, 5*, 531–533.

Skinner, B. F. (1984). The shame of American education. *American Psychologist, 39*, 947–954.

Solomon, R. L., & Wynne, L. C. (1953). Traumatic avoidance learning: Acquisition in normal dogs. *Psychological Monographs, 67*, No. 354, 1–19.

Solomon, R. L., & Wynne, L. D. (1954). Traumatic avoidance learning: The principle of anxiety conservation and partial irreversibility. *Psychological Review, 61*, 353–385.

Solomon, R. L., Kamin, L. D., & Wynne, L. C. (1953). Traumatic avoidance learning: The outcomes of several extinction procedures with dogs. *Journal of Abnormal and Social Psychology, 48*, 291–302.

Spear, N. E. (1978). *The processing of memories: Forgetting and retention*. Hillsdale, NJ: Lawrence Erlbaum Associates.

Spence, K. W. (1966). Cognitive and drive factors in the extinction of the conditioned eye-blink in human subjects. *Psychological Review, 73*, 445–458.

Spence, K. W., & Runquist, W. N. (1958). Temporal effects of conditioned fear on the eyelid reflex. *Journal of Experimental Psychology, 55*, 613–616.

Stampfl, T. G. (1966). Implosive therapy, Part I: The theory. In S. G. Armitage (Ed.), *Behavioral modification techniques in the treatment of emotional disorders* (pp. 12–21). Battle Creek, MI: V.A. Hospital Publications.

Stampfl, T. G. (1970). Implosive therapy: An emphasis on covert stimulation. In D. J. Levis (Ed.), *Learning approaches to therapeutic behavior change*. Chicago: Aldine.

Stampfl, T. G. (1987). Theoretical implications of the neurotic paradox as a problem in behavior therapy: An experimental resolution. *The Behavior Analyst, 10,* 161–173.

Stampfl, T. G., & Levis, D. J. (1967). The essentials of implosive therapy: A learning-theory based psychodynamic behavioral therapy. *Journal of Abnormal Psychology, 72,* 496–503.

Stampfl, T. G., & Levis, D. J. (1969). Learning theory: An aid to dynamic therapeutic practice. In L. D. Eron & R. Callahan (Eds.), *Relationship of theory to practice in psychotherapy.* Chicago: Aldine.

Stampfl, T. G., & Levis, D. J. (1973). *Implosive therapy: Theory and technique.* Morristown, NJ: General Learning Press.

Stampfl, T. G., & Levis, D. J. (1976). Implosive therapy: A behavioral therapy. In J. T. Spence, R. D. Carson, & J. W. Thibaut (Eds.), *Behavioral approaches to therapy.* Morristown, NJ: General Learning Press.

Starr, M. D., & Mineka, S. (1977). Determinants of fear over the course of avoidance learning. *Learning and Motivation, 8,* 332–350.

Strouthes, A., & Hamilton, H. C. (1959). Fear conditioning as a function of the number and timing of reinforcements. *Journal of Psychology, 48,* 131–139.

Theios, J., & Dunaway, J. E. (1964). One-way versus shuttle avoidance conditioning. *Psychonomic Science, 1,* 251–252.

Theios, J., Lynch, A. D., & Lowe, W. F., Jr. (1966). Differential effects of shock intensity on one-way and shuttle avoidance conditioning. *Journal of Experimental Psychology, 72,* 294–299.

Thompson, C. P., Sachson, S. M., & Higgins, R. L. (1969). Distribution of intertrial responses in shuttlebox avoidance conditioning. *Journal of Comparative and Physiological Psychology, 69,* 563–572.

Thorndike, E. L. (1935). *The psychology of wants, interests, and attitudes.* New York: Appleton-Century-Crofts.

Tolman, E. C. (1932). *Purposive behavior in animals and man.* New York: Macmillan.

Valenstein, E. S. (1959). The effects of reserpine on the conditioned emotional response in the guinea pig. *Journal of the Experimental Analysis of Behavior, 2,* 219–225.

Wagner, A. R. (1963). Conditioned frustration as a learned drive. *Journal of Experimental Psychology, 66,* 142–148.

Warner, L. H. (1932). The association span of the white rat. *Journal of Genetic Psychology, 41,* 57–90.

Watson, J. B. (1919). *Psychology from the standpoint of a behaviorist.* Philadelphia: Lippincott.

Weinberger, N. M. (1965). Effects of detainment on extinction of avoidance responses. *Journal of Comparative and Physiological Psychology, 60,* 135–138.

Weisman, R. G., & Litner, J. S. (1969). Positive conditioned reinforcement of Sidman avoidance behavior in rats. *Journal of Comparative and Physiological Psychology, 68,* 597–603.

Weiss, J. M., Krieckhaus, E. E., & Conte, R. (1968). Effects of fear conditioning on subsequent avoidance behavior and movement. *Journal of Comparative and Physiological Psychology, 65,* 413–421.

Weitzman, R. A. (1966). Statistical learning model and individual difference. *Psychological Review, 73,* 357–364.

Wilson, G. T. (1973). Counterconditioning versus forced exposure in extinction of avoidance responding and conditioned fear in rats. *Journal of Comparative and Physiological Psychology, 82,* 105–114.

Wolpe, J. (1958). *Psychotherapy by reciprocal inhibition.* Standford: Stanford University Press.

9 Expectancy Theory in Animal Conditioning

Anthony Dickinson
University of Cambridge

The most perverse feature of stimulus-response theories has always been their claim that knowledge about the consequences of actions and about the predictive implications of stimuli plays no role in the genesis of conditioned behavior. The natural interpretation of conditioning is that an animal comes to expect the reinforcer following either an established conditioned stimulus or an instrumental action and that such expectations act as causal agents in performance. In one form or another this position was vigorously defended throughout the heyday of stimulus-response theory by Tolman (1932, 1951, 1959) and his collaborators, but by the 1950s the parties to the dispute appeared to despair of a resolution with the result that the question of "what is learned" came to have less and less prominence in discussions of conditioning. Some with positivist inclinations (e.g., Kendler, 1952) abandoned the issue altogether because it was thought to be closed to empirical resolution (but see Ritchie, 1953, for an interesting rejoinder), whereas others (e.g., Thistlethwaite, 1951) were disillusioned by the variability of the empirical evidence.

Over the intervening years attempts have been made to resurrect expectancy theory (e.g., Bolles, 1972; Irwin, 1971), although, by and large, contemporary students of animal conditioning (e.g., Mackintosh, 1975; Rescorla & Wagner, 1972) have been content to leave the nature of the knowledge underlying conditioning unspecified within the term associative strength. The last decade or so, however, has seen a reawakening of interest in animal cognition, and so it seems once more opportune to ask whether we need an expectancy theory of animal conditioning. To this end, I shall discuss some of our recent studies bearing on this issue, but before doing so it is necessary to establish what is meant by the concept of an expectancy in the present context.

I. THE CONCEPT OF EXPECTANCY

Like so many intentional concepts, that of expectancy may appear to be a slippery one and a variety of attempts have been made to capture this idea within a theory of conditioning. All seemed agreed that expectancies are mental or cognitive states, but there is less unanimity about the ontological and causal status of such states. In perhaps the most sophisticated presentation of expectancy theory Irwin (1971) adopted what was effectively the stance of a logical behaviorist by identifying an expectancy as a dispositional state and he made clear his Rylean (Ryle, 1949) interpretation of this mental predicate when he characterized it by an analogy to the inflammability of a dry match (Irwin, 1971, p. 106). Thus, for Irwin, an expectancy is a disposition to act in a particular way in certain "diagonistic" situations just as inflammability is the disposition of a dry match to ignite when struck. Given this interpretation of mentality, the job of the theorist becomes that of specifying the logic and rules for the use of this predicate, a task that Irwin undertakes in his monograph. By identifying expectancies with intervening variables, Tolman often seemed to ally himself with such a position; indeed, at one point he defined expectancy operationally in terms of performance in a particular spatial task (Tolman, Ritchie, & Kalish, 1946, p. 15).

The contrasting view assumes that mental predicates refer to states and processes which transcend their behavioral manifestations, although acting as causal agents in the production of this behavior. Such an interpretation is implicated by MacCorquodale and Meehl (1954, p. 236), for instance, when they identify an expectancy with the capacity of a particular stimulus to "arouse a central state," for the state's arousablity and centrality clearly refer to properties that transcend any simple reference to behavioral dispositions. Tolman himself often seemed to endorse, at least implicitly, such a realist interpretation of mentality in many of his theoretical statements (Amundson, 1986), and it is from this stance that I shall discuss the analysis of animal conditioning in terms of expectancy.

But what sort of mental state is an expectancy? Although expectancies are often discussed as though they are beliefs, I think that is best to follow Tolman in distinguishing between an expectancy and the knowledge upon which it is based. He drew this distinction by contrasting the term "mean-end readiness" with that of expectancy; for Tolman (1959):

> A mean-end readiness, as I conceive it, is a condition in the organism which is equivalent to what in ordinary parlance we call a "belief" . . . to the effect that an instance of this *sort* of stimulus situation, if reacted to by an instance of this *sort* of response, will lead to an instance of that *sort* of further stimulus situation, or else, that an instance of this *sort* of stimulus situation will simply by itself be accompanied, or followed, by an instance of that *sort* of stimulus situation. Further, I assume that different readinesses or beliefs . . . are stored up (in the nervous system). When they are concretely activated in the form of expectancies they tend to interact and/or consolidate with one another. (p. 113; the italics are Tolman's)

Thus, for Tolman an expectancy is an activated means-end readiness or belief or, if we are unhappy with the idea that a belief is the sort of thing that can be *activated*, we can rephrase this claim by saying an expectancy is an occurrent mental state by which a dispositional mental state of belief interacts with other mental states. But, however we wish to characterize the relationship between a belief and an expectancy, it seems clear that the nature of the expectancy is determined by the content of the belief. As we have seen, Tolman identified two different representational contents which I shall designate as (S,R,S*) and (S,S*); these two representational structures are clearly intended to distinguish beliefs about instrumental and Pavlovian contingencies, respectively, with S referring to the discriminative or conditioned stimulus ("this sort of stimulus situation"), R the instrumental response or action, and S* the reinforcer ("that sort of stimulus situation"). These structures have at least three important features.

Elements of an Expectancy

An important feature that distinguishes the representational structure of the underlying belief from the associative structure implicated by stimulus-response theory is the presence of a representation of the reinforcer. Tolman clearly specifies that a reinforcer representation is an element of the content of beliefs about both instrumental and Pavlovian contingencies, and so there is no need to invoke an expectancy to explain either form of conditioning unless it can be demonstrated that performance depends on knowledge of the reinforcer.

Form of an Expectancy

Sometime ago I (Dickinson, 1980) suggested that Winograd's (1975) distinction between procedural and declarative knowledge could also be used to illuminate the difference between stimulus-response and expectancy theories. Whereas procedural knowledge consists of an instruction to perform a given action under a certain condition, declarative knowledge stands in a descriptive relationship to a state of affairs. Clearly a stimulus-response associative structure is the prototypical procedural representation, whereas the content of an expectancy has a declarative structure in the sense that it describes or represents an instrumental or Pavlovian contingency. It contains terms that refer to each element of the contingency and relates them in a way that reflects the associations arranged by the contingency.

The declarative form of the representations mediating conditioning is central to an expectancy account for there are two-factor stimulus-response theories of instrumental conditioning with associative structures that could be interpreted as containing an element representing the reinforcer. Trapold and Overmier (1972), for example, argue for a structure of the form $S \rightarrow S^* \rightarrow R$ so that presentation of the discrimimative stimulus activates a representation of the reinforcer which in turn activates the response. What distinguishes this associative structure from the content of an expectancy is the representational status of the link between the terms referring to the action and reinforcer. In the case of an expectancy this link has its origins in the experience of a causal (or perhaps just contiguous) relationship between the instrumental action and the reinforcer and thus can be regarded as representing this relationship. In the two-factor case, by contrast, the link is formed simply because the response is reinforced in the presence of an activated representation of the reinforcer which means that it cannot be taken as standing in a descriptive relationship to the instrumental contingency. To qualify as the content of an expectancy, a relational term in a representational structure must arise directly from the contingency that it describes.

Nature of an Expectancy

Although we have determined that the content of an expectancy must have a declarative structure, we are still left with the problem of specifying the nature of the elements of this structure: the stimulus, action, and reinforcer representations and the relational connections between them. It is now generally recognized that the nature of representations cannot be discussed independently of the processes that operate on them (Anderson, 1978). This means that questions about the representations that carry the content of expectancies are intimately bound up with the issue of how these expectancies control action.

Stung by Guthrie's renowned jibe that expectancy theory leaves the animal buried in thought, the Tolmanians came to be acutely aware of this problem, but in the end simply finessed it. Both Tolman himself (1949b, 1955) and MacCorquodale and Meehl (1954) suggested that performance is simply a function of the product of the strength of the expectancy and the current value or *valence* of the reinforcer without stating the nature of the psychological processes that mediate such an interaction. Subsequent presentations of expectancy-type theories have made little advance, being content, by and large, to state simply that conditioning reflects the fact that animals learn about stimulus-reinforcer and response-reinforcer associations. The problem of performance is then solved by claiming that "An expectancy explains movement because it is postulated to do so" (Bolles, 1972, p. 404). To a mental realist this claim seems to be in danger of leading us back to behavioral dispositions, and it is clear that we need to say something more about the nature and deployment of expectancies. There are two representation-process systems that seem to be particularly appropriate for conditioning, and I shall consider each in turn.

Mechanistic Systems. In this type of system the relational term between the elements is simply a link that allows one element to exert an excitatory (or inhibitory) influence upon another element when the first is activated or excited either by an external input via a sensory system or by excitation in another link to which the first element is also connected. I refer to such associative networks as mechanistic because the psychological processes that operate on them gain their explanatory force by analogy to the causal influence of physical processes.

Classic examples of this type of representational system are to be found in both Pavlov's (1927) and Konorski's (1948) theories of Pavlovian conditioning. When translated from neural- to mental-ese, both these theories maintain that Pavlovian conditioning consists of the formation of an excitatory link between the representations of the conditioned stimulus and reinforcer, yielding an associative representation of the form $S \rightarrow S^*$. When excited by the presentation of the conditioned stimulus, S, this system produces the conditioned response by activation of the reinforcer representation, S^*.

Pavlov (1932) also proposed a parallel $S \rightarrow S^* \rightarrow R$ structure for the generation of instrumental performance which came to be known as the "bidirectional" theory (Asratyan, 1974). Note that this structure is identical to that of the two-factor stimulus-response theory that we considered earlier; the critical difference, however, is that in bidirectional theory the $S^* \rightarrow R$ link comes about, not through the reinforcement of the response in the presence of an activated reinforcer representation, but rather from the direct experience of the response-reinforcer contiguities produced by the instrumental contingency. It is for this reason that the link can be taken as standing in a declarative relationship to the contingency, albeit a somewhat distorted one in that the direction of activation is opposite to that of the causal influence in the instrumental contingency. This fact presents problems for bidirectional theory (see Dickinson, 1980; Mackintosh & Dickinson, 1979), although they will not be taken up here; Gormezano and Tait (1976) have discussed the empirical arguments against the idea that an instrumental contingency results in the formation of such a backward link.

Within an excitatory-link account a Tolmanian "means-end readiness" or belief is the latent associative structure which becomes an expectancy when activated. To complete the model, we need an account of how expectancies interact with the current value of reinforcer to determine performance. Konorski (1948, pp. 103–104) argued that the current drive state of the animal affects performance because it has direct control over the "excitability" of the reinforcer representation and hence its sensitivity to activation via excitatory links. An increase in excitability will thus enhance the strength of responses mediated via the reinforcer representation whether of the Pavlovian or instrumental variety. It is in this way that a change in value of the reinforcer brought about by a shift in drive state will be immediately reflected in behavior.

Bolles (1972) offered a nice conceit for characterizing this type of expectancy theory when he suggested that it retained the semantics of stimulus-response theory while liberalizing its syntax so that not only may a stimulus be linked to a response but also a stimulus to a stimulus and a response to a stimulus. The problem with excitatory-link theory, however, is that it does not really have a semantics; when subject to the process of excitation, an associative structure of this type is just a reactive system whose behavioral effect is not due to the fact its associative structure stands in a representational relationship to the conditioning contingency for the animal. It could be argued that, properly speaking, one should not refer to such a structure and its elements and links as representations (although I shall continue to follow the convention of doing so in the present chapter). In order for an element or structure in a psychological theory to merit the term "representation," its role in the theory should depend on the fact that it serves a representational function for the agent or, in other words, upon the fact that it has a semantic content for the agent. By this criterion mechanistic structures do not represent a state of affairs in the world for the agent; all they do is to control the transmission of excitation (or inhibition).

It is unclear whether Tolman's concept of expectancy and its underlying belief can be embodied within a mechanistic system of the type I have been considering. The fact that he talked about beliefs being "activated" certainly suggests that his concept could be mapped onto such a system. However, he also seemed to imply, at least in the definition that I have quoted, that these beliefs carry semantic or representational content; he explicity identifies this content as being of the form that an action "will lead to" a reinforcer or a stimulus will "be accompanied, or followed," by a reinforcer. To the extent that we take this attribution of semantic content to beliefs and expectancies seriously, a mechanistic system will not do.

Intentional Systems.   An alternative interpretation of expectancy can be expressed in terms of Brentano's (1874/1973) concept of intentionality. In this technical sense intentionality refers to the property of mental states to possess a content or, in Searle's (1983) words, to be "directed at or about or of objects and states of affairs in the world." Typical of such states are the so-called propositional attitudes in which the agent takes a certain psychological relationship to a content that can be expressed in a propositional form, such as believing that "action R causes reinforcer S*" or desiring that "reinforcer S* occurs."

This view of knowledge about the world allows us to conceive of the interaction between an expectancy and the current value of the reinforcer as a form of practical inference. This inference takes the content of a belief about the conditioning contingency and the content of a desire for the reinforcer as premises and yields as a conclusion a command to perform the conditioned response or action. The Tolmanian distinction between beliefs and expectations could then be preserved by viewing an expectation as the deployment of the content of the relevant belief in the practical inference.

In contrast to the associative structures of a mechanistic system, the content of intentional states is truly representational because the deployment of this content by the inference process to control action depends directly upon the semantic or representational nature of that content. The performance of an action can only be rationally related to an agent's belief or expectation about the consequences of that act and his or her desire for the consequences by virtue of the capacity of the content to carry meaning for the agent. It is in this sense that a strong version of expectancy theory requiries an interpretation in terms of intentionality.

In summary, then, the validity of an expectancy theory of conditioning depends on meeting a series of increasingly stringent empirical criteria. First, it must be shown that a representation of the training reinforcer is encoded in the knowledge underlying conditioning, and second, that this knowledge stands in a declarative relationship to the conditioning contingency. Even these two criteria, however, establish only a weak form of the theory; the strong form requires compelling arguments for the intentional nature of this declarative knowledge.

Finally, it should be noted that considerations of brevity restrict this chapter to the discussion of conditioning under a positive contingency or, in other words, to excitatory conditioning in the Pavlovian case and positive reinforcement in the instrumental case. There is no reason, however, why an expectancy account should not also be given of conditioning under negative contingencies (see: Konorski 1948; Seligman & Johnston, 1973).

II. LATENT LEARNING

Over the years a variety of empirical findings have been advanced to demonstrate the role of expectancies in conditioning. One of the first arose from Tinklepaugh's (1928) observations on the effects of changing or omitting the reinforcer. He found that when he substituted a less preferred reward for the training reinforcer, his monkeys would refuse to consume this new reward although it was perfectly effective as a reinforcer if used from the outset of training. Moreover, complete omission of the training reinforcer led to apparent searching behavior at the reinforcement source. These reactions Tinklepaugh interpreted as evidence that his animals expected to receive the reward at the reinforcement source. This may well be so, but what they do not show is that any such expectancy plays a role in the processes generating the conditioned response itself. In fact, when frustration theory (Amsel, 1958) was subsequently developed in an attempt to relate such reactions to instrumental performance, it was assumed that the reaction to reinforcer omission resulted from a process that plays no more than a modulatory role in instrumental performance.

Many have taken the apparent anticipatory nature of classically conditioned responses as evidence that in the presence of the conditioned stimulus the animals expect the reinforcer. Such an interpretation was first advanced by Zener (1937) when he noted the diversity of conditioned responses when his dogs were freed from the restraint of their Pavlovian harness. Once again, however, this observation does not meet the criteria for an expectancy, and an account of the apparent anticipatory nature of conditioned responses can be advanced which makes no reference to expectancies, at least, in the sense I am discussing. Behavior systems theory (Timberlake and Lucas, 1989) is perhaps the best example of such an account.

The major empirical battleground for expectancy theory has been that of latent learning, which usually involves revealing knowledge about a training reinforcer by a shift in the motivational or drive state of the animal. When MacCorquodale and Meehl reviewed the topic in 1954 one particular procedure predominated, the so-called irrelevant incentive procedure.

Irrelevant Incentive Learning

To demonstrate an irrelevant incentive effect, animals are trained to perform an instrumental action that produces an incentive or reinforcer with a property which is supposedly irrelevant to their motivational state at the time of training. Thus, for instance, if hungry rats are taught to press a lever for access to a sucrose solution, the liquidity of this reinforcer is irrelevant to their state of hunger. Following this training, the performance of these experimental animals can be measured in an extinction test under a drive state relevant to this critical property, in this case thirst, and compared to that of control animals originally trained with a reinforcer, such as food pellets, that lacks this property. Figure 9.1 shows that in our hands (Dickinson & Dawson, 1987a) the animals trained with the sucrose solution press reliably more than those trained with food pellets when the test is conducted under thirst.

The intuitive interpretation of this finding is that animals learn what their instrumental actions produce and can use this expectancy to adjust their behavior appropriately when faced with a drive shift. The difficulty for simple stimulus-response theory arises from the fact that there is no reason to believe that the training schedule established a stronger lever-press response in one group rather than the other. In fact, when the extinction test was conducted while animals in a second pair of groups were hungry, performance was unaffected by the type of reinforcer used during training (see Fig. 9.1), suggesting that the sucrose solution and food pellets were equally effective reinforcers under hunger.

Although this effect lies outside the scope of simple stimulus-response learning, theorists of this persuasion soon developed a mechanism to encompass latent learning, the fractional antedating or anticipatory goal response (see Hull, 1952, pp. 148–150; Spence, Bergmann, & Lippitt, 1950). The basic idea is that some component of the consummatory response, drinking in the case of the sucrose solution and eating in the case of the food pellets, will become conditioned to the contextual and drive stimuli during training. This means that lever pressing will often be reinforced while the animals are performing these fractional consummatory responses, so that their stimulus-feedback will become capable of eliciting lever pressing. As a result, lever pressing should be produced by drinking movements following training with the sucrose solution and by eating movements after reinforcement by the pellets. When the drive is shifted to thirst, fractional drinking should predominate through the past history of reinforcement

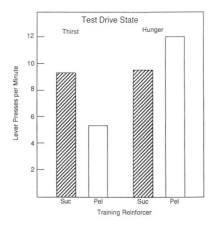

Fig. 9.1. Mean rates of lever pressing during an extinction test under either thirst or hunger following reinforcement of lever pressing by either the sucrose solution (Suc) or the food pellets (Pel).

of this consummatory response in this drive state and, as a result, the most vigorous lever pressing should occur in the group rewarded with the sucrose solution.

Until recently, the only real advance in the study of the irrelevant incentive effect was Krieckhaus and Wolf's (1968) demonstration of the implausibility of this stimulus-response mechanism. I shall illustrate their findings by one of our experiments (Dickinson & Nicholas, 1983) that replicates and extends their study. Again two groups of rats were trained to press a lever, but in this case while they were thirsty. For one group the reinforcer was a sodium solution whereas the other received a potassium solution. Figure 9.2 shows that when the animals were tested in extinction following the induction of a sodium appetite, those trained with the sodium solution pressed more than those for which the reinforcer was potassium. Again the effect was drive specific and did not emerge under control states in which the animls were either sated or thirsty. Here the irrelevant incentive effect occurred even though the same fractional antedating goal response, drinking, should have been conditioned by the two reinforcers. In addition, it is most unlikely that these animals had previously experienced a sodium appetite and thus this drive state could not have gained control over the drinking response through a prior history of reinforcement. In the absence of a plausible stimulus-reponse account of this effect, it is reasonable to conclude that this study meets the first criterion for attributing an expectancy, namely that some representation of the reinforcer is involved in the knowledge controlling behavior. It is difficult to see how the test drive states could bring about differential performance unless the animals had knowledge of the training reinforcers.

Role of the Instrumental Contingency

In fact, many might think that this evidence establishes the case for an expectan-

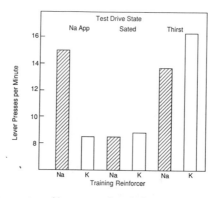

Fig. 9.2.   Mean rates of lever pressing during an extinction test following reinforcement by either the sodium (Na) or potassium solutions (K).
Different groups of animals were tested under a sodium appetite, sated
for water, or thirsty.

cy theory of instrumental conditioning. It is clear, however, that, as they stand,
such demonstrations of the irrelevant incentive effect fail to meet even the second criterion for the attribution of an expectancy in that they do not show that
the knowledge relating to the reinforcer stands in a declarative relationship to
the instrumental contingency. The early students of the effect were not in a position to undertake such a demonstration because of their reliance upon the maze.
A maze procedure inevitably confounds the instrumental and Pavlovian contingencies; not only is reinforcement dependent upon approaching its location in
the maze, but it is also associated with the cues specifying that location. With
an operant procedure, however, we are in a position to dissociate the roles of
the Pavlovian and instrumental relationships in the effect, and this we have done
in a number of experiments.

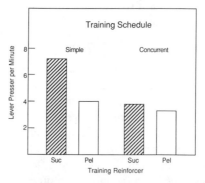

Fig. 9.3.   Mean rates of lever pressing during an extinction test following reinforcement by either the sucrose solution (Suc) or the food pellets
(Pel). In one condition the animals received simple lever-press training,
whereas in the other lever pressing was reinforced concurrently with chain
pulling during training.

In one of these experiments (Dickinson & Dawson, 1987a), hungry rats were trained to press a lever and pull a chain concurrently. For one group lever pressing was reinforced by the sucrose solution and chain pulling by food pellets, whereas the second group received the opposite assignment; sucrose was earned by chain pulling and pellets by lever pressing. Finally, lever pressing alone was tested in extinction following a drive shift to thirst. If the irrelevant incentive effect is mediated by the instrumental contingency, pressing should have been greater on test when it had been reinforced by the sucrose solution during training. Much to our surprise this was not so. Figure 9.3 shows that after concurrent training lever pressing on test was unaffected whether reinforced with sucrose solution or food pellets. This failure to demonstrate the irrelevant incentive effect was not due to the training schedule associated with lever pressing. Two further groups were trained under identical conditions except for the fact that the chain was withdrawn from the chamber so that the rats could neither perform this action nor earn the reinforcers associated with it. Now test performance was affected by the training reinforcer with greater lever pressing occurring when it had been rewarded with the sucrose solution. The insensitivity of the irrelevant incentive effect to the instrumental contingency is not peculiar to this particular drive shift from hunger to thirst for it is also observed following a shift from thirst to a sodium appetite (Dickinson, 1986; Dickinson & Nicholas, 1983).

In summary, it appears that we cannot take the irrelevant incentive effect as evidence for an instrumental expectancy for it is clear that the knowledge upon which the effect is based does not stand in a declarative relationship to the instrumental contingency. This conclusion leaves open the question of the nature of the knowledge that does mediate the effect, the issue to which I now turn.

Role of the Pavlovian Contingency

If the irrelevant incentive effect is not mediated by the instrumental contingency, the next obvious candidate is the Pavlovian association between the incentive and the contextual cues. There are at least two reasons for thinking that this association might be important. First, there is some evidence that an irrelevant incentive effect can be observed with a purely Pavlovian procedure (e.g., Holman, 1980), and second, as I have already mentioned, two-factor theories (e.g., Rescorla & Solomon, 1967; Trapold & Overmier, 1972) identify a role for a Pavlovian process in instrumental performance. The normal procedure for demonstrating such a role is the Pavlovian instrumental transfer design. Initially, instrumental performance and Pavlovian conditioning are established independently before testing the effect of presenting the conditioned stimulus for the first time while the animals are performing the instrumental action. With this design it is found that under certain circumstances the presentation of an appetitive conditioned stimulus accelerates the performance of an instrumental action trained under positive reinforcement (e.g., Estes, 1943). Such findings raise the possibility that the association between the contextual cues and the irrelevant incentive endow these cues with the capacity to bring about a general enhancement of performance under the relevant drive state.

To investigate this possibility, we (Dickinson & Dawson, 1987b) performed a Pavlovian instrumental transfer experiment within the context of the irrelevant incentive procedure. Hungry rats were trained on a three-component multiple schedule. In two of the components, signaled by different stimuli, the animals received either sucrose solution or food pellets noncontingently with the lever withdrawn from the chamber. Thus, both these components involved pure Pavlovian contingencies. The third component was instrumental and signaled by the insertion of the lever; during this component lever pressing was reinforced by food pellets. The components were separated by intervals during which neither stimuli nor reinforcers were presented. Finally, lever pressing in extinction was tested in the presence of the two conditioned stimuli while the animals were either hungry or thirsty. When the animals were thirsty, we saw a clear effect in that they pressed more in the presence of the stimulus associated with the sucrose solution during training (see Fig. 9.4). A comparable effect was not seen when the animals were hungry.

This finding suggests that the instrumental irrelevant incentive effect can be mediated by a Pavlovian association. In fact, we (Dickinson & Dawson, 1987b) have evidence suggesting that almost all the effect is due to such an association. In this study the hungry rats were trained with two Pavlovian components identical to those of the previous experiment and two instrumental components. Each instrumental component was signaled by a distinctive discriminative stimulus during which lever pressing was reinforced with the sucrose solution in one component and the food pellets in the other. Thus, the animals experienced two stimuli associated with each type of reinforcer: one, Pavlovian signaling the free deliv-

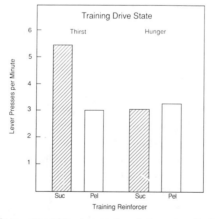

Fig. 9.4.   Mean rates of lever pressing during an extinction test in the presence of a Pavlovian conditioned stimulus that had been paired with either the sucrose solution (Suc) or the food pellets (Pel) during training. Different groups of animals were tested under thirst and hunger.

ery of the appropriate reward, the other, the instrumental or discriminative stimulus, signaling that lever pressing would be reinforced with this reward. Finally, all animals were tested in extinction for lever pressing in the presence of all four stimuli while thirsty.

The difference between test performance in the two discriminative stimuli indicates the size of the instrumental effect. If this effect is entirely due to the Pavlovian relationship between these stimuli and the reinforcers, we should have observed a comparable difference between performance in the presence of the two conditioned stimuli. Figure 9.5 shows that the pattern of pressing on test matched this prediction with no significant interaction between the type of training reinforcer (sucrose solution vs. food pellets) and the type of stimulus (discriminative vs. Pavlovian). This result implies that the simple irrelevent incentive effect is entirely due to the association between the stimuli accompanying instrumental performance and the reinforcers rather than to the causal relationship between the instrumental actions and the reinforcers.

Although the classic irrelevant incentive effect cannot be used to support the concept of an instrumental expectancy, there is little doubt that it provides good evidence for, at least, the weak version of a Pavlovian expectancy. The effect could not occur unless information about the reinforcer was encoded in the associative structure mediating the Pavlovian influence. Moreover, the fact that the elevated performance in the presence of a conditioned stimulus depends on whether or not this conditioned stimulus has been directly paired with the incentive indicates that the underlying associative structure is declarative in form.

There is little reason, however, to argue for the intentional version of the theory in which the knowledge-action translation process is one of practical inference. In fact, the present data provides evidence against such an interpretation.

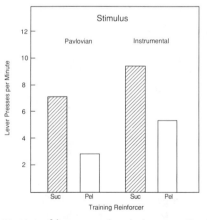

Fig. 9.5. Mean rates of lever pressing during an extinction test in the presence of either a Pavlovian conditioned stimulus or an instrumental discriminative stimulus. These stimuli had been associated with either the sucrose solution (Suc) or the food pellets (Pel) during training.

The hallmark of an inference process is, of course, rationality, so to support an intentional account, we should have to demonstrate, at very least, that the behavior controlled by a conditioned stimulus could be plausibly considered to be rational with respect to the information that this signal provides and the current motivational state of the animal. It is not clear, however, that a plausible inference can be constructed to support an enhancement under thirst of an instrumental action, which was reinforced by food pellets during training, by a conditioned stimulus that predicts the sucrose solution. And yet this appears to be the consequence of a Pavlovian expectancy. Apparent irrationality appears to be a general feature of Pavlovian conditioning. It is well established, for instance, that animals will persist in performing a Pavlovian response even though it causes the omission of the appetitive reinforcer that is used to establish it (e.g., Holland, 1979).

In conclusion, the classic instrumental irrelevant incentive effect is mediated by Pavlovian knowledge that meets the criteria for an expectancy only in the weak, mechanistic sense. Presenting a conditioned stimulus activates a *representation* of the reinforcer whose sensitivity to the activation is directly enhanced by the presence of a relevant drive state. The excited representation then appears to have a potentiating effect on any prepotent actions. This conclusion is also in accord with an established account, namely Rescorla and Solomon's (1967) motivational version of two-factor theory, which assumes that instrumental performance reflects the motivational modulation of an instrumental stimulus-response process by a Pavlovian influence.

III.   INSTRUMENTAL EXPECTANCIES

So far, our analysis of the irrelevant incentive effect points to the conclusion that expectancies play no more than a modulatory role in instrumental performance. Before embracing stimulus-response theory, however, we should consider the outcome of other techniques for evaluating whether or not the reinforcer is represented in the knowledge directly controlling instrumental action. It may well be that the motivational manipulations that we have considered so far simply fail to contact the reinforcer representation in an instrumental expectancy. One technique that has received increasing attention recently is that of reinforcer devaluation (Rozeboom, 1958).

Reinforcer Devaluation

To the best of my knowledge, Tolman (1933) was the first to attempt a reinforcer devaluation experiment. He trained rats to choose the white goal box in a black–white discrimination apparatus in order to get access to food. He then placed the animals in the white goal box and gave them a shock, anticipating that if the animals had learned which choice led to this goal box, associating it with the shock should reduce further choice of this stimulus. It did not. Subsequently, however, both Miller (1935) and then Tolman himself (Tolman & Gleitman, 1949) provided successful demonstrations of a reinforcer devaluation effect in T-mazes.

Once again, however, the interpretative significance of these classic reinforcer devaluation studies is limited by their use of maze procedures. As we have already noted, it is difficult to dissociate the contribution of the Pavlovian and instrumental contingencies to performance in a maze, a dissociation that is necessary if we are to determine the nature of the knowledge underlying any devaluation effect. It is now clear, however, that this effect can be mediated by the instrumental relationship. Adams and I (Adams & Dickinson, 1981) found that performance of an instrumental action is reduced to a greater extent by postconditioning devaluation of a contingent reinforcer rather than one that was presented independently of this action during training, a finding that was subsequently replicated by Colwill and Rescorla (1985a). We used a training procedure in which one reinforcer was presented contingent upon the target action and the other independently of any action; whereas Colwill and Rescorla employed a concurrent training procedure in which the different reinforcers were earned by different actions, as in our concurrent irrelevant incentive study. In both cases subsequent devaluation of one of the reinforcers by establishing a food aversion to it reduced later, nonreinforced performance of the action that had earned this reinforcer training. As both our contingent/noncontingent training procedure and Colwill and Rescorla's concurrent schedule equated any Pavlovian influences, it would appear that, unlike the irrelevant incentive effect, the consequences of reinforcer devaluation can be mediated by the instrumental contingency.

Acquisition of Reinforcer Value

Clearly the results of this devaluation procedure stand in marked contrast to those of the irrelevant incentive studies that we considered previously. Following the same instrumental training a change in reinforcer value brought about by food-aversion learning did affect subsequent performance whereas a change in value resulting from a motivational shift did not. A possible resolution of this discrepancy may be found in Tolman's own analysis of how reinforcers acquire value. As already noted, for Tolman performance is a function of the product of the expectancy and the "valence" of the reinforcer at that time, an interaction that we have interpreted in terms of a practical inference in the case of intentional theory. Valence in turn is a product of the current drive state of the animal and what Tolman (1949a, 1949b) called the "cathexis" attached to the reinforcer. The cathexis of a reinforcer is a belief about the value of a reinforcer in a given drive state that is based on prior consummatory experience with that reinforcer in the relevant drive state. In other words, according to Tolman, animals have to learn about the value of a reinforcer under a particular drive state.

This analysis of reinforcer value would not anticipate an irrelevant incentive effect unless the animals had prior experience of the irrelevant incentive under the test drive state. As we typically use novel incentives, such as sucrose solution and saline, and sometimes novel drive states, such as a sodium appetite, our animals would not have had the opportunity to form the appropriate cathexes for these reinforcers relevant to the test drive state. Thus, our simple irrelevant incentive effect, which is mediated by the Pavlovian contingency, lies outside the scope of Tolman's account of the acquisition of reinforcer value in that it occurs in immediate response to a drive shift.

Tolman's analysis, however, may hold for the effects of changes in reinforcer value that are mediated by the instrumental contingency. If it is true that in these cases it is necessary to have had experience of the revalued reinforcer before an appropriate adjustment of instrumental performance occurs, we could understand why the reinforcer devaluation procedure produces an instrumental effect, whereas a drive shift does not. Because complete devaluation requires a number of pairings of the reinforcer and the toxic agent, during this procedure the animals will be exposed to the reinforcer at a time when it is, at least, partially devalued, an experience that should change its cathexis according to Tolman.

The obvious prediction from this analysis is that if we had given our animals prior experience of the irrelevant incentive under the test drive state, we should have observed an effect of the instrumental contingency. To test this prediction, we (Dickinson & Dawson, 1988) trained hungry rats on the concurrent lever-press chain-pull schedule used in our previous irrelevant incentive studies. The sucrose solution acted as the reinforcer for one action and food pellets for the other in a counterbalanced assignment. After performance was established, the lever and chain were withdrawn from the chamber and the drive state was alternated daily between hunger and thirst for 10 days. During this phase half of the animals received free or noncontingent presentations of the sucrose solution and food pellets on days when they were thirsty. As neither the lever nor the chain was present during this noncontingent training, the rewards delivered during this phase could not have exerted any direct reinforcing effect on these instrumental actions. Even so, this experience should have allowed the rats to form an appropriate cathexis for the irrelevant incentive, sucrose solution, under the test drive state, thirst, and for that matter also have allowed them to learn that the food pellets have little value in this drive state. Thus, we should expect these animals to have a greater desire for the sucrose solution than for the food pellets when they were thirsty once again on test. By contrast, the remaining, control animals, which received the noncontingent rewards on days when they were hungry should not have had the opportunity to acquire cathexes for the two reinforcers appropriate for the state of thirst. Following this noncontingent training the lever and chain were then reinserted and the baseline level of instrumental performance reestablished under hunger prior to test. In this test the chain was removed and lever pressing measured without any rewards under thirst.

If control of the irrelevant incentive effect by the instrumental contingency

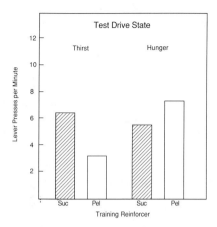

Fig. 9.6.   Mean rates of lever pressing during the extinction test following reinforcement by either the sucrose solution (Suc) or food pellets (Pel).
During training the animals had received non-contingent presentations of
the reinforcers under either thirst or hunger.

depends on establishing the appropriate cathexes for the incentives, we should
not expect to have observed an effect in the control animals that received the
noncontingent reinforcer presentations under hunger; they had no opportunity
to find out the relative value of the incentives when thirsty. Fig. 9.6 bears out
this expectation; the performance of the rats which received noncontingent training under hunger was unaffected by the type of reward used to reinforcer lever
pressing. By contrast, the animals trained under thirst showed a clear irrelevant
incentive effect in that they pressed more when this action had been rewarded
by the sucrose solution rather than the food pellets. Thus, it would appear that
knowledge of an instrumental contingency can mediate the effects of a drive shift
on performance, but only if the animals have had prior experience of the training
reinforcers under the new motivational state.

What then are the implications of this analysis for the nature of instrumental
knowledge? First, the reinforcer devaluation effect and this final demonstration
of an irrelevant incentive effect dependent upon the instrumental contingency show
that we need an expectancy theory in which a representation of the reinforcer
is encoded in declarative knowledge about the instrumental relationship. Second,
and this is probably the most important implication of the present data, the expectancies based on knowledge of Pavlovian and instrumental contingencies appear to be different; the former can mediate the effects of drive shifts directly,
whereas the latter cannot. The significance of this dissociation for expectancy
theory in general lies with the implication that there are two different forms of
expectancies, one mediating the effect of Pavlovian relationships and the other
knowledge about instrumental contingencies.

This dissociation also has implications for the nature of these expectancy systems. As we have already noted, the properties of Pavlovian expectancies are well captured by Konorski's (1948) mechanistic model, which specifically anticipates that changes in drive state should have a direct effect on the excitability of the reinforcer *representation* and hence upon performance. Moreover, the fact that the representation mediating performance via an instrumental contingency does not show a similar direct modulation by drive state casts doubt upon whether a comparable mechanistic theory is sufficient in the instrumental case. If, as a result, one was to advocate by default an intentional interpretation of instrumental performance, what the present results indicate is that a desire for a particular reinforcer under a given drive state depends on prior experience with that incentive in the appropriate motivational state. This, in turn, suggests that desires must be based on beliefs about the value of reinforcers which have their origin in experience.

IV. BEHAVIORAL AUTONOMY

In spite of the general claim that instrumental actions can be purposive and goal-directed, expectancy theory has always recognized a role for responses whose executions are autonomous or independent of their original goals. Such responses, Tolman (1932) argued, 'may through repetition come to lose their original truly cognitive, or *sign* characters and become merely "mechanical", "fixated", "conditioned", "stamped-in" ' (p. 300). Similarly, Bolles (1972) acknowledged that under certain circumstances a direct stimulus-response connection might be formed and that "A reinforcement process might be invoked at this point. But perhaps sheer repetition of a response . . . suffices to connect it with the prevailing stimuli" (pp. 405–406). The general idea seems to be that an instrumental action usually starts out under the control of an expectancy, but that with further training a transition occurs whereby the same activity becomes a stimulus-response habit, autonomous of the current value of the training reinforcer.

Overtraining

Until recently, however, there was little or no evidence for the popular belief that overtraining establishes behavioral autonomy. Adams (1982) provided such evidence when he compared the effects of various training conditions on the susceptibility of instrumental performance to reinforcer devaluation. In one experiment he trained two groups of rats to lever press for sucrose. One group was allowed to make only 100 presses, each of which was rewarded, whereas for the other group conditioning was extended for 500 presses. Training occurred at the rate of 50 presses per daily session so that it was spread over only 2 days for one group but over 10 days for the other. For half the subjects in both training conditions the reinforcer was then devalued by pairing its consumption with induction of illness in a food-aversion procedure. The remaining animals in the control condition (N) received the sucrose and the lithium injections on alternate days. After the food-aversion procedure had completely suppressed sucrose intake in the devaluation condition (D), the levers were reinserted in the operant chambers and the rate of pressing was measured in an extinction test.

Not surprisingly, on the last session of training the animals in the 500 condition performed twice as fast on average as those in the 100 condition. Consequently, the lever-press rates in the extinction test were expressed as a percentage of the rates on the last training session for display in the left-hand panel of Fig. 9.7. At first sight, these results appear to support the contention that simple repetition produces behavioral autonomy. A devaluation effect was observed in the 100 condition but not following extended training. A third condition run by Adams, however, suggested that the number of times that the instrumental action was performed during training is not the critical factor leading to behavioral autonomy. In this 500/100 condition, each of the first 50 presses was rewarded but thereafter the reinforcement schedule was changed to a variable ratio 9 so that 450 presses were required to earn the final 50 sucrose reinforcer. Thus the training in this condition was matched to that in the 500 condition in terms of the number of lever presses, whereas the number of rewards received was the same as that in the 100 condition. Fig. 9.7 shows that the number of lever presses is not the critical factor in that rats in the 500/100 condition produced a large devaluation effect. This finding also rules out the performance rate at the end of training as an important variable for the 500/100 animals pressed at a rate comparable to that of the rats in the 500 condition on the last training session.

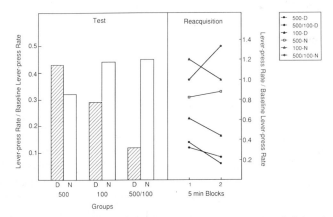

Fig. 9.7 Mean rates of lever pressing during the extinction (left-hand panel) and reacquisition tests (right-hand panel) expressed as a ratio of the rate on the last baseline or training session following either the devaluation (D) or nondevaluation (N) of the reward. During training different groups of animals were allowed to make 100 rewarded presses, 500 rewarded presses, or 500 presses for 100 rewards (500/100).

Adams' (1982) results suggest that the number of training rewards may be important although they allow us to rule out a trivial explanation in terms of this variable, namely that the greater prior exposure to the sucrose under extended training prevented the development of a strong aversion to it. The food-aversion procedure continued until all animals stopped consuming any sucrose; this did in fact require one extra day of conditioning in the 500 condition. Moreover, the right-hand panel of Fig. 9.7 shows that in the reacquisition test when each lever press produced the sucrose reward, rats in the 500 condition pressed no faster than those in the 500/100 condition following devaluation. Clearly, in this case behavioral autonomy could not be attributed simply to the retention of reward value.

An alternative account can be derived from Holland and Rescorla's (1975) obervation that appetitive Pavlovian second-order conditioning often shows behavioral autonomy in the face of reinforcer devaluation, whereas first-order conditioning does not. Rescorla (1977) has noted that if the same is true of the instrumental parallel of second-order conditioning, namely conditioned reinforcement, instrumental behavior should show autonomy to the extent that its maintenance depends on sources of conditioned reinforcement arising from cues associated with the presentation of the primary reinforcer. We should expect the conditioned reinforcing power of these cues to strengthen with the number of times that they paired with the primary reinforcer so their role in instrumental performance should increase with the number of reinforcers given during training.

Another possibility is that the development of a stimulus-response habit depends on a reinforcement process (e.g., Hull, 1943) which means, of course, that the strength of such a habit should be a direct function of the number of training reinforcers. The problem for all these accounts, however, is that behavioral autonomy can be produced by varying the training schedule even when the number of training reinforces is controlled.

Training Schedule

Adams' (1982) instrumental devaluation study employed ratio schedules. In contrast to the reliable effect that can be detected following such training, behavioral autonomy is typically observed following reinforcement on simple interval schedules (Adams, 1980; Holman, 1975; Morrison & Collyer, 1974). This suggested to us that the development of autonomy might be affected by the type of instrumental contingency upon which performance was based. To investigate this idea, we (Dickinson, Nicholas, & Adams, 1983) decided to compare directly the effects of reinforcer devaluation following training in which only 110 reinforcers were delivered on either a ratio or interval schedule. Thus, one group of animals was trained on a ratio schedule for the sucrose reward and another on a variable interval schedule before this reinforcer was devalued by the food-aversion procedure. In order to ensure that any differences in the effect of this devaluation were due to the differing contingencies arranged by the two schedules, an attempt was made to match other features of ratio and interval training, namely the probability that a press would be rewarded and the reward rate, by using a yoking procedure (for details see Dickinson et al., 1983). On the whole the matching was successful in that there was no significant difference between the reward probability under the two schedules, although the reward rate was, on average, 28% higher during ratio rather than interval training.

The results of a subsequent extinction test of lever pressing essentially replicated those of previous studies. As the left-hand panel of Fig. 9.8 shows, when the animals were trained on a ratio schedule a devaluation effect was observed. Following interval training, by contrast, the instrumental action appeared to be entirely autonomous of the current value of the reinforcer. This difference once again cannot be simply due to variations in devaluation; the results of a reacquisition test, displayed in the right-hand panel of Fig. 9.8, show that devaluation was just as effective in the interval condition as following ratio training. More importantly, these results cannot be explained in terms of the factor that we thought might be critical in producing behavioral autonomy following extended training, namely the number of training reinforcers, for this was the same under the two schedules. There is no reason to believe, moreover, that performance on the two schedules should have received differential contributions from conditioned and stimulus-response reinforcement processes. The factors that should determine these contributions, the number, probability, and rate of reinforcement, were matched across the schedules. This conclusion thus leaves us in search of a theory that will explain why both extended training and interval schedules lead to behavioral autonomy.

Behavior-Reward Correlation

Sometime ago Baum (1973) suggested that free-operant performance is determined by the experienced correlation between the rate of performance and the

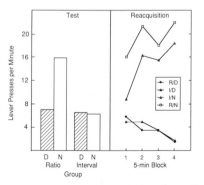

Fig. 9.8 Mean rates of lever pressing during the extinction (left-hand panel) and reacquisition tests (right-hand panel) following either the devaluation (D) or nondevaluation (N) of the reward. Different groups of animals were trained on ratio and interval schedules. (After Dickinson, 1985.)

rate of reinforcement over some time interval. It is but a small step from this correlation-based law of effect to suggest that the content of an instrumental expectancy represents the currently experienced correlation between performance and reinforcement rates. Recently, I (Dickinson, 1985) have suggested that this idea could account for the effects of both overtraining and reinforcement schedule on behavioral autonomy. This point can be illustrated by reference to Fig. 9.9, which displays the feedback functions for ratio and interval schedules.

Let us consider first the effect of overtraining on a ratio schedule. There is a consistent correlation between performance rate and reward rate on a ratio schedule in that reward rate will always increase by the same amount for a constant increment in performance. An animal's experience of this correlation, however, should change with training. Plotted on the feedback function for the ratio schedule are points representing the mean relative performances of the animals on each of the 10 sessions of training in the 500 condition of the overtraining experiment. Also included are the points representing performance on the two sessions of training received by animals in 100 condition. From Fig. 9.9 it can be seen that because animals varied their rate of lever pressing over a wide range during early training sessions, they experienced the strong behavior-reward correlation arranged by a ratio schedule and therefore they should have entertained an instrumental expectancy to the effect that lever pressing causes sucrose delivery. In turn, such knowledge should have rendered their performance susceptible to reinforcer devaluation. By contrast, during the last few sessions of extended training in the 500 condition the animals showed little variation in their rate of lever pressing. Consequently, during these sessions they did not experience the behavior-reward correlation, or in other words, the way in which the reward rate would have altered if they had varied their rate of lever pressing. As a result, their experience

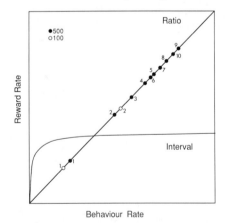

Fig. 9.9 Reward rate as a function of behavior rate for ratio and interval schedules. The points on the ratio feedback function represent the relative performance in each succesive session for the groups allowed to make either 100 or 500 rewarded responses in the overtraining study. (After Dickinson, 1985.)

during the final stages of overtraining should not have sustained an instrumental expectancy to the effect that lever pressing causes reinforcer delivery, thus rendering performance impervious to reinforcer devaluation.

Overtraining is but one way to restrict an animal's experience of a behavior-reward correlation. Another way is to employ a schedule that arranges only a weak correlation in the first place, and this is what an interval schedule does. Whereas on a random ratio schedule there is a fixed probability that each press will be reinforced, a random interval schedule arranges that a reward will become available for collection by a press with a constant probability in each unit of time. This schedule results in a different feedback function, also illustrated in Fig. 9.9, which, unlike that for a ratio schedule, is nonlinear. At low levels of performance there is a strong positive correlation between behavior and reward rates, but this relationship rapidly weakens at modest levels of performance until a stage is reached where the reinforcement rate is relatively unaffected by variations in performance. This is, of course, because the reinforcement rate cannot exceed the fixed rate at which rewards become available however fast the animal presses. The consequence of this analysis is that if the animals are performing at a rate at which the slope of the feedback function for the interval schedule is lower than that for the ratio schedule, the instrumental expectancy supported by the interval contingency will represent a weaker causal relationship between lever pressing and reinforcement than will that engendered by the ratio schedule. As a result, the interval expectancy will be capable of mediating only a smaller devaluation effect.

An analysis of the interval schedule used in our experiment showed that this condition was fulfilled on the last session of training. When the computer program that actually controlled the random interval schedule used during the final training session was driven at different rates by simulated, randomly spaced lever presses, it was found that a five fold increase in performance from 5 to 25 presses per min only increased the reward rate, on average, from 0.92 to 1.06 pellets per min. The mean actual rate of 12.4 presses per min on the interval schedule during the last training session places the animals' performance right in the range where there is little or no behavior-reward correlation. And what correlation there is remains small by comparison to that for the ratio schedule; the 15% increase in reward across this range for the interval schedule contrasts with the 400% rise that would be produced by the same increment in performance under the ratio contingency.

There is, in fact, further evidence that the critical feature of interval schedules and overtraining in producing behavioral autonomy is the lack of experienced behavior-reward correlation. Colwill and Rescorla have shown that performance remains susceptible to reinforcer devaluation under both these conditions if one ensures that animals continue to experience such a correlation. In one set of studies (Colwill & Rescorla, 1985a) they demonstrated a reinforcer devaluation effect following training on interval schedules in which lever pressing led to one reward and chain pulling to another either within the same training session or on alternate sessions. Such training schedules, of course, ensure that the animals always experience a behavior-reward correlation in that different actions lead to different outcomes. This means that overtraining on these schedules should fail to establish autonomy, a fact confirmed by Colwill and Rescorla (1985b) in a second series of studies.

In conclusion, we have seen that degrading the experienced behavior-reward correlation by overtraining and the use of an interval schedule both result in behavior autonomy, a finding which suggests that this is the condition for the absence of control by an instrumental expectancy. Such an account also makes theoretical sense. If, as we have argued, the content of an expectancy is a declarative representation of the experienced contingency, a weak behavior-reward correlation is not going to produce an expectancy that will sustain an inference leading to a command for the instrumental action. To explain the autonomous instrumental performance that is seen after overtraining and simple interval training, one can appeal to the development of stimulus-response habits either as a function of exercise or reinforcement. As Colwill and Rescorla (1985b) have noted, even complete reinforcer devaluation never appears to result in a complete abolition of performance. This suggests that habits may develop when the instrumental action is also being controlled by an expectancy, and it is perhaps significant that in our experiment contrasting ratio and interval training, reinforcer devaluation in the ratio condition reduced performance to the level seen after interval training (see Fig. 9.8). This level may simply reflect the habit strength acquired after this limited amount of training.

V.   CONCLUSIONS

In contrast to the associative knowledge mediating Pavlovian conditioning, that underlying instrumental performance appears to be complex and various. Pavlovian conditioning of the first-order type, at least, appears to be mediated by what I have called a mechanistic version of expectancy theory. This is one that fulfils two criteria: first, that a *representation* of the reinforcer should be encoded in the associative structure mediating the conditioned response and, second, that the form of this structure should be declarative with respect to the conditioning contingency. In the present chapter these conclusions are based on the the stimulus-specificity of the irrelevant incentive effect, although there are also many other sources of evidence for this conclusion (e.g., Holland & Rescorla, 1975). We need only appeal to an excitatory-link representation and an activation process to explain the property of Pavlovian stimuli in this effect.

This is not to say, of course, that Pavlovian contingencies fail to support intentional expectancies. In fact, the finding that in human conditioning there is often a close relationship between beliefs about the Pavlovian contingency and the development of a conditioned response (e.g., Brewer, 1974; Dawson & Furedy, 1976) suggests that it does. But unless there is a rational action that can be taken on the basis of this knowledge, there is no way that the process operating upon this expectancy, namely practical inference, could generate behavior. And the only way to provide the opportunity for rational action is to arrange for an instrumental contingency; in the absence of such a contingency, beliefs about Pavlovian relationships will remain forever behaviorally silent.

Our analysis of the irrelevant incentive effect indicates that instrumental behavior is also affected by mechanistic expectancies, but only via the Pavlovian relationship that is embedded in any instrumental contingency. In fact, for autonomous behavior that is maintained in the presence of a weak behavior-reward correlation this should be the only contribution of an expectancy system to instrumental performance. But the reinforcer devaluation effects make clear that under certain circumstances performance can be controlled by an expectancy about the instrumental contingency. There is reason to believe, however, that this expectancy has different properties to that mediating the Pavlovian effects; unlike the Pavlovian case, the behavioral expression of instrumental expectancies are not affected by changes of motivational state without prior experience of the reinforcers in that state. One could thus argue by default for an intentional account of instrumental conditioning.

As in the Pavlovian case, however, I do not claim that instrumental contingencies result in only one form of expectancy. In fact, there is evidence that an instrumental relationship can produce in a mechanistic, Pavlovian-type expectancy in that performance of instrumental action under certain circumstances can elicit a Pavlovian conditioned response (e.g., Williams, 1965), but this does not imply that such expectancies play a central role in generating instrumental action.

In summary, then, Pavlovian and instrumental relationships both result in the formation of mechanistic and intentional expectancies, although in each case the observed conditioning is primarily controlled by only one kind of expectancy, the mechanistic type for Pavlovian responses and the intentional type for nonautonomous instrumental actions.[1] This position joins a long tradition of distinctions between Pavlovian and instrumental conditioning (see Mackintosh, 1974; Rescorla & Solomon, 1967). For instance, it has been argued that the two forms of conditioning are governed by different principles of reinforcement, Pavlov's principle of "stimulus substitution" in the case of classical conditioning and the "law of effect" in the case of instrumental conditioning (Mackintosh, 1974). This distinction is respected by the present position in that the activation of an excitatory-

---

[1]This dual expectancy theory has been presented as though the two types of expectancies set up by a conditioning experience are independent mental entities. It makes little substantive difference for the present analysis, however, if it were assumed that the two types of expectancies are based upon a common representation of the conditioning contingency, but are differentiated by the type of process that operates on this representation. One possible problem with such a unified account is that it would not allow for the claim that beliefs about contingencies and the strength of conditioning can be dissociated under certain circumstances (e.g., Hugdahl & Ohmann, 1977).

link structure leads to stimulus substitution, whereas the rationality of intentional processes ensures in the selection of an instrumental action by its consequences.

Similarly, this version of expectancy theory also accords with Skinner's (1938) characterization of the Pavlovian responses as "elicited" and instrumental actions or operant as "emitted." The knowledge-action translation process in the case of Pavlovian conditioning is one whereby the response is elicited directly by the activation of the reinforcer representation, whereas an instrumental action is a consequence of a command generated by the practical inference process. For this reason the present position also anticipates that nonautonomous instrumental actions should also be subject to voluntary control for the practical inference system can only control actions that are executable on command. By contrast, Pavlovian responses, being elicited by conditioned stimulus via the activation of the excitatory-link structure, should be involuntary.

There is a danger that these distinctions might be taken to imply that the two forms of conditioning are subject to different laws of association. In fact, the argument that both Pavlovian and instrumental contingencies result in both types of expectancy suggests that the two forms of conditioning are governed by the same learning mechanisms, and what relevant evidence we have supports this conclusion (e.g., Dickinson & Charnock, 1985; Mackintosh & Dickinson, 1979). The two forms of conditioning differ simply in terms of the type of expectancy that exerts primary control over performance.

My final point concerns the question of whether the contrast between mechanistic and intentional expectancies is really appropriate, for it might be argued that they represent theoretical accounts at different levels of discourse. As I have already noted, the mechanistic account gains its explanatory force by analogy to the transmission of energy in a physical system, whereas the strong version of expectancy theory with its appeal to the role of inference is couched in terms of semantic and computational processes, the end point of which is a command to action. Given this distinction, a case could be made that the mechanistic theory (and for that matter stimulus-response/reinforcement theory) should really be juxtaposed to a comparable account of the inference processes invoked by the strong version of expectancy theory rather than to a statement of the theory at the intentional level.[2]

It was an unformulated concern about the disjunction between levels of discourse that, I suspect, led Tolman to mix, quite inappropriately, intentional and mechanistic terms. This can be seen in the earlier quotation from Tolman (1959)

---

[2]Much play is often made of the fact that even apparently mechanistic theories use intentionally- or goal-defined terms. When, for example, such theories refer to the activation of some response, this response is usually specified in terms of the achievement of some goal or state of affairs, such as pressing a lever or pulling a chain, a fact that is captured by Skinner's concept of an operant. Thus, it is clear that the mechanistic-intentional distinction, in the sense that I am discussing, must be drawn with respect to a certain level of analysis, namely that level at which the conditioning contingency and phenonmena are specified. This means that when we observe that arranging an instrumental contingency between lever pressing and the delivery of a food reinforcer strengthens that behavior, we must allow these specifications of the action and reinforcer to enter into both mechanistic theories of the psychological kind and intentional accounts as unanalyzed terms.

in which he defines expectancies as "activated" beliefs. This confusion probably arose from a desire to gain the teleological power of the intentional system without sacrificing the mechanistic level of explanation. Another manifestation of this desire is to be found in the emergence of a number of what Estes (1969) has called contiguity-cybernetic accounts of instrumental conditioning in the era following the demise of the traditional stimulus-response/reinforcement theories. Such theories (King, 1979; Miller, 1963; Mowrer, 1960a, 1960b; Sheffield, 1965; Sutton & Barto, 1981) invoked the presence of an excitatory-link from the representation of the instrumental response (or possibly its stimulus consequences) to that of the reinforcer. Activation of the reinforcer representation could in turn exert an excitatory or inhibitory modulation upon performance through a feedforward or -backward influence. Whatever the details of these accounts they all seem to be attempts to capture the goal-directed nature of instrumental behavior without sacrificing the mechanistic level of psychological theorizing.

One possible reason for the reluctance to entertain an intentional account of animal behavior in general and conditioning in particular may stem from a widespread belief that the use of representations with semantic content depends on natural language, thus restricting intentionality to being a solely a human attribute. Many cognitive theorists and philosophers (e.g., Fodor, 1977; Pylyshyn, 1984; Searle, 1983), however, have argued that intentionality is prior to natural language and therefore is not only capable of being, but also very likely to be, a property of animal mentality, at least in certain cases. Given that there is, at present, no reason to choose between the mechanistic/cybernetic and intentional approaches to instrumental action on empirical grounds, my own preference (Adams & Dickinson, 1981; Dickinson, 1980; Mackintosh & Dickinson, 1979) is for the strong expectancy theory if only because it draws a clear distinction between the reflexive and elicited character of Pavlovian responses and the purposive and rational nature of nonautonomous instrumental action. It is an important distinction between the two forms of conditioning that, unlike Pavlovian responses, instrumental actions will support an intentional interpretation (Dickinson, 1988). Whether or not it is possible to capture the full intentionality of instrumental conditioning by a psychological *mechanism* must at present remain an open question.

ACKNOWLEDGMENT

The work reported in this chapter and its preparation was supported by a grant from the United Kingdom Science and Engineering Research Council. I should like to thank Paula Durlach, Cecelia Hayes, and N.J. Mackintosh for their helpful and often critical comments upon a draft of this chapter.

REFERENCES

Adams, C. D. (1980). Post-conditioning devaluation of an instrumental reinforcer has no effect on extinction performance. *Quarterly Journal of Experimental Psychology, 32*, 447–458.

Adams, C. D. (1982). Variations in the sensitivity of instrumental responding to reinforcer devaluation. *Quarterly Journal of Experimental Psychology, 34B*, 77–98.

Adams, C. D., & Dickinson, A. (1981). Instrumental responding following reinforcer devaluation. *Quarterly Journal of Experimental Psychology, 33B*, 109–122.

Amsel, A. (1958). The role of frustrative nonreward in noncontinuous reward situations. *Psychological Bulletin, 55*, 102–119.

Amundson, R. (1986). The unknown epistemology of E. C. Tolman. *British Journal of Psychology, 77*, 525–531.

Anderson, J. R. (1978). Arguments concerning representations for mental imagery. *Psychological Review, 85*, 249–277.

Asratyan, E. A. (1974). Conditioned reflex theory and motivational behavior. *Acta Neurobiologiae Experimentalis, 34*, 15–31.

Baum, W. M. (1973). The correlation-based law of effect. *Journal of the Experimental Analysis of Behavior, 20*, 137–153.

Bolles, R. C. (1972). Reinforcement, expectancy, and learning. *Psychological Review, 95*, 394–409.

Brentano, F. (1874/1973). *Psychology from an empirical standpoint*. London: Routledge & Kegan Paul.

Brewer, W. F. (1974). There is no convincing evidence for operant or classical conditioning in adult humans. In W. B. Weimer & D. S. Palermo (Eds.)., *Cognition and the symbolic processes* (pp. 1–42). Hillsdale, NJ: Lawrence Erlbaum Associates.

Colwill, R. C., & Rescorla, R. A. (1985a). Postconditioning devaluation of a reinforcer affects instrumental responding. *Journal of Experimental Psychology: Animal Behavor Processes, 11*, 120–132.

Colwill, R. C., & Rescorla, R. A. (1985b). Instrumental responding remains sensitive to reinforcer devaluation after extensive training. *Journal of Experimental Psychology: Animal Behavior Processes, 11*, 520–536.

Dawson, M. E., & Furedy, J. J. (1976). The role of awareness in human differential autonomic classical conditioning. *Psychophysiology, 13*, 50–53.

Dickinson, A. (1980). *Contemporary animal learning theory*. Cambridge, England: Cambridge University Press.

Dickinson, A. (1985). Actions and habits: the development of behavioural autonomy. *Philosophical Transactions of the Royal Society (London), B308*, 67–78. See also, L. Weiskrantz (Ed.), *Animal intelligence* (pp. 67–78). Oxford: Clarendon Press.

Dickinson, A. (1986). Re-examination of the role of the instrumental contingency in the sodium-appetite irrelevant incentive effect. *Quarterly Journal of Experimental Psychology, 38B*, 161–172.

Dickinson, A. (1988). Intentionality in animal conditioning. In L. Weiskrantz (Ed.), *Thought without language*. Oxford: Oxford University Press.

Dickinson, A., & Charnock, D. J. (1985). Contingency effects with maintained instrumental reinforcement. *Quarterly Journal of Experimental Psychology, 37B*, 397–416.

Dickinson, A., & Dawson, G. R. (1987a). The role of the instrumental contingency in the motivational control of performance. *Quarterly Journal of Experimental Psychology, 39B*, 77–93.

Dickinson, A., & Dawson, G. R. (1987b). Pavlovian processes in the motivational control of instrumental performance. *Quarterly Journal of Experimental Psychology, 39B*, 201–213.

Dickinson, A., & Dawson, G. R. (1988). Motivational control of instrumental performance: The role of prior experience of the reinforcer. *Quarterly Journal of Experimental Psychology, 400*, 113–134.

Dickinson, A., & Nicholas, D. J. (1983). Irrelevant incentive learning during instrumental conditioning: The role of drive-reinforcer and response-reinforcer relationships. *Quarterly Journal of Experimental Psychology, 35B*, 249–263.

Dickinson, A., Nicholas, D. J., & Adams, C. D. (1983). The effect of the instrumental training contingency on susceptibility to reinforcer devaluation. *Quarterly Journal of Experimental Psychology, 35B*, 35–51.

Estes, W. K. (1943). Discriminative conditioning. I. A discriminative property of conditioned anticipation. *Journal of Experimental Psychology, 32*, 150–155.

Estes, W. K. (1969). New perspectives on some old issues in association theory. In N. J. Mackintosh & W. K. Honig (Eds.), *Fundamental issues in associative learning* (pp. 162–189). Halifax: Dalhousie University Press.

Fodor, J. A. (1977). *The language of thought.* Hassocks, Sussex: Harvester Press.

Gormezano, I., & Tait, R. W. (1976). The Pavlovian analysis of instrumental conditioning. *Pavlovian Journal of Biological Sciences*, *11*, 37–55.

Holland, P. C., (1979). Differential effects of omission contingencies on various components of Pavlovian appetitive responding in rats. *Journal of Experimental Psychology: Animal Behavior Process*, *5*, 178–193.

Holland, P. C., & Rescorla, R. A. (1975). The effect of two ways of devaluing the unconditioned stimulus after first- and second-order appetitive conditioning. *Journal of Experimental Psychology: Animal Behavior Processes*, *1*, 355–363.

Holman, E. W. (1975). Some conditions for the dissociation of consummatory and instrumental behavior in rats. *Learning and Motivation*, *6*, 358–366.

Holman, E. W. (1980). Irrelevant-incentive learning with flavors in rats. *Journal of Experimental Psychology: Animal Behavior Processes*, *6*, 126–136.

Hugdahl, K., & Ohman, A. (1977). Effects of instructions on acquisition and extinction of electrochemical responses to fear-relevant stimuli. *Journal of Experimental Psychology: Human Learning and Memory*, *3*, 608–618.

Hull, C. L. (1943). *Principles of behavior.* New York: Appleton-Century-Crofts.

Hull, C. L. (1952). *A behavior system.* New Haven: Yale University Press.

Irwin, F. W., (1971). *Intentional behavior and motivation: A cognitive theory.* Philadelphia: Lippincott.

Kendler, H. M. (1952). "What is learned?''—A theoretical blind alley. *Psychological Review*, *59*, 269–277.

King, D. L. (1979). *Conditioning: An image approach.* New York: Gardner.

Krieckhaus, E. E., & Wolf, G. (1968). Acquisition of sodium by rats: Interaction of innate mechanisms and latent learning. *Journal of Comparative and Physiological Psychology*, *65*, 197–201.

Konorski, J. (1948). *Conditioned reflex and neuron organization.* Cambridge, England: Cambridge University Press.

MacCorquodale, K., & Meehl, P. E. (1954). Edward C. Tolman. In W. K. Estes et al. (Eds.), *Modern learning theory* (pp. 177–266). New York: Appleton-Century-Crofts.

Mackintosh, N. J. (1974). The psychology of animal learning. London: Academic Press.

Mackintosh, N. J. (1975). A theory of attention: Variations in the associability of stimuli with reinforcement. *Psychological Review*, *82*, 276–298.

Mackintosh, N. J. & Dickinson, A. (1979). Instrumental (Type II) conditioning. In A. Dickinson & R.A. Boakes (Eds.), *Mechanisms of learning and motivation* (pp. 143–170). Hillsdale, NJ: Lawrence Erlbaum Associates.

Miller, N. E. (1935). A reply to 'sign-gestalt or conditioned reflex.' *Psychological Review*, *42*, 280–292.

Miller, N. E. (1963). Some reflections on the law of effect produce a new alternative to drive reduction. In M. R. Jones (Ed.), *Nebraska symposium on motivation* (pp. 65–112). Lincoln: Nebraska University Press.

Morrison, G. R., & Collyer, R. (1974). Taste-mediated conditioned aversion to an exteroceptive stimulus following LiCl poisoning. *Journal of Comparative and Physiological Psychology*, *86*, 51–55.

Mowrer, O. H. (1960a). *Learning theory and behavior.* New York: Wiley.

Mowrer, O. H. (1960b). *Learning theory and symbolic processes.* New York: Wiley.

Pavlov, I. P. (1927). *Conditioned reflexes.* Oxford: Oxford University Press.

Pavlov, I. P. (1932). The reply of a physiologist to a psychologist. *Psychological Review*, *39*, 91–127.

Pylyshyn, Z. W. (1984). *Computation and cognition.* Cambridge, MA: The MIT Press.

Rescorla, R. A. (1977). Pavlovian second-order conditioning: Some implications for instrumental behavior. In. H. Davis & H. M. B. Hurwitz (Eds.), *Operant Pavlovian interactions.* Hillsdale, NJ: Lawrence Erlbaum Associates.

Rescorla, R. A., & Solomon, R. L. (1967). Two-process learning theory: Relationship between Pavlovian conditioning and instrumental learning. *Psychological Review, 74*, 151–182.

Rescorla, R. A., & Wagner, A. R. (1972). A theory of Pavlovian conditioning: Variations in the effectiveness of reinforcement and nonreinforcement. In A. H. Black & W. F. Prokasy (Eds.), *Classical conditioning II: Current research and theory* (pp. 64–99). New York: Appleton-Century-Crofts.

Ritchie, B. F. (1953). The circumnavigation of cognition. *Psychological Review, 60*, 216–221.

Rozeboom, W. W. (1958). "What is learned?"—An empirical enigma. *Psychological Review, 65*, 22–33.

Ryle, G. (1949). *The concept of mind*. London: Hutchinson House.

Searle, J. R. (1983). *Intentionality*. Cambridge, England: Cambridge University Press.

Seligman, M. E. P., & Johnston, J. C. (1973). A cognitive theory of avoidance learning. In F. J. McGuigan & D. B. Lumsden (Eds.), *Contemporary approaches to conditioning and learning* (pp. 69–110). Washington, DC: V.H. Winston.

Sheffield, F. D. (1965). Relation between classical conditioning and instrumental learning. In W. F. Prokasy (Ed.), *Classical conditioning: A symposium.* (pp. 302–322). New York: Appleton-Century-Crofts.

Skinner, B. F. (1938). *The behavior of organisms*. New York: Appleton-Century-Crofts.

Spence, K. W., Bergmann, G., & Lippitt, R. (1950). A study of simple learning under irrelevant motivational-reward conditions. *Journal of Experimental Psychology, 40*, 539–551.

Sutton, R. S., & Barto, A. G. (1981). An adaptive network that constructs and uses an internal model of its world. *Cognition and Brain Theory, 4*, 217–246.

Thistlethwaite, D. (1951). A critical review of latent learning and related experiments. *Psychological Review, 48*, 97–129.

Timberlake, W., & Lucas, G. A. (1989). *Behavior systems and learning: From misbehavior to general principles*. In S. B. Klein & R. R. Mowrer (Eds.), *Contemporary learning theories: Instrumental conditioning theory and the impact of biological constraints on learning*. Hillsdale, NJ: Lawrence Erlbaum Associates.

Tinklepaugh, O. L. (1928). An experimental study of representative factors in monkeys. *Journal of Comparative Psychology, 8*, 197–236.

Tolman, E. C. (1932). *Purposive behavior in animals and men*. New York: Appleton-Century-Crofts.

Tolman, E. C. (1933). Sign-gestalt or conditioned reflex? *Psychological Review, 40*, 246–255.

Tolman, E. C. (1949a). There is more than one kind of learning. *Psychological Review, 56*, 144–155.

Tolman, E. C. (1949b). The nature and functioning of wants. *Psychological Review, 56*, 357–369.

Tolman, E. C. (1951). *Collected papers in psychology*. Berkeley and Los Angeles: University of California Press.

Tolman, E. C. (1955). Principles of performance. *Psychological Review, 62*, 315–326.

Tolman, E. C. (1959). Principles of purposive behavior. In S. Koch (Ed.), *Psychology: A study of a science* (Vol. 2, pp. 92–157). New York: McGraw-Hill.

Tolman, E. C., & Gleitman, H. (1949). Studies in learning and motivation: I. Equal reinforcement in both end-boxes, followed by shock in one end-box. *Journal of Experimental Psychology, 39*, 810–819.

Tolman, E. C., Ritchie, B. F., & Kalish, D. (1946). Studies in spatial learning. I. Orientation and the short-cut. *Journal of Experimental Psychology, 36*, 13–24.

Trapold, M. A., & Overmier, J. B. (1972). The second learning process in instrumental learning. In A. H. Black & W. F. Prokasy (Eds.), *Classical Conditioning II: Current Research and Theory* (pp. 427–452). New York: Appleton-Century-Crofts.

Williams, D. R. (1965). Classical conditioning and incentive motivation. In W. F. Prokasy (Ed.), *Classical conditioning: A symposium* (pp. 340–357). New York: Appleton-Century-Crofts.

Winograd, T. (1975). Frames and the declarative-procedural controversy. In D. G. Bobrow & A. Collins (Eds.), *Representation and understanding* (pp. 185–210). New York: Academic Press.

Zener, K. (1937). The significance of behavior accompanying conditioned salivary secretion for theories of the conditioned response. *American Journal of Psychology, 50*, 384–403.

Author Index

Numbers in *italics* indicate pages with complete
bibliographic information.

Subject Index